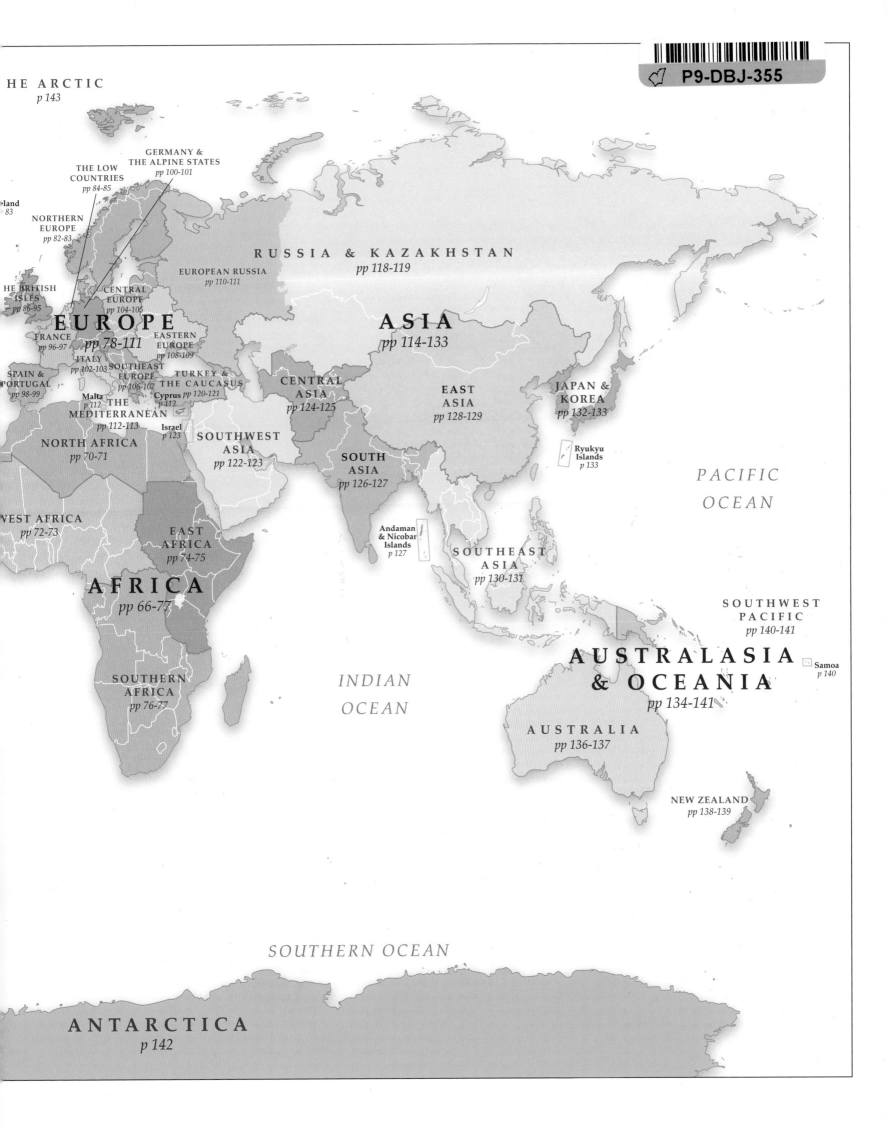

STUDENT
ATLAS

DK | Penguin Random House

Penguin
Random
House

FOR THE EIGHTH EDITION

Senior Cartographic Editor Simon Mumford

Senior Producer Vivienne Yong   Producer, Pre-Production Luca Frassinetti

Jacket Design Development Manager Sophia MTT   Publisher Andrew Macintyre   Art Director Karen Self

Publishing Director Jonathan Metcalf   Associate Publishing Director Liz Wheeler

FOR PREVIOUS EDITIONS

MANAGING EDITOR
Lisa Thomas

MANAGING ART EDITOR
Philip Lord

PROJECT EDITORS
Debra Clapson, Wim Jenkins, Jill Hamilton (US)

PROJECT DESIGNERS
Rhonda Fisher, Karen Gregory

EDITORIAL CONTRIBUTORS
Thomas Heath, Kevin McRae, Constance Novis,
Iris Rossoff (US), Siobhan Ryan

DESIGNERS
Carol Ann Davis, David Douglas,
Nicola Liddiard

MANAGING CARTOGRAPHER
David Roberts

SENIOR CARTOGRAPHIC EDITOR
Roger Bullen

DATABASE MANAGER
Simon Lewis

DIGITAL MAPS CREATED IN DK CARTOPIA BY
Phil Rowles, Rob Stokes

PLACENAMES DATABASE TEAM
Natalie Clarkson, Julia Lynch,

EDITORIAL DIRECTION
Andrew Heritage

CARTOGRAPHERS
Pamela Alford, James Anderson, Chris Atkinson, Dale Buckton, Tony Chambers, Jan Clark,
Martin Darlison, Damien Demaj, Paul Eames, Sally Gable, Jeremy Hepworth, Michael Martin,
Ed Merritt, Simon Mumford, John Plumer, Gail Townsley, Julie Turner,
Sarah Vaughan, Jane Voss, Peter Winfield

PICTURE RESEARCH
Louise Thomas

EDUCATIONAL CONSULTANTS
Dr. David Lambert, Institute of Education, University of London, David R Wright, BA MA

TEACHER REVIEWERS
US: Ramani DeAlwis; UK: Kevin Ball, Pat Barber, Stewart Marson

First American Edition, 1998. Reprinted with Revisions 1999,
Second Edition (revised) 2002, Reprinted 2003, Third Edition (revised) 2004,
Fourth Edition (revised) 2006, Fifth Edition (revised) 2008, Sixth Edition (revised) 2011,
Reprinted with Revisions 2012, Seventh Edition (revised) 2013, Eighth Edition (revised) 2015

Published in the United States by DK Publishing, 345 Hudson Street, New York, New York, 10014

15 16 17 18 19   10 9 8 7 6 5 4 3 2 1

264841 - November 2015

ISBN 978-1-4654-3876-8

Printed and bound in Hong Kong

A WORLD OF IDEAS:
SEE ALL THERE IS TO KNOW

www.dk.com

ACKNOWLEDGMENTS
The publishers are grateful for permission to reproduce the following photographs:

t=top, b=bottom, a=above, l=left, r=right, c=centre
Axiom: Jiri Rezac 64br; J Spaull 92br. **Bridgeman Art Library**: Hereford Cathedral, Trustees of the Hereford Mappa Mundi 8tr. **J Allan Cash**: 120cr. **Bruce Coleman Ltd:** C Ott 28cr (below); Dr E Pott 4bc; R Heinhard 19cr; J Murray 130bl; Peter Terry 19cr. **Colourific**: Black Star/R Rogers 113br; Frank Herrmann 119bc. **Comstock**: 17tc. **Corbis**: Bob Daemmrich 30bl. **James Davis Travel Photography**: 44tr, 119tr. **Robert Harding Picture Library**: 6tr (below); 21c, 21cr, 22br, 92cr (above), 28bl, 30cr, 30br, 31bl, 38tr, 118bl; A Tovy 120br; Adam Woolfitt 62br; C Bowman 112tr; Charcrit Boonson 90cr (below); David Lomax 20tr; Franz Joseph Land 19tr; G Boutin 120cl (below); G Renner 17c, 118cr(above); Gavin Hellier 31tr; Geoff Renner 39cr (above); H P Merten 23tl; Jane Sweeney 23bl; Louise Murray 93tr; Peter Scholey 91tr; Robert Francis 23cr; Schuster/Keine 62cr (above); Simon Westcott 90br. **Hutchison Library**: A Zvoznikov 19cl; J Nowell 93bl; R Ian Lloyd 10cl. **Image Bank**: Carlos Navajas 17bl; M Isy-Schwart 17bc; P Grumann 64cr (below); Steve Proehl 30cr (below); Terje Rakke 17br. **Images Colour Library**: 19c, 62cr (below), 118br. **Impact**: Jeremy Nicholl 121cl (below); Mark Henley 20bl; Paul O'Driscoll 63cr; Robin Lubbock 118br. **Frank Lane Picture Agency**: D Smith 19bc; W Wisniewsli 17cr. **Magnum**: Chris Steele Perking 120tr (below); Jean Gaumy 65cl. **N.A.S.A**: 9tc. **N.H.P.A**: M Wendler 4cl, 110bl. **Oxford Scientific Films**: Konrad Wothe 19tc; L Gould 4tr; Nobert Rosing 28cl. **Panos Pictures**: Alain le Garsheur 92cr; Alain le Garsmeur 31cl (above); Alberto Arzoz 63tr; Bruce Paton 121bl; Jeremy Hartley 120bl; Maria Luiza M Cavalho 112cl (below); Paul Smith 111cr; Rhodri Jones 113bl; Ron Gilling 119cr; Trygve Bolstad 22bl. **Edward Parker**: 17cr (above). **Pictor International**: 4tc, 10bc, 18tr, 20br, 36bc, 38br. **Planet Earth Pictures**: J Waters 113bc. **South American Pictures**: Robert Francis 29br; Tony Morrison 110cr, 111cl. **Spectrum Colour Library**: 29br. **Frank Spooner Pictures**: Gamma/E Baitel 91cl. **Still Pictures**: J Frebet 113cr; R Seitre 90cr (above). **Tony Stone Images**: 17tr, 112cl; A Sacks 28cr; Alan Levenson 92cr; Charles Thatcher 39tr; D Austen 131cr; D Hanson 17cl; Donald Johnson 62bc; Earth Imaging 6tr (above); G Johnson 90bl; H Strand 113tr; Hans Schlapfer 38bc; J Jangoux 19bcr; J Warden 110bc; John Garrett 121br; L Resnick 121tr; Larry Ulrich 37br; P Chesley 130tr; Paul Chesley 36br; Randy Wells 19br; Robert Frerck 65tr; Tom Walker 36bl; Tony Craddock 65cr. **Telegraph Colour Library**: 29tr. **Travel Ink**: Colin Marshall 22bc. **Trip**: A Kuznetsov 92bc; H Rogers 90cr; M Barlow 112bl; N Ray 10tr; Robert Belbin 92bl; V Kolpakov 93cr (below); V Sidoropolev 64cr; W Jacobs 130c. **World Pictures**: 131tr. **ZEFA Picture Library**: 19bcl, 19cll, 63bc; Damm 119cl; Heilman 110cr (below); K Siewert 110cl; Kitchen 19bll; Sunak 91cr; Surpress 11tr. **JACKET IMAGES**: Front: **Corbis**: Richard Berenholtz br; Bob Krist tc, bl; JamesRandklev tr, bl; Keren Su tl; **Science Photo Library/NOAA**. Back: **Corbis**: Robert Y. Ono bc; James Randklevbl; Paul A. Souders br; Royalty Free Images: Cobis tc; Corbis tr. Spine: **Corbis**: Robert Y. Ono.

CONTENTS

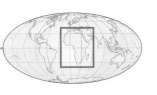

AMAZING EARTH

Earth is unique among the nine planets that circle the Sun. It is the only one that can support life, because it has enough oxygen in its atmosphere and plentiful water. In fact, seen from space, the Earth looks almost entirely blue. This is because about 70% of its surface is under water, submerged beneath four huge oceans: the Pacific, Atlantic, Indian and Arctic oceans. Land makes up about 30% of the Earth's surface. It is divided into seven landmasses of varying shapes and sizes called continents. These are, from largest to smallest: Asia, Africa, North America, South America, Antarctica, Europe, and Australia.

THE SHAPE OF THE EARTH

Photographs taken from space by astronauts in the 1960s, and more recently from orbiting satellites, have proven beyond doubt what humans had worked out long ago – that the Earth is shaped like a ball. But it is not perfectly round. The force of the Earth's rotation makes the world bulge very slightly at the Equator and go a little flat at the North and South Poles. So the Earth is actually a flattened sphere, or a "geoid."

WET EARTH

Tropical rain forests grow in areas close to the Equator, where it is wet and warm all year round. Although they cover just 7% of the Earth's land, these thick, damp forests form the richest ecosystems on the planet. More plant and animal species are found here than anywhere else on Earth.

DRY EARTH

Deserts are among the most inhospitable places on the planet. Some deserts are scorching hot, others are freezing cold, but they have one thing in common – they are all dry. Very few plant and animal species can survive in these harsh conditions. The world's coldest and driest continent, Antarctica (*left*), is a cold desert.

WATERY WORLD

The Earth's oceans and seas cover more than 142 million sq miles – that is twice the surface of Mars and nine times the surface of the moon.

Beneath the ocean waves lies the biggest and most unexplored landscape on Earth. Here are coral reefs, enormous, open plains, deep canyons, and the longest mountain range on Earth – the Mid-Atlantic Ridge – which stretches almost from pole to pole.

HEIGHTS AND DEPTHS

The Pacific Ocean contains the deepest places on the Earth's surface – the ocean trenches. The very deepest is Challenger Deep in the Mariana Trench which plunges 35,827 ft into the Earth's crust. If Mount Everest, the highest point on land at 29,029 ft, was dropped into the trench, its peak wouldn't even reach the surface of the Pacific.

WATER

Over 97% of the Earth's water is salt water. The total amount of salt in the world's oceans and seas would cover all of Europe to a depth of three miles. Less than 3% of the Earth's water is fresh. Of this, 2.06% is frozen in ice sheets and about 0.9% is stored underground as groundwater. The remainder is in lakes and rivers.

COASTS

The total length of the Earth's coastlines is more than 217,500 miles – that is the equivalent of 8.75 times around the globe. A high percentage of the world's people live in coastal zones: of the ten most populated cities on Earth, seven are situated on estuaries or the coast.

BIODIVERSITY

Today, around 7,200,000,000 humans, an estimated 7.7 million animal species and 300,000 known plant species depend on the air, water and land of planet Earth.

VANISHING FORESTS

10,000 years ago, thick forests covered about half of the Earth's land surface. Today, 33% of those forests no longer exist, and more than half of what remains has been dramatically altered. During the 20th century, more than 50% of the Earth's rainforests were felled.

DIFFERENT WORLD VIEWS

Because the Earth is round, we can only see half of it at any one time. This half is called a hemisphere, which means "half a sphere." There are always two hemispheres – the half that you see and the other half that you don't see. Two hemispheres placed together will always make a complete sphere.

PLANET WATER, PLANET LAND

The Earth can also be divided into land and water hemispheres. The land hemisphere shows most of the land on the Earth's surface. The water hemisphere is dominated by the vast Pacific Ocean – from this view, the Earth appears to be almost entirely covered by water.

Equator 0°

NORTH AND SOUTH

The Equator is an imaginary line drawn around the middle of the Earth, where its circumference is greatest. If we cut along the Equator, the Earth separates into two hemispheres: the Northern and Southern Hemispheres. Most of the Earth's land is the Northern Hemisphere. Europe and North America are the only continents that lie entirely in the northern hemisphere. Australia and Antarctica are the only continents that lie entirely in the southern hemisphere.

The Southern Hemisphere contains three of the Earth's four great oceans: the Pacific, Indian, and Atlantic Oceans.

Prime Meridian (0°)

North Pole

EAST AND WEST

The Earth can also be divided along two other imaginary lines – the Prime Meridian (0°) and 180° – which run opposite each other between the North and South Poles. This creates eastern and western hemispheres. The continents in the eastern hemisphere are traditionally called the Old World, while those in the western hemisphere – the Americas – were named the New World by the Europeans who explored them in the 15th century.

180°

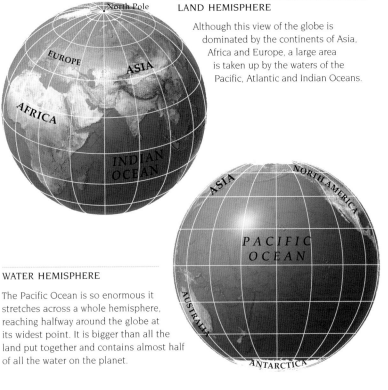

LAND HEMISPHERE

Although this view of the globe is dominated by the continents of Asia, Africa and Europe, a large area is taken up by the waters of the Pacific, Atlantic and Indian Oceans.

WATER HEMISPHERE

The Pacific Ocean is so enormous it stretches across a whole hemisphere, reaching halfway around the globe at its widest point. It is bigger than all the land put together and contains almost half of all the water on the planet.

THE SEASONS

As the Earth orbits the Sun, it is also spinning around an imaginary line called its axis, which joins the North and South Poles. The Earth's axis is not quite at right angles to the Sun, but tilts over at an angle of 23.5°. As a result, each place gradually moves closer to the Sun and then farther away from it again. Summer in the Northern Hemisphere is when the north is closest to the Sun. In winter, the Northern Hemisphere tilts away from the Sun, receiving far less heat and light. In the Southern Hemisphere the seasons are reversed, with summer in December and winter in June.

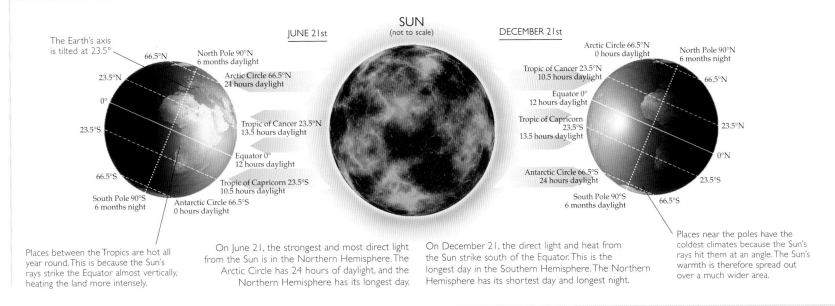

SUN (not to scale)

JUNE 21st

The Earth's axis is tilted at 23.5°
66.5°N
23.5°N
0°
23.5°S
66.5°S
North Pole 90°N 6 months daylight
Arctic Circle 66.5°N 24 hours daylight
Tropic of Cancer 23.5°N 13.5 hours daylight
Equator 0° 12 hours daylight
Tropic of Capricorn 23.5°S 10.5 hours daylight
South Pole 90°S 6 months night
Antarctic Circle 66.5°S 0 hours daylight

DECEMBER 21st

Arctic Circle 66.5°N 0 hours daylight
North Pole 90°N 6 months night
Tropic of Cancer 23.5°N 10.5 hours daylight
66.5°N
Equator 0° 12 hours daylight
Tropic of Capricorn 23.5°S 13.5 hours daylight
23.5°N
0°N
Antarctic Circle 66.5°S 24 hours daylight
23.5°S
South Pole 90°S 6 months daylight
66.5°S

Places between the Tropics are hot all year round. This is because the Sun's rays strike the Equator almost vertically, heating the land more intensely.

On June 21, the strongest and most direct light from the Sun is in the Northern Hemisphere. The Arctic Circle has 24 hours of daylight, and the Northern Hemisphere has its longest day.

On December 21, the direct light and heat from the Sun strike south of the Equator. This is the longest day in the Southern Hemisphere. The Northern Hemisphere has its shortest day and longest night.

Places near the poles have the coldest climates because the Sun's rays hit them at an angle. The Sun's warmth is therefore spread out over a much wider area.

MAPPING THE WORLD

The main purpose of a map is to show, or locate, where things are. The only truly accurate map of the whole world is a globe – a round model of the Earth. But a globe is impractical to carry around, so mapmakers (cartographers) produce flat paper maps instead. Changing the globe into a flat map is not simple. Imagine cutting a globe in half and trying to flatten the two hemispheres. They would be stretched in some places, and squashed in others. In fact, it is impossible to make a map of the round Earth on flat paper without some distortion of area, distance, or direction.

Satellite images can show the whole world as it appears from space. However, this image shows only one half of the world, and is distorted at the edges.

A globe (*right*) is the only way to illustrate the shape of the Earth accurately. A globe also shows the correct positions of the continents and oceans and how large they are in relation to one another.

LATITUDE

We can find out exactly how far north or south, east or west any place is on Earth by drawing two sets of imaginary lines around the world to make a grid. The horizontal lines on the globe below are called lines of latitude. They run from east to west. The most important is the Equator, which is given the value 0°. All other lines of latitude run parallel to the Equator. and are numbered in degrees either north or south of the Equator.

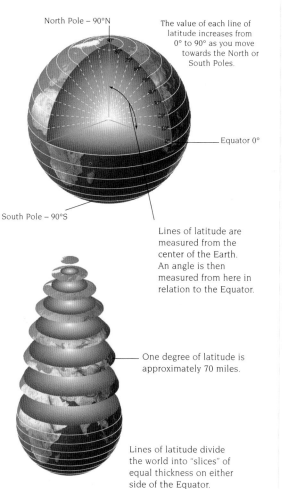

North Pole – 90°N

The value of each line of latitude increases from 0° to 90° as you move towards the North or South Poles.

Equator 0°

South Pole – 90°S

Lines of latitude are measured from the center of the Earth. An angle is then measured from here in relation to the Equator.

One degree of latitude is approximately 70 miles.

Lines of latitude divide the world into "slices" of equal thickness on either side of the Equator.

LONGITUDE

The vertical lines on the globe below run from north to south between the poles. They are called lines of longitude. The most important passes through Greenwich, England, and is numbered 0°. It is called the Prime Meridian. All other lines of longitude are numbered in degrees either east or west of the Prime Meridian. The line directly opposite the Prime Meridian is numbered 180°.

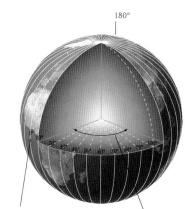

180°

Prime Meridian – 0°

Lines of longitude are also measured from the center of the Earth. This time, the angle is taken in relation to the Prime Meridian.

Lines of longitude divide the world into segments, like those of an orange – wide near the Equator, but narrow at the poles.

WHERE ON EARTH?

When lines of latitude and longitude are combined on a globe, or as here, on a flat map, they form a grid. Using this grid, we can locate any place on land, or at sea, by referring to the point where its line of latitude intersects with its line of longitude. Even when a place is not located exactly where the lines cross, you can still find its approximate position.

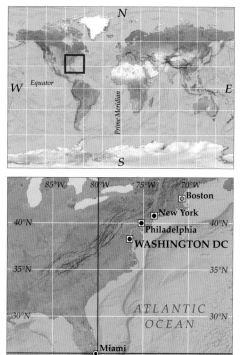

N

W Equator E

Prime Meridian

S

85°W 80°W 75°W 70°W

Boston
New York
40°N Philadelphia 40°N
WASHINGTON DC

35°N 35°N

30°N ATLANTIC OCEAN 30°N

Miami

25°N 25°N

85°W 80°W 75°W 70°W

The map above is of the eastern US. It is too small to show all the lines of latitude and longitude, so they are given at intervals of 5°. Miami is located at about 26° north of the Equator and 80° west of the Prime Meridian. We write its location 26°N 80°W.

MAKING A FLAT MAP FROM A GLOBE

Cartographers use a technique called projection to show the Earth's curved surface on a flat map. Many different map projections have been designed. The distortion of one feature – either area, distance, or direction – can be minimized, while other features become more distorted. Cartographers must choose which of these things it is most important to show correctly for each map that they make. Three major families of projections can be used to solve these questions.

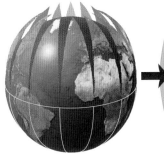
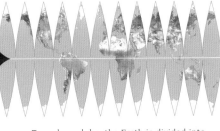

To make a globe, the Earth is divided into segments or 'gores' along lines of longitude.

1 CYLINDRICAL PROJECTIONS

These projections are "cylindrical" because the surface of the globe is transferred onto a surrounding cylinder. This cylinder is then cut from top to bottom and "rolled out" to give a flat map. These maps are very useful for showing the whole world.

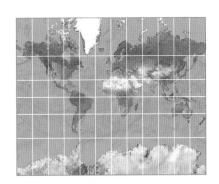

The cylinder touches the globe at the Equator. Here, the scale on the map will be exactly the same as it is on the globe. At the northern and southern edges of the cylinder, which are farthest away from the surface of the globe, the map is most distorted. The Mercator projection (*above*), created in the 16th century, is a good example of a cylindrical projection.

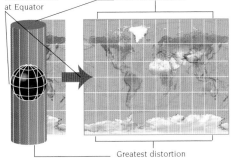

Scale accurate at Equator — Greatest distortion

Greatest distortion

2 AZIMUTHAL PROJECTIONS

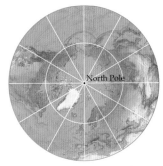
North Pole

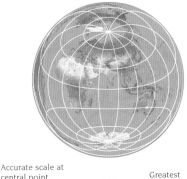

Azimuthal projections put the surface of the globe onto a flat circle. "Azimuthal" means that the direction or "azimuth" of any line coming from the center point of that circle is correct. Azimuthal maps are useful for viewing hemispheres, continents, and the polar regions. Mapping any area larger than a hemisphere gives great distortion at the outer edges of the map.

Accurate scale at central point — Greatest distortion

The circle only touches the globe's surface at one central point. The scale is only accurate at this point and becomes less and less accurate the farther away the circle is from the globe. This kind of projection is good for maps centering on a major city or on one of the poles.

3 CONIC PROJECTIONS

Conic projections are best used for smaller areas of the world, such as country maps. The surface of the globe is projected onto a cone which rests on top of it. After cutting from the point to the bottom of the cone, a flat map in the shape of a fan is left behind.

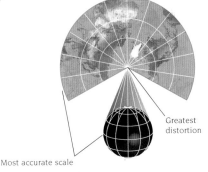

The conic projection touches the globe's surface at one latitude. This is where the scale of the map will be most accurate. The parts of the cone farthest from the globe will be the most distorted and are usually omitted from the map itself.

Greatest distortion

Most accurate scale

PROJECTIONS USED IN THIS ATLAS

The projections that are appropriate for showing maps at a world, continental, or country scale are quite different. The projections for this atlas have been carefully chosen. They are ones that show areas as familiar shapes that are distorted as little as possible.

1 World Maps

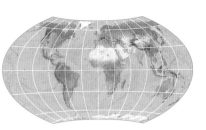

The Wagner VII projection is used for our world maps as it shows all the countries at their correct sizes relative to one another.

2 Continents

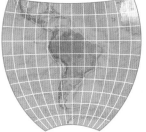

The Lambert Azimuthal Equal Area is used for continental maps. The shape distortion is relatively small and countries retain their correct sizes relative to one another.

3 Countries

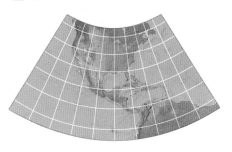

The Lambert Conformal Conic shows countries with as little distortion as possible. The angles from any point on the map are the same as they would be on the surface of the globe.

HOW MAPS ARE MADE

New technologies have revolutionized mapmaking. Computers and information from satellites have replaced drawing boards and drafting pens, and the process of creating new maps is now far easier. But mapmaking is still a skilled and often time-consuming process. Information about the world must be gathered, sorted, and checked. The cartographer must make decisions about the function of the map and what information to select in order to make it as clear as possible.

THE MAPPA MUNDI

Maps have been made for thousands of years. The 13th-century Mappa Mundi, meaning "known world" shows the Mediterranean Sea and the Don and Nile rivers. Asia is at the top, with Europe on the left, and Africa to the right. The oceans are shown as a ring surrounding the land. The map reflects a number of biblical stories.

HISTORICAL MAP MAKING

This detailed hand-drawn map of the southern coast of Spain was made in about 1750. The mountains are illustrated as small hills and the labels have been hand lettered.

For centuries, maps were drawn by hand. Very early maps were no more than a pictorial representation of what the surface of the ground looked like. Where there were hills, pictures were drawn to represent them. Later maps were drawn using information gathered by survey teams. They would carefully mark out and calculate the height of the land, the positions of towns, and other geographical features. As knowledge and techniques improved, maps became more accurate.

NEW TECHNIQUES

Computers make it easier to change map information and styles quickly. This map of the southern coast of Spain, made in 1997 has been made using digital terrain modeling (see below) and traditional cartography.

Today, cartographers have access to far more data about the Earth than in the past. Satellites collect and process information about its surface. Further elements may then be added in the traditional way. Computers are now widely used to combine these different sorts of map information. More recently, the use of Global Positioning Systems (GPS) linked to satellites, and the increased availability of Internet based mapping, has revolutionised the way that maps are created and used.

MODERN MAP MAKING

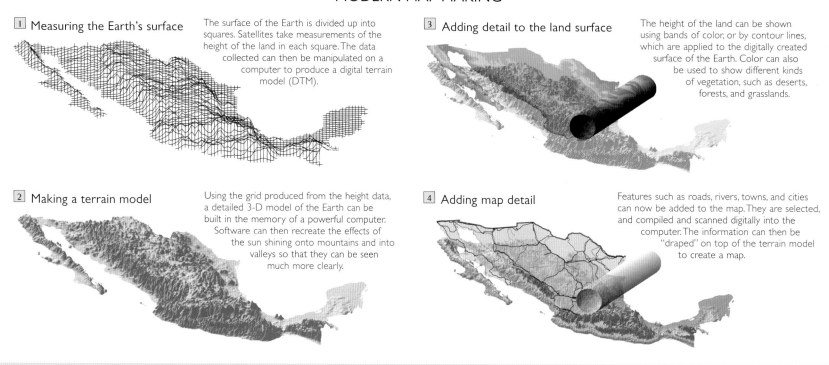

1 Measuring the Earth's surface

The surface of the Earth is divided up into squares. Satellites take measurements of the height of the land in each square. The data collected can then be manipulated on a computer to produce a digital terrain model (DTM).

3 Adding detail to the land surface

The height of the land can be shown using bands of color, or by contour lines, which are applied to the digitally created surface of the Earth. Color can also be used to show different kinds of vegetation, such as deserts, forests, and grasslands.

2 Making a terrain model

Using the grid produced from the height data, a detailed 3-D model of the Earth can be built in the memory of a powerful computer. Software can then recreate the effects of the sun shining onto mountains and into valleys so that they can be seen much more clearly.

4 Adding map detail

Features such as roads, rivers, towns, and cities can now be added to the map. They are selected, and compiled and scanned digitally into the computer. The information can then be "draped" on top of the terrain model to create a map.

SHOWING INFORMATION ON A MAP

A map is a selective diagram of a place. It is the cartographer's job to decide what kind of information to show on a map. They can choose to highlight certain kinds of features – such as roads, rivers, and land height. They can also show other features such as sea depth, place names, and borders that would be impossible to see either on the ground or from a photograph. The information that can be shown on a map is influenced by a number of factors, most notably by its scale.

This is a satellite photograph of the harbor area of Rio de Janeiro in Brazil. Although you can see the bay and where most of the housing is, it is impossible to see roads or get any sense of the position of places relative to one another.

This is a map of the same area as you can see in the photograph. Much of the detail has been greatly simplified. Towns are named and marked; contours indicate the height of the land; and roads, railways and borders between districts have been added.

SCALE

To make a map of an area it needs to be greatly reduced in size. This is known as drawing to scale. The scale of the map shows us by how much the area has been reduced. The smaller the scale, the greater the area of land that can be shown on the map. There will be far less detail and the map will not be as accurate. The maps below show the different kinds of information that can be shown on maps of varying scales.

WAYS TO SHOW SCALE

When using a map to work out what areas or distances are in reality, we need to refer to the scale of that particular map. Map scales can be shown in several ways.

1 Representative fraction

One unit on the map would be equal to 1,000,000 units on the ground.

1:1,000,000

2 Linear scale

The line is marked off in units which represent the real distances of the map, given in both miles and kilometers.

SCALE BAR

0 km   10   20

0 miles   10   20

3 Statement of scale

It means that 1 inch on the map represents 1 mile on the ground.

1 inch represents 1 mile

LONDON 1:21,000,000

This small-scale map shows the position of London in relation to Europe. Very little detail can be seen at this scale – only the names of countries and the largest towns.

LONDON 1:5,500,000

At a scale of 1 to 5,500,000 you can see the major road network in the southeast of the UK. Many towns are named and you can see the difference in size and status.

LONDON 1:900,000

This map is at a much larger scale. You can see the major roads that lead out from London and the names of many suburbs, places of interest, and airports.

LONDON 1:12,500

This is a street map of central London. The streets are named, as are places of interest, train and subway stations. The scale is large enough to show plenty of detail.

READING MAPS

Maps use a unique visual language to convey a great deal of detailed information in a relatively simple form. Different features are marked out using special symbols and styles of print. These symbols are explained in the key to the map and you should always read a map alongside its key or legend. This page explains how to look for different features on the map and how to unravel the different layers of information that you can find on it.

PHYSICAL FEATURES

All the regional and country maps in this atlas are based on a model of the Earth's surface. The computer-generated relief gives an accurate picture of the surface of the land. Colors are used to show the relative heights of the land; green is for low-lying land, and yellows, browns, and grays are for higher land. Water features like streams, rivers, and lakes are also shown

1 WATER FEATURES

On this map extract, the blue lines show a number of rivers, including the Salween and the Irrawaddy. The Irrawaddy forms a huge delta, splitting into many streams as it reaches the sea.

2 RELIEF

These mountains are in the north of Southeast Asia. The underlying relief on the map and the colored bands help you to see the height of the land..

HUMAN FEATURES

Maps also reveal a great deal about the human geography of an area. In addition to showing the location of towns and roads, different symbols can tell you more about the size of towns and the importance of a road. Borders between countries or regions can only be seen on a map.

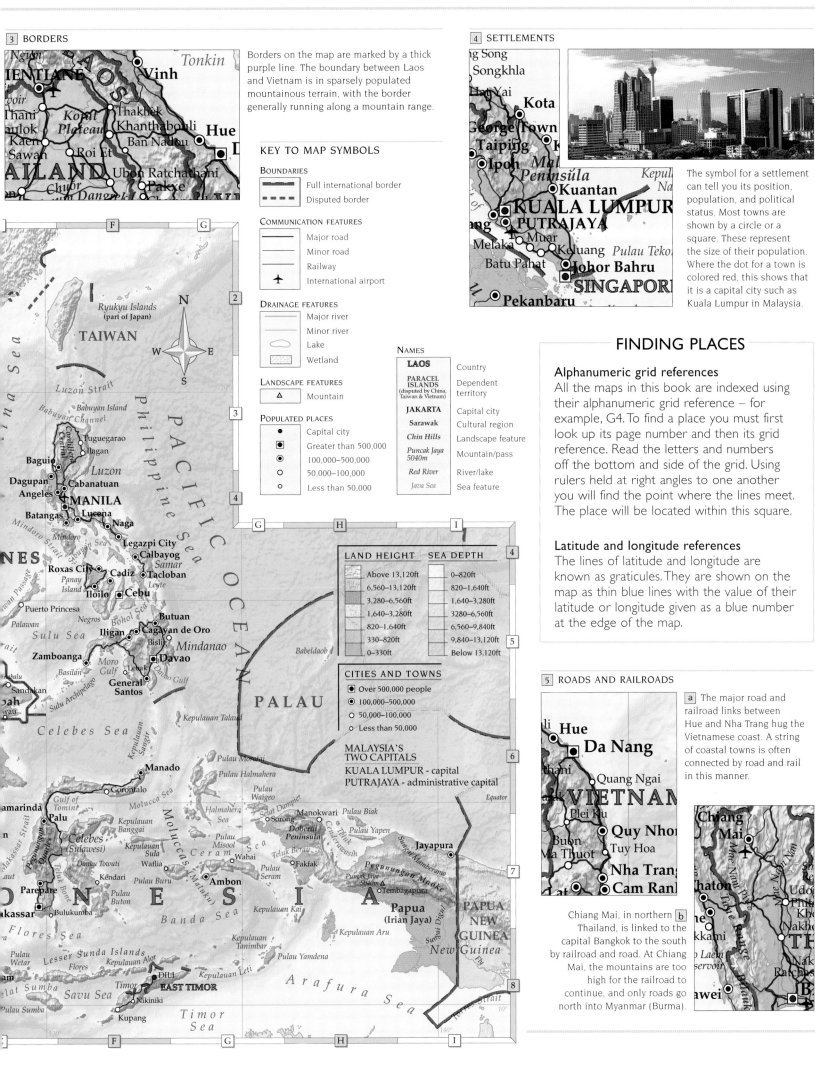

3 BORDERS

Borders on the map are marked by a thick purple line. The boundary between Laos and Vietnam is in sparsely populated mountainous terrain, with the border generally running along a mountain range.

KEY TO MAP SYMBOLS

BOUNDARIES

▬▬▬	Full international border
▪▪▪▪	Disputed border

COMMUNICATION FEATURES

	Major road
	Minor road
	Railway
✈	International airport

DRAINAGE FEATURES

	Major river
	Minor river
	Lake
	Wetland

LANDSCAPE FEATURES

△	Mountain

POPULATED PLACES

●	Capital city
◉	Greater than 500,000
◉	100,000–500,000
○	50,000–100,000
○	Less than 50,000

NAMES

LAOS	Country
PARACEL ISLANDS (disputed by China, Taiwan & Vietnam)	Dependent territory
JAKARTA	Capital city
Sarawak	Cultural region
Chin Hills	Landscape feature
Puncak Jaya 5040m	Mountain/pass
Red River	River/lake
Java Sea	Sea feature

4 SETTLEMENTS

The symbol for a settlement can tell you its position, population, and political status. Most towns are shown by a circle or a square. These represent the size of their population. Where the dot for a town is colored red, this shows that it is a capital city such as Kuala Lumpur in Malaysia.

FINDING PLACES

Alphanumeric grid references

All the maps in this book are indexed using their alphanumeric grid reference – for example, G4. To find a place you must first look up its page number and then its grid reference. Read the letters and numbers off the bottom and side of the grid. Using rulers held at right angles to one another you will find the point where the lines meet. The place will be located within this square.

Latitude and longitude references

The lines of latitude and longitude are known as graticules. They are shown on the map as thin blue lines with the value of their latitude or longitude given as a blue number at the edge of the map.

LAND HEIGHT | SEA DEPTH

Above 13,120ft	0–820ft
6,560–13,120ft	820–1,640ft
3,280–6,560ft	1,640–3,280ft
1,640–3,280ft	3280–6,560ft
820–1,640ft	6,560–9,840ft
330–820ft	9,840–13,120ft
0–330ft	Below 13,120ft

CITIES AND TOWNS

■	Over 500,000 people
◉	100,000–500,000
○	50,000–100,000
○	Less than 50,000

MALAYSIA'S TWO CAPITALS

KUALA LUMPUR - capital
PUTRAJAYA - administrative capital

5 ROADS AND RAILROADS

a The major road and railroad links between Hue and Nha Trang hug the Vietnamese coast. A string of coastal towns is often connected by road and rail in this manner.

Chiang Mai, in northern **b** Thailand, is linked to the capital Bangkok to the south by railroad and road. At Chiang Mai, the mountains are too high for the railroad to continue, and only roads go north into Myanmar (Burma).

USING THE ATLAS

This Atlas has been designed to develop map-reading skills and to introduce readers to a wide range of different maps. It also provides a wealth of detailed geographic information about the world today. The Atlas is divided into four sections: **Learning Map Skills**; **The World About Us**, covering global geographic patterns; the **World Atlas**, dealing with the world's regions and an **Index**.

LEARNING MAP SKILLS

Maps show the Earth – which is three-dimensional – in just two dimensions. This section shows how maps are made; how different kinds of information are shown on maps; how to choose what to put on a map and the best way to show it. It also explains how to read the maps in this Atlas.

THE WORLD ABOUT US

These pages contain a series of world maps that show important themes, such as physical features, climate, life zones, population, and the world economy, on a global scale. They give a worldwide picture of concepts that are explored in more detail later in the book.

Text introduces themes and concepts in each spread.

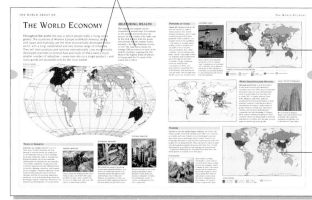

Photographs illustrate examples of places or topics shown on the main map.

World maps show geographic patterns on a global scale.

Introduction to projections: different projections and how they work.

Choosing the best projections: the map projections used in this book.

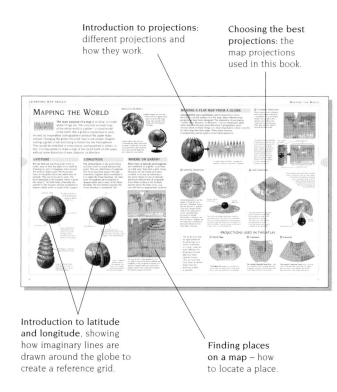

Introduction to latitude and longitude, showing how imaginary lines are drawn around the globe to create a reference grid.

Finding places on a map – how to locate a place.

CONTINENTAL MAPS

A cross section through the continent shows the relative height of certain features.

A detailed physical map of the continent shows major natural geographic features, including mountains, lakes and rivers.

Photographs and locator maps illustrate the main geographic regions and show you where they are.

The industry map shows the main industrial towns and cities and the main industries in each continent. It also shows the wealth of each country relative to the rest of the world.

CONTINENTAL GEOGRAPHY PAGES

Humans have colonized and changed all the continents except Antarctica. These pages show the factors which have affected this process: climate, the availability of resources such as coal, oil, and minerals, and varying patterns of land use. Mineral resources are directly linked to many industries, and most agriculture is governed both by the quality of the land and the climate.

CONTINENTAL PAGES

These pages show the physical shape of each continent and the impact that humans have made on the natural landscape – building towns and roads and creating borders between countries. They show where natural features such as mountain ranges and rivers have created physical boundaries, and where humans have created their own political boundaries between states.

The political map of the continent shows country boundaries and country names.

The climate map shows the main types of climate across the continent and where the hottest and coldest, wettest and driest places are.

The mineral resources map shows where the most important reserves of minerals, including coal and precious metals, are found.

The land use map shows different types of land and the main kinds of farming that take place in each area.

REGIONAL MAPS

The main part of the Atlas contains detailed maps of countries and regions. Each of these is accompanied by a series of small thematic maps, models, and charts, which give information about the climate, where people live, how they use the land, the different kinds of industry, and important environmental issues.

TERRAIN MODEL

A computer-generated landscape model shows what the land really looks like. There are no roads or towns to mask the physical geography of the country or region. Mountain ranges, plains, and river basins can be easily seen.

COLORED THUMB TAGS

Each section has its own color code.

Learning Map Skills

The World About Us

North America

South America

Africa

Europe

Asia

Australasia and Oceania

Antarctica and the Arctic

CLIMATE MAPS

These maps show the temperature and rainfall patterns in January and July. Colored bands indicate temperatures: blue for low temperatures, orange for high ones. Rainfall is represented by black lines with a number giving the average amount of rain. These are called isohyets.

Isohyets show the rainfall patterns in inches per year. The areas between the lines are either over or under the figures shown on the isohyets.

JANUARY

JULY

The hottest areas are colored orange.

Here the rainfall is between 2 and 4 inches per year.

LOCATOR GLOBE

This shows the location of the country or region both within its continent and in relation to the rest of the world.

EUROPE

MAP GRID

Each main map has a grid. Using the grid will help you to find a place on the map. Grid references are expressed as letters (running from left to right across the frame), and numbers (running from the top to the bottom of the frame), for example, A-4, G-6. Everything on the map is referenced in the **Index** at the back of the book.

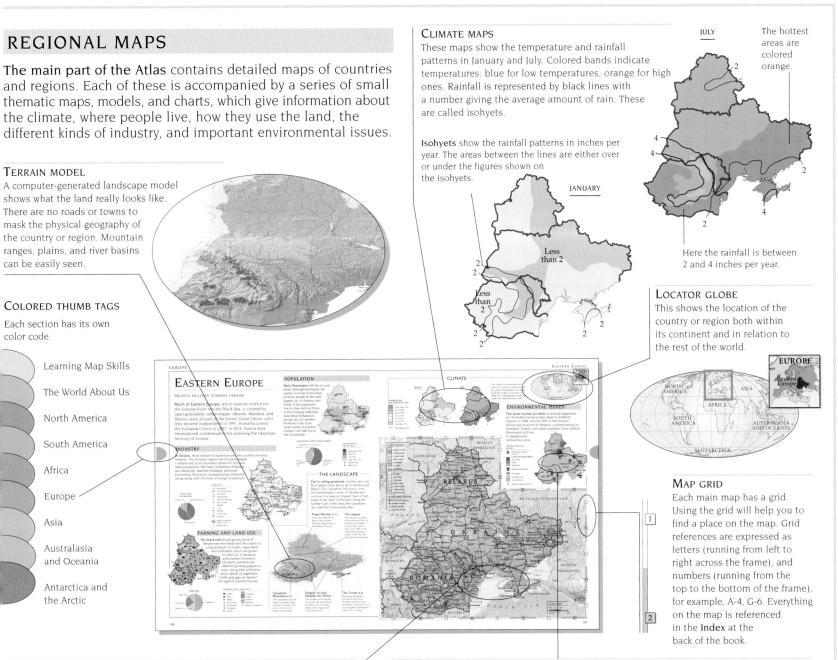

REGIONAL MAPS

The main map on each regional page shows the main topographical features of the area: the height of the land, the major roads, the rivers and lakes. It also shows the main cities and towns in the region – represented by different symbols.

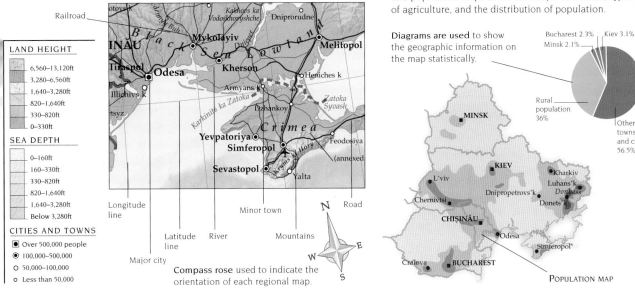

Railroad

LAND HEIGHT

	6,560–13,120ft
	3,280–6,560ft
	1,640–3,280ft
	820–1,640ft
	330–820ft
	0–330ft

SEA DEPTH

	0–160ft
	160–330ft
	330–820ft
	820–1,640ft
	1,640–3,280ft
	Below 3,280ft

CITIES AND TOWNS

◉ Over 500,000 people
◉ 100,000–500,000
○ 50,000–100,000
○ Less than 50,000

Longitude line

Latitude line

River

Major city

Minor town

Mountains

Road

Compass rose used to indicate the orientation of each regional map.

THEMATIC MAPS

These small maps show various aspects of the geography of the country or region. The environment maps cover topics such as the effects of pollution. Industry, land use, and population maps locate the major industries, types of agriculture, and the distribution of population.

Diagrams are used to show the geographic information on the map statistically.

Bucharest 2.3%   Kiev 3.1%
Minsk 2.1%

Rural population 36%

Other towns and cities 56.5%

POPULATION MAP

INDUSTRY MAP

LAND USE MAP

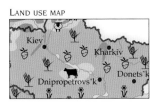

ENVIRONMENT MAP

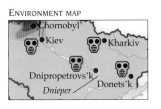

THE PHYSICAL WORLD

This map shows the main physical features of the world: the mountain ranges, the great rivers and lakes, deserts, grassland plains, seas and oceans. No human settlements are named on this map – only the physical or landscape features.

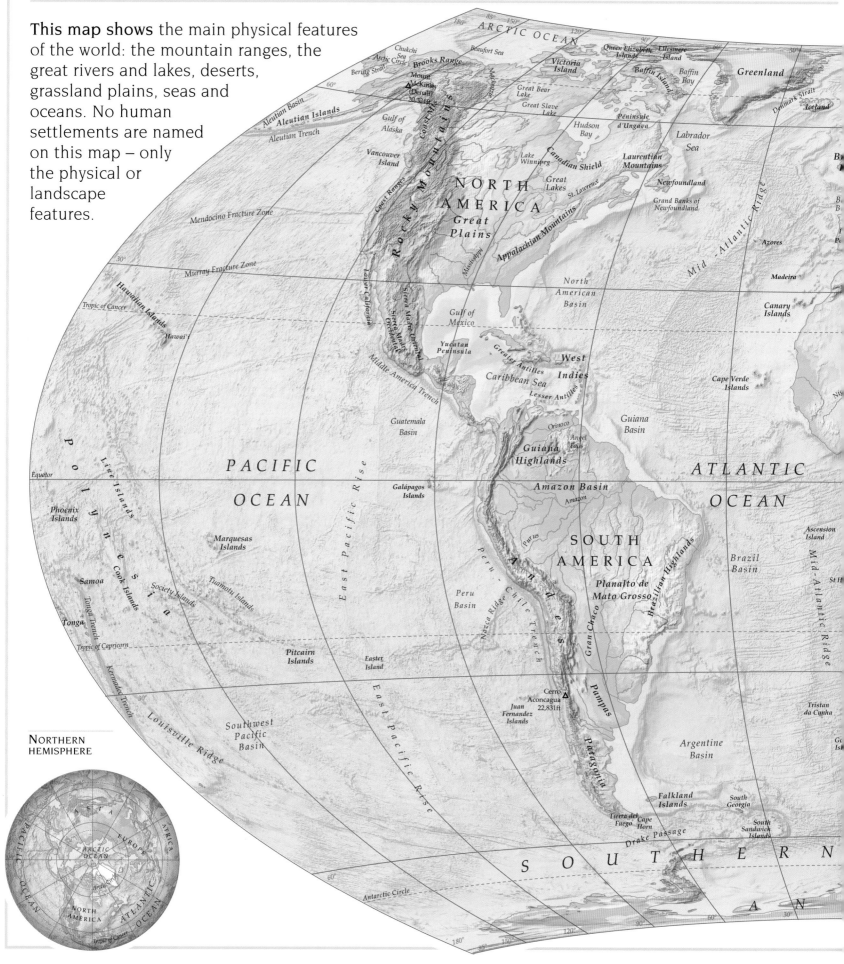

ARCTIC OCEAN

Chukchi Sea
Arctic Circle
Bering Strait
Beaufort Sea
Brooks Range
Mount McKinley (Denali) 20,324ft
Gulf of Alaska
Aleutian Basin
Aleutian Islands
Aleutian Trench

Victoria Island
Queen Elizabeth Islands
Ellesmere Island
Baffin Island
Baffin Bay
Greenland
Denmark Strait
Iceland

Mackenzie
Great Bear Lake
Great Slave Lake
Hudson Bay
Péninsule d'Ungava
Labrador Sea

Vancouver Island
Lake Winnipeg
Canadian Shield
Laurentian Mountains
Newfoundland

NORTH AMERICA
Great Lakes
St. Lawrence
Grand Banks of Newfoundland

Mendocino Fracture Zone
Great Plains
Appalachian Mountains
Mid-Atlantic Ridge

Azores

Murray Fracture Zone
Mississippi
North American Basin
Madeira

Hawaiian Islands
Tropic of Cancer
Canary Islands

Hawai'i
Sierra Madre Occidental
Gulf of Mexico

Yucatan Peninsula
Greater Antilles
West Indies
Cape Verde Islands

Middle America Trench
Caribbean Sea
Lesser Antilles

Guatemala Basin
Guiana Basin

PACIFIC OCEAN
Galápagos Islands
Orinoco
Angel Falls
Guiana Highlands

ATLANTIC OCEAN

Equator
Line Islands
East Pacific Rise
Amazon Basin
Amazon

Phoenix Islands
Ascension Island

Marquesas Islands
Purus
SOUTH AMERICA
Brazilian Highlands
Brazil Basin

Samoa
Society Islands
Tuamotu Islands
Peru Basin
Planalto de Mato Grosso
Mid-Atlantic Ridge

Tonga
Tonga Trench
Nazca Ridge
Gran Chaco

Tropic of Capricorn
Pitcairn Islands
Easter Island
Cerro Aconcagua 22,831ft
Pampas
Tristan da Cunha

Juan Fernandez Islands
Kermadec Trench
Louisville Ridge
Southwest Pacific Basin
East Pacific Rise
Argentine Basin

Patagonia

Falkland Islands
South Georgia

Tierra del Fuego
Cape Horn
South Sandwich Islands

Drake Passage

SOUTHERN
Antarctic Circle

NORTHERN HEMISPHERE

ASIA
EUROPE
AFRICA
ARCTIC OCEAN
PACIFIC OCEAN
ATLANTIC OCEAN
NORTH AMERICA
Tropic of Cancer

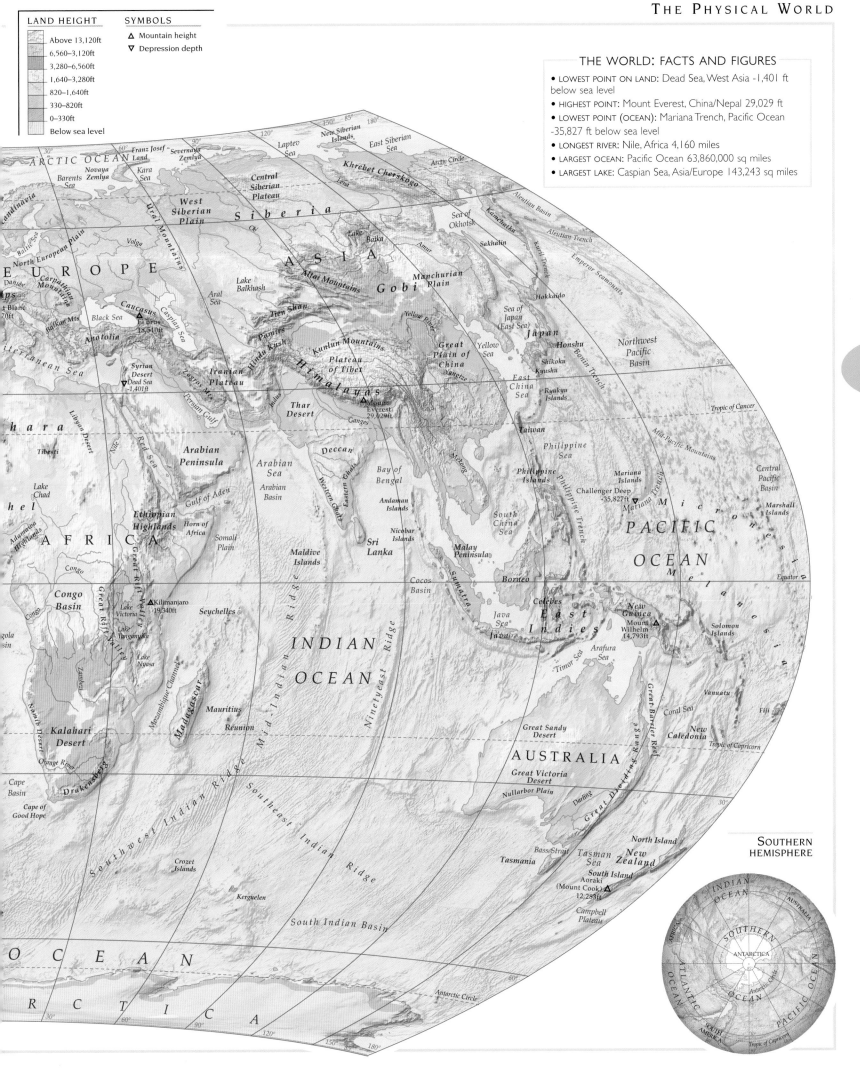

LAND HEIGHT
Above 13,120ft
6,560–3,120ft
3,280–6,560ft
1,640–3,280ft
820–1,640ft
330–820ft
0–330ft
Below sea level

SYMBOLS
△ Mountain height
▽ Depression depth

THE WORLD: FACTS AND FIGURES

- **LOWEST POINT ON LAND:** Dead Sea, West Asia -1,401 ft below sea level
- **HIGHEST POINT:** Mount Everest, China/Nepal 29,029 ft
- **LOWEST POINT (OCEAN):** Mariana Trench, Pacific Ocean -35,827 ft below sea level
- **LONGEST RIVER:** Nile, Africa 4,160 miles
- **LARGEST OCEAN:** Pacific Ocean 63,860,000 sq miles
- **LARGEST LAKE:** Caspian Sea, Asia/Europe 143,243 sq miles

SOUTHERN HEMISPHERE

15

THE EARTH'S STRUCTURE

The shape and position of the Earth's oceans and continents make a familiar pattern. This is just the latest in a series of forms that the Earth has taken in the hundreds of millions of years since its creation. Massive forces inside the Earth cause the continents and oceans to move apart and together again, forming larger landmasses and then breaking them apart – a process known as plate tectonics. The movement is very slow – but over millions of years, the changes can be enormous.

DYNAMIC EARTH

The heart of the Earth is a solid core of iron surrounded by several layers of very hot – sometimes liquid – rock. The crust is relatively thin and is made up of a series of "plates" that fit closely together. Movement of the molten rock deep within the mantle of the Earth causes the plates to move, creating changes in the surface features of the Earth.

THE EARTH'S PLATES

Continental plate

Oceanic plate

Plate boundary or margin

Continental and oceanic plates are tectonic plates are made from crustal rock

INSIDE THE EARTH

Rocky crust

Outer core – liquid iron and nickel

Inner core – made of iron

Mantle – m from solid molten

TECTONIC PLATES, VOLCANOES AND EARTHQUAKES

▲ Volcanic zone

▮ Earthquake zone on land

⇨ Direction of plate movement

〰️ Rift valley

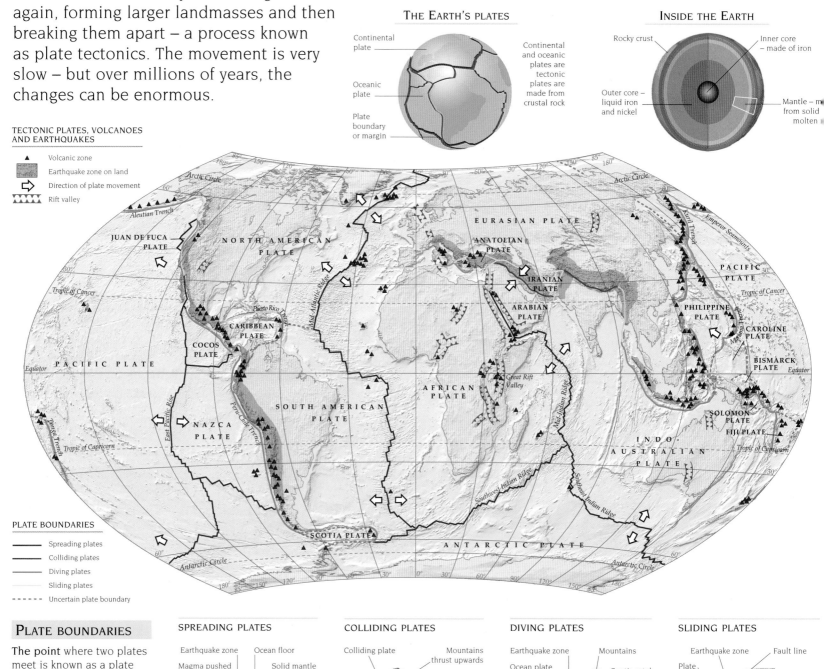

EURASIAN PLATE

ANATOLIAN PLATE

Aleutian Trench

JUAN DE FUCA PLATE

NORTH AMERICAN PLATE

IRANIAN PLATE

ARABIAN PLATE

PACIFIC PLATE

PHILIPPINE PLATE

CARIBBEAN PLATE

CAROLINE PLATE

COCOS PLATE

Puerto Rico

Mid-Atlantic Ridge

BISMARCK PLATE

PACIFIC PLATE

AFRICAN PLATE

Great Rift Valley

SOLOMON PLATE

FIJI PLATE

NAZCA PLATE

Peru-Chile Trench

SOUTH AMERICAN PLATE

East Pacific Rise

Tonga Trench

Mid-Indian Ridge

INDO-AUSTRALIAN PLATE

Southwest Indian Ridge

Southeast Indian Ridge

SCOTIA PLATE

ANTARCTIC PLATE

Arctic Circle

Tropic of Cancer

Equator

Tropic of Capricorn

Antarctic Circle

PLATE BOUNDARIES

——— Spreading plates

——— Colliding plates

——— Diving plates

——— Sliding plates

- - - - Uncertain plate boundary

PLATE BOUNDARIES

The point where two plates meet is known as a plate boundary. As the Earth's plates move together or apart or slide alongside one another, the great forces that result cause great changes in the landscape. Mountains can be created, earthquakes occur, and there may be frequent volcanic eruptions.

SPREADING PLATES

Earthquake zone   Ocean floor

Magma pushed upwards   Solid mantle

As plates move apart, magma rises through the outer mantle. When it cools, it forms new crust. The Mid-Atlantic Ridge is caused by spreading plates.

COLLIDING PLATES

Colliding plate   Mountains thrust upwards

Earthquake zone

When two plates bearing landmasses collide with one another, the land is crumpled upward into high mountain peaks such as the Alps and the Himalayas.

DIVING PLATES

Earthquake zone   Mountains

Ocean plate   Continental plate

When an ocean-bearing plate collides with a continental plate it is forced downward under the other plate and into the mantle. Volcanoes occur along these boundaries.

SLIDING PLATES

Earthquake zone   Fault line

Plate   Plate

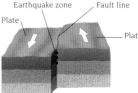

As two plates slide past each other, great friction is set up along the fault line that lies between them. This can lead to powerful earthquakes.

SHAPING THE LANDSCAPE

The Earth's surface is made from solid rock or water. The land is constantly reshaped by external forces. Water flowing as rivers or in the oceans erodes and deposits material to create valleys and lakes and to shape coastlines. When water is built up and compressed into solid sheets of ice, it can erode more deeply, creating deeper, wider valleys. Wind also has a powerful effect: stripping away vegetation and transporting rock particles vast distances.

RIVERS

Most rivers have their sources in mountain areas. They flow fast through the mountains, eroding deep V-shaped valleys. As they reach flatter areas they begin to meander in great loops, both eroding and then depositing rock particles as they slow down.

GLACIERS

In cold areas, close to the poles or on mountaintops, snow is built up into rivers of ice called glaciers. They move slowly, eroding deep U-shaped valleys. When the glacier melts, ridges of eroded rock called moraines are left at the sides and end of the glacier.

SEA ACTION

The oceans change the landscape in two major ways. They batter cliffs, causing rock to break away and the land to retreat, and they carry eroded material along the coast, to make beaches and sandbars.

WIND

Wind can erode and break down rock into smaller boulders and stones and eventually into sand. Desert sand dunes are shaped by the force of the wind and vary from ripples to hills 650 ft high.

LANDSLIDES

Heavy rain can loosen soil and rock beneath the surface of slopes. As this moves, the top layers slip, forming heaps of rubble at the base of the slope.

THE WORLD'S OCEANS

Just over two-thirds of the Earth's surface is covered by water and more than 97% of this water is contained in the oceans. Movements within the Earth shape the ocean floor in the same way they do the land surface, creating mountain ranges, trenches, and plateaus, and changing the shape and size of the oceans. The difference between an ocean and a sea is simply its size; oceans are much bigger.

POLAR OCEANS

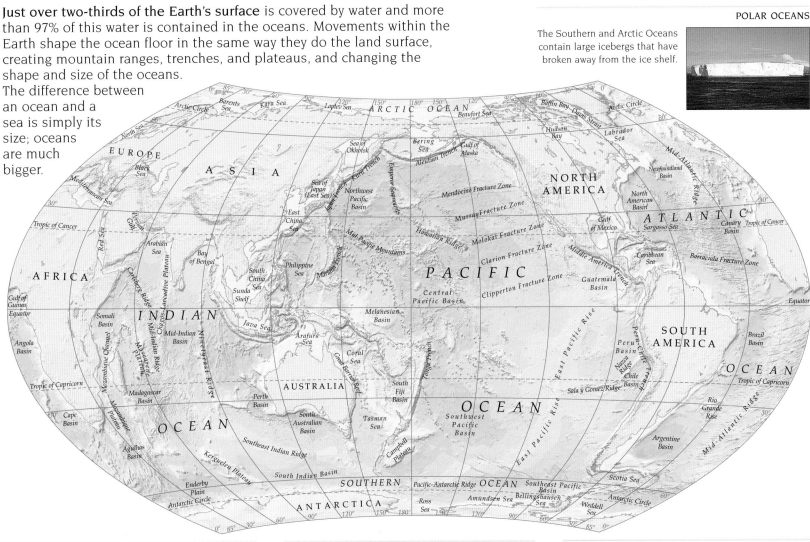

The Southern and Arctic Oceans contain large icebergs that have broken away from the ice shelf.

INDIAN OCEAN

The Indian Ocean covers about 20% of the world's surface. Ocean swells, starting deep in the Southern Ocean, often cause flooding in Sri Lanka and the Maldives.

PACIFIC OCEAN

The Pacific is the largest and deepest ocean in the world. It is surrounded by an arc of volcanoes, including Japan, Indonesia, and the Andes, known as the "Ring of Fire."

ATLANTIC OCEAN

The Atlantic Ocean was formed about 180 million years ago. The land that now forms Europe and Africa pulled apart from the Americas to create an ocean 1,900 miles wide.

CLIMATE AND LIFE ZONES

HURRICANES

This map shows the different climates found around the world. Climates are particular combinations of temperature and humidity. Climates are affected by latitude, the height of the land, winds, and ocean currents. Climates can change, but not overnight. Weather is local and consists of short-term events such as thunderstorms, hurricanes, and blizzards.

HURRICANES

Hurricanes are violent cyclonic windstorms, driven by heat energy gathered from tropical seas. The Caribbean islands and the east coast of the US are particularly prone to hurricanes.

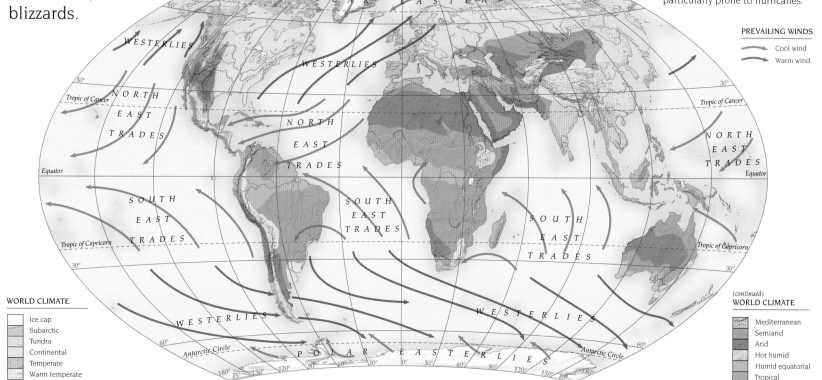

PREVAILING WINDS

- Cool wind
- Warm wind

WORLD CLIMATE

- Ice cap
- Subarctic
- Tundra
- Continental
- Temperate
- Warm temperate

(continued)
WORLD CLIMATE

- Mediterranean
- Semiarid
- Arid
- Hot humid
- Humid equatorial
- Tropical

CLIMATE CHANGE

The Earth's climate is a constantly changing system resulting from a complex interaction of different geographical factors. Throughout history there have been several periods when the Earth's climate has been either hotter or colder than today. However, many scientists think that human activity is causing problems to this system by increasing levels of "greenhouse gases" in the atmosphere. These gases, including carbon dioxide (CO_2), allow heat from the Sun to enter the atmosphere and then trap some of this heat like a greenhouse. Most scientists believe that unless action is taken to reduce greenhouse gases, temperatures will rise in a process known as global warming.

MAP KEY

Predicted change in average surface air temperature between 1960–1990 and 2070–2100

- 7.2 to 9.0°F
- 5.4 to 7.2°F
- 3.6 to 5.4°F
- 1.8 to 3.6°F
- 0 to 1.8°F

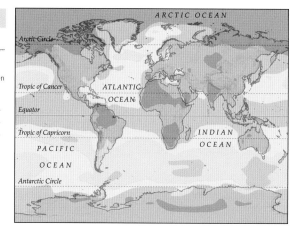

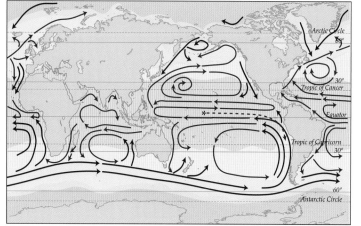

OCEAN CURRENTS

Ocean currents help distribute heat around the Earth and have a great influence on climate. Convection currents circulate massive amounts of warm and cold water around the oceans. Warm water is moved away from the tropics to higher latitudes and cold water is moved toward the tropics.

OCEAN CURRENTS AND SURFACE TEMPERATURES

- Cold currents
- Warm currents
- El Niño

- 68 to 86°F
- 50 to 68°F
- 32 to 50°F
- Seawater 28 to 32°F
- Sea ice (average) below 28°F

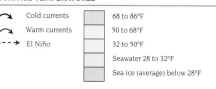

LIFE ZONES

The map below shows the Earth divided into different biomes – also called biogeographical regions. The combination of climate, the type of landscape, and the plants and animals that live there are used to classify a region. Similar biomes are found in very different places around the world.

POLAR REGIONS
The North and South Poles are permanently covered by ice. Only a few plants and animals can live here.

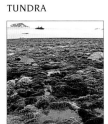

TUNDRA
Tundra is flat, cold, and dry, with few trees. Plants such as mosses and lichens grow close to the ground.

DESERTS
Very little rain falls in desert areas, whether they are hot deserts such as the Sahara or cold deserts like the Gobi.

CONIFEROUS FORESTS
Tall coniferous trees such as pine and spruce, with spines or needles instead of leaves, grow in the far north of Scandinavia, Canada, and the Russian Federation.

BROADLEAF FORESTS
Broadleaf or deciduous forests once covered temperate regions over most of the Northern Hemisphere. They contain trees of many varieties – all of which shed their leaves every year.

TEMPERATE RAIN FORESTS
Evergreen, broadleaved trees need a warmer, wetter climate than deciduous trees. They are known as temperate rain forests.

MEDITERRANEAN
Close to the shores of the Mediterranean Sea, the vegetation consists mainly of herbs, shrubs, and drought-resistant trees.

BIOME TYPES
- Mountains
- Polar regions
- Tundra
- Tropical rainforests
- Dry woodlands
- Savannah
- Temperate grasslands

(continued)
BIOME TYPES
- Mediterranean
- Coniferous forests
- Temperate rain forests
- Broadleafs forests
- Cold deserts
- Hot deserts
- Wetlands

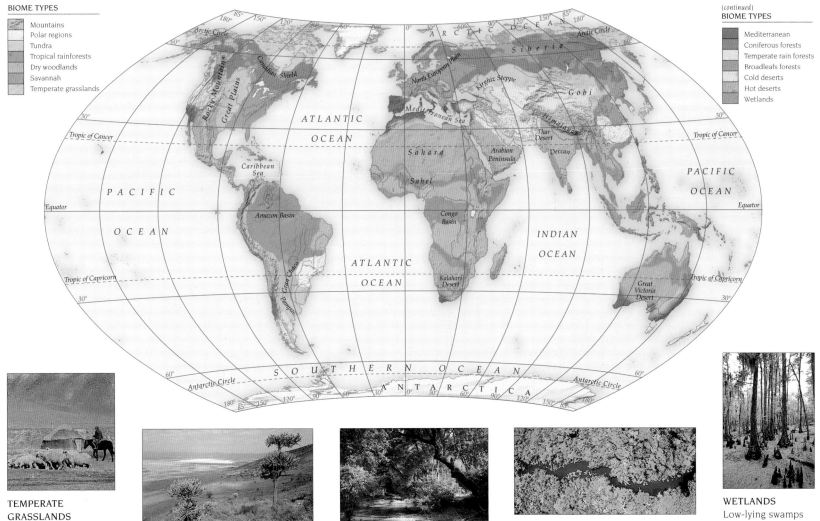

TEMPERATE GRASSLANDS
Grasslands cover the central areas of the continents. They are known in the middle latitudes as prairies, steppe, and pampas.

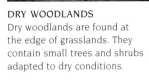

SAVANNA
The savanna consists of woodland interspersed with grassland. These regions lie between the tropical rain-forest and hot desert regions.

DRY WOODLANDS
Dry woodlands are found at the edge of grasslands. They contain small trees and shrubs adapted to dry conditions.

TROPICAL RAIN FORESTS
Around the Equator, where temperatures are high and there is plenty of rain, tropical rain forests flourish. Trees grow continuously and are tall with huge, broad leaves.

WETLANDS
Low-lying swamps and marshes are known as wetlands. They are often home to a rich variety of animal, plant, and bird species.

WORLD POPULATION

Favelas – or shanty towns – have grown up around many South American cities because of overcrowding.

There are now an estimated **7.2 billion people** on Earth. The population has increased to nearly four times that of 1900. Before that date, the number of people increased slowly because people were born and died at similar rates. With improved living conditions, better medical care, and more efficient food production, more people survived to adulthood, and the population began to grow much faster. If growth continues at the present rate, the world's population is likely to reach 7,700,000,000 by the year 2020.

POPULATION STRUCTURES

Measuring the numbers of old and young people gives the age structure of a country or continent. If there are large numbers of young people and a high birthrate, the population is said to be youthful – as is the case in many African, Asian, and South American countries. If the birthrate is low but many people survive into old age, the population distribution is said to be aging – this is true of much of Europe, Japan, Canada, and the US. Extreme events like wars can distort the population, leading to a loss of population in certain age groups.

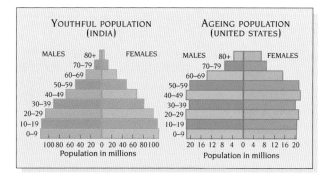

POPULATION DENSITY

The main map (*center*) and the map below both show population density – the number of people who live in a given area. The map below shows the average population density per country. You can see that European countries and parts of Asia are very densely populated. The large map shows where people actually live. While the average population density in Brazil and Egypt is quite low, the coasts of Brazil and the areas close to the Nile River in Egypt are very densely populated.

DENSE POPULATION

Huge crowds near the Haora Bridge in Kolkata (Calcutta), India – one of the world's most densely populated cities.

POPULATION DENSITY (BY COUNTRY)

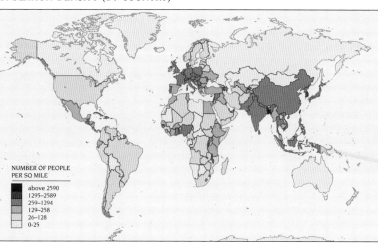

NUMBER OF PEOPLE
PER SQ MILE

- above 2590
- 1295–2589
- 259–1294
- 129–258
- 26–128
- 0–25

SPARSE POPULATION

The cold north of Canada has one of the lowest population densities in the world. Some people live in extreme isolation, separated from others by lakes and forests.

URBAN GROWTH

The 20th century saw a huge increase in the number of people living in urban areas. This has led to more large cities and the development of some "super cities" such as Mexico City and Tokyo, each with more than 20 million people. In 1900, only about 10% of the population lived in cities. Now it is closer to 50% and soon the figure may be nearer two in three people. Some continents are far more "urbanized" than others: in South America nearly 80% of people live in cities, whereas in Africa the figure is only about 30%.

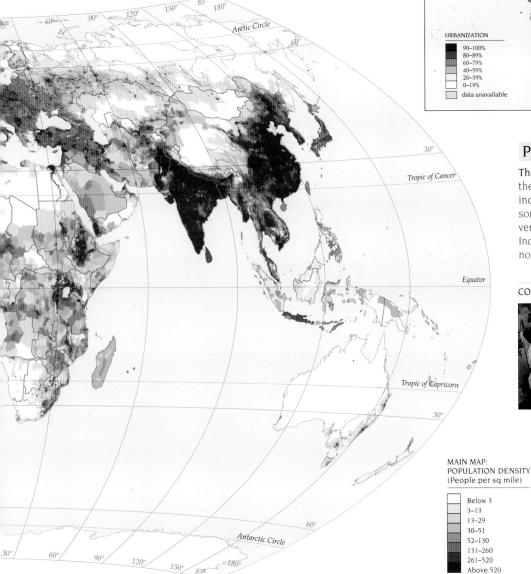

MAIN MAP:
POPULATION DENSITY
(People per sq mile)

- Below 3
- 3–13
- 13–29
- 30–51
- 52–130
- 131–260
- 261–520
- Above 520

LEVELS OF URBANIZATION

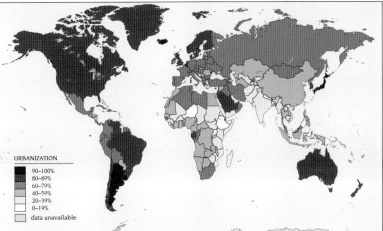

URBANIZATION
- 90–100%
- 80–89%
- 60–79%
- 40–59%
- 20–39%
- 0–19%
- data unavailable

POPULATION GROWTH

The rate of population growth varies dramatically between the continents. Europe has a large population but it is increasing slowly. Africa is still sparsely populated, but in some countries such as Kenya, the population is growing very rapidly, increasing pressure on the land. China and India have the world's largest populations. Both countries now have laws designed to curb the birthrate.

CONTROLLING GROWTH

In 1980, fewer than 25% of women in less-developed countries used birth control. Education programs and more widely available contraceptives are thought to have doubled this figure. But many families still have no access to contraception.

AN AGEING POPULATION

In some countries, a low birthrate and an increasingly long-lived elderly population have greatly increased the ratio of old people to younger people, putting a strain on health and social services. For example, in Japan, most people can now expect to live to at least 80 years of age.

BIRTH RATE

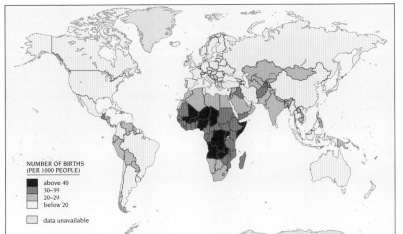

NUMBER OF BIRTHS
(PER 1000 PEOPLE)
- above 40
- 30–39
- 20–29
- below 20
- data unavailable

LIFE EXPECTANCY

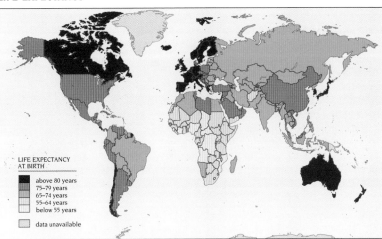

LIFE EXPECTANCY
AT BIRTH
- above 80 years
- 75–79 years
- 65–74 years
- 55–64 years
- below 55 years
- data unavailable

THE WORLD ECONOMY

Throughout the world, the way in which people make a living varies greatly. The countries of Western Europe and North America, along with Japan and Australia, are the most economically developed in the world, with a long- established and very diverse range of industries. They sell their products and services internationally. Less economically developed countries in Central Asia and much of Africa have a much smaller number of industries – some may rely on a single product – and many goods are produced only for the local market.

MEASURING WEALTH

The wealth of a country can be measured in several ways: for example, by the average annual income per person; by the volume of its trade; and by the total income from the goods and services that the country trades annually – its Gross National Income or GNI. The map below shows the average GNI per person for each of the world's countries, expressed in US$. Most of the highest levels of GNI are in Europe and the US; most of the lowest are in Africa.

WORLD ECONOMIES

GNI per capita (in US$)

- above 45,000
- 30,000–45,000
- 15,000–30,000
- 6,500–15,000
- below 6,500
- data unavailable

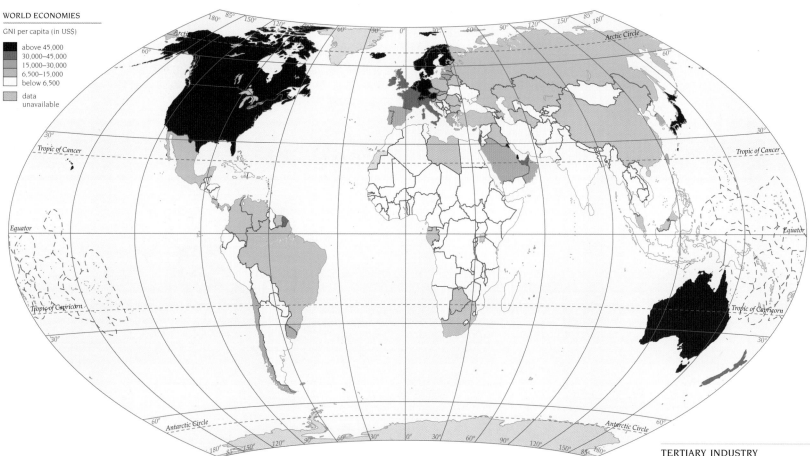

TYPES OF INDUSTRY

Industries are usually defined in one of three ways. Primary industries such as farming or mining involve the production of raw materials such as food or minerals. Secondary industries make or manufacture finished products out of raw materials: clothing and car manufacture are examples of secondary industries. People who work in tertiary industries provide different kinds of services. Banking, insurance, and tourism are all examples of tertiary industries. Some economically advanced nations such as Germany and the US now have quaternary industries, such as biotechnology which are knowledge-creation industries, devoted to the research and development of new products.

PRIMARY INDUSTRY

Tobacco leaves are picked and laid out for drying in Cuba, one of the world's great producers of cigars. Many countries rely on one or two high-value "cash crops" like tobacco to earn foreign currency.

SECONDARY INDUSTRY

This skilled Thai weaver is producing an intricately patterned silk fabric on a hand loom. Fabric manufacture is an important industry throughout South and Southeast Asia. In India and Pakistan, vast quantities of cotton are produced in highly mechanized factories, but many fabrics are still hand woven.

TERTIARY INDUSTRY

The City of London is one of the world's great finance centers. Branches of many banks and insurance companies, including the world-famous Lloyds of London, are clustered into the City's "square mile."

PATTERNS OF TRADE

Almost all countries trade goods with one another in order to obtain products they cannot produce themselves, and to make money from goods they have produced. Some countries – for example those in the Caribbean – rely mainly on a single export, usually a food or mineral, and can suffer a loss of income when world prices drop. Other countries, such as Germany and Japan, export a vast range of both raw materials and manufactured goods throughout the world. A number of huge companies, known as multinational corporations or MNCs, are responsible for more than 70% of world trade, with divisions all over the world. They include firms like BP, Coca Cola, and Microsoft.

CONTAINER SHIPS

Many products are transported around the world on container ships. Containers are of a standard size so that they can be efficiently transported to their destinations. Some ships are specially designed to carry perishable goods such as fruit and vegetables.

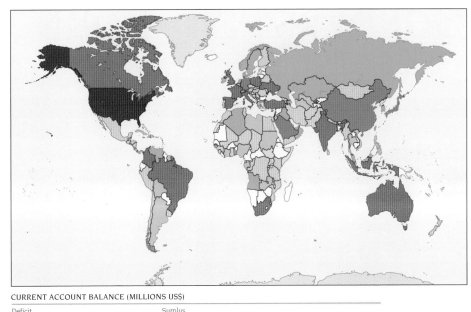

CURRENT ACCOUNT BALANCE (MILLIONS US$)

Deficit
- Over 450,000
- 10,000–450,000
- 1,000–10,000
- 0–1,000

Surplus
- 0–10,000
- 10,000–100,000
- Over 100,000
- Data unavailable

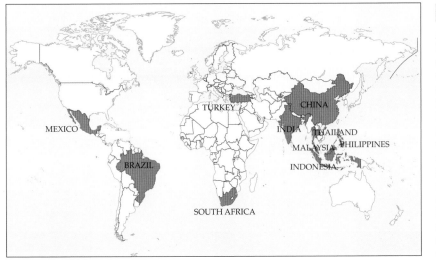

MEXICO · TURKEY · CHINA · INDIA · THAILAND · PHILIPPINES · MALAYSIA · INDONESIA · BRAZIL · SOUTH AFRICA

NEWLY INDUSTRIALIZED NATIONS

Although world trade is still dominated by the more economically developed countries, since the 1970s, less economically developed countries have increased their share of world trade from less than 10% to nearly 30%. Countries such as China, India, Malaysia, and Brazil, aided by investment from their governments or from wealthier countries, have become able to manufacture and export a wide variety of goods. Products include cars, electronics, clothing, and footwear. Multinational companies can take advantage of cheaper labor costs to manufacture goods in these countries. Moves are being made to limit the exploitation of workers who are paid very low wages for producing luxury goods.

ASIAN "TIGER" ECONOMIES

The economies of Malaysia, Taiwan, and South Korea boomed in the late 1980s, attracting investment for buildings such as the Petronas Towers (*above*).

TOURISM

Tourism is now the world's largest industry. More than 700 million people travel both abroad and in their own countries as tourists each year. People in more developed countries have more money and leisure time to travel. Tourism can bring large amounts of cash into the local economy, but local people do not always benefit. They may have to take low-paid jobs and experience great intrusions into their lives. Tourist development and pollution may damage the environment – sometimes destroying the very attractions that led to the development of tourism in the first place.

ECOTOURISM

These tourists are being introduced to a giant tortoise, one of the many unique animals found in the Galapagos Islands. A number of places with special animals and ecosystems have introduced programs to teach visitors about them. This not only educates people about the need to safeguard these environments, but brings in money to help protect them.

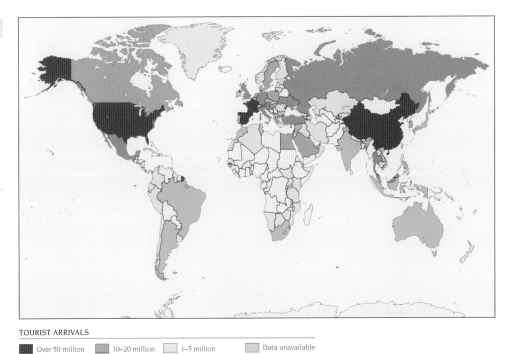

TOURIST ARRIVALS

- Over 50 million
- 20–50 million
- 10–20 million
- 5–10 million
- 1–5 million
- below 1 million
- Data unavailable

BORDERS AND BOUNDARIES

There are more countries in the world today than ever before – almost 200 – whereas in 1950, there were only 82. Since then, many former European colonies and Soviet states have become independent. The establishment of borders for each of these countries has often been the subject of disagreement.

Military borders
At the end of wars, new borders are often drawn up between the countries – frequently along cease-fire lines. They may remain there for many years. At the end of the Korean War in 1953, North and South Korea were divided close to the 38° line of latitude. This border has remained heavily fortified.

Enclaves
If part of a country's territory has become separated from the rest of the country, and is surrounded by foreign territory, it is called an enclave. Kaliningrad is part of the Russian Federation, but is cut off from it by Lithuania and Belarus.

River borders
Over one-sixth of the world's national borders are formed by rivers. Long stretches of the Danube form natural borders in southeastern Europe.

Long borders
The border between the USA and Canada is the second longest continuous border in the world. It cuts through the center of the Great Lakes. To the west of the Great Lakes, the border runs along the 49° line of latitude.

Mountain borders
Mountain ranges such as the Pyrenees, Alps and Himalayas form natural borders between many countries. In the Andes, border disputes between Chile and Argentina centered on finding the highest point in the mountain range that divided them.

Straight line borders
The borders of many countries in Africa and other former colonial territories are straight lines. This was the simplest solution for colonial administrators, who often knew little of the country's geography or population.

Lake boundaries
Countries which lie next to lakes usually fix their borders in the middle of the lake. Complicated agreements between colonial powers led to the awkward division of Lake Nyasa in Africa.

Territorial disputes
There are still many disputed territories and borders. One of the most serious territorial disputes is between India and Pakistan over Jammu and Kashmir, which has led to three wars since 1947.

THE ATLAS
OF THE
WORLD

THE NATIONS OF THE WORLD

The world is divided into 196 independent countries, and about 60 overseas territories or dependencies. The largest country is the Russian Federation covering 6,592,735 sq miles; the smallest is Vatican City in Rome, with an area of 0.17 sq miles.

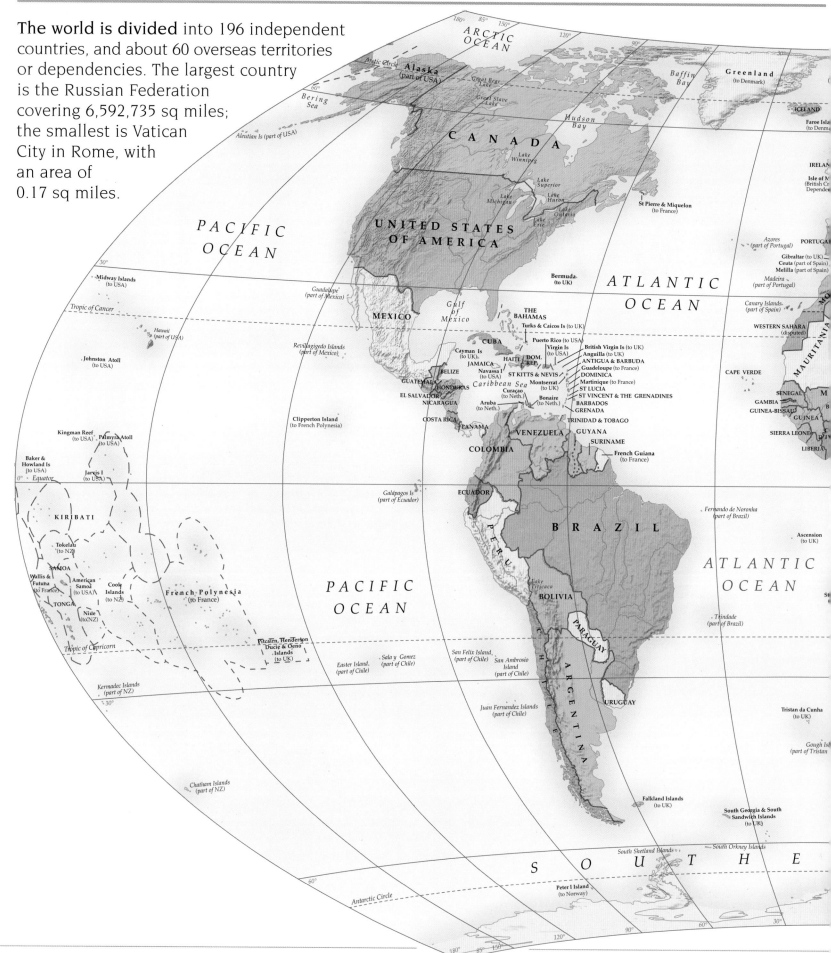

ARCTIC OCEAN

Arctic Circle **Alaska** (part of USA)

Bering Sea

Aleutian Is (part of USA)

Great Bear Lake

Great Slave Lake

CANADA

Hudson Bay

Lake Winnipeg

Lake Superior

Lake Michigan

Lake Huron

Lake Ontario

Lake Erie

Baffin Bay

Greenland (to Denmark)

ICELAND

Faroe Islands (to Denmark)

IRELAND

Isle of Man (British Crown Dependency)

PACIFIC OCEAN

30°

• Midway Islands (to USA)

Tropic of Cancer

• Hawaii (part of USA)

• Johnston Atoll (to USA)

UNITED STATES OF AMERICA

St Pierre & Miquelon (to France)

Guadalupe (part of Mexico)

MEXICO

Gulf of Mexico

Bermuda (to UK)

ATLANTIC OCEAN

Azores (part of Portugal)

PORTUGAL

Gibraltar (to UK)
Ceuta (part of Spain)
Melilla (part of Spain)

Madeira (part of Portugal)

Canary Islands (part of Spain)

WESTERN SAHARA (disputed)

MAURITANIA

THE BAHAMAS

Turks & Caicos Is (to UK)

CUBA

Puerto Rico (to USA)

Virgin Is (to USA)

British Virgin Is (to UK)
Anguilla (to UK)
ANTIGUA & BARBUDA
Guadeloupe (to France)
DOMINICA
Martinique (to France)
ST LUCIA
ST VINCENT & THE GRENADINES
BARBADOS
GRENADA

Revillagigedo Islands (part of Mexico)

Cayman Is (to UK)

JAMAICA

HAITI

DOM. REP.

BELIZE

Navassa I (to USA)

ST KITTS & NEVIS

Montserrat (to UK)

GUATEMALA

HONDURAS

Curaçao (to Neth.)

Caribbean Sea

EL SALVADOR

NICARAGUA

Aruba (to Neth.)

Bonaire (to Neth.)

CAPE VERDE

SENEGAL

GAMBIA

GUINEA-BISSAU

GUINEA

SIERRA LEONE

LIBERIA

Clipperton Island (to French Polynesia)

COSTA RICA

PANAMA

TRINIDAD & TOBAGO

VENEZUELA

GUYANA

SURINAME

COLOMBIA

French Guiana (to France)

Kingman Reef (to USA)

Palmyra Atoll (to USA)

Baker & Howland Is (to USA)

0° Equator

Jarvis I (to USA)

KIRIBATI

Galápagos Is (part of Ecuador)

ECUADOR

Fernando de Noronha (part of Brazil)

PERU

BRAZIL

Ascension (to UK)

ATLANTIC OCEAN

Tokelau (to NZ)

SAMOA

Wallis & Futuna (to France)

American Samoa (to USA)

Cook Islands (to NZ)

French Polynesia (to France)

PACIFIC OCEAN

TONGA

Niue (to NZ)

Lake Titicaca

BOLIVIA

Trindade (part of Brazil)

Tropic of Capricorn

Pitcairn, Henderson, Ducie & Oeno Islands (to UK)

Easter Island (part of Chile)

Sala y Gomez (part of Chile)

San Felix Island (part of Chile)

San Ambrosio Island (part of Chile)

CHILE

PARAGUAY

ARGENTINA

Kermadec Islands (part of NZ)

30°

Juan Fernandez Islands (part of Chile)

URUGUAY

Tristan da Cunha (to UK)

Gough Island (part of Tristan)

Chatham Islands (part of NZ)

Falkland Islands (to UK)

South Georgia & South Sandwich Islands (to UK)

South Shetland Islands

South Orkney Islands

SOUTHE

60°

Antarctic Circle

Peter I Island (to Norway)

60°

30°

180° 85° 150°

120°

90°

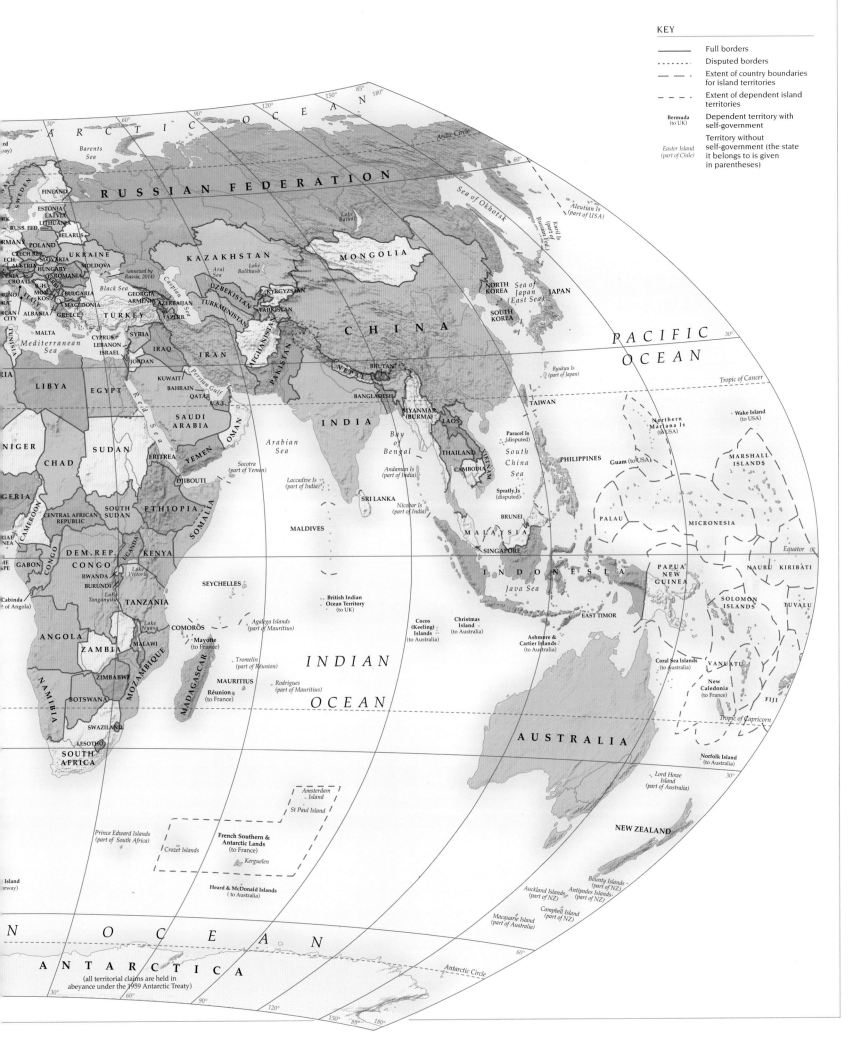

KEY

——————— Full borders

·········· Disputed borders

– – – – Extent of country boundaries
for island territories

– – – Extent of dependent island
territories

Bermuda   Dependent territory with
(to UK)   self-government

Easter Island   Territory without
(part of Chile) self-government (the state
           it belongs to is given
           in parentheses)

ARCTIC OCEAN

Barents
Sea

Arctic Circle

SWEDEN
FINLAND
ESTONIA
LATVIA
RUSS. FED.
LITHUANIA
BELARUS
GERMANY
POLAND
CZECH REP.
SLOVAKIA
UKRAINE
MOLDOVA
AUSTRIA HUNGARY
SLOVENIA ROMANIA
CROATIA
B-H.
MON. SERBIA
KOS.
BULGARIA
MACEDONIA
ALBANIA GREECE
ITALY
SAN MARINO
VATICAN CITY
MALTA
TUNISIA

RUSSIAN FEDERATION

Sea of Okhotsk

Aleutian Is
(part of USA)

Lake
Baikal

KAZAKHSTAN

(annexed by
Russia, 2014)

Aral
Sea

Lake
Balkhash

MONGOLIA

Kuril Is
(part of
Russian Fed.)

Black Sea

GEORGIA

Caspian Sea

UZBEKISTAN

KYRGYZSTAN

NORTH
KOREA

Sea of
Japan
(East Sea)

JAPAN

ARMENIA AZERBAIJAN
TURKMENISTAN
AZERB.
TAJIKISTAN

SOUTH
KOREA

TURKEY

CYPRUS
LEBANON
SYRIA
ISRAEL
IRAQ
JORDAN

AFGHANISTAN

PAKISTAN

CHINA

PACIFIC
OCEAN

Mediterranean
Sea

NEPAL

BHUTAN

Ryukyu Is
(part of Japan)

Tropic of Cancer

LIBYA
EGYPT

KUWAIT
BAHRAIN
QATAR
U.A.E.

Persian Gulf

INDIA

BANGLADESH

MYANMAR
(BURMA)

TAIWAN

LAOS

Wake Island
(to USA)

Red Sea

SAUDI
ARABIA

OMAN

Arabian
Sea

Bay
of
Bengal

THAILAND

Northern
Mariana Is
(to USA)

NIGER
CHAD

SUDAN

ERITREA
YEMEN

DJIBOUTI

Socotra
(part of Yemen)

Laccadive Is
(part of India)

Andaman Is
(part of India)

South
China
Sea

VIETNAM

CAMBODIA

PHILIPPINES

Guam (to USA)

MARSHALL
ISLANDS

NIGERIA

SOUTH
SUDAN

ETHIOPIA

SOMALIA

Nicobar Is
(part of India)

SRI LANKA

Paracel Is
(disputed)

BRUNEI

PALAU

MICRONESIA

CAMEROON

CENTRAL AFRICAN
REPUBLIC

MALDIVES

Spratly Is
(disputed)

MALAYSIA

EQUATORIAL GUINEA

GABON

DEM. REP.
CONGO

UGANDA

KENYA

Lake
Victoria

SINGAPORE

INDONESIA

PAPUA
NEW
GUINEA

NAURU

KIRIBATI

Equator

CONGO

RWANDA
BURUNDI

SEYCHELLES

Cabinda
(of Angola)

Lake
Tanganyika

TANZANIA

British Indian
Ocean Territory
(to UK)

Java Sea

SOLOMON
ISLANDS

TUVALU

Agalega Islands
(part of Mauritius)

EAST TIMOR

ANGOLA

ZAMBIA

MALAWI

Lake
Nyasa

COMOROS

Mayotte
(to France)

Cocos
(Keeling)
Islands
(to Australia)

Christmas
Island
(to Australia)

Ashmore &
Cartier Islands
(to Australia)

Coral Sea Islands
(to Australia)

VANUATU

New
Caledonia
(to France)

FIJI

NAMIBIA

ZIMBABWE

MOZAMBIQUE

MADAGASCAR

MAURITIUS

Tromelin
(part of Réunion)

Rodrigues
(part of Mauritius)

INDIAN
OCEAN

BOTSWANA

Réunion
(to France)

Tropic of Capricorn

SWAZILAND

AUSTRALIA

Norfolk Island
(to Australia)

LESOTHO

SOUTH
AFRICA

Lord Howe
Island
(part of Australia)

Amsterdam
Island

St Paul Island

Prince Edward Islands
(part of South Africa)

French Southern &
Antarctic Lands
(to France)

Crozet Islands

Kerguelen

NEW ZEALAND

Bounty Islands
(part of NZ)

Island
(Norway)

Heard & McDonald Islands
(to Australia)

Auckland Islands
(part of NZ)

Antipodes Islands
(part of NZ)

Campbell Island
(part of NZ)

Macquarie Island
(part of Australia)

OCEAN

ANTARCTICA

(all territorial claims are held in
abeyance under the 1959 Antarctic Treaty)

Antarctic Circle

CONTINENTAL NORTH AMERICA

North America is the world's third largest continent, stretching from icy Greenland to the tropical Caribbean. The first people came from Asia more than 20,000 years ago. Their descendants spread across the continent, ate fish, meat, and wild and cultivated plants, and developed a wide variety of cultures and languages. About 500 years ago, immigrants from Europe, Africa, and Asia began to arrive in North America, bringing their own languages and cultures to the "New World."

4,600 miles

3,540 miles

CROSS-SECTION THROUGH NORTH AMERICA

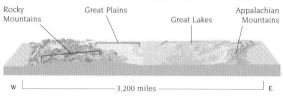

Rocky Mountains | Great Plains | Great Lakes | Appalachian Mountains

W   3,200 miles   E

In the west the land rises from the Pacific Ocean to the coastal ranges and the Rocky Mountains. Farther east, the continent flattens into the Great Plains and the Great Lakes – gouged out by glaciers at the end of the last Ice Age. The Appalachian Mountains are older than the Rockies, and are very worn down.

PHYSICAL NORTH AMERICA

The high peaks of the Rocky Mountains of Canada and the US tower above the lower ranges of the western coasts. These ranges stretch from the icy north of Alaska, south to Mexico and Central America. The heart of the continent is flatter, and much of it is drained by the mighty Mississippi-Missouri river system.

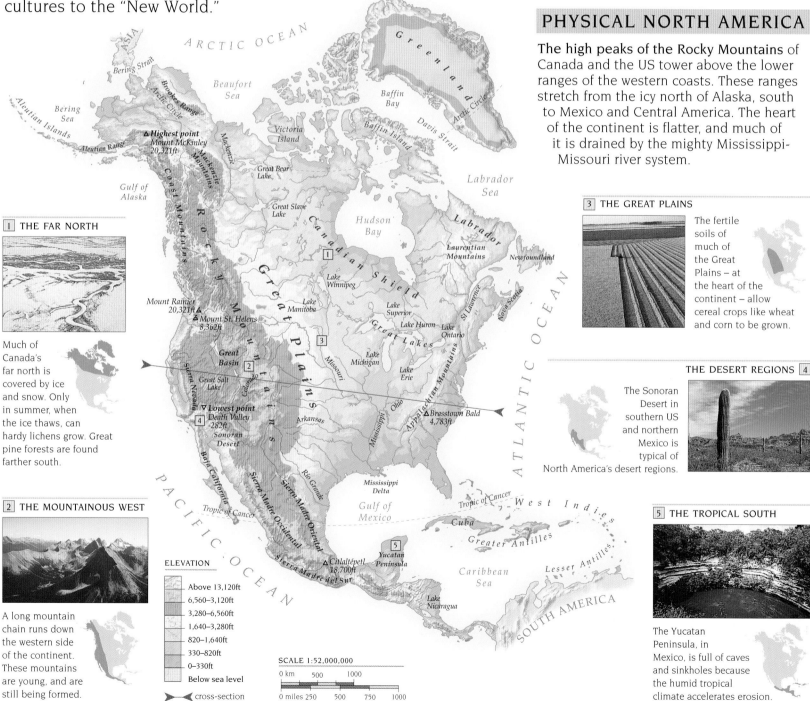

1 THE FAR NORTH

Much of Canada's far north is covered by ice and snow. Only in summer, when the ice thaws, can hardy lichens grow. Great pine forests are found farther south.

2 THE MOUNTAINOUS WEST

A long mountain chain runs down the western side of the continent. These mountains are young, and are still being formed.

3 THE GREAT PLAINS

The fertile soils of much of the Great Plains – at the heart of the continent – allow cereal crops like wheat and corn to be grown.

THE DESERT REGIONS 4

The Sonoran Desert in southern US and northern Mexico is typical of North America's desert regions.

5 THE TROPICAL SOUTH

The Yucatan Peninsula, in Mexico, is full of caves and sinkholes because the humid tropical climate accelerates erosion.

Map labels:

ARCTIC OCEAN
ASIA
Bering Strait
Brookes Range
Arctic Circle
Beaufort Sea
Aleutian Islands
Bering Sea
Aleutian Range
▲ Highest point Mount McKinley 20,321ft
Mackenzie
Mackenzie Mountains
Gulf of Alaska
Coast Mountains
Great Bear Lake
Victoria Island
Baffin Island
Davis Strait
Arctic Circle
Greenland
Baffin Bay
Labrador Sea
Rocky Mountains
Canadian Shield
Great Slave Lake
Hudson Bay
Laurentian Mountains
Newfoundland
Lake Winnipeg
Mount Rainier 20,321ft ▲
Mount St. Helens 8,362ft
Lake Manitoba
Lake Superior
Lake Huron
St. Lawrence
Nova Scotia
Great Basin 2
Great Salt Lake
Colorado
Great Plains
Missouri
Lake Michigan
Lake Ontario
Lake Erie
Great Lakes
Sierra Nevada
▽ Lowest point Death Valley -282ft
4
Sonoran Desert
Arkansas
Ohio
Mississippi
Appalachian Mountains
▲ Brasstown Bald 4,783ft
ATLANTIC OCEAN
Baja California
Sierra Madre Occidental
Rio Grande
Sierra Madre Oriental
Mississippi Delta
Gulf of Mexico
Tropic of Cancer
West Indies
Cuba
Greater Antilles
Lesser Antilles
Caribbean Sea
PACIFIC OCEAN
▲ Citlaltépetl 18,700ft
Yucatan Peninsula
Sierra Madre del Sur
Lake Nicaragua
SOUTH AMERICA

ELEVATION

- Above 13,120ft
- 6,560–3,120ft
- 3,280–6,560ft
- 1,640–3,280ft
- 820–1,640ft
- 330–820ft
- 0–330ft
- Below sea level
- ➤◄ cross-section

SCALE 1:52,000,000

0 km   500   1000

0 miles 250   500   750   1000

POLITICAL NORTH AMERICA

The US, Canada, and Mexico are all federal countries. This means that political power is shared between the national government and the state or provincial governments. Canada and the US are democracies with a long history of freedom and equal rights. Governments in the countries south of the US have been less stable, often ruled by dictators or harsh regimes. Many people have suffered for their political beliefs. During the 1960s and 70s many of the Caribbean islands gained independence from their European colonial rulers.

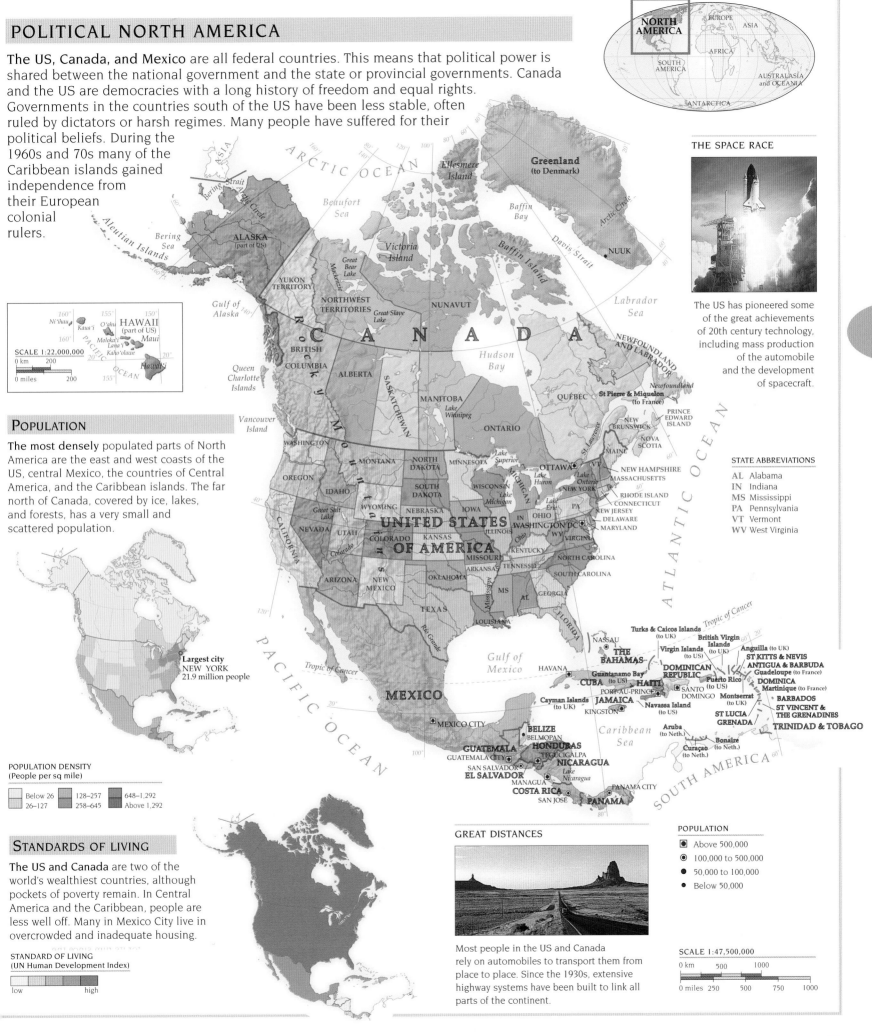

THE SPACE RACE

The US has pioneered some of the great achievements of 20th century technology, including mass production of the automobile and the development of spacecraft.

POPULATION

The most densely populated parts of North America are the east and west coasts of the US, central Mexico, the countries of Central America, and the Caribbean islands. The far north of Canada, covered by ice, lakes, and forests, has a very small and scattered population.

Largest city
NEW YORK
21.9 million people

POPULATION DENSITY
(People per sq mile)

Below 26	128–257	648–1,292
26–127	258–645	Above 1,292

STANDARDS OF LIVING

The US and Canada are two of the world's wealthiest countries, although pockets of poverty remain. In Central America and the Caribbean, people are less well off. Many in Mexico City live in overcrowded and inadequate housing.

STANDARD OF LIVING
(UN Human Development Index)

low   high

STATE ABBREVIATIONS

AL Alabama
IN Indiana
MS Mississippi
PA Pennsylvania
VT Vermont
WV West Virginia

GREAT DISTANCES

Most people in the US and Canada rely on automobiles to transport them from place to place. Since the 1930s, extensive highway systems have been built to link all parts of the continent.

POPULATION

◉ Above 500,000
◎ 100,000 to 500,000
● 50,000 to 100,000
• Below 50,000

SCALE 1:47,500,000

0 km   500   1000

0 miles 250   500   750   1000

NORTH AMERICAN GEOGRAPHY

Canada and the US are among the world's wealthiest countries. They have rich natural resources, good farmland, and thriving, varied industries. The range of different industries in Mexico is growing, but other Central American countries and the Caribbean islands rely on one or two important cash crops and tourism for most of their incomes. They have a lower standard of living than the US and Canada.

MINERAL RESOURCES

North America still has large amounts of mineral resources. Canada has important nickel reserves, Mexico is renowned for its silver, and bauxite – used to make aluminum – is found in Jamaica. Oil and gas are plentiful, particularly in the Arctic northwest by the Beaufort Sea, and farther south by the Gulf of Mexico.

INDUSTRY

The US and Canada have an extremely wide range of industries, from mining and the processing of farm produce, to heavy and light manufacturing and service industries like banking. A variety of goods are produced, including airplanes, cars, and computers. Oil exports and machine assembly are Mexico's main industries. In Central America and the Caribbean nations, most industry is based on agricultural produce.

MINERAL RESOURCES

- Bauxite
- Copper
- Iron
- Nickel
- Phosphates
- Silver
- Uranium
- Oil/gas field
- Coal field

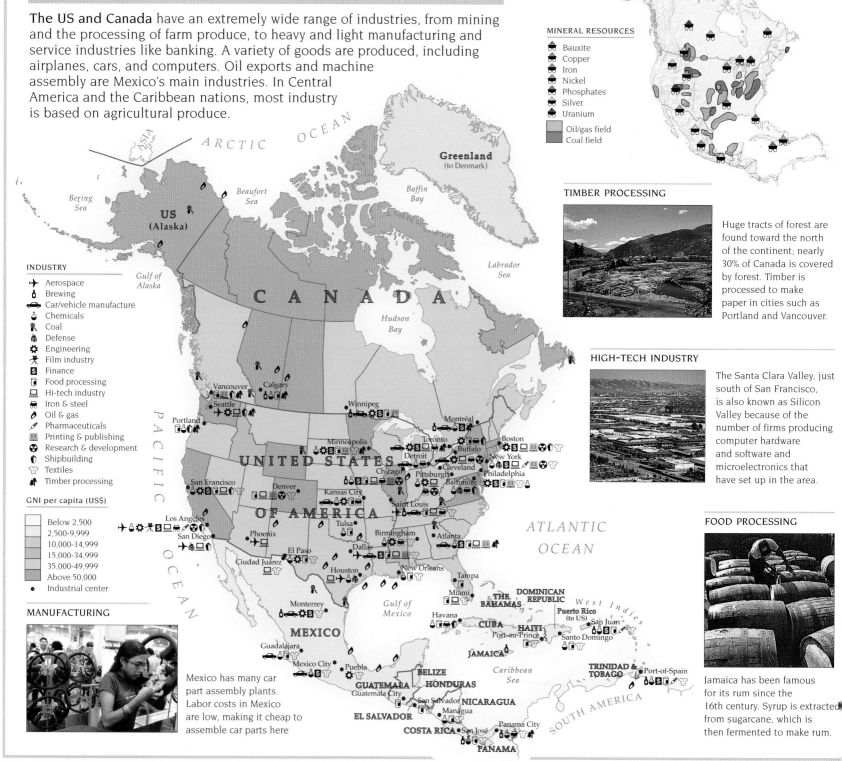

INDUSTRY
- Aerospace
- Brewing
- Car/vehicle manufacture
- Chemicals
- Coal
- Defense
- Engineering
- Film industry
- Finance
- Food processing
- Hi-tech industry
- Iron & steel
- Oil & gas
- Pharmaceuticals
- Printing & publishing
- Research & development
- Shipbuilding
- Textiles
- Timber processing

GNI per capita (US$)
- Below 2,500
- 2,500-9,999
- 10,000-14,999
- 15,000-34,999
- 35,000-49,999
- Above 50,000
- • Industrial center

TIMBER PROCESSING

Huge tracts of forest are found toward the north of the continent; nearly 30% of Canada is covered by forest. Timber is processed to make paper in cities such as Portland and Vancouver.

HIGH-TECH INDUSTRY

The Santa Clara Valley, just south of San Francisco, is also known as Silicon Valley because of the number of firms producing computer hardware and software and microelectronics that have set up in the area.

MANUFACTURING

Mexico has many car part assembly plants. Labor costs in Mexico are low, making it cheap to assemble car parts here

FOOD PROCESSING

Jamaica has been famous for its rum since the 16th century. Syrup is extracted from sugarcane, which is then fermented to make rum.

CLIMATE

Much of northern Canada lies within the Arctic Circle and is permanently covered by ice or the sparse vegetation known as tundra. Southern Canada and much of central US have a continental climate, with hot summers and cold winters. The southern parts of the US, Central America, and the Caribbean have a hot, humid tropical climate. The Caribbean and the eastern and central states of the US often experience hurricane-force winds, waterspouts, and tornadoes.

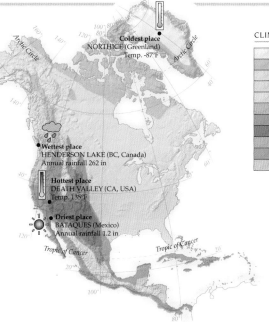

Coldest place
NORTHICE (Greenland)
Temp. -87°F

Wettest place
HENDERSON LAKE (BC, Canada)
Annual rainfall 262 in

Hottest place
DEATH VALLEY (CA, USA)
Temp. 135°F

Driest place
BATAQUES (Mexico)
Annual rainfall 1.2 in

EXTREME WEATHER EVENTS

Symbols indicate climatic extremes

CLIMATE

- Ice cap
- Tundra
- Subarctic
- Cool continental
- Warm temperate
- Mediterranean
- Semiarid
- Arid
- Humid equatorial
- Tropical
- Hot humid

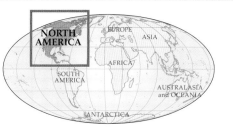

NORTH AMERICA'S HOTTEST PLACE

Death Valley in California is the hottest and driest place in the US. Strong, dry winds sweep through the valley, constantly reshaping the sand and salt deposits that cover its floor.

LAND USE AND AGRICULTURE

On the Great Plains and prairies of the US and Canada, vast quantities of cereal crops, including corn and wheat, grow in the fertile soils. Cattle are also raised on great ranches throughout these regions and on the foothills of the Rocky Mountains. In California, vegetables and fruits are grown with the aid of irrigation. Bananas, coffee, and sugarcane are grown for export in Central America and the Caribbean, while sorghum and corn are grown as subsistence crops.

BANANA PLANTATION

Banana plantations are common in the Caribbean and Central America. The fruit is grown for local consumption and for export to the US and Europe, where they are valued for their flavor and nutritional qualities.

FISHING

The Grand Banks off the eastern coast of Canada were once home to almost limitless fish stocks. Overfishing has reduced the number of fish to very low levels. Quotas limiting the numbers of fish caught help the numbers to rise.

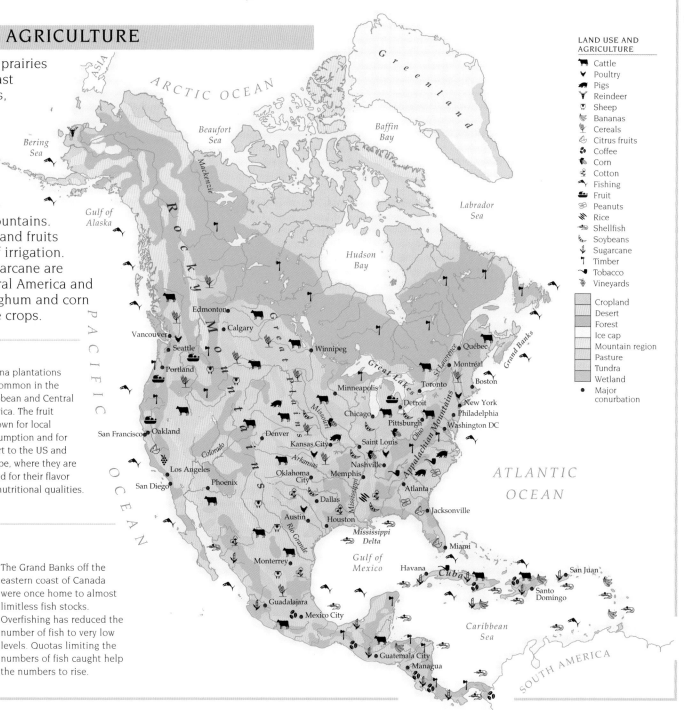

LAND USE AND AGRICULTURE

- Cattle
- Poultry
- Pigs
- Reindeer
- Sheep
- Bananas
- Cereals
- Citrus fruits
- Coffee
- Corn
- Cotton
- Fishing
- Fruit
- Peanuts
- Rice
- Shellfish
- Soybeans
- Sugarcane
- Timber
- Tobacco
- Vineyards

- Cropland
- Desert
- Forest
- Ice cap
- Mountain region
- Pasture
- Tundra
- Wetland
- Major conurbation

WESTERN CANADA

ALBERTA, BRITISH COLUMBIA, MANITOBA, NORTHWEST
TERRITORIES, NUNAVUT, SASKATCHEWAN, YUKON TERRITORY

The first inhabitants of Canada's western provinces
were Native Americans. By the late 1800s, the Canadian
Pacific Railroad was completed and European settlers
moved west, turning most of the prairie into huge grain
farms. North of the prairies lie the vast, empty territories
that have significant Native American populations.
In 1999, part of the Northwest Territories, known as
Nunavut, became a self-governing Inuit homeland.

FARMING AND LAND USE

More than 20% of the world's wheat is
grown in Canada's prairie provinces:
Manitoba, Alberta, and
Saskatchewan. Beef cattle graze
on the ranches of Alberta and
British Columbia. Fruits,
especially apples, flourish
in the sheltered southern
valleys of British Columbia,
and Pacific salmon and
herring are caught off
the west coast.

LAND USE

Pasture 5%
Cropland 4%
Forest 38%
Other (including mountains) 53%

FARMING AND LAND USE

- Cattle
- Fishing
- Cereals
- Fruit
- Timber
- Major conurbation
- Pasture
- Cropland
- Forest
- Mountain region
- Barren
- Tundra

INDUSTRY

The major industries in the prairie provinces
are related to agriculture, such as
meat-processing in Manitoba. Alberta
has huge reserves of fossil fuels,
and the other provinces are rich in
minerals, including zinc, nickel,
silver, and uranium. British
Columbia's economy depends
on manufacturing, especially
automobiles, chemicals, and
machinery, along
with paper and
timber industries.

Resolute

Kitimat
Edmonton
Flin Flon
Calgary
Vancouver
Regina
Winnipeg

STRUCTURE OF INDUSTRY

Primary 6%
Services 64%
Manufacturing 30%

INDUSTRY

- Car manufacturing
- Chemicals
- Engineering
- Food processing
- Metal refining
- Oil and gas
- Mining
- Timber processing
- Tourism
- Major industrial center / area
- Major road

THE LANDSCAPE

The prairie provinces are mostly flat. Occasionally,
the level plains are broken up by river valleys such
as that of the Qu'Appelle in Saskatchewan. In the
west, the jagged peaks and steep passes of the Rocky
Mountains and the Coast Mountains are covered
in snow for months on end. West of the Rockies,
the land descends sharply toward the coast of
British Columbia. The far north is covered by dense
forests and many glacial lakes.

The Arctic
Most of Canada's northern
islands are within the Arctic
Circle. They are covered by
ice year-round.

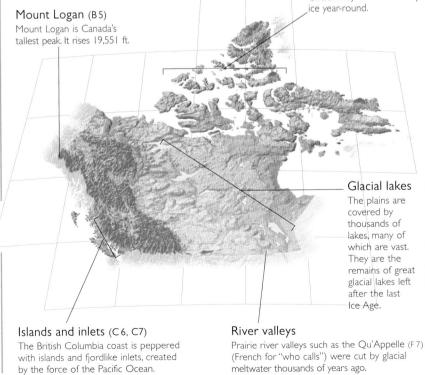

Mount Logan (B 5)
Mount Logan is Canada's
tallest peak. It rises 19,551 ft.

Glacial lakes
The plains are
covered by
thousands of
lakes, many of
which are vast.
They are the
remains of great
glacial lakes left
after the last
Ice Age.

Islands and inlets (C 6, C7)
The British Columbia coast is peppered
with islands and fjordlike inlets, created
by the force of the Pacific Ocean.

River valleys
Prairie river valleys such as the Qu'Appelle (F 7)
(French for "who calls") were cut by glacial
meltwater thousands of years ago.

ENVIRONMENTAL ISSUES

For hundreds of years sailors have searched in vain for
a route from Europe to Asia via the Northwest Passage,
through the north of this region. In recent summers the sea
ice has retreated further north, and in 2007 the route was
completely navigable.
Many of the extensive forests in
British Columbia are used for
commercial lumbering. The
province produces more than
half of Canada's timber.

Vancouver
Winnipeg

ENVIRONMENTAL ISSUES

- Lumbering activity
- Permafrost zone
- Major industrial center
- - - - Northwest Passage - direct route

POPULATION

Most of the people in western Canada live near the Canada/US border, taking advantage of the warmer climate and convenient transportation routes. In the cold, forested north, the population is sparse, with only a few people per 100 sq miles – many of them Native Americans such as the Inuit.

Edmonton
Saskatoon
Vancouver
Calgary
Regina
Winnipeg

CLIMATE

Parts of northern Canada are frozen all year round. The prairie provinces have warm summers and cold winters. Coastal British Columbia is mild and wet.

January

July

NORTH AMERICA

Western Canada

EUROPE
ASIA
AFRICA
SOUTH AMERICA
AUSTRALASIA AND OCEANIA
ANTARCTICA

TEMPERATURE AND PRECIPITATION

More than 68°F	23 to 32°F
59 to 68°F	14 to 23°F
50 to 59°F	5 to 14°F
41 to 50°F	Less than 5°F
32 to 41°F	4 — Precipitation (in)

URBAN/RURAL POPULATION DIVISION

Vancouver 22.7%
Other towns and cities 38%
Calgary 10.8%
Edmonton 10.5%
Rural population 18%

INHABITANTS PER SQ MILE

More than 30
3–30
Less than 3
• Major city

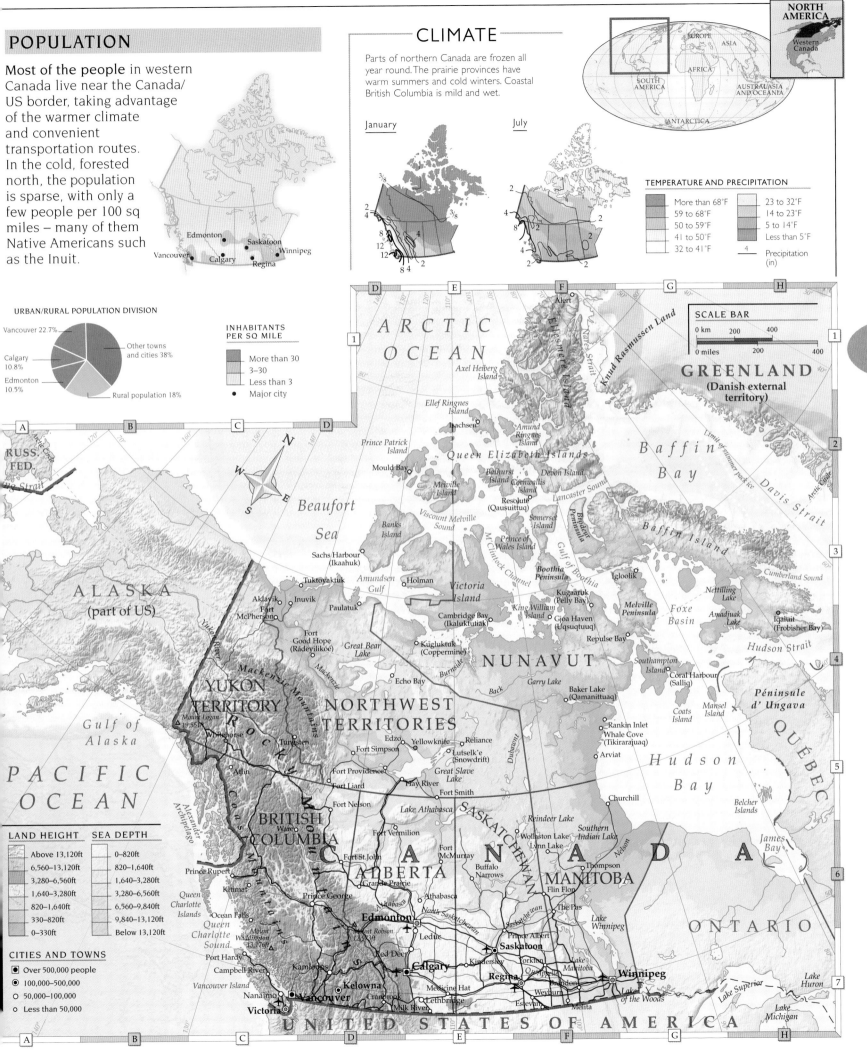

LAND HEIGHT

	Above 13,120ft
	6,560–13,120ft
	3,280–6,560ft
	1,640–3,280ft
	820–1,640ft
	330–820ft
	0–330ft

SEA DEPTH

	0–820ft
	820–1,640ft
	1,640–3,280ft
	3,280–6,560ft
	6,560–9,840ft
	9,840–13,120ft
	Below 13,120ft

CITIES AND TOWNS

■ Over 500,000 people
◉ 100,000–500,000
○ 50,000–100,000
○ Less than 50,000

SCALE BAR

0 km 200 400
0 miles 200 400

ARCTIC OCEAN

GREENLAND (Danish external territory)

Ellesmere Island
Knud Rasmussen Land
Naves Strait
Axel Heiberg Island
Ellef Ringnes Island
Amund Ringnes Island
Isachsen
Prince Patrick Island
Queen Elizabeth Islands
Baffin Bay
Mould Bay
Bathurst Island
Devon Island
Cornwallis Island
Lancaster Sound
Melville Island
Resolute (Qausuittuq)
Somerset Island
Viscount Melville Sound
Prince of Wales Island
Brodeur Peninsula
Baffin Island
Banks Island
Sachs Harbour (Ikaahuk)
Boothia Peninsula
Igloolik
Cumberland Sound
Nettilling Lake
Tuktoyaktuk
Amundsen Gulf
Holman
Victoria Island
M'Clintock Channel
Gulf of Boothia
Kugaaruk (Pelly Bay)
Melville Peninsula
Foxe Basin
Amadjuak Lake
Iqaluit (Frobisher Bay)
Aklavik
Inuvik
Paulatuk
Cambridge Bay (Ikaluktutiak)
King William Island
Gjoa Haven (Uqsuqtuuq)
Fort McPherson
Fort Good Hope (Rádeyilikóé)
Great Bear Lake
Kugluktuk (Coppermine)
Repulse Bay
Hudson Strait
Mackenzie
Burnside
NUNAVUT
Southampton Island
Mansel Island
Coral Harbour (Salliq)
Péninsule d' Ungava
YUKON TERRITORY
Echo Bay
Back
Garry Lake
Coats Island
Whitehorse
Mount Logan 19,551ft
NORTHWEST TERRITORIES
Baker Lake (Qamanittuaq)
QUÉBEC
Tungsten
Edzo
Yellowknife
Reliance
Rankin Inlet
Whale Cove (Tikirajuaq)
Fort Simpson
Lutselk'e (Snowdrift)
Dubawnt
Arviat
Hudson Bay
Atlin
Fort Providence
Great Slave Lake
Fort Liard
Hay River
Fort Smith
Churchill
Fort Nelson
Lake Athabasca
Reindeer Lake
Belcher Islands
BRITISH COLUMBIA
Fort Vermilion
SASKATCHEWAN
Wollaston Lake
Southern Indian Lake
James Bay
Prince Rupert
Fort St.John
Fort McMurray
Lynn Lake
Thompson
Kitimat
ALBERTA
Buffalo Narrows
MANITOBA
Grande Prairie
Flin Flon
Queen Charlotte Islands
Prince George
Athabasca
The Pas
ONTARIO
Ocean Falls
Mount Waddington
Edmonton
Mount Robson 12,972ft
North Saskatchewan
Lake Winnipeg
Queen Charlotte Sound
Ledue
Prince Albert
Port Hardy
Red Deer
Saskatoon
Yorkton
Lake Manitoba
Campbell River
Kamloops
Calgary
Kindersley
Lake Winnipeg
Lake Superior
Nanaimo
Kelowna
Medicine Hat
Regina
Brandon
Winnipeg
Lake of the Woods
Vancouver
Cranbrook
Lethbridge
Weyburn
Melita
Lake Huron
Victoria
Milk River
Estevan
Lake Michigan

ALASKA (part of US)
Yukon River
Mackenzie Mountains
Rocky Mountains
Coast Mountains
Alexander Archipelago
Gulf of Alaska
PACIFIC OCEAN
RUSS. FED.
Bering Strait
Arctic Circle
Beaufort Sea
CANADA
Vancouver Island

UNITED STATES OF AMERICA

EASTERN CANADA

NEW BRUNSWICK, NEWFOUNDLAND AND LABRADOR,
NOVA SCOTIA, ONTARIO, PRINCE EDWARD ISLAND, QUÉBEC

The first European settlements grew up in the Atlantic provinces, and along the St. Lawrence River, where Québec City and Montréal were founded. People gradually migrated farther west along the St. Lawrence River and the Great Lakes, establishing other cities including Toronto. Although the majority of Canadians speak English, people in Québec speak mainly French, and both English and French are official languages in Canada.

INDUSTRY

In the Atlantic provinces the traditional fishing industry has declined, causing unemployment. However, Newfoundland has a thriving food processing industry. Ontario and Québec have a wide range of industries, including the generation of hydroelectricity, mining, and chemicals, car manufacturing and fruit canning in the great cities. Large amounts of wood pulp and paper are also produced.

STRUCTURE OF INDUSTRY

Primary 7%
Services 64%
Manufacturing 29%

INDUSTRY

🚗	Car manufacturing	⚶	Timber processing
⚗	Chemicals	💻	High-tech industry
🐟	Fish processing	⚓	Tourism
📦	Food processing		
⚡	Hydroelectric power	▪	Major industrial center / area
△	Metal refining		Major road
⛏	Mining		

FARMING AND LAND USE

The best farmland lies on the flat, fertile plains close to the St. Lawrence River and on the strip of land between Lake Erie and Lake Ontario. It is used to grow fruits such as grapes, cherries, and peaches, and to raise cattle. Nova Scotia has fruit farms, and the rich red soils of Prince Edward Island produce a big potato crop. The vast forests that grow across the north are a major source of timber.

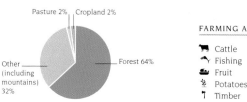

LAND USE

Pasture 2%   Cropland 2%
Other (including mountains) 32%
Forest 64%

FARMING AND LAND USE

🐂	Cattle		Pasture
🐟	Fishing		Cropland
🍒	Fruit		Forest
⚘	Potatoes		Tundra
⚶	Timber	●	Major conurbation

ENVIRONMENTAL ISSUES

Acid rain caused by emissions from factories in the US and along the St. Lawrence River destroys forests and kills marine life. Massive hydro-electric power projects in James Bay on Hudson Bay have flooded huge areas of land, affecting the environment and the local Cree people. Overfishing in the Atlantic has led to limits being set on the number of fish that can be caught.

ENVIRONMENTAL ISSUES

🐟	Depleted fish stocks
〰	Major dam
👥	Urban air pollution
	Affected by acid rain
	Severe sea/lake pollution
●	Major industrial center

THE LANDSCAPE

A huge, ancient mass of rock called the Canadian Shield lies beneath much of eastern Canada. It is covered by low hills, rocky outcrops, thousands of lakes, and huge areas of forest. Much of the Canadian Shield is permanently frozen. The St. Lawrence River flows out of Lake Ontario and into the Atlantic Ocean. It is surrounded by rolling hills and flat areas of very fertile farmland.

Scoured by ice
About 20,000 years ago, Labrador and northern Québec were completely covered by ice. The glaciers scraped hollows in the rock beneath. When the ice melted, lakes were left in the hollows that remained.

Lake Superior (B5)
Lake Superior is the largest freshwater lake in the world. It covers an area of 32,150 sq miles and lies between Canada and the US.

St. Lawrence River (E5)
The St. Lawrence River is 744 miles long. Parts of it have become silted up, causing it to be braided into many different channels. Between December and mid-April the river freezes over.

Highlands
The highlands of New Brunswick, Nova Scotia, and Newfoundland are the most northerly part of the Appalachian mountain chain.

The Bay of Fundy (F5)
This bay has the world's highest tides. It is shaped like a funnel, and as the Atlantic flows into it, the ever narrowing shores cause the water level to rise 20–50 ft at every high tide.

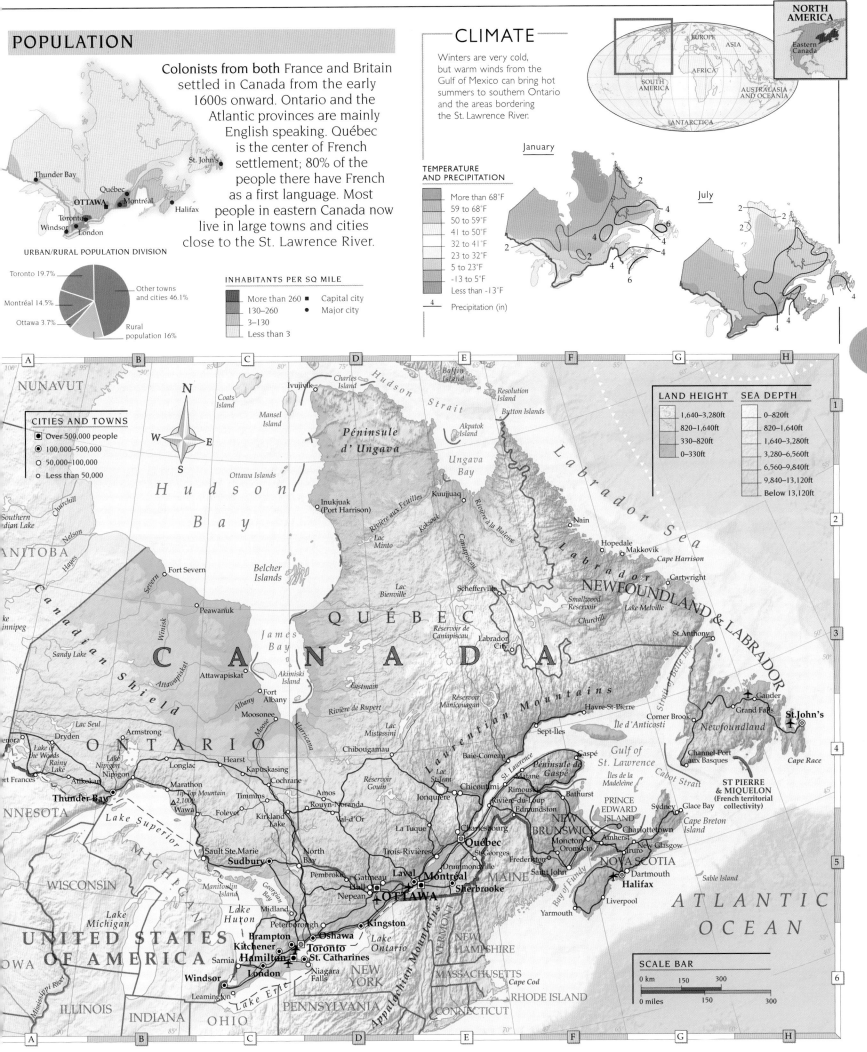

POPULATION

Colonists from both France and Britain settled in Canada from the early 1600s onward. Ontario and the Atlantic provinces are mainly English speaking. Québec is the center of French settlement; 80% of the people there have French as a first language. Most people in eastern Canada now live in large towns and cities close to the St. Lawrence River.

URBAN/RURAL POPULATION DIVISION

Toronto 19.7%
Montréal 14.5%
Ottawa 3.7%
Other towns and cities 46.1%
Rural population 16%

INHABITANTS PER SQ MILE

More than 260
130–260
3–130
Less than 3

■ Capital city
● Major city

CLIMATE

Winters are very cold, but warm winds from the Gulf of Mexico can bring hot summers to southern Ontario and the areas bordering the St. Lawrence River.

NORTH AMERICA
Eastern Canada

TEMPERATURE AND PRECIPITATION

More than 68°F
59 to 68°F
50 to 59°F
41 to 50°F
32 to 41°F
23 to 32°F
5 to 23°F
-13 to 5°F
Less than -13°F

4 Precipitation (in)

January
July

CITIES AND TOWNS

■ Over 500,000 people
◉ 100,000–500,000
◎ 50,000–100,000
○ Less than 50,000

LAND HEIGHT

1,640–3,280ft
820–1,640ft
330–820ft
0–330ft

SEA DEPTH

0–820ft
820–1,640ft
1,640–3,280ft
3,280–6,560ft
6,560–9,840ft
9,840–13,120ft
Below 13,120ft

SCALE BAR

0 km   150   300
0 miles   150   300

US: THE NORTHEASTERN STATES

CONNECTICUT, DELAWARE, MAINE, MASSACHUSETTS, NEW-HAMPSHIRE, NEW JERSEY, NEW YORK, PENNSYLVANIA, RHODE ISLAND, VERMONT

The dynamic 200-year boom of the northeastern states has been the result of a combination of factors. Between 1855 and 1924, over 20 million people poured into the region from all over the world, hoping to build a new life. Natural resources, including coal and iron, fueled new industries and fertile farmland provided food for the region's growing population. The "gateway" cities of the Atlantic seaboard, New York and Boston, enabled manufacturers to export their goods worldwide.

INDUSTRY

Boston, New York, and Philadelphia are international centers of industry and commerce. Electronics and communications are growing throughout the Northeast alongside traditional industries such as fishing and wood products. Tourism is vital for the northeastern states, particularly along the Atlantic coast.

STRUCTURE OF INDUSTRY

Manufacturing 16.5%
Primary 0.5%
Services 83%

INDUSTRY

- Chemicals
- Engineering
- Food processing
- Iron and steel
- Pharmaceuticals
- Textiles
- Timber processing
- Defense
- Finance
- High-tech
- Research and development
- Tourism

▪ Major industrial center / area
— Major road

ENVIRONMENTAL ISSUES

The high level of industry and the large population puts great pressure on the environment. Air pollution from automobiles and industry led to poor air quality in many cities and caused acid rain. The problem is worse toward the Great Lakes, where severe lake pollution has occurred.

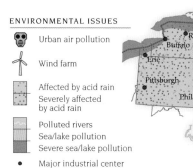

ENVIRONMENTAL ISSUES

- Urban air pollution
- Wind farm
- Affected by acid rain
- Severely affected by acid rain
- Polluted rivers
- Sea/lake pollution
- Severe sea/lake pollution
- Major industrial center

FARMING AND LAND USE

The varied landscape of the northeastern states supports a great range of farming. Livestock, including cattle, horses, poultry, and pigs, are raised throughout the region. The main crops are fruits and vegetables. Fishing is important, especially off the Atlantic coast of Maine.

FARMING AND LAND USE

- Cattle
- Pigs
- Poultry
- Fishing
- Cereals
- Cranberries
- Fruit
- Maple syrup
- Timber
- Cropland
- Forest
- Pasture
- Major conurbation

LAND USE

Pasture 6%
Cropland 14%
Other 16%
Forest 64%

THE LANDSCAPE

The Appalachian and Adirondack Mountains form a barrier between the marshy lowlands of the Atlantic coast and the lowlands farther west. The interior consists of rolling hills, fertile valleys, and thousands of lakes created by the movement of glaciers.

Appalachians (E3)
The Appalachian Mountains, which run through most of this region, are the eroded remnants of peaks that were once much higher.

Rocky coastline (G3)
The coast of Maine is made up of rocky bays, islands, and inlets. If the shoreline were stretched out, it would be 2,500 miles long.

Adirondacks (E3)
The Adirondacks are a broad, wide mountain range, formed when older rocks were forced into a "dome" shape by movements in the Earth's crust many millions of years ago.

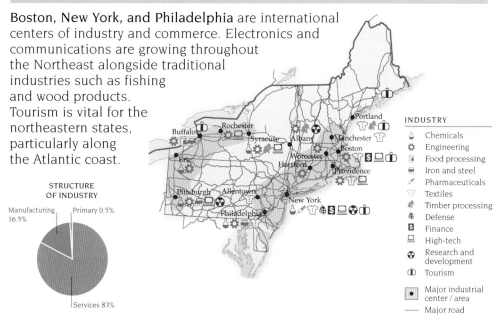

Long Island Sound (F5)
Long Island Sound is a river valley that was drowned by rising sea levels.

Finger Lakes (D3)
The long, narrow Finger Lakes lie in upper New York state. They were cut by glaciers.

Delaware Bay (D6)
Deep bays such as Delaware Bay are often surrounded by salt marshes and barrier beaches that create ideal breeding conditions for a wide variety of birds and animals.

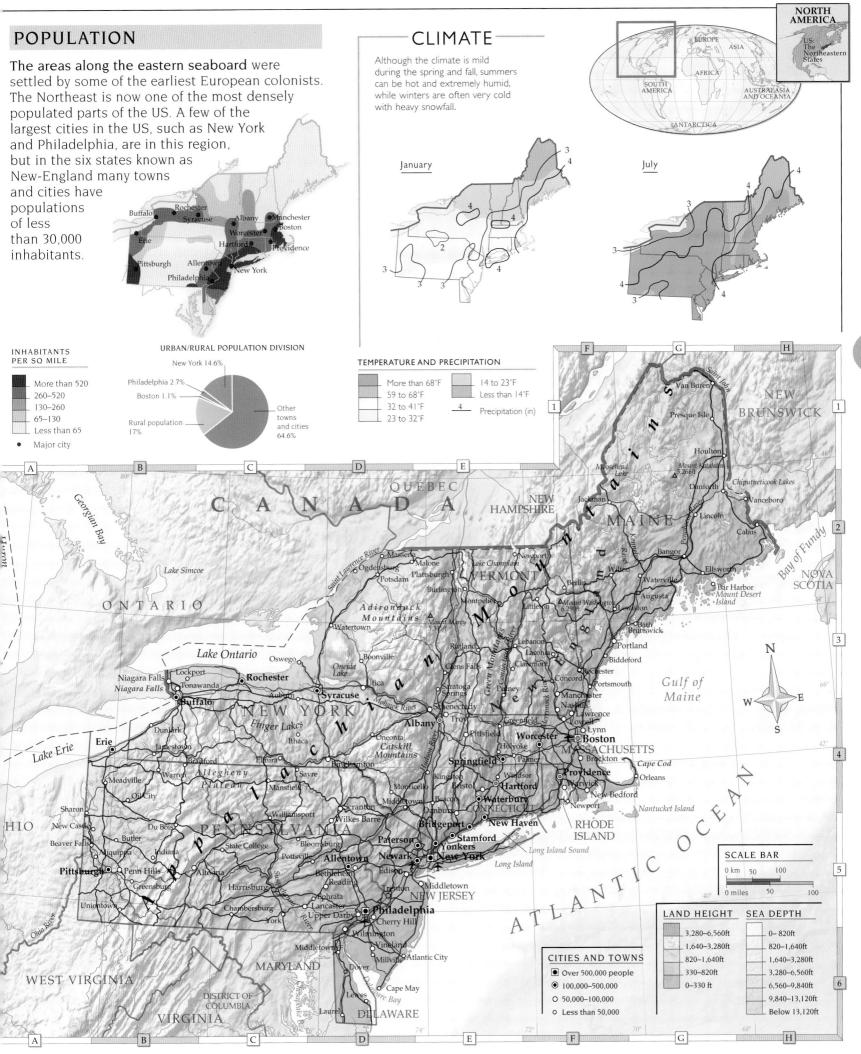

POPULATION

The areas along the eastern seaboard were settled by some of the earliest European colonists. The Northeast is now one of the most densely populated parts of the US. A few of the largest cities in the US, such as New York and Philadelphia, are in this region, but in the six states known as New-England many towns and cities have populations of less than 30,000 inhabitants.

CLIMATE

Although the climate is mild during the spring and fall, summers can be hot and extremely humid, while winters are often very cold with heavy snowfall.

January

July

NORTH AMERICA

US: The Northeastern States

INHABITANTS PER SQ MILE

- More than 520
- 260–520
- 130–260
- 65–130
- Less than 65
- • Major city

URBAN/RURAL POPULATION DIVISION

New York 14.6%
Philadelphia 2.7%
Boston 1.1%
Rural population 17%
Other towns and cities 64.6%

TEMPERATURE AND PRECIPITATION

- More than 68°F
- 59 to 68°F
- 32 to 41°F
- 23 to 32°F
- 14 to 23°F
- Less than 14°F
- 4 — Precipitation (in)

SCALE BAR

0 km 50 100
0 miles 50 100

LAND HEIGHT

- 3,280–6,560ft
- 1,640–3,280ft
- 820–1,640ft
- 330–820ft
- 0–330 ft

SEA DEPTH

- 0–820ft
- 820–1,640ft
- 1,640–3,280ft
- 3,280–6,560ft
- 6,560–9,840ft
- 9,840–13,120ft
- Below 13,120ft

CITIES AND TOWNS

- Over 500,000 people
- 100,000–500,000
- 50,000–100,000
- Less than 50,000

CANADA
QUÉBEC
ONTARIO
NEW HAMPSHIRE
VERMONT
MAINE
NEW BRUNSWICK
NOVA SCOTIA
NEW YORK
MASSACHUSETTS
RHODE ISLAND
CONNECTICUT
PENNSYLVANIA
NEW JERSEY
MARYLAND
DELAWARE
WEST VIRGINIA
VIRGINIA
OHIO
DISTRICT OF COLUMBIA

Appalachian Mountains
New England Mountains
Green Mountains
Adirondack Mountains
Catskill Mountains
Allegheny Plateau
Finger Lakes

Lake Ontario
Lake Erie
Lake Simcoe
Georgian Bay
Gulf of Maine
ATLANTIC OCEAN
Bay of Fundy
Long Island Sound
Long Island
Nantucket Island
Cape Cod
Chesapeake Bay
Delaware Bay

Van Buren, Presque Isle, Houlton, Danforth, Vanceboro, Chiputneticook Lakes, Mount Katahdin 5,266ft, Moosehead Lake, Jackman, Lincoln, Calais, Bangor, Ellsworth, Bar Harbor, Mount Desert Island, Waterville, Augusta, Lewiston, Bath, Brunswick, Portland, Biddeford, Rochester, Portsmouth, Concord, Manchester, Nashua, Laconia, Claremont, Lebanon, Littleton, Mount Washington 6,290ft, Berlin, Montpelier, Burlington, Newport, Plattsburgh, Malone, Massena, Ogdensburg, Potsdam, Watertown, Lake Champlain, Mount Marcy 5,344ft, Oswego, Boonville, Utica, Oneida Lake, Rome, Rutland, Glens Falls, Saratoga Springs, Schenectady, Troy, Albany, Pittsfield, Greenfield, Putney, Lawrence, Lowell, Lynn, Boston, Worcester, Holyoke, Springfield, Palmer, Windsor, Brockton, Orleans, Providence, Warwick, Newport, New Bedford, Hartford, Waterbury, Bristol, Middletown, New Haven, Bridgeport, Stamford, Danbury, Beacon, Kingston, Monticello, Binghamton, Oneonta, Ithaca, Elmira, Sayre, Mansfield, Williamsport, Scranton, Wilkes Barre, Bloomsburg, Pottsville, Allentown, Bethlehem, Reading, Lancaster, York, Harrisburg, Chambersburg, Altoona, State College, Indiana, Greensburg, Uniontown, Penn Hills, Pittsburgh, Aliquippa, Beaver Falls, Butler, New Castle, Sharon, Oil City, Meadville, Warren, Bradford, Du Bois, Jamestown, Dunkirk, Erie, Buffalo, Niagara Falls, Tonawanda, Lockport, Rochester, Auburn, Syracuse, Paterson, Newark, Yonkers, New York, Edison, Trenton, Middletown, Philadelphia, Upper Darby, Cherry Hill, Wilmington, Vineland, Millville, Atlantic City, Middletown, Dover, Lewes, Laurel, Cape May

Saint Lawrence River, Saint John, Kennebec River, Penobscot River, Merrimack River, Connecticut River, Hudson River, Mohawk River, Susquehanna River, Ohio River, Niagara Falls

37

US: THE SOUTHERN STATES

ALABAMA, ARKANSAS, DISTRICT OF COLUMBIA, FLORIDA, GEORGIA, KENTUCKY, LOUISIANA, MARYLAND, MISSISSIPPI, NORTH CAROLINA, SOUTH CAROLINA, TENNESSEE, VIRGINIA, WEST VIRGINIA

The southern states suffered great devastation and poverty as a result of the Civil War (1861–65). Recovery has come with the discovery and exploitation of resources and the development of major commercial and industrial centers. Yet these states retain the vibrant mix of cultures that reflect their French, Spanish, English, and African heritage.

INDUSTRY

Tourism is a major industry in the "sunbelt" states, especially Florida, and many people move to the area when they retire to enjoy the climate. Oil and gas are extracted along the coast of the Gulf of Mexico, and there are many related chemical industries. Textiles are still produced in North and South Carolina, but aerospace and other high-tech industries have been established as well.

STRUCTURE OF INDUSTRY

Primary 2%
Services 78%
Manufacturing 20%

INDUSTRY

- ✈ Aerospace
- 🛢 Chemicals
- ⚙ Engineering
- 🏭 Food processing
- Iron and steel
- 👕 Textiles
- Coal
- ⬙ Oil and gas
- 💻 High-tech
- ☢ Research and development
- 🏛 Tourism
- • Major industrial center / area
- — Major road

POPULATION

Creoles, descended from Spanish and French colonizers, and Cajuns, of French-Canadian ancestry, live in the south of this region. Florida has a large Hispanic population, increased by migration from the Caribbean. In the early 20th century, five million black people, the descendants of slaves, left the South for cities in the North.

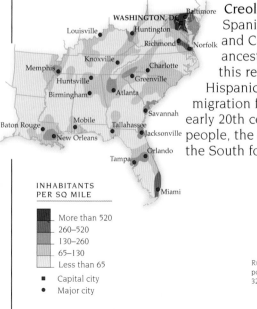

INHABITANTS PER SQ MILE

- More than 520
- 260–520
- 130–260
- 65–130
- Less than 65
- ■ Capital city
- • Major city

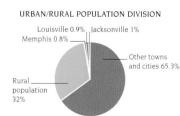

URBAN/RURAL POPULATION DIVISION

Louisville 0.9% Jacksonville 1%
Memphis 0.8%
Other towns and cities 65.3%
Rural population 32%

FARMING AND LAND USE

Cotton is still the South's main crop, but many old cottonfields are now pastures where all types of livestock are raised. Florida is famous for citrus fruits, while Georgia is renowned for peanuts. Sugarcane, soybeans, tobacco, corn, fruits, and rice are grown in other areas.

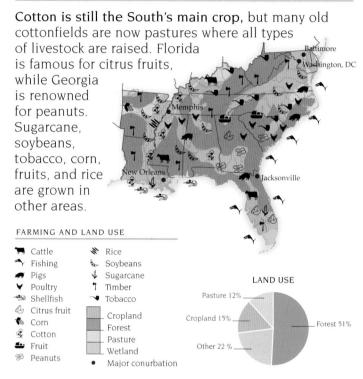

FARMING AND LAND USE

- 🐄 Cattle
- Fishing
- 🐖 Pigs
- Poultry
- Shellfish
- Citrus fruit
- Corn
- Cotton
- Fruit
- Peanuts
- Rice
- Soybeans
- Sugarcane
- Timber
- Tobacco
- Cropland
- Forest
- Pasture
- Wetland
- • Major conurbation

LAND USE

Pasture 12%
Cropland 15%
Other 22%
Forest 51%

THE LANDSCAPE

The South is a land of contrasts, the uplands of the Appalachians, the foothills of the Piedmont, and low-lying coastal regions are all featured. The interior lowlands are drained by the Mississippi. Florida is dotted with thousands of lakes and is home to the Everglades, a giant sawgrass swamp.

Mississippi River (C4)
A major transportation artery, the Mississippi was an essential route in opening up the interior region. With its main tributary, the Missouri, it is nearly 3,800 miles long, making it the world's fourth-longest river.

Kentucky Bluegrass (E2)
The gently rolling bluegrass landscape of northern Kentucky is ideal horse- and livestock-raising country.

Barrier beaches (I3)
Sandy barrier beaches and islands line the eastern and southern coasts, along with sheltered lagoons and salt marshes.

The Everglades (G8)
The Everglades cover 5,000 sq miles and support abundant wild animals and plants, many unique to the area.

Thermal springs (B4)
Hot Springs National Park in Arkansas has 47 thermal springs and is a popular tourist and health resort. Visitors relax here in the hot water that trickles from the hillsides.

Tennessee River (D4)
The Tennessee River is 625 miles long. Dams along the river generate hydro-electricity to provide most of the region's energy needs.

Limestone caves (E4)
Cathedral Caverns in Alabama is a collection of enormous limestone caves. The main entrance is more than 1,000 ft high and 150 ft wide.

ENVIRONMENTAL ISSUES

Factories in the Great Lakes region have contributed to the large blanket of acid rain across the northern part. Toward the south, hurricanes sweep in from the Atlantic Ocean and Gulf of Mexico during the hurricane season, which lasts from May to October each year.

ENVIRONMENTAL ISSUES

- Path of recent, devastating hurricane
- Affected by acid rain
- Polluted river
- Sea pollution
- Major city

NORTH AMERICA
US: The Southern States

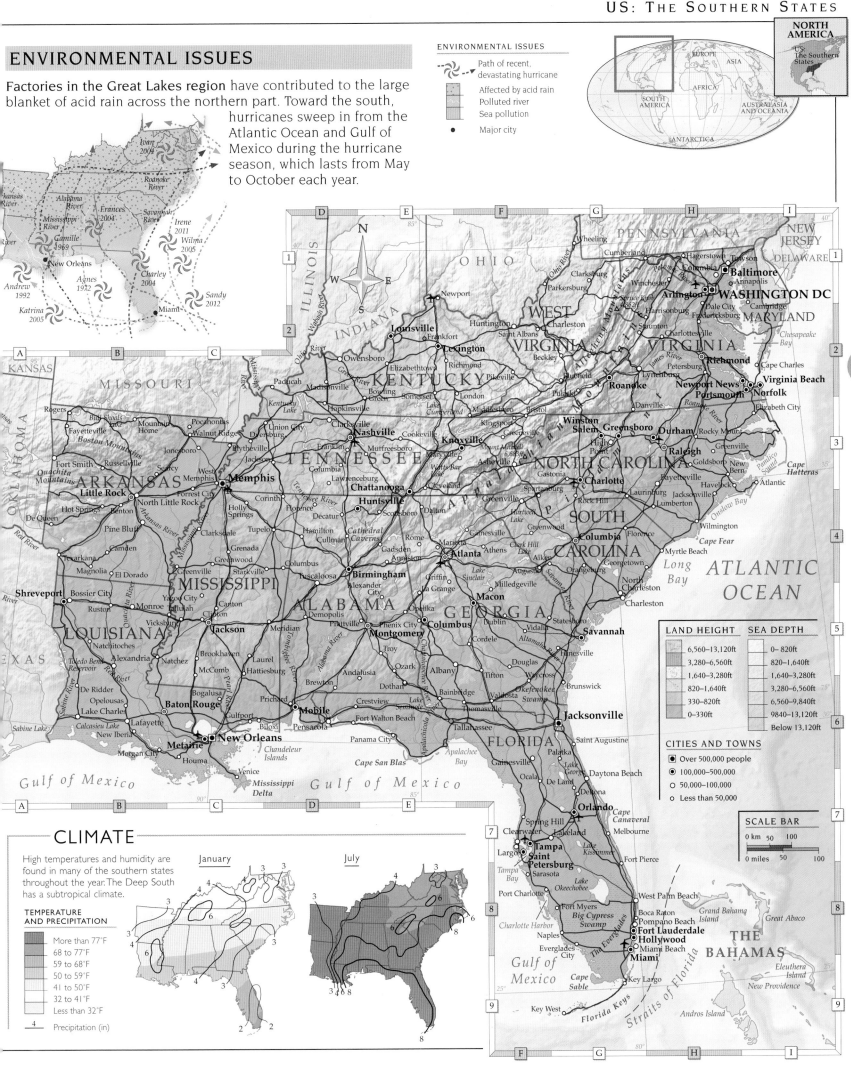

CLIMATE

High temperatures and humidity are found in many of the southern states throughout the year. The Deep South has a subtropical climate.

TEMPERATURE AND PRECIPITATION

- More than 77°F
- 68 to 77°F
- 59 to 68°F
- 50 to 59°F
- 41 to 50°F
- 32 to 41°F
- Less than 32°F

4 — Precipitation (in)

January

July

LAND HEIGHT
- 6,560–13,120ft
- 3,280–6,560ft
- 1,640–3,280ft
- 820–1,640ft
- 330–820ft
- 0–330ft

SEA DEPTH
- 0–820ft
- 820–1,640ft
- 1,640–3,280ft
- 3,280–6,560ft
- 6,560–9,840ft
- 9840–13,120ft
- Below 13,120ft

CITIES AND TOWNS
- Over 500,000 people
- 100,000–500,000
- 50,000–100,000
- Less than 50,000

SCALE BAR
0 km   50   100
0 miles   50   100

39

US: THE GREAT LAKES STATES

ILLINOIS, INDIANA, MICHIGAN, OHIO, WISCONSIN

Good transportation links, excellent farmland, and a wealth of natural resources drew settlers from Europe and the south and east of the US to the Great Lakes states during the late 19th century. By the 1930s, they had become one of the world's most prosperous industrial and agricultural regions. In recent years, the decline in traditional heavy industries has hit some cities hard, leading to unemployment and a rising crime rate.

POPULATION

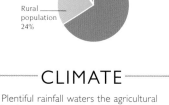

The Great Lakes states are one of the most densely populated parts of the US. Many of the largest cities in this region – Chicago, Detroit, and Milwaukee – grew up on the banks of the lakes and are connected to each other and the rest of the US by an impressive road and rail network.

INHABITANTS PER SQ MILE
- More than 520
- 260–520
- 130–260
- 65–130
- Less than 65
- • Major city

URBAN/RURAL POPULATION DIVISION
- Detroit 2%
- Chicago 6.3%
- Indianapolis 1.7%
- Other towns and cities 66%
- Rural population 24%

CLIMATE

Plentiful rainfall waters the agricultural lands. In winter, strong winds sweep across the lakes, and water close to the shore may freeze.

January

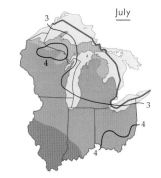

July

TEMPERATURE AND PRECIPITATION
- More than 77°F
- 68 to 77°F
- 59 to 68°F
- 32 to 41°F
- 23 to 32°F
- 14 to 23°F
- Less than 14°F
- 4 — Precipitation (in)

SCALE BAR
0 km 50 100
0 miles 50 100

CITIES AND TOWNS
- ◉ Over 500,000 people
- ◉ 100,000–500,000
- ○ 50,000–100,000
- ○ Less than 50,000

LAND HEIGHT
- 1,640–3,280ft
- 820–1,640ft
- 330–820ft
- 0–330ft

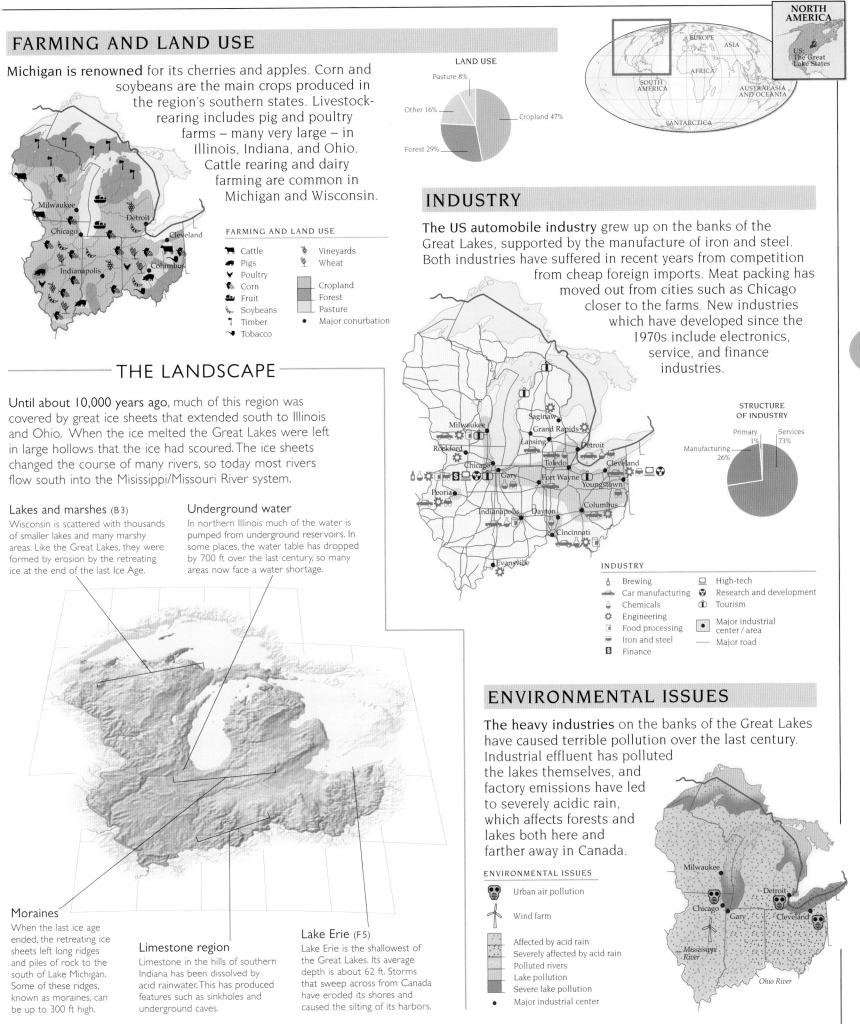

FARMING AND LAND USE

Michigan is renowned for its cherries and apples. Corn and soybeans are the main crops produced in the region's southern states. Livestock-rearing includes pig and poultry farms – many very large – in Illinois, Indiana, and Ohio. Cattle rearing and dairy farming are common in Michigan and Wisconsin.

LAND USE

Pasture 8%
Other 16%
Cropland 47%
Forest 29%

Milwaukee
Detroit
Chicago
Cleveland
Indianapolis
Columbus

FARMING AND LAND USE

- Cattle
- Pigs
- Poultry
- Corn
- Fruit
- Soybeans
- Timber
- Tobacco
- Vineyards
- Wheat
- Cropland
- Forest
- Pasture
- Major conurbation

THE LANDSCAPE

Until about 10,000 years ago, much of this region was covered by great ice sheets that extended south to Illinois and Ohio. When the ice melted the Great Lakes were left in large hollows that the ice had scoured. The ice sheets changed the course of many rivers, so today most rivers flow south into the Misissippi/Missouri River system.

Lakes and marshes (B 3)

Wisconsin is scattered with thousands of smaller lakes and many marshy areas. Like the Great Lakes, they were formed by erosion by the retreating ice at the end of the last Ice Age.

Underground water

In northern Illinois much of the water is pumped from underground reservoirs. In some places, the water table has dropped by 700 ft over the last century, so many areas now face a water shortage.

Moraines

When the last ice age ended, the retreating ice sheets left long ridges and piles of rock to the south of Lake Michigan. Some of these ridges, known as moraines, can be up to 300 ft high.

Limestone region

Limestone in the hills of southern Indiana has been dissolved by acid rainwater. This has produced features such as sinkholes and underground caves.

Lake Erie (F 5)

Lake Erie is the shallowest of the Great Lakes. Its average depth is about 62 ft. Storms that sweep across from Canada have eroded its shores and caused the silting of its harbors.

INDUSTRY

The US automobile industry grew up on the banks of the Great Lakes, supported by the manufacture of iron and steel. Both industries have suffered in recent years from competition from cheap foreign imports. Meat packing has moved out from cities such as Chicago closer to the farms. New industries which have developed since the 1970s include electronics, service, and finance industries.

STRUCTURE OF INDUSTRY

Primary 1%
Services 73%
Manufacturing 26%

Milwaukee
Saginaw
Grand Rapids
Rockford
Lansing
Detroit
Chicago
Toledo
Cleveland
Gary
Fort Wayne
Peoria
Youngstown
Indianapolis
Dayton
Columbus
Cincinnati
Evansville

INDUSTRY

- Brewing
- Car manufacturing
- Chemicals
- Engineering
- Food processing
- Iron and steel
- Finance
- High-tech
- Research and development
- Tourism
- Major industrial center / area
- Major road

ENVIRONMENTAL ISSUES

The heavy industries on the banks of the Great Lakes have caused terrible pollution over the last century. Industrial effluent has polluted the lakes themselves, and factory emissions have led to severely acidic rain, which affects forests and lakes both here and farther away in Canada.

ENVIRONMENTAL ISSUES

- Urban air pollution
- Wind farm
- Affected by acid rain
- Severely affected by acid rain
- Polluted rivers
- Lake pollution
- Severe lake pollution
- Major industrial center

Milwaukee
Detroit
Chicago
Gary
Cleveland
Mississippi River
Ohio River

US: THE CENTRAL STATES

IOWA, KANSAS, MINNESOTA, MISSOURI, NEBRASKA,
NORTH DAKOTA, OKLAHOMA, SOUTH DAKOTA

The prairie states of the central US became one of America's richest agricultural regions in the mid-19th century. Despite the "Dustbowl" crisis of the 1930s, which led many farmers to leave their ruined lands, agriculture is still crucial to the economy, and one third of the people still live in rural areas rather than large cities.

FARMING AND LAND USE

Wheat and corn grow on the fertile plains. Kansas is the leading grower of wheat in the entire US, while Iowa is one of the leaders in corn and livestock. Irrigation projects to combat drought are crucial in large areas. Livestock – including cattle in vast herds; pigs, particularly in Iowa, the Dakotas, and Nebraska; sheep; and turkeys – are raised throughout these states.

INDUSTRY

Industries related to agriculture, such as food processing and the production of farm machinery, are traditional in these states but high-tech industries – such as aeronautical engineering – are increasing and large aerospace plants are found in Wichita and Saint Louis. Oil and gas are extracted in great quantities toward the south of the region, especially in Oklahoma and Kansas.

LAND USE

Other 37%
Cropland 43%
Forest 11%
Pasture 9%

FARMING AND LAND USE

- Cattle
- Pigs
- Poultry
- Sheep
- Corn
- Soybeans
- Wheat
- Cropland
- Forest
- Pasture
- Major conurbation

INDUSTRY

- ✈ Aerospace
- 🚗 Car manufacturing
- Chemicals
- ⚙ Engineering
- Food processing
- Iron and steel
- Textiles
- Oil and gas
- $ Finance
- ▣ Major industrial center / area
- — Major road

STRUCTURE OF INDUSTRY

Primary 4%
Services 76%
Manufacturing 20%

THE LANDSCAPE

Most of the eastern edge of this region is marked by the Mississippi River, while the Missouri bisects it, running from northwest to southeast. The Great Plains cover most of this area, gradually rising toward the Rocky Mountains at the far western edge of the Central States.

The Badlands (A 4)
The Badlands cover an area of about 2,000 sq miles in South Dakota. Heavily eroded by wind and water, almost nothing grows there.

Minnesota
Minnesota is filled with lakes, hills strewn with boulders, and mineral-rich deposits that have been left behind by the scouring movement of glaciers.

ENVIRONMENTAL ISSUES

Intensive agriculture requires large quantities of water to grow crops. Overintensive use of the land has destroyed the balance of soil and water in the past, leading to fertile farmland being turned into useless areas of "Dustbowl." These states have a great underground store of water known as the Ogallala Aquifer, but overextraction for irrigation is reducing the amount of available water.

Chimney Rock (A-5)
Chimney Rock stands 500 ft above the plains. It is a remnant of an ancient land surface that was eroded by the North Platte River.

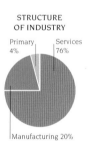

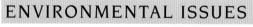

ENVIRONMENTAL ISSUES

- Urban air pollution
- Wind farm
- Affected by acid rain
- Aquifer
- Polluted river
- Risk of desertification
- Major industrial center

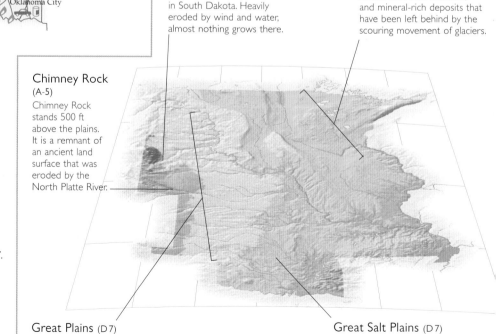

Great Plains (D 7)
Little more than a century ago the great flat plains that cover most of these states were home to wild grasses and massive herds of buffalo. In areas where lack of water has made farming impossible, large tracts of land are being allowed to return to grassland.

Great Salt Plains (D 7)
These arid salt plains cover about 45 sq miles of northern Oklahoma. An ancient salt lake once occupied the area. When the salt evaporated, only the salt flats were left.

POPULATION

The inhabitants are largely the descendants of Europeans who came to the region in the late 1800s. The entire region is primarily rural, with enormous tracts of land devoted to growing crops. North Dakota has no city with a population greater than 100,000.

URBAN/RURAL POPULATION DIVISION

Kansas City 1.9%   Oklahoma City 2.3%
Omaha 1.8%

Other towns and cities 60%

Rural population 34%

NORTH AMERICA

US: The Central States

INHABITANTS PER SQ MILE

More than 130
65–130
Less than 65
● Major city

CLIMATE

The Central States have a continental climate, with hot, dry summers and long, cold winters. Unreliable rainfall can be a problem for farmers on the Great Plains.

January

July

TEMPERATURE AND PRECIPITATION

More than 77°F
68 to 77°F
59 to 68°F
50 to 59°F
41 to 50°F
32 to 41°F

23 to 32°F
14 to 23°F
5 to 14°F
Less than 5°F
—4— Precipitation (in)

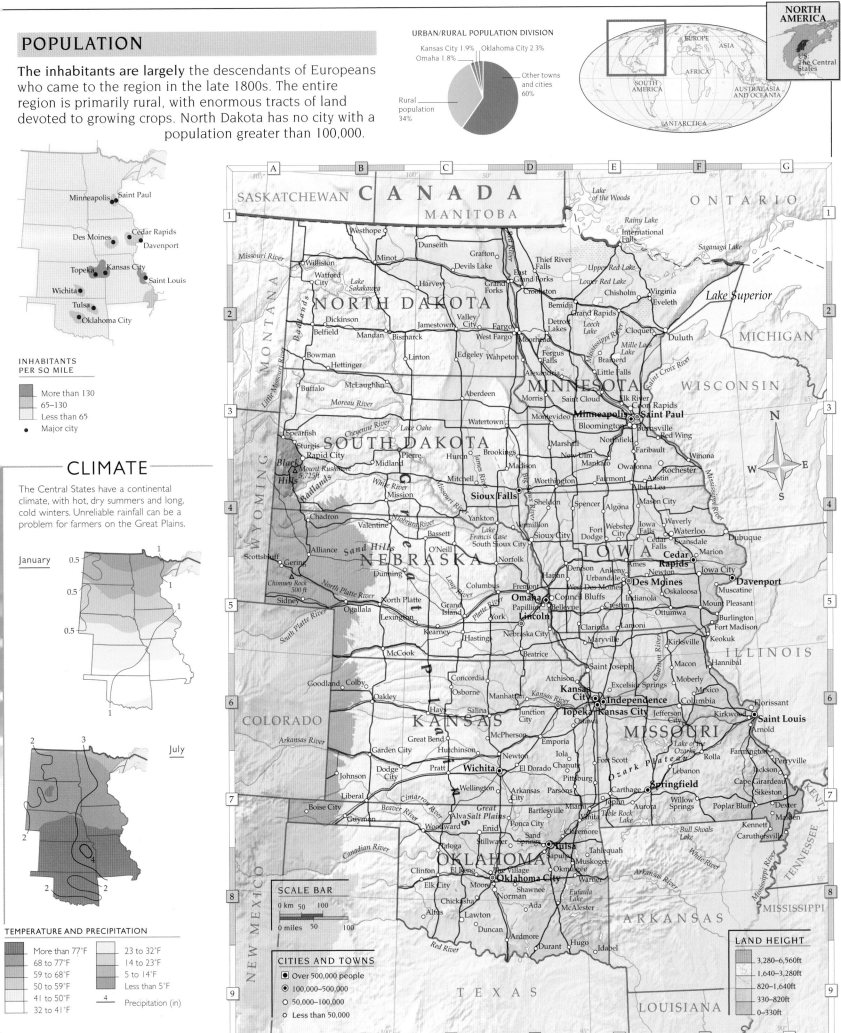

SCALE BAR

0 km   50   100

0 miles   50   100

CITIES AND TOWNS

■ Over 500,000 people
◉ 100,000–500,000
◎ 50,000–100,000
○ Less than 50,000

LAND HEIGHT

3,280–6,560ft
1,640–3,280ft
820–1,640ft
330–820ft
0–330ft

US: THE SOUTHWESTERN STATES

ARIZONA, NEW MEXICO, TEXAS

Large parts of the southwestern states were purchased from Mexico in 1848. This land of expansive plateaus, spectacular canyons, prairies, and deserts is home to several distinct peoples, whose customs and traditions are still practiced. The Navaho and Hopi own one-third of the land in Arizona, and the ruins of thousand-year-old cliff dwellings built by the Anasazi people are still preserved there today.

ENVIRONMENTAL ISSUES

Desertification is a serious problem in the southwestern states. Lack of water combined with intensive farming has allowed soils to erode. Drought is held at bay by irrigation, but falling water table levels are a cause for concern. New Mexico was the site for many early nuclear weapons tests, and some places remain contaminated.

ENVIRONMENTAL ISSUES

- Urban air pollution
- Former nuclear test site
- Path of recent, devastating hurricane
- Wind farm
- Desert area
- Risk of desertification
- Polluted river
- Major industrial center

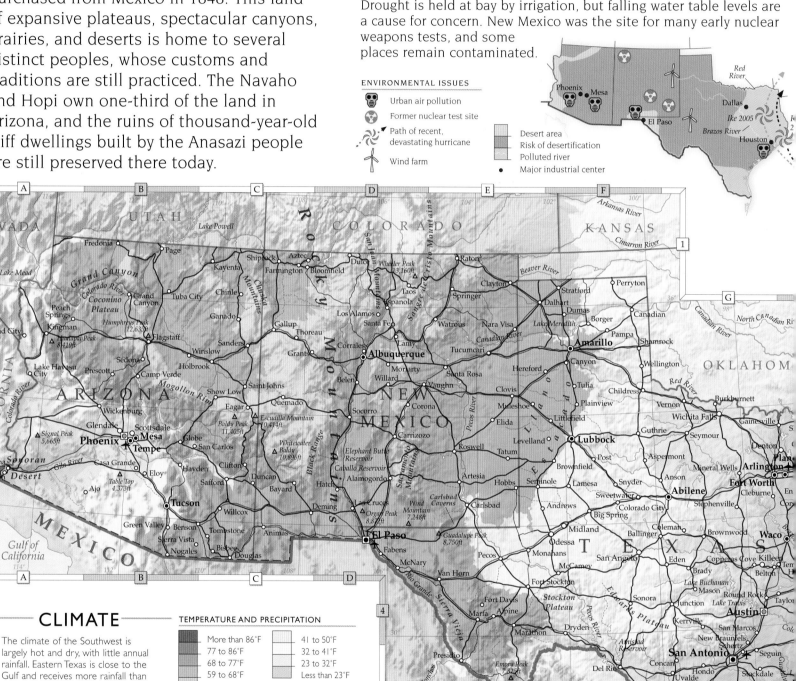

CLIMATE

The climate of the Southwest is largely hot and dry, with little annual rainfall. Eastern Texas is close to the Gulf and receives more rainfall than elsewhere in this region.

TEMPERATURE AND PRECIPITATION

- More than 86°F
- 77 to 86°F
- 68 to 77°F
- 59 to 68°F
- 50 to 59°F
- 41 to 50°F
- 32 to 41°F
- 23 to 32°F
- Less than 23°F
- 4 — Precipitation (in)

January

July

LAND HEIGHT | SEA DEPTH

LAND HEIGHT	SEA DEPTH
Above 13,120ft	0–820ft
6,560–13,120ft	820–1,640ft
3,280–6,560ft	1,640–3,280ft
1,640–3,280ft	3,280–6,560ft
820–1,640ft	6,560–9,840ft
330–820ft	9,840–13,120ft
0–330 ft	Below 13,120ft

CITIES AND TOWNS

- Over 500,000 people
- 100,000–500,000
- 50,000–100,000
- Less than 50,000

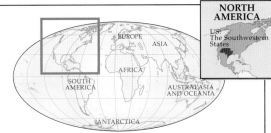

THE LANDSCAPE

The arid, mountainous Colorado Plateau covers nearly half of Arizona, dipping toward the south to form desert basins. Parts of northern New Mexico are forested, but the south consists primarily of semiarid plains. Eastern Texas is bordered by the waters of the Gulf of Mexico, and the farmland of this area is well watered. Western Texas is covered by the Llano Estacado and, in the south, much of the land is arid.

Big Bend (E 5)
Big Bend National Park gets its name from the 90° bend that the Rio Grande makes there.

Invading sea
The crust of southeastern Texas is warping, causing the land to subside and allowing the sea to invade. Hurricanes make the situation worse.

Grand Canyon (B I)
The Grand Canyon is a dramatic gorge cut in the rock by the Colorado River. It is about 217 miles long, 418 miles wide, and up to one-mile deep.

Carlsbad Caverns (B 3)
Carlsbad Caverns are a series of underground caves, consisting of a three-level chain of limestone chambers studded with towering stalactites and stalagmites. They are millions of years old.

Rio Grande (G 5)
The Rio Grande, or "Great River" forms all of the border between Texas and Mexico. It flows from its source high up in the Rocky Mountains, to the Gulf of Mexico.

INDUSTRY

Mining and related industries are one of the most important sources of income in the Southwest. Great deposits of oil lie under about 65% of Texas; copper and coal are mined in Arizona and New Mexico. Defense-related industries, including NASA have encouraged the development of many high-tech companies in Texas – and high-tech is also growing in larger cities such as Santa Fe and Phoenix.

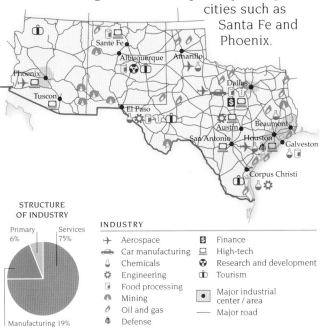

STRUCTURE OF INDUSTRY
Primary 6%
Services 75%
Manufacturing 19%

INDUSTRY
- ✈ Aerospace
- 🚗 Car manufacturing
- ⚗ Chemicals
- ⚙ Engineering
- Food processing
- ⛏ Mining
- ⬤ Oil and gas
- Defense
- 💲 Finance
- 💻 High-tech
- ⚙ Research and development
- 🎫 Tourism
- ▪ Major industrial center / area
- — Major road

FARMING AND LAND USE

Many cattle and sheep ranches have been set up on the open plateaus. Fruit and vegetables, grown in hothouses and cotton, hay, and wheat are among the major crops. Beef cattle and broiler chickens are raised on huge farms while sheep graze the drier parts of Texas. Extensive irrigation has made farming possible in even the most arid areas.

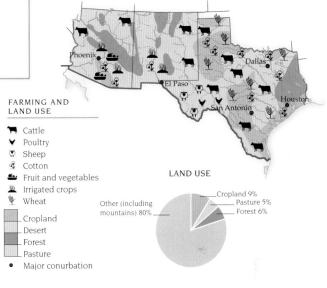

FARMING AND LAND USE
- Cattle
- Poultry
- Sheep
- Cotton
- Fruit and vegetables
- Irrigated crops
- Wheat
- Cropland
- Desert
- Forest
- Pasture
- ● Major conurbation

LAND USE
Other (including mountains) 80%
Cropland 9%
Pasture 5%
Forest 6%

POPULATION

The descendants of Mexican and Spanish settlers and numerous groups of Native Americans live in the southwestern states. The great cities of Texas grew up on income from cattle-ranching and the oil industry. Much of Arizona and New Mexico is sparsely populated, but today people are moving to these states to escape the cold winters elsewhere.

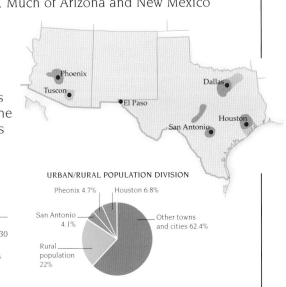

INHABITANTS PER SQ MILE
- More than 130
- 65–130
- Less than 65
- ● Major city

URBAN/RURAL POPULATION DIVISION
Pheonix 4.7%
Houston 6.8%
San Antonio 4.1%
Rural population 22%
Other towns and cities 62.4%

US: THE MOUNTAIN STATES

COLORADO, IDAHO, MONTANA, NEVADA, UTAH, WYOMING

These states are home to some of the nation's most fantastic landscapes: endless treeless plains, craggy peaks, incredible desert landforms, and the salt flats of Utah. Although this was one of the last regions of the US to be settled, great mineral reserves have been exploited here in recent years, and new industries have grown up in some of the larger cities. Utah is the headquarters of the Mormon religion.

INDUSTRY

Rich mineral reserves, including coal, oil, and gas, are mined throughout the region and forests are a source of good-quality timber. In the larger cities of Colorado and Utah, growing industries include high-tech computer firms. Many tourists are drawn to this region to ski in the resorts of Colorado and to explore the wilderness.

INDUSTRY

Icon	Industry
⚗	Chemicals
🥫	Food processing
▽	Textiles
⚒	Coal
⛏	Mining
◔	Oil and gas
♣	Timber processing
♨	Gambling
🖥	High-tech
☢	Research and development
⬧	Tourism

- Major industrial center / area
- — Major road

STRUCTURE OF INDUSTRY

Manufacturing 16%
Primary 4%
Services 80%

FARMING AND LAND USE

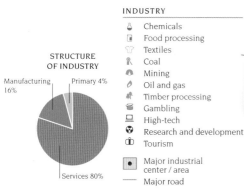

In the southern mountain states, cattle ranching is the main form of farming. Wheat and corn are grown in the eastern states, and the fertile soils of the Snake River valley in Idaho produce large crops of potatoes and many other vegetables. The northern states have many large commercial forests.

FARMING AND LAND USE

- 🐂 Cattle
- 🌽 Corn
- Irrigated crops
- Potatoes
- Timber
- Wheat
- Cropland
- Desert
- Forest
- Pasture
- Major conurbation

LAND USE

Other (including mountains) 85%
Cropland 9%
Pasture 2%
Forest 4%

POPULATION

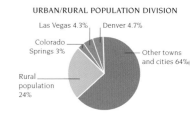

Colorado, with the growing city of Denver, is the most populous of the mountain states. In other states, people have settled close to sources of water such as Great Salt Lake in Utah. Many towns have less than 10,000 people and are far apart.

INHABITANTS PER SQ MILE

- More than 130
- 65–130
- Less than 65
- • Major city

URBAN/RURAL POPULATION DIVISION

Las Vegas 4.3%
Denver 4.7%
Colorado Springs 3%
Other towns and cities 64%
Rural population 24%

THE LANDSCAPE

The great Rocky Mountains and many smaller mountain ranges cover almost all of this region. Only eastern Montana is not mountainous. Here western parts of the Great Plains rise to meet the mountains. Parts of the southern mountain states are very arid with spectacular scenery, including blocklike *mesas*, formed by erosion.

Continental Divide

From this watershed, crossing the Lewis Range, rivers flow in different directions across North America. Some flow east to Hudson Bay, some south to the Gulf of Mexico and others west to the Pacific Ocean.

Yellowstone National Park (D 3)

Yellowstone was set up in 1872 as the first national park in the US. Water from hot springs has deposited minerals as it cools, forming white rock terraces close to the springs.

Snake River (C 4)

Great Plains (E 2)

North Platte River (F 4)

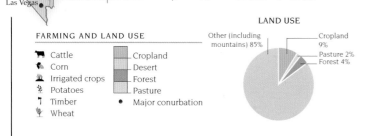

Artificial lake (C 7)

Lake Mead – more than 177 miles long, is one of the largest artificial lakes in the world. It was formed in 1936, when the Hoover Dam was built across the Colorado River.

Great Salt Lake (C 5)

Mountainous state

Colorado has more than 1,500 peaks more than 9,840 ft high – this is six times the number of high mountains found in the Swiss Alps.

ENVIRONMENTAL ISSUES

Parts of the Rocky Mountains, including the National Parks, have become major centers for outdoor pursuits. The sheer number of people puts pressure on the land leading to soil erosion, and increasing the possibility of landslides. Nevada remains the main testing ground for the US nuclear arsenal, and there are many older, disused sites here.

ENVIRONMENTAL ISSUES

- Former nuclear test site
- Nuclear test site
- Urban air pollution
- Wind farm
- National Park
- Winter tourist resort
- Major industrial center

NORTH AMERICA

US: The Mountain States

CLIMATE

In the lowland areas, particularly in the south, summers are often very hot and dry. Parts of the Rocky Mountains are permanently covered by snow, and some of the high passes are cut off by snow in the winter.

January

July

TEMPERATURE AND PRECIPITATION

More than 86°F	32 to 41°F
77 to 86°F	23 to 32°F
68 to 77°F	14 to 23°F
59 to 68°F	Less than 14°F
50 to 59°F	
41 to 50°F	4 — Precipitation (in)

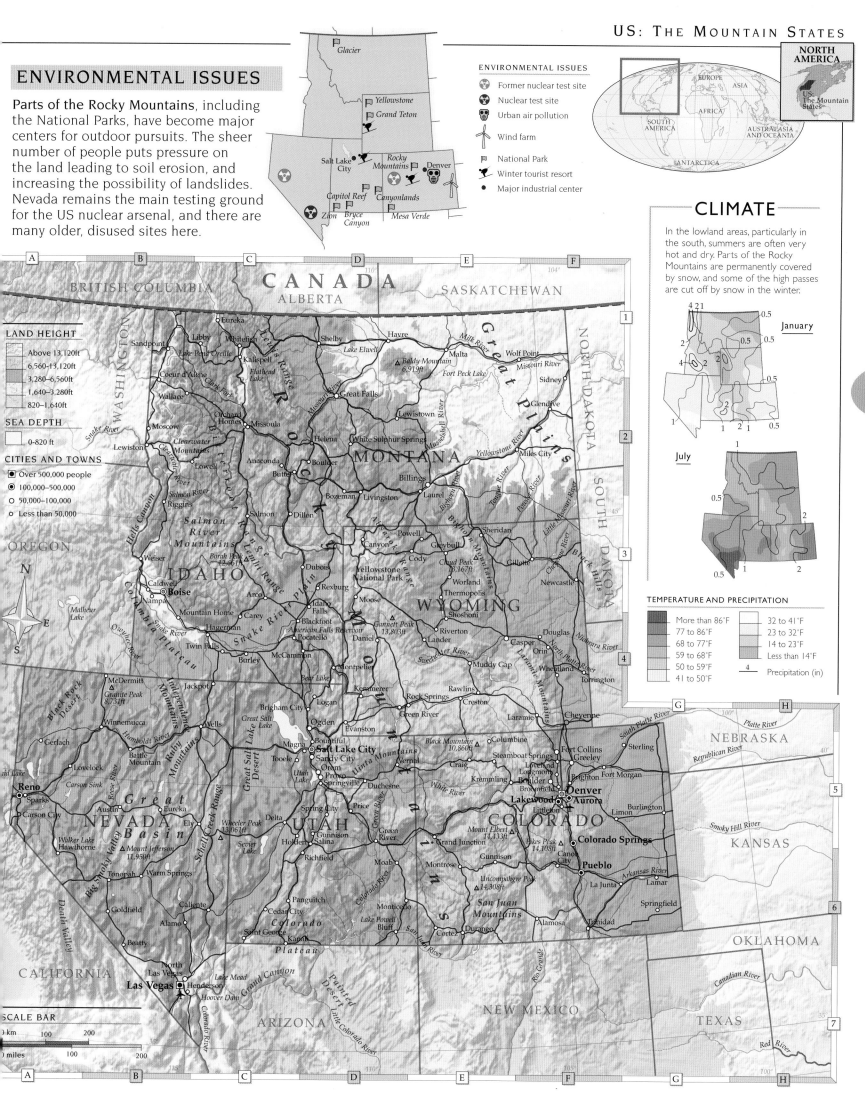

LAND HEIGHT

- Above 13,120ft
- 6,560–13,120ft
- 3,280–6,560ft
- 1,640–3,280ft
- 820–1,640ft

SEA DEPTH

- 0–820 ft

CITIES AND TOWNS

- Over 500,000 people
- 100,000–500,000
- 50,000–100,000
- Less than 50,000

US: THE PACIFIC STATES

CALIFORNIA, OREGON, WASHINGTON

The earliest European visitors to the West Coast were fur-trappers and miners, but the Gold Rush of 1849 brought in the first major wave of settlers. Drawn by tales of the beautiful scenery, pleasant climate, and fertile valleys, more people arrived on the newly built railroads. People from all over the world are still moving into this region, seeking jobs in the dynamic economy and the famous laid-back lifestyle.

INDUSTRY

The Pacific States are the center of the high-tech computer industry with Silicon Valley between San Francisco and San Jose, and electronics industries growing in Portland and Seattle. Other major industries include research and development for the defense industry, filmmaking in Los Angeles, food processing and lumbering. Tourism is well developed throughout the Pacific States.

STRUCTURE OF INDUSTRY

Primary 2%
Services 81%
Manufacturing 17%

INDUSTRY

- ✈ Aerospace
- ♨ Chemicals
- ✿ Engineering
- ▤ Food processing
- ♢ Iron and steel
- ⚓ Shipbuilding
- ▽ Textiles
- ✿ Timber processing
- ✳ Film industry
- ▱ High-tech
- ☢ Research and development
- ⌼ Tourism
- ▣ Major industrial center / area
- — Major road

FARMING AND LAND USE

California's Central Valley and the river valleys of Washington and Oregon provide ideal conditions for a wide range of fruit and vegetables, including citrus fruit and grapes. Poultry farming is widespread in the northwest and there are many large cattle ranches. Millions of acres of commercial forest are located in this region.

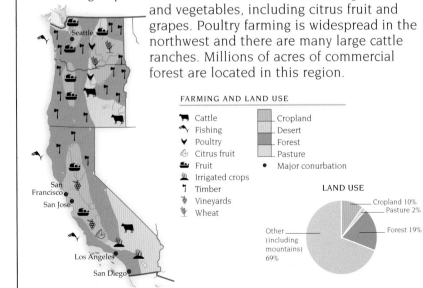

FARMING AND LAND USE

- 🐂 Cattle
- ⌁ Fishing
- ▾ Poultry
- ⌕ Citrus fruit
- ⬢ Fruit
- ⚖ Irrigated crops
- ⌁ Timber
- ⚘ Vineyards
- ⍦ Wheat
- ▨ Cropland
- ▨ Desert
- ▨ Forest
- ▨ Pasture
- • Major conurbation

LAND USE

Cropland 10%
Pasture 2%
Forest 19%
Other (including mountains) 69%

ENVIRONMENTAL ISSUES

Some of the great national parks of the US, including Yosemite and Sequoia, are found here. The immense numbers of visitors put great pressure on the landscape. Water is in short supply in large parts of California, and desertification, caused by overintense farming methods, is a problem. Wind farms have been set up on the hills above the San Joaquin valley to provide alternative energy.

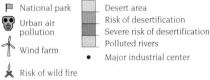

ENVIRONMENTAL ISSUES

- ⚑ National park
- ☻ Urban air pollution
- ✦ Wind farm
- ✗ Risk of wild fire
- ▨ Desert area
- ▨ Risk of desertification
- ▨ Severe risk of desertification
- ▨ Polluted rivers
- • Major industrial center

THE LANDSCAPE

The Coast and Cascade ranges run north–south through Oregon and Washington while further south, the high Sierra Nevada run along California's eastern fringes. Two broad valleys, the Sacramento and San Joaquin, are known as the Central Valley, and form a trough beneath the Sierra Nevada. The south is extremely dry – Death Valley is the hottest place in the entire US.

Northern rain forest (B 2)
The ocean-facing side of the Olympic Mountains receives 142 in of rain every year, supporting the only true temperate rain forest in the Northern Hemisphere.

Hells Canyon (D 3)
Hells Canyon is North America's deepest gorge. Running through part of Oregon, it was created as the Snake River cut down through the land.

Volcanic eruption (B 2)
Mount St. Helens erupted in 1980, killing 57 people and destroying a vast area.

San Andreas Fault
The San Andreas Fault runs for 650 miles underneath California. When both sides of the fault move at different rates, tremors and earthquakes result.

Hottest place (D 7)
In 1913, Death Valley set the record for the highest temperature ever recorded in the US, at 134° F.

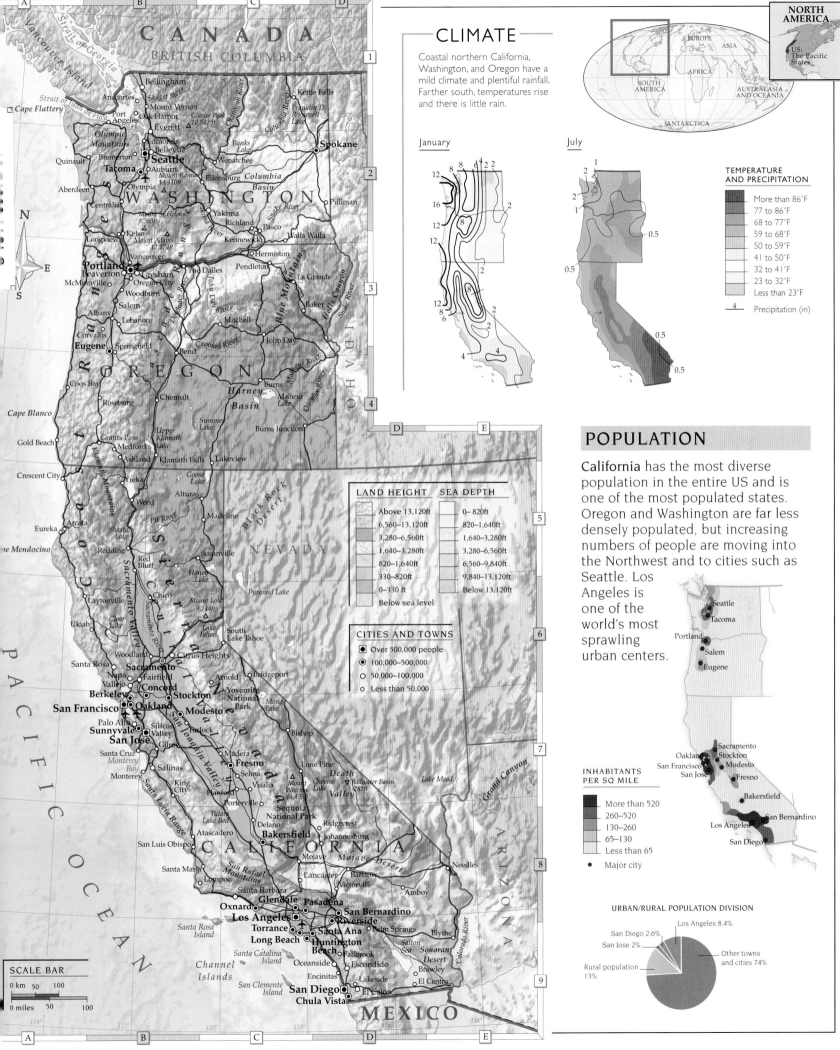

NORTH AMERICA

US: The Pacific States

CLIMATE

Coastal northern California, Washington, and Oregon have a mild climate and plentiful rainfall. Farther south, temperatures rise and there is little rain.

January

July

TEMPERATURE AND PRECIPITATION

- More than 86°F
- 77 to 86°F
- 68 to 77°F
- 59 to 68°F
- 50 to 59°F
- 41 to 50°F
- 32 to 41°F
- 23 to 32°F
- Less than 23°F
- —4— Precipitation (in)

LAND HEIGHT
- Above 13,120ft
- 6,560–13,120ft
- 3,280–6,560ft
- 1,640–3,280ft
- 820–1,640ft
- 330–820ft
- 0–330 ft
- Below sea level

SEA DEPTH
- 0–820ft
- 820–1,640ft
- 1,640–3,280ft
- 3,280–6,560ft
- 6,560–9,840ft
- 9,840–13,120ft
- Below 13,120ft

CITIES AND TOWNS
- Over 500,000 people
- 100,000–500,000
- 50,000–100,000
- Less than 50,000

POPULATION

California has the most diverse population in the entire US and is one of the most populated states. Oregon and Washington are far less densely populated, but increasing numbers of people are moving into the Northwest and to cities such as Seattle. Los Angeles is one of the world's most sprawling urban centers.

INHABITANTS PER SQ MILE
- More than 520
- 260–520
- 130–260
- 65–130
- Less than 65
- Major city

URBAN/RURAL POPULATION DIVISION

- Los Angeles 8.4%
- San Diego 2.6%
- San Jose 2%
- Other towns and cities 74%
- Rural population 13%

49

ALASKA

A **magnificent land** of mountains, forests, and snowfields, with rich oil and mineral reserves, Alaska was purchased from Russia for $1 million in 1867. Almost 650,000 people live here, many drawn by the oil industry. Some of Alaska's native peoples like the Aleuts and Inupiaq still live by hunting and fishing.

ENVIRONMENTAL ISSUES

Much of northern Alaska is covered by permafrost (permanently frozen ground). The Trans-Alaska Pipeline, which brings oil from Prudhoe Bay to Valdez, was built above ground to stop the permafrost melting. A number of major oil spills have threatened Alaska's unique envrionment.

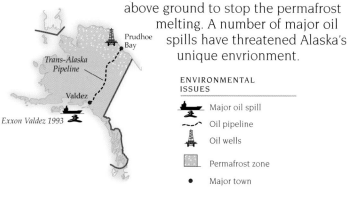

Trans-Alaska Pipeline

Prudhoe Bay

Valdez

Exxon Valdez 1993

ENVIRONMENTAL ISSUES

- ⚓ Major oil spill
- Oil pipeline
- Oil wells
- Permafrost zone
- ● Major town

INDUSTRY

Prudhoe Bay

Anchorage

Valdez

Juneau

The Alaskan economy is dominated by the oil business. The oilfields of Alaska are of a similar size to those in the Persian Gulf. Minerals including gold are mined in the mountains, and paper products are exported to countries on the Pacific Rim.

INDUSTRY

- ⚗ Chemicals
- ⛏ Mining
- ◊ Oil and gas
- 🌲 Timber processing
- ● Major industrial center
- — Major road

FARMING AND LAND USE

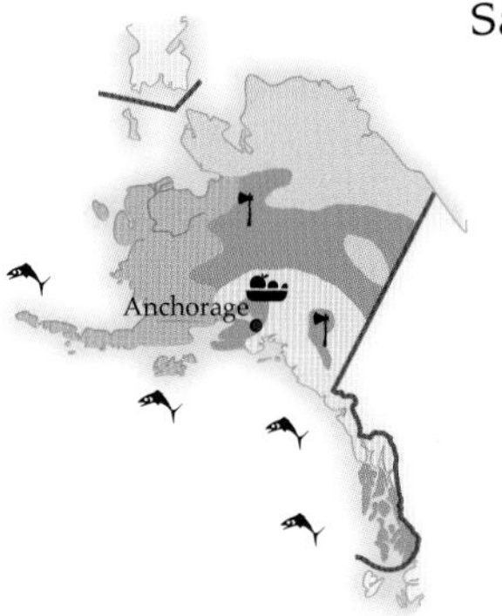

Anchorage

Salmon are caught in great numbers in the waters of the north Pacific. Much of the state – more than 22.2 million acres – is covered by forest which is commercially lumbered. Most food must be imported, although fruit is grown in hothouses near the larger cities.

FARMING AND LAND USE

- 🐟 Fishing
- 🚢 Fruit
- 🌲 Timber
- Barren
- Forest
- Mountains
- Tundra
- ● Major conurbation

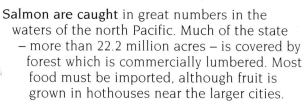

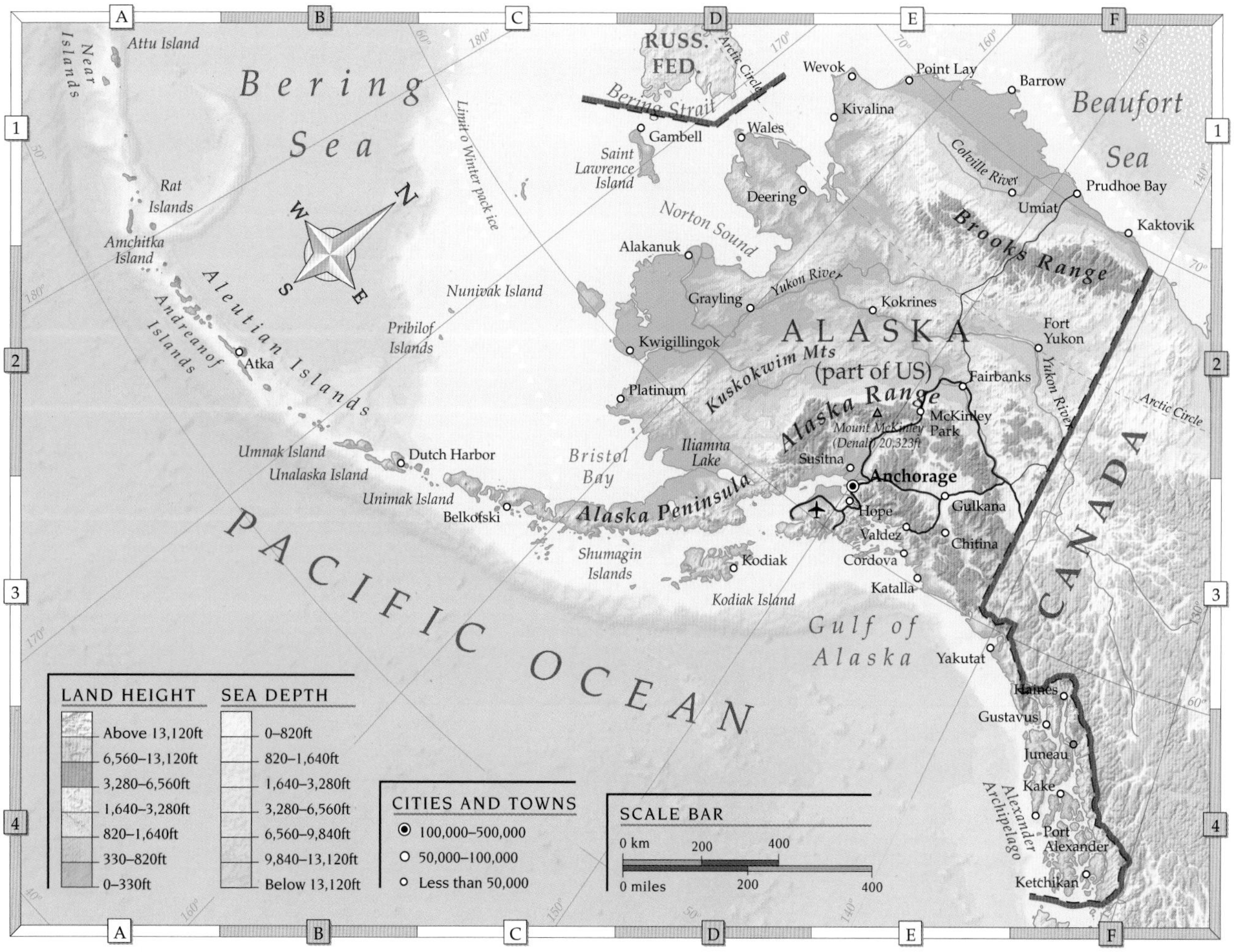

CLIMATE

Parts of northern Alaska are frozen year-round and can be cut off entirely in the winter. Summers are milder – especially in the Aleutians.

January

July

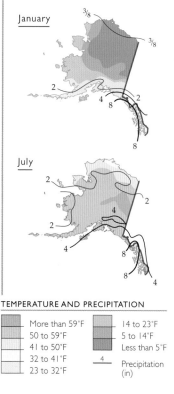

TEMPERATURE AND PRECIPITATION

- More than 59°F
- 50 to 59°F
- 41 to 50°F
- 32 to 41°F
- 23 to 32°F
- 14 to 23°F
- 5 to 14°F
- Less than 5°F
- 4 — Precipitation (in)

Main map labels

Near Islands · Attu Island · Bering Sea · Limit of Winter Pack ice · RUSS. FED. · Arctic Circle · Bering Strait · Wevok · Point Lay · Barrow · Beaufort Sea · Kivalina · Gambell · Wales · Saint Lawrence Island · Deering · Colville River · Umiat · Prudhoe Bay · Kaktovik · Brooks Range · Rat Islands · Amchitka Island · Aleutian Islands · Andreanof Islands · Atka · Norton Sound · Alakanuk · Grayling · Yukon River · Kokrines · Fort Yukon · Nunivak Island · Pribilof Islands · Kwigillingok · ALASKA (part of US) · Fairbanks · Yukon River · Arctic Circle · Umnak Island · Unalaska Island · Dutch Harbor · Platinum · Kuskokwim Mts · Alaska Range · McKinley Park · Mount McKinley (Denali) 20,323ft · Unimak Island · Belkofski · Bristol Bay · Iliamna Lake · Susitna · Anchorage · Hope · Gulkana · Valdez · Chitina · Shumagin Islands · Kodiak · Cordova · Katalla · CANADA · Kodiak Island · Gulf of Alaska · Yakutat · PACIFIC OCEAN · Haines · Gustavus · Juneau · Kake · Alexander Archipelago · Port Alexander · Ketchikan

LAND HEIGHT

- Above 13,120ft
- 6,560–13,120ft
- 3,280–6,560ft
- 1,640–3,280ft
- 820–1,640ft
- 330–820ft
- 0–330ft

SEA DEPTH

- 0–820ft
- 820–1,640ft
- 1,640–3,280ft
- 3,280–6,560ft
- 6,560–9,840ft
- 9,840–13,120ft
- Below 13,120ft

CITIES AND TOWNS

- ◉ 100,000–500,000
- ○ 50,000–100,000
- ○ Less than 50,000

SCALE BAR

0 km   200   400

0 miles   200   400

HAWAII

Hawaii is the 50th US state. It lies far from the mainland in the middle of the Pacific Ocean. The island chain was formed by volcanoes, only one of which, Mauna Loa, remains active today. The islands' indigenous peoples are Polynesians, but continued immigration means that they now make up only 9% of the population.

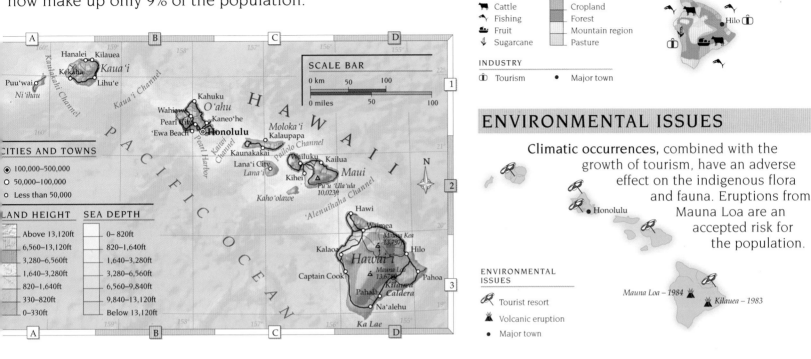

CITIES AND TOWNS
- ⦿ 100,000–500,000
- ○ 50,000–100,000
- ○ Less than 50,000

LAND HEIGHT
- Above 13,120ft
- 6,560–13,120ft
- 3,280–6,560ft
- 1,640–3,280ft
- 820–1,640ft
- 330–820ft
- 0–330ft

SEA DEPTH
- 0–820ft
- 820–1,640ft
- 1,640–3,280ft
- 3,280–6,560ft
- 6,560–9,840ft
- 9,840–13,120ft
- Below 13,120ft

SCALE BAR
0 km 50 100
0 miles 50 100

INDUSTRY AND LAND USE

Tourism is the most important industry in Hawaii, accounting for one in every three jobs. The naval base at Pearl Harbor also provides jobs for numerous people. The many large plantations grow sugarcane, bananas, and tropical fruit for export.

FARMING AND LAND USE
- Cattle
- Fishing
- Fruit
- Sugarcane
- Cropland
- Forest
- Mountain region
- Pasture

INDUSTRY
- Tourism
- Major town

ENVIRONMENTAL ISSUES

Climatic occurrences, combined with the growth of tourism, have an adverse effect on the indigenous flora and fauna. Eruptions from Mauna Loa are an accepted risk for the population.

ENVIRONMENTAL ISSUES
- Tourist resort
- Volcanic eruption
- Major town

Mauna Loa – 1984
Kilauea – 1983

US OVERSEAS TERRITORIES

America's overseas territories have traditionally been seen as strategically or economically important. In most cases, the local population has been given a say in deciding whether it wants to govern itself. A US commonwealth territory has a greater level of independence than a US unincorporated or external territory. The US has 13 overseas territories: the four largest are shown here.

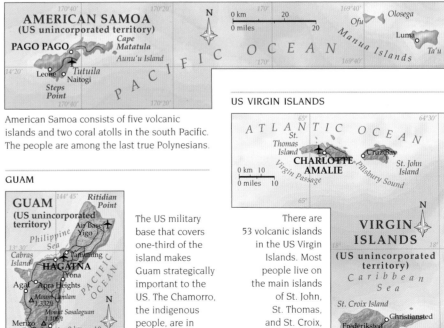

AMERICAN SAMOA

AMERICAN SAMOA (US unincorporated territory)
PAGO PAGO

American Samoa consists of five volcanic islands and two coral atolls in the south Pacific. The people are among the last true Polynesians.

GUAM

GUAM (US unincorporated territory)
HAGÅTÑA

The US military base that covers one-third of the island makes Guam strategically important to the US. The Chamorro, the indigenous people, are in charge of political and social life.

US VIRGIN ISLANDS

CHARLOTTE AMALIE

VIRGIN ISLANDS (US unincorporated territory)

There are 53 volcanic islands in the US Virgin Islands. Most people live on the main islands of St. John, St. Thomas, and St. Croix, which has a vast oil refinery.

PUERTO RICO

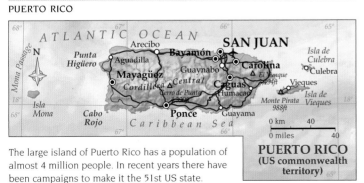

SAN JUAN

PUERTO RICO (US commonwealth territory)

The large island of Puerto Rico has a population of almost 4 million people. In recent years there have been campaigns to make it the 51st US state.

MEXICO

Mexico is a large country with a rich mixture of traditions and cultures. The ancient civilization of the Aztecs that flourished here was crushed by Spanish invaders in the 16th century. Spain ruled Mexico until its independence in 1836, and today the country has the world's largest Spanish-speaking population. Mexico is mostly dry and mountainous, and farmland is limited, so the country has to import most of the basic foods it needs to feed its people.

FARMING AND LAND USE

Most of the land suitable for farming is planted with corn – a big part of the Mexican diet. Along the Gulf coast coffee, sugarcane, and cotton are grown on plantations for export. Parts of the dry north are irrigated to grow cotton, but most of the land is taken up by large cattle ranches. Fishing, especially for shellfish such as lobster and shrimp is important in coastal areas.

FARMING AND LAND USE

- 🐂 Cattle
- 🎣 Fishing
- 🐑 Sheep
- 🍌 Bananas
- ☕ Coffee
- 🌽 Corn
- Cotton
- Fruit
- Grapes
- 🦞 Shellfish
- ⚓ Sugarcane
- Timber

- Cropland
- Desert
- Forest
- Pasture
- Wetland
- • Major conurbation

LAND USE

Cropland 14%
Other 15%
Forest 29%
Pasture 42%

THE LANDSCAPE

Much of Mexico is made up of a high plateau. The climate there is very dry and varies between true desert in the north, and semidesert farther south. The plateau is separated from the coastal plains by two long, rugged mountain chains: the Eastern Sierra Madre and the Western Sierra Madre. Toward the south, the mountain ranges join, meeting in the region of high volcanic peaks that surround Mexico City.

Baja (Lower) California (B 3)
This long and very dry peninsula separates the Gulf of California from the Pacific Ocean. The Gulf was formed after the last Ice Age, when the sea rose to flood a major rift valley.

The Rio Grande (D 2)
This river flows from Colorado in the US and forms much of Mexico's northern border. It crosses a vast arid area on its way to the Gulf of Mexico.

Earthquakes and volcanoes
Volcanic activity is common in Mexico. Popocatépetl (F5) and Volcán El Chichónal (G5) have erupted recently, and Mexico City was hit by a devastating earthquake in 1985.

Eastern Sierra Madre (D 5).

Yucatan Peninsula (H 4)
The Yucatan Peninsula is a low, wide tableland, formed by layers of limestone. Limestone absorbs water, so there are few rivers on the peninsula, and the tropical rainforests found there are fed mainly by streams and underground water.

Western Sierra Madre (C 3).

POPULATION

Most of the north is sparsely populated due to the hot, dry climate and lack of cultivable farmland. As people have migrated from the countryside in search of work, the cities have grown dramatically; almost 75% of Mexicans now live in urban areas. Mexico City is home to almost a fifth of the population and is one of the world's largest cities.

INHABITANTS PER SQ MILE

- More than 520
- 260–520
- 130–260
- Less than 130
- ■ Capital city
- • Major city

URBAN/RURAL POPULATION DIVISION

Mexico City 17.1%
Guadalajara 3.5%
Monterrey 3.1%
Other towns and cities 50.3%
Rural population 26%

ENVIRONMENTAL ISSUES

Fast, unplanned growth has led to poor sanitation and water supplies in Mexico City, while the wall of mountains that surrounds the city traps pollution from cars and factories, giving it some of the world's worst air pollution. Much of Mexico's tropical rainforest has been felled, leading to increased soil erosion. Land clearance farther north is also causing desertification.

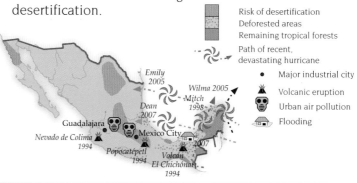

ENVIRONMENTAL ISSUES

- Risk of desertification
- Deforested areas
- Remaining tropical forests
- Path of recent, devastating hurricane
- • Major industrial city
- Volcanic eruption
- Urban air pollution
- Flooding

INDUSTRY

Oil and gas on the Gulf coast are the biggest source of income. Mexico is also rich in other minerals; it is the world's top silver producer. Manufacturing is centered around Mexico City and along the US border, where mainly foreign-owned factories assemble products for export.

Tourism is also very important to Mexico.

**STRUCTURE
OF INDUSTRY**

Primary 4%
Services 70%
Manufacturing 26%

INDUSTRY

- 🚗 Car manufacturing
- ⚙ Electronics
- ⚙ Engineering
- 🍴 Food processing
- Iron and steel
- Oil refining
- Textiles
- Mining
- Oil and gas
- Tourism
- ▣ Major industrial center / area
- — Major road

CLIMATE

Northern Mexico and the peninsula of Baja California are dry, hot, and largely desert. Toward the south, rainfall increases, especially in July. Moist, warm conditions allow rainforests to grow.

January

July

**TEMPERATURE
AND PRECIPITATION**

- More than 86°F
- 77 to 86°F
- 68 to 77°F
- 59 to 68°F
- 50 to 59°F
- 41 to 50°F
- Less than 41°F
- 4 Precipitation (in)

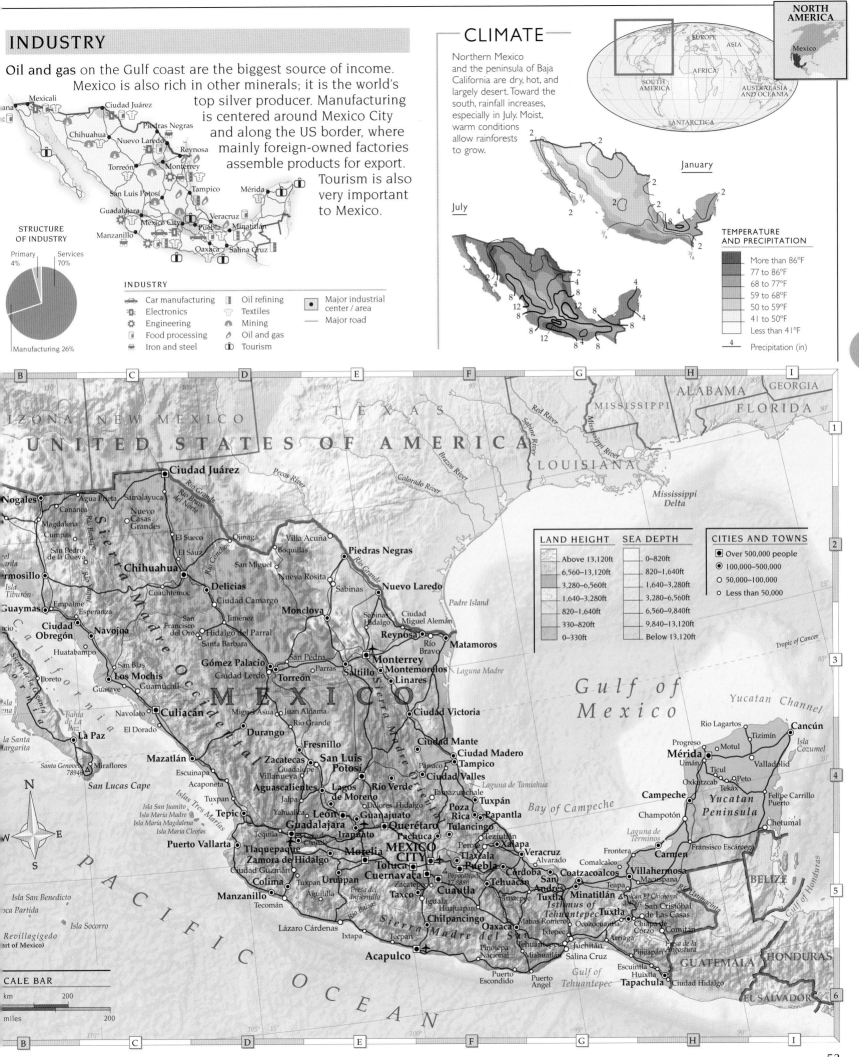

LAND HEIGHT
- Above 13,120ft
- 6,560–13,120ft
- 3,280–6,560ft
- 1,640–3,280ft
- 820–1,640ft
- 330–820ft
- 0–330ft

SEA DEPTH
- 0–820ft
- 820–1,640ft
- 1,640–3,280ft
- 3,280–6,560ft
- 6,560–9,840ft
- 9,840–13,120ft
- Below 13,120ft

CITIES AND TOWNS
- Over 500,000 people
- 100,000–500,000
- 50,000–100,000
- Less than 50,000

SCALE BAR

km   200

miles   200

CENTRAL AMERICA

BELIZE, COSTA RICA, EL SALVADOR, GUATEMALA, HONDURAS, NICARAGUA, PANAMA

Central America lies on a narrow bridge of land which links North and South America. All the countries here, except Belize, were once governed by Spain. Today, most of their people are *mestizos* – a mix of the original Maya Indian inhabitants and Spanish settlers. The hot, steamy climate is ideal for growing tropical crops, such as coffee and bananas, which are exported worldwide.

FARMING AND LAND USE

About half of all the agricultural products grown here are exported. The Pacific coast has fertile, well-watered land suitable for growing cotton and sugarcane. In the central highlands are big coffee plantations and ranches where beef cattle are raised. Bananas grow well along the humid Caribbean coastal plain, and shrimp and lobster are caught offshore.

FARMING AND LAND USE

🐂 Cattle
🦐 Shellfish
🍌 Bananas
☕ Coffee
🌽 Corn
🌿 Cotton
⚓ Sugarcane
🌲 Timber

- Cropland
- Forest
- Pasture
- Major conurbation

Guatemala City
Tegucigalpa
San Salvador
Managua
San José
Colón
Panama City

LAND USE

Pasture 27%
Forest 35%
Cropland 15%
Other 23%

ENVIRONMENTAL ISSUES

Central America's rain forests are rapidly being cut down for timber and to make way for farmland and land for building. Over half of Guatemala's forests have been felled, mostly in the last 30 years. The situation is also bleak in Honduras, Costa Rica, and Nicaragua. Central America has a line of volcanoes running through the region which, are still active.

Mitch 1998
Felix 2007
Volcán Tacaná 1986
Volcán de Fuego 1974
Volcán de Izalco 1958
Volcán San Cristobal 2000
Volcán Cerro Negro 1995
Volcán Masaya 2001
Volcán Concepcion 1986
Volcán Arenal 1998, 2000
Volcán Rincon de la Vieja 1998

ENVIRONMENTAL ISSUES

🌋 Volcanic eruption
Deforested areas
Remaining forests
Path of recent, devastating hurricane

POPULATION

Central America's people live mainly in the valleys of the central highlands or along the Pacific coastal plains. Despite the threat of volcanic eruptions and earthquakes, towns and cities were developed in these areas because of the fertile volcanic soils found there. Around half the population still lives in rural areas, mostly in small villages or remote settlements, but the cities have expanded rapidly and overcrowding has become a serious problem.

BELMOPAN
GUATEMALA CITY
TEGUCIGALPA
SAN SALVADOR
MANAGUA
SAN JOSÉ
PANAMA CITY

INHABITANTS PER SQ MILE

- More than 130
- 52–130
- Less than 52
- Capital city

URBAN/RURAL POPULATION DIVISION

San Salvador 3.3%
Tegucigalpa 3.2%
Managua 3.5%
Other towns and cities 37%
Rural population 53%

THE LANDSCAPE

The Sierra Madre in the north and the Cordillera Central to the south form a mountainous ridge that stretches down most of Central America. Along the Pacific coast north of Panama is a belt of more than 40 active volcanoes. The mountains are broken by valleys and basins with large, fertile areas of rich, volcanic soil.

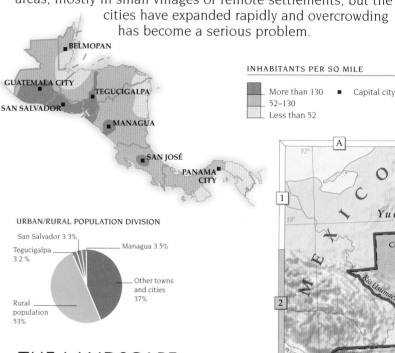

Coral reef (C 2)
Off the coast of Belize is a 180 mile-long coral reef – the second longest in the world. Its waters contain spectacular marine life. In places, the reef has become built up into dozens of small sandy islands called cayes.

Sierra Madre (A 3)

The Mosquito Coast (E 4)
The Mosquito Coast is a remote area of tropical rain forests, lagoons, and rivers lined with mangroves. Most of it is uninhabited by humans, but there is a huge variety of animal species, including monkeys and alligators.

Lake Nicaragua (E 5)
This large freshwater lake contains about 400 islands, some of which are active volancoes like Volcán Concepcion. The lake is also home to the world's only freshwater sharks.

Cordillera Central (G 6)

Panama Canal (H 6)
The Panama Canal links the Atlantic and Pacific oceans along a distance of 51 miles. Half of its route passes through Lake Gatún, a freshwater lake that acts as a reservoir for the canal, providing water to operate the locks.

MEXICO
Yuc
Río Usumacin
A
1
2
3
4
92°
18°
14°
Barillas
Jacaltenango GUA
Chajul
Nebaj
Huehuetenango
Volcán Tacaná 13,429ft
Santa Cruz del Quiché
San Marcos
Quezaltenan
GUATEMALA CH
Champerico
San Jo

NORTH AMERICA

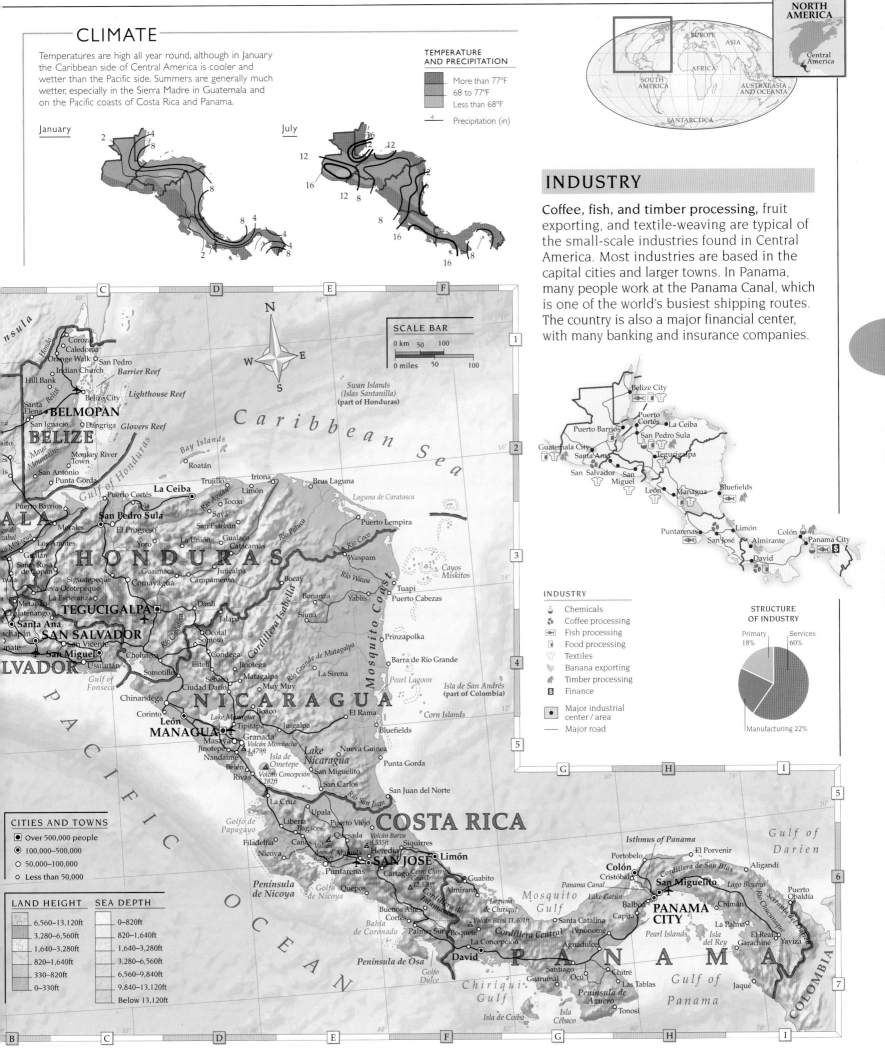

CLIMATE

Temperatures are high all year round, although in January the Caribbean side of Central America is cooler and wetter than the Pacific side. Summers are generally much wetter, especially in the Sierra Madre in Guatemala and on the Pacific coasts of Costa Rica and Panama.

TEMPERATURE AND PRECIPITATION

More than 77°F
68 to 77°F
Less than 68°F
Precipitation (in)

January

July

INDUSTRY

Coffee, fish, and timber processing, fruit exporting, and textile-weaving are typical of the small-scale industries found in Central America. Most industries are based in the capital cities and larger towns. In Panama, many people work at the Panama Canal, which is one of the world's busiest shipping routes. The country is also a major financial center, with many banking and insurance companies.

INDUSTRY

Chemicals
Coffee processing
Fish processing
Food processing
Textiles
Banana exporting
Timber processing
Finance
● Major industrial center / area
— Major road

STRUCTURE OF INDUSTRY

Primary 18%
Services 60%
Manufacturing 22%

SCALE BAR

0 km   50   100
0 miles   50   100

CITIES AND TOWNS

■ Over 500,000 people
● 100,000–500,000
◐ 50,000–100,000
○ Less than 50,000

LAND HEIGHT

6,560–13,120ft
3,280–6,560ft
1,640–3,280ft
820–1,640ft
330–820ft
0–330ft

SEA DEPTH

0–820ft
820–1,640ft
1,640–3,280ft
3,280–6,560ft
6,560–9,840ft
9,840–13,120ft
Below 13,120ft

THE CARIBBEAN

The Caribbean Sea is enclosed by an arc of many hundreds of islands, islets, and offshore reefs that reach from Florida in the US, round to Venezuela in South America. From 1492, Spain, France, Britain, and the Netherlands claimed the islands as colonies. Most of the islands' original inhabitants were wiped out by disease and a wide mixture of peoples – of African, Asian, and European descent – now make up the population. In 2010, a huge earthquake killed around 250,000 people in Haiti.

THE LANDSCAPE

The Bahamas
The Bahamas are low-lying islands formed from limestone rock. Their coastlines are fringed by coral reefs, lagoons, and mangrove swamps. Some of the bigger islands are covered by forests.

The islands are formed from two main mountain chains: the Greater Antilles, which are part of a chain running from west to east, and the Lesser Antilles, which run from north to south. The mountains are now almost submerged under the Atlantic Ocean and Caribbean Sea. Only the higher peaks reach above sea level to form islands.

Hispaniola (F4)
Two countries, Haiti and the Dominican Republic, occupy the island of Hispaniola. The land is mostly mountainous, broken by fertile valleys.

Cuba (C3)
Cuba is the largest island in the Antilles. Its landscape is made up of wide, fertile plains with rugged hills and mountains in the southeast.

The Lesser Antilles
Most of these small volcanic islands have mountainous interiors. Barbados and Antigua & Barbuda are flatter, with some higher volcanic areas. Montserrat was evacuated in 1997, following volcanic eruptions on the island.

FARMING AND LAND USE

Agriculture is an important source of income, with over half of all produce exported. Many islands have fertile, well-watered land and large areas are set aside for commercial crops such as sugarcane, tobacco, and coffee. Some islands rely heavily on a single crop; in Dominica, bananas provide over half the country's income. Cuba is one of the world's biggest sugar producers.

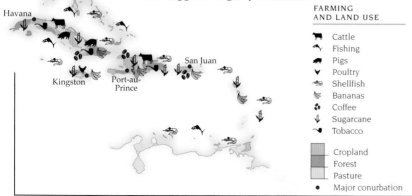

FARMING AND LAND USE

- 🐄 Cattle
- Fishing
- Pigs
- Poultry
- Shellfish
- Bananas
- Coffee
- Sugarcane
- Tobacco
- Cropland
- Forest
- Pasture
- • Major conurbation

ENVIRONMENTAL ISSUES

The islands of the Caribbean are often under threat from hurricane storm systems which sweep in from the Atlantic Ocean between May and October. The winds can reach speeds of up to 185 miles per hour, devastating everything that lies in their path and causing severe flooding. The storms themselves are enormous; a hurricane can extend outward for 400 miles from its calm center, which is known as the "eye."

TOURISM

Tourism is thriving in the Caribbean, often bringing more income to the region than other, traditional industries. Long sandy beaches, clear, warm waters, and the climate are the main attractions. In Cuba and the Dominican Republic, tourism is expanding at some of the fastest rates in North America. As hotel complexes and new roads and airports are developed, the environment is often damaged. Local people who work in the industry often receive little of the extra cash brought in by the tourists.

TOURISM

Major tourist destinations

NORTH AMERICA
The Caribbean

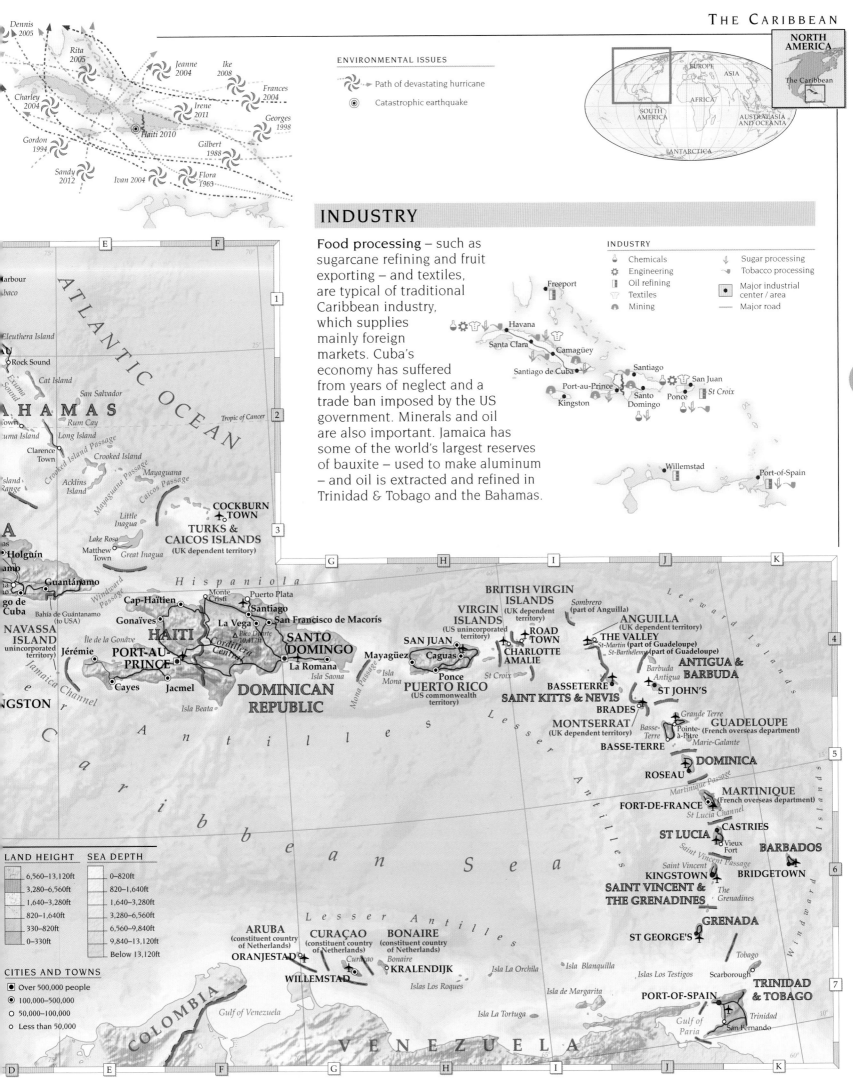

ENVIRONMENTAL ISSUES

🌀 Path of devastating hurricane

◎ Catastrophic earthquake

Dennis 2005
Rita 2005
Jeanne 2004
Ike 2008
Frances 2004
Charley 2004
Irene 2011
Georges 1998
Gordon 1994
Haiti 2010
Gilbert 1988
Sandy 2012
Ivan 2004
Flora 1963

INDUSTRY

Food processing – such as sugarcane refining and fruit exporting – and textiles, are typical of traditional Caribbean industry, which supplies mainly foreign markets. Cuba's economy has suffered from years of neglect and a trade ban imposed by the US government. Minerals and oil are also important. Jamaica has some of the world's largest reserves of bauxite – used to make aluminum – and oil is extracted and refined in Trinidad & Tobago and the Bahamas.

INDUSTRY

- 🧪 Chemicals
- ⚙ Engineering
- Oil refining
- 👕 Textiles
- Mining
- ↓ Sugar processing
- Tobacco processing
- ■ Major industrial center / area
- — Major road

Freeport
Havana
Santa Clara
Camagüey
Santiago de Cuba
Santiago
San Juan
St Croix
Port-au-Prince
Santo Domingo
Ponce
Kingston
Willemstad
Port-of-Spain

LAND HEIGHT
- 6,560–13,120ft
- 3,280–6,560ft
- 1,640–3,280ft
- 820–1,640ft
- 330–820ft
- 0–330ft

SEA DEPTH
- 0–820ft
- 820–1,640ft
- 1,640–3,280ft
- 3,280–6,560ft
- 6,560–9,840ft
- 9,840–13,120ft
- Below 13,120ft

CITIES AND TOWNS
- ■ Over 500,000 people
- ◉ 100,000–500,000
- ○ 50,000–100,000
- · Less than 50,000

ATLANTIC OCEAN

Harbour
Abaco
Eleuthera Island
Rock Sound
Cat Island
San Salvador
BAHAMAS
Town
Rum Cay
uma Island
Long Island
Clarence Town
Crooked Island
Crooked Island Passage
Mayaguana
Acklins Island
Caicos Passage
Mayaguana Passage
island Range
Little Inagua
Lake Rosa
Matthew Town
Great Inagua
COCKBURN TOWN
TURKS & CAICOS ISLANDS
(UK dependent territory)

Tropic of Cancer

Holguín
amo
Guantánamo
go de Cuba
Bahía de Guántanamo (to USA)
Hispaniola
Windward Passage
Cap-Haïtien
Monte Cristi
Puerto Plata
Santiago
San Francisco de Macorís
NAVASSA ISLAND
unincorporated territory
Île de la Gonâve
Gonaïves
HAITI
La Vega
Jérémie
PORT-AU-PRINCE
▲ Pico Duarte 10,417ft
Cordillera Central
SANTO DOMINGO
La Romana
Cayes
Jacmel
DOMINICAN REPUBLIC
Isla Beata
Isla Saona
Jamaica Channel
ngston

SAN JUAN
Mayagüez
Caguas
Ponce
PUERTO RICO
(US commonwealth territory)
St Croix
Isla Mona
Mona Passage

VIRGIN ISLANDS
(US unincorporated territory)
CHARLOTTE AMALIE
BRITISH VIRGIN ISLANDS
(UK dependent territory)
ROAD TOWN
Sombrero (part of Anguilla)
THE VALLEY
ANGUILLA
(UK dependent territory)
St-Martin (part of Guadeloupe)
St-Barthélemy (part of Guadeloupe)
Leeward Islands
BASSETERRE
SAINT KITTS & NEVIS
BRADES
MONTSERRAT
(UK dependent territory)
Barbuda
Antigua
ANTIGUA & BARBUDA
ST JOHN'S
Grande Terre
Basse-Terre
Pointe-à-Pitre
GUADELOUPE
(French overseas department)
BASSE-TERRE
Marie-Galante
DOMINICA
ROSEAU
Martinique Passage
MARTINIQUE
(French overseas department)
FORT-DE-FRANCE
St Lucia Channel
ST LUCIA
CASTRIES
Vieux Fort
Saint Vincent Passage
BARBADOS
BRIDGETOWN
Saint Vincent
KINGSTOWN
SAINT VINCENT & THE GRENADINES
The Grenadines
Windward Islands
GRENADA
ST GEORGE'S
Tobago
Scarborough
TRINIDAD & TOBAGO

Caribbean Sea

Lesser Antilles
Antilles

ARUBA
(constituent country of Netherlands)
ORANJESTAD
CURAÇAO
(constituent country of Netherlands)
Curaçao
BONAIRE
(constituent country of Netherlands)
Bonaire
WILLEMSTAD
KRALENDIJK
Islas Los Roques
Isla La Orchila
Isla Blanquilla
Islas Los Testigos
Isla de Margarita
Isla La Tortuga
PORT-OF-SPAIN
Trinidad
San Fernando
Gulf of Paria

COLOMBIA
Gulf of Venezuela
VENEZUELA

CONTINENTAL SOUTH AMERICA

The towering peaks of the Andes stand high above the western side of South America. They act as a barrier to the sparsely inhabited interior of the continent, which includes the dense rain forest of the Amazon Basin – one of the Earth's last great wildernesses. Most people live on South America's coastal fringes. Brazil is both the largest country and the most populous. Over half the continent's land area and half of its people are found there.

3,100 miles
4,750 miles

CROSS-SECTION ACROSS SOUTH AMERICA

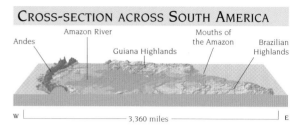

Andes
Amazon River
Guiana Highlands
Mouths of the Amazon
Brazilian Highlands

W — 3,360 miles — E

The high peaks of the Andes rise up from a narrow strip of land bordering the Pacific Ocean. East of the Andes, the land flattens into a broad, shallow basin into which the Amazon River flows. To the north are the older Guiana Highlands where rock has been eroded to form flat-topped "table" mountains.

PHYSICAL SOUTH AMERICA

Ancient masses of rocks, like the Guiana and Brazilian highlands, which are known as shields, form the core of South America. The Andes are the solid backbone of the continent. They are relatively young, formed by collisions between different plates of the Earth's crust. The major rivers: the Paraná and the mighty Amazon, flow in deep depressions to the east of the mountains.

ELEVATION

Above 13,120ft
6,560–3,120ft
3,280–6,560ft
1,640–3,280ft
820–1,640ft
330–820ft
0–330ft
Below sea level

cross-section

SCALE 1:40,000,000

0 km 400 800
0 miles 400 800

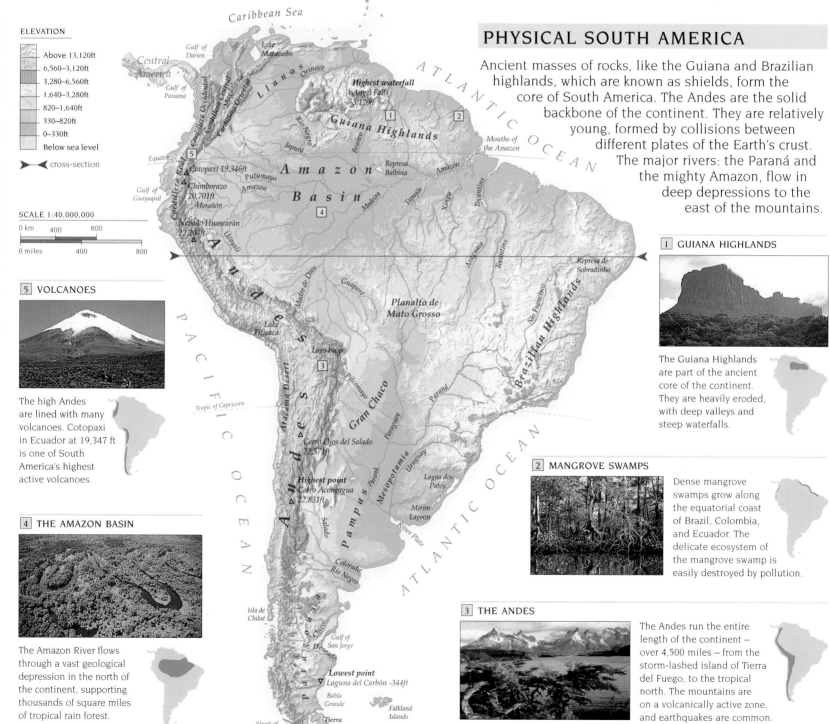

Caribbean Sea
Central America
Gulf of Darien
Lake Maracaibo
Gulf of Panama
Llanos
Orinoco
Cordillera Occidental
Cordillera Central
Magdalena
Cordillera Oriental
Rio Negro
Guiana Highlands
Highest waterfall Angel Falls 3,120ft
ATLANTIC OCEAN
Mouths of the Amazon
Japurá
Equator
Cordillera Real
Cotopaxi 19,346ft
Putumayo
Amazon
Chimborazo 20,701ft
Marañón
Gulf of Guayaquil
Amazon Basin
Branco
Represa Balbina
Amazon
Madeira
Tapajós
Xingu
Tocantins
Nevado Huascarán 22,204ft
Ucayali
Madre de Dios
Araguaia
Tocantins
Represa de Sobradinho
Andes
Guaporé
Planalto de Mato Grosso
São Francisco
Brazilian Highlands
Lake Titicaca
Lago Poopó
Atacama Desert
Pilcomayo
Gran Chaco
Paraná
Tropic of Capricorn
Cerro Ojos del Salado 22,571ft
Pilcomayo
Paraguay
Uruguay
Mesopotamia
Lagoa dos Patos
Highest point Cerro Aconcagua 22,831ft
Paraná
Pampas
Mirim Lagoon
Salado
River Plate
PACIFIC OCEAN
Isla de Chiloé
Chiloé
Colorado
Río Negro
Gulf of San Jorge
Lowest point Laguna del Carbón -344ft
Patagonia
Bahía Grande
Falkland Islands
Strait of Magellan
Tierra del Fuego
Cape Horn
ATLANTIC OCEAN

5 VOLCANOES

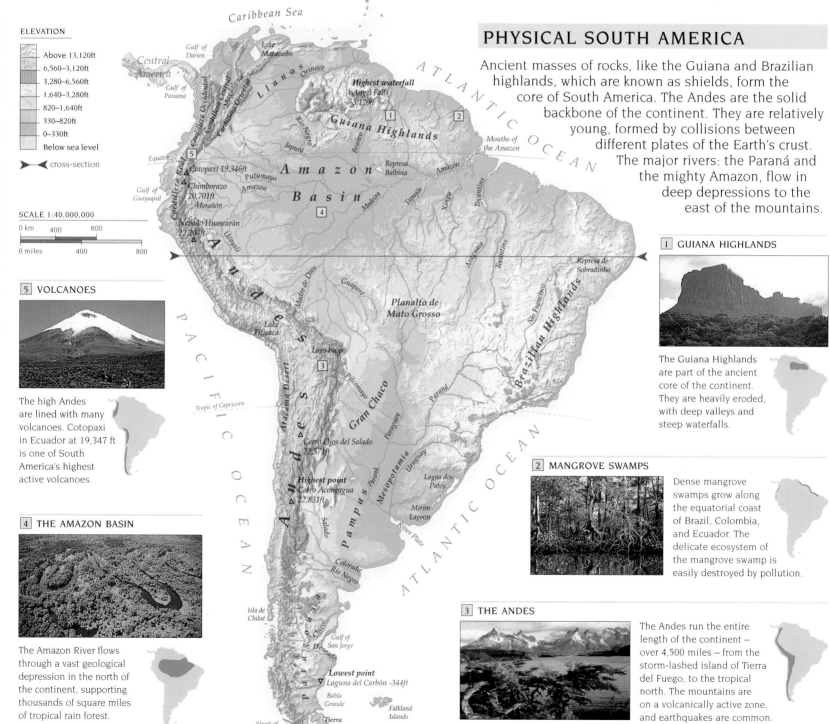

The high Andes are lined with many volcanoes. Cotopaxi in Ecuador at 19,347 ft is one of South America's highest active volcanoes.

4 THE AMAZON BASIN

The Amazon River flows through a vast geological depression in the north of the continent, supporting thousands of square miles of tropical rain forest.

1 GUIANA HIGHLANDS

The Guiana Highlands are part of the ancient core of the continent. They are heavily eroded, with deep valleys and steep waterfalls.

2 MANGROVE SWAMPS

Dense mangrove swamps grow along the equatorial coast of Brazil, Colombia, and Ecuador. The delicate ecosystem of the mangrove swamp is easily destroyed by pollution.

3 THE ANDES

The Andes run the entire length of the continent – over 4,500 miles – from the storm-lashed island of Tierra del Fuego, to the tropical north. The mountains are on a volcanically active zone, and earthquakes are common.

58

POLITICAL SOUTH AMERICA

In the 17th century, explorers from Spain and Portugal claimed most of South America for their rulers in Europe. Their influences are still strong today: Brazilians speak Portuguese, while much of the rest of the continent is Spanish-speaking. The small nations of the north, Suriname and Guyana, were Dutch and British colonies, and French Guiana is a French overseas department. The mix of peoples is mainly European, Native American, and African. Some native peoples still live in the dense Amazon rain forest.

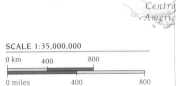

TRANSPORTATION LINKS

The Pan American Highway is a vital transportation link, running from the far south of the continent, northward along the Pacific coast. Its route takes it through sparsely populated areas like the Atacama Desert.

POPULATION

Many South American countries have a similar pattern of population distribution. The largest concentrations of people are found near the coasts. Migration to the coastal cities has led to rocketing population figures and growing social problems. São Paulo is now one of the world's largest cities; its outskirts are fringed with sprawling, shanty town suburbs, known as *favelas*.

Largest city
SÃO PAULO
21.7 million people

POPULATION DENSITY
(People per sq mile)

Below 13	24–36	51–76
13–23	37–50	Above 76

SCALE 1:35,000,000

0 km   400   800

0 miles   400   800

BORDER DISPUTES

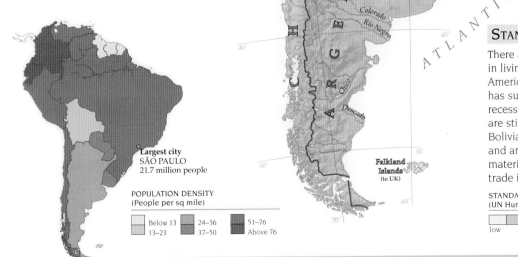

Many of South America's borders have been, or remain, disputed. Bolivia is landlocked as a result of a dispute with Chile in 1883, when it lost its lands bordering the Pacific Ocean.

URBAN GROWTH

Urban growth has transformed São Paulo into a major population and industrial center. Its rapid growth has created many problems, such as traffic congestion, overcrowding, and inadequate sewerage.

POPULATION

Capital cities
- ◉ Above 500,000
- ◉ 100,000 to 500,000
- ● 50,000 to 100,000
- ● Below 50,000

Other cities
- ⊡ Above 500,000
- ○ 50,000 to 100,000

STANDARDS OF LIVING

There are many inequalities in living standards across South America. Argentina's economy has suffered during the regional recession but living standards are still above those of Guyana and Bolivia, which have weak economies and are heavily reliant upon trade in raw materials. The booming black-market drugs trade increases crime and corruption.

STANDARD OF LIVING
(UN Human Development Index)

low   high   no data

SOUTH AMERICAN GEOGRAPHY

Agriculture is still the most common form of employment in South America. Cattle and cash crops of coffee, cocoa, and, in some places, coca for cocaine, provide the main sources of income. Brazil has the greatest range of industries, followed by Argentina, Venezuela, and Chile. The large coastal cities such as Rio de Janeiro, Lima, and Buenos Aires are where most of the jobs are found. This encourages people to migrate from the country to the city, in search of employment.

INDUSTRY

Brazil is the continent's leading industrial producer, and São Paulo is the major industrial city. Manufactured products include iron and steel, automobiles, chemicals, textiles, and meat and leather products from the continent's vast cattle herds. In the mountains of Bolivia and Colombia, coca plants are grown to make cocaine, which has created a black market for this illegal drug.

OIL AND GAS

Under the waters of Lake Maracaibo, Venezuela, lie some of South America's biggest oil reserves. Oil exploitation has brought great wealth to Venezuela. The money has helped the country to build new roads and develop other industries.

INDUSTRIAL CENTER

São Paulo, Brazil, is the largest city in South America and a leading industrial center. A wide range of goods is manufactured here, including automobiles, chemicals, textiles, and electronic products. São Paulo is also a leading financial center. Hundreds of people flock to the city daily in search of work.

TRADE AND EXPORTS

The Chilean port of Valparaíso ships many different products out of South America. Trade is growing with Japan and other countries around the Pacific Ocean.

MINERAL RESOURCES

South America's mineral resources are highly localized. Few countries have both fossil fuels and metallic ores. The richest oilfields are in the north, especially in Venezuela. Coal, however, is scarce. When the Andes were formed, heat helped create the many metallic minerals that are mined today.

MINERAL RESOURCES
- Bauxite
- Copper
- Iron
- Lead
- Silver
- Tin
- Oil/Gas field
- Coal field

COPPER MINES

Metallic mineral reserves are abundant in the Andes. Chuquicamata, northern Chile, is one of the world's largest copper mines.

ECONOMIC ACTIVITY
- Aerospace
- Brewing
- Car/vehicle manufacture
- Chemicals
- Coal
- Electronics
- Engineering
- Finance
- Fish processing
- Food processing
- Hi-tech industry
- Iron & steel
- Metal refining
- Narcotics
- Oil and gas
- Pharmaceuticals
- Printing & publishing
- Shipbuilding
- Textiles
- Timber processing
- Tobacco processing

GNI per capita (US$)
- Below 3,000
- 3,000-4,999
- 5,000-6,999
- 7,000-8,999
- 9,000-10,999
- Above 11,000
- Industrial center

Caribbean Sea
Central America
Barranquilla
Cartagena
Maracaibo
Barquisimeto
Caracas
Valencia
Ciudad Guayana
Georgetown
Paramaribo
French Guiana (to France)
SURINAME
GUYANA
VENEZUELA
Medellín
Bogotá
Cali
COLOMBIA
Quito
ECUADOR
Guayaquil
Belém
Manaús
Amazon Basin
Fortaleza
Natal
Recife
Maceió
Salvador
ATLANTIC OCEAN
Chiclayo
Chimbote
Lima
PERU
Cusco
BRAZIL
Brasília
BOLIVIA
La Paz
Santa Cruz
Arequipa
Sucre
Arica
Iquique
Chuquicamata
Antofagasta
PARAGUAY
Belo Horizonte
Rio de Janeiro
São Paulo
Asunción
San Miguel de Tucumán
Corrientes
Curitiba
PACIFIC OCEAN
Porto Alegre
URUGUAY
Córdoba
Santa Fe
Valparaíso
Mendoza
Rosario
Rio Grande
Santiago
Buenos Aires
Montevideo
Talca
Concepción
ARGENTINA
Neuquén
Bahía Blanca
Valdivia
ATLANTIC OCEAN
Comodoro Rivadavia
Falkland Islands (to UK)
Punta Arenas
Cape Horn

CLIMATE

South America has four main climatic regions: tropical, arid, temperate, and the cold climate of the far south. The Amazon Basin, covered by massive rain forests, and the Guiana Highlands have a humid, tropical climate that allows vegetation to flourish. West of the Andes the climate tends to be very dry. Moist air flowing west from the Atlantic Ocean is prevented from reaching the shores of the Pacific Ocean by the Andes, and rain falls before it can pass over the mountains. This creates arid deserts like the Atacama.

EXTREME WEATHER EVENTS

Symbols indicate climatic extremes

Wettest place
QUIBDÓ (Colombia)
Annual rainfall 354in

Equator

Driest place
ARICA (Chile)
Annual rainfall 1/4in

Hottest place
RIVADAVIA (Argentina)
Temp 120°F

Tropic of Capricorn

Coldest place
SARMIENTO (Argentina)
Temp -27°F

CLIMATE

- Subarctic
- Cool continental
- Warm temperate
- Semiarid
- Arid
- Temperate
- Tropical
- Humid equatorial

NORTH AMERICA · EUROPE · ASIA · AFRICA · SOUTH AMERICA · AUSTRALASIA and OCEANIA · ANTARCTICA

PATAGONIAN ICEFIELDS

Toward the south of the continent, the climate becomes very cold. Large expanses of ice, forming glaciers, are found in southern Patagonia and on islands such as Tierra del Fuego at the tip of South America.

LAND USE AND AGRICULTURE

- Cattle
- Pigs
- Sheep
- Bananas
- Corn
- Citrus fruits
- Coca
- Cocoa
- Cotton
- Coffee
- Fishing
- Oil palms
- Peanuts
- Rubber
- Shellfish
- Soybeans
- Sugarcane
- Vineyards
- Wheat

- Barren land
- Cropland
- Desert
- Forest
- Mountain region
- Pasture
- Wetland
- Major conurbation

LAND USE AND AGRICULTURE

Many plants now found throughout the world originated in South America, like the tomato, potato, and cassava. Today, coffee, cocoa, rubber, soybeans, corn, and sugarcane are widely cultivated, and grapes are grown in sheltered valleys in the Andes. Much of the Amazon Basin is covered by dense rain forest and is unsuitable for cultivation, although some farmers practice "slash and burn" techniques to make land for crops and cattle farming, which destroy ancient forest.

COFFEE

South America, and Brazil in particular, is a major producer of coffee. The plants thrive in the rich red soils of southern Brazil and are grown on huge plantations on the mountain slopes.

LOCAL MARKETS

At traditional markets such as this one in Ecuador, high in the Andes, local people trade fruit, vegetables, and goods such as clothing, rugs, and blankets. Some goods produced by Ecuadorean Indians are now exported worldwide.

CATTLE

The vast plains of the Pampas, to the west of Buenos Aires, support large herds of cattle. Meat processing and canning is a major industry in Argentina, Paraguay, and Uruguay.

NARCOTICS

Coca, grown in forest clearings in remote mountain areas, is used to make the drug cocaine. Government troops burn any coca plants they discover to discourage production.

Map labels: Caribbean Sea, Central America, Barranquilla, Maracaibo, Caracas, Llanos, Orinoco, Medellín, Bogotá, Cali, Guiana Highlands, Rio Negro, Amazon Basin, Putumayo, Amazon, Manaus, Belém, Marañón, Amazon, Fortaleza, Purus, Madeira, Tapajós, Xingu, Tocantins, Recife, Lima, São Francisco, Brasília, Salvador, Brazilian Highlands, Belo Horizonte, Pilcomayo, Gran Chaco, Paraguay, Paraná, Rio de Janeiro, São Paulo, Curitiba, Uruguay, Porto Alegre, Córdoba, Rosario, Santiago, Pampas, Montevideo, Buenos Aires, Colorado, Rio Negro, Patagonia, Gulf of San Jorge, Falkland Islands, Cape Horn, Pacific Ocean, Atlantic Ocean, Andes

NORTHERN SOUTH AMERICA

BRAZIL, COLOMBIA, ECUADOR, GUYANA, PERU,
SURINAME, VENEZUELA

High mountains, rain forests, and hot, grassy plains
cover much of northern South America. From the 16th
century, after the conquest of the Incas, the western
countries were ruled by Spain. Brazil was governed
by Portugal, Guyana by Britain, and Suriname by
the Dutch. The more recent history of some of these
countries has included periods of civil war and military
rule. Most are still troubled by widespread poverty.

FARMING AND LAND USE

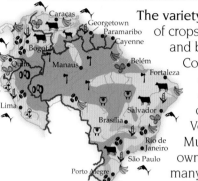

The variety of climates allows a wide range
of crops, including sugarcane, cocoa,
and bananas, to be grown for export.
Coffee is the most important cash
crop; Brazil is the world's leading
coffee grower. Cattle are farmed
on the plains of Colombia,
Venezuela, and southern Brazil.
Much of the good farmland is
owned by a few rich landowners:
many peasant farmers do not have
enough land to make a living.

FARMING AND LAND USE

Cattle	Sugarcane
Fishing	Timber
Goats	
Sheep	Cropland
Bananas	Forest
Cocoa	Mountain region
Cotton	Pasture
Coffee	Wetland
Rubber	Major conurbation

LAND USE

Cropland 6%
Other (including mountains) 15%
Pasture 23%
Forest 56%

INDUSTRY

Important oil reserves are found in
Venezuela and parts of the Amazon
Basin; Venezuela is one of the world's
top oil producers. Brazil's cities have
a wide range of industries including
chemicals, clothes and shoes,
and textiles. Metallic minerals,
particularly iron ore, are mined
throughout the area and specially built
industrial centers like Ciudad Guayana
have been developed to refine them.

STRUCTURE OF INDUSTRY

Primary 11%
Services 50%
Manufacturing 39%

INDUSTRY

Aerospace	Oil
Chemicals	Timber processing
Food processing	Tourism
Iron and steel	
Metal refining	Major industrial center / area
Textiles	
Mining	Major road

POPULATION

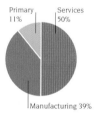

Most of the population lives in urban
areas. Many cities are extremely
overcrowded, with poor housing.
São Paulo in Brazil is one of
the world's fastest-growing
cities. The rain forests of
the interior and high Andes
are sparsely populated. The
few Native American peoples
live in remote areas.

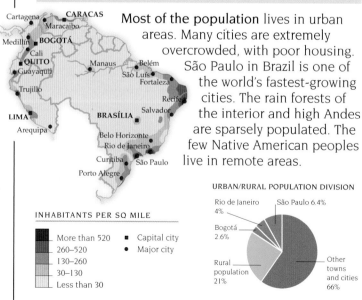

URBAN/RURAL POPULATION DIVISION

Rio de Janeiro 4%
São Paulo 6.4%
Bogotá 2.6%
Rural population 21%
Other towns and cities 66%

INHABITANTS PER SQ MILE

- More than 520
- 260–520
- 130–260
- 30–130
- Less than 30
- Capital city
- Major city

THE LANDSCAPE

The Andes run down the western side of South
America. There are many volcanoes among their peaks,
and earthquakes are common. The tropical rain forests
surrounding the Amazon River take up most of western
Brazil. Huge, dry, flat grasslands called *llanos* cover
central Venezuela and part of eastern Colombia.

Angel Falls (D 2)
Venezuela's Angel Falls is the
world's highest waterfall. Twenty
times as high as Niagara Falls, it
drops 3,212 ft from a spectacular
plateau deep in the Guiana Highlands.

Amazon River (D 4)
The Amazon is the longest
river in South America, and
the second longest in
the world. It flows over
4,049 miles from the
Peruvian Andes to the
coast of Brazil. One-fifth of
the world's freshwater is
carried by the river.

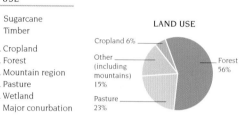

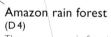

Andes (B 5)
The snow-capped
Andes are the
longest mountain
range on Earth.
They stretch
4,500 miles down
the whole length
of South America.

Lake Titicaca (C 6)
South America's
largest lake is the
highest navigable
lake in the world
at 12,500 ft
above sea level.
It lies across the
border between
Peru and Bolivia.

Pantanal (E 6)
This is the largest area of
wetlands in the world. It spreads
across 50,000 sq miles of Brazil.
Many hundreds of plant and
animal species are found here.

Amazon rain forest (D 4)
The enormous rain forest
surrounding the Amazon
River and its tributaries
covers 2,510,000 sq miles,
an area almost as big as
Australia. It is estimated
that at least half of all
known living species
are found in the forest.

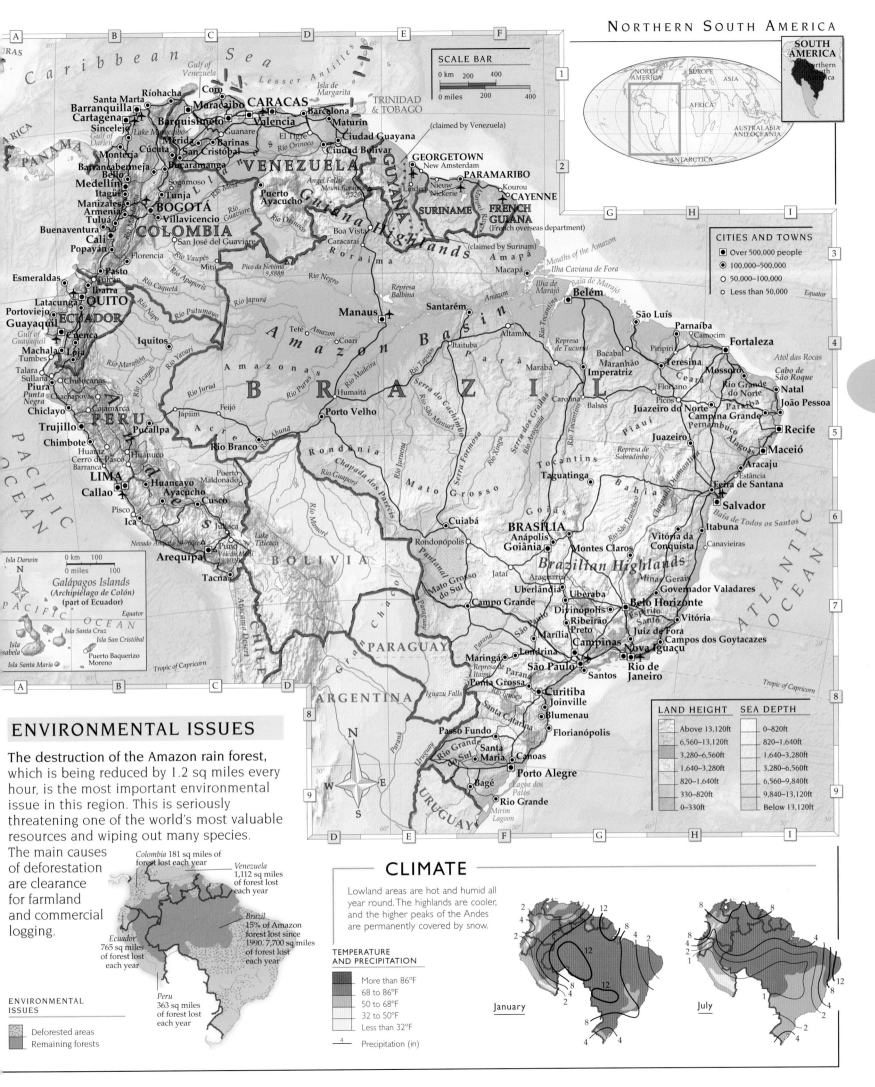

ENVIRONMENTAL ISSUES

The destruction of the Amazon rain forest, which is being reduced by 1.2 sq miles every hour, is the most important environmental issue in this region. This is seriously threatening one of the world's most valuable resources and wiping out many species.

The main causes of deforestation are clearance for farmland and commercial logging.

Colombia 181 sq miles of forest lost each year

Venezuela 1,112 sq miles of forest lost each year

Brazil 15% of Amazon forest lost since 1990. 7,700 sq miles of forest lost each year

Ecuador 765 sq miles of forest lost each year

Peru 363 sq miles of forest lost each year

ENVIRONMENTAL ISSUES

Deforested areas
Remaining forests

CLIMATE

Lowland areas are hot and humid all year round. The highlands are cooler, and the higher peaks of the Andes are permanently covered by snow.

TEMPERATURE AND PRECIPITATION

- More than 86°F
- 68 to 86°F
- 50 to 68°F
- 32 to 50°F
- Less than 32°F

— Precipitation (in)

January

July

SOUTH AMERICA
Northern South America

CITIES AND TOWNS
- Over 500,000 people
- 100,000–500,000
- 50,000–100,000
- Less than 50,000

SCALE BAR
0 km 200 400
0 miles 200 400

LAND HEIGHT	SEA DEPTH
Above 13,120ft	0–820ft
6,560–13,120ft	820–1,640ft
3,280–6,560ft	1,640–3,280ft
1,640–3,280ft	3,280–6,560ft
820–1,640ft	6,560–9,840ft
330–820ft	9,840–13,120ft
0–330ft	Below 13,120ft

SOUTHERN SOUTH AMERICA

ARGENTINA, BOLIVIA, CHILE, PARAGUAY, URUGUAY

The southern half of South America forms a long, narrow cone, with landscapes ranging from barren desert in the west to frozen glaciers in the far south. The whole area was governed by Spain until the early 19th century, and Spanish is still the main language spoken, although the few remaining Native American groups use their own languages. Most people now live in vast cities such as Buenos Aires and Santiago.

POPULATION

Since the 1950s, there has been a tremendous move from the countryside to the cities. In Argentina, Chile, and Uruguay more than 85% of the people are now city dwellers. The capital cities of all these countries have grown enormously – Buenos Aires holds a third of Argentina's population, and two fifths of Uruguay's people live in the capital, Montevideo.

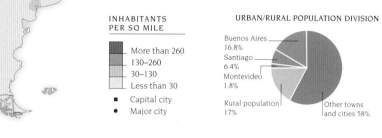

INHABITANTS PER SQ MILE

- More than 260
- 130–260
- 30–130
- Less than 30
- ■ Capital city
- ● Major city

URBAN/RURAL POPULATION DIVISION

- Buenos Aires 16.8%
- Santiago 6.4%
- Montevideo 1.8%
- Rural population 17%
- Other towns and cities 58%

INDUSTRY

Rich deposits of minerals – especially copper – in the Andes have led to the development of large metal refining industries in Chile. The capital cities, Buenos Aires and Santiago, are home to a wide range of industries, and Argentina is an important producer of processed foods like canned beef. There are fewer industries in the south, although oil and gas are extracted in southern Argentina and Chile.

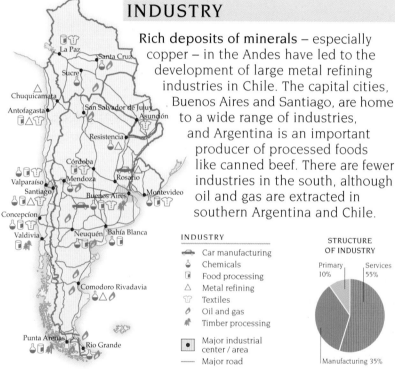

INDUSTRY

- 🚗 Car manufacturing
- Chemicals
- Food processing
- △ Metal refining
- Textiles
- Oil and gas
- Timber processing
- ⊡ Major industrial center / area
- — Major road

STRUCTURE OF INDUSTRY

- Primary 10%
- Services 55%
- Manufacturing 35%

THE LANDSCAPE

Southern South America's landscape varies from tropical forest and dry desert in the north to subantarctic conditions in the south. The towering Andes divide Chile from Argentina. East of the Andes lie forests and rolling grasslands. To the west is a thin coastal strip. The wet, windswept, freezing southern tip of the continent has volcanoes alongside glaciers and fjords.

Gran Chaco (C3)
This huge stretch of forest and grassland runs from Bolivia, through Paraguay and into Argentina. The south and east provide grazing for cattle.

Paraná River (C4)
South America's second-longest river is the Paraná. It stretches 2,485 miles from the Brazilian Highlands, finally flowing into the Plate River near Buenos Aires in Argentina.

Iguazu Falls (D4)
The Iguazu River drops 860 ft over the Iguazu Falls. When the river is at its fullest, the water flowing over the falls could fill six Olympic swimming pools every second.

Atacama Desert (A3)
The Atacama Desert in northern Chile is the driest place on Earth. In some parts, rain has not fallen for hundreds of years.

Pampas (B5)
The grassy plains in central Argentina – known as the Pampas – cover 251,000 sq miles. The western part is semidesert, but the east gets plenty of rain.

Chile
The far south of Chile has a dramatic landscape of fjords, lakes, jagged mountain peaks, and spectacular glaciers.

Patagonia (B8)
The high, windswept plateau of Patagonia covers 297,000 sq miles of southern Argentina. The south is dry and freezing cold, with very little vegetation.

ENVIRONMENTAL ISSUES

Many of southern South America's rivers are polluted, particularly close to Buenos Aires. The Itaipú Dam on the Paraná River is the world's largest hydroelectric power plant. Deforestation is a persistent problem in Bolivia, Paraguay and northern Argentina with 2,320 sq miles cut down every year. Air quality in Buenos Aires and Santiago is poor, especially in Santiago, which is surrounded by mountains, making it difficult for pollution to escape.

ENVIRONMENTAL ISSUES

- Major dam
- Urban air pollution
- Deforested areas
- Polluted river
- ● Major industrial center

SOUTH
AMERICA
Southern
South America

CLIMATE

Temperature patterns are similar in January and July; warmer to the north and east, colder to the south and west, although January is much warmer than July. Temperatures are always low, high in the Andes.

January

July

TEMPERATURE AND PRECIPITATION

More than 68°F	4 Precipitation (in)
50 to 68°F	
32 to 50°F	
Less than 32°F	

LAND HEIGHT / SEA DEPTH

LAND HEIGHT	SEA DEPTH
Above 13,120ft	0–820ft
6,560–13,120ft	820–1,640ft
3,280–6,560ft	1,640–3,280ft
1,640–3,280ft	3,280–6,560ft
820–1,640ft	6,560–9,840ft
330–820ft	9,840–13,120ft
0–330ft	Below 13,120ft

CITIES AND TOWNS

- ■ Over 500,000 people
- ◉ 100,000–500,000
- ○ 50,000–100,000
- ○ Less than 50,000

BOLIVIA'S TWO CAPITALS
LA PAZ – legislative and administrative capital
SUCRE – legal capital

SCALE BAR

| 0 km | 200 | 400 |
| 0 miles | 200 | 400 |

FARMING AND LAND USE

The enormous grasslands to the east of the Andes provide good grazing for cattle and sheep, and Argentina is one of the world's leading suppliers of meat, milk, and hides. The country is also an important grower of wheat and fruit. Chile grows grapes for its successful wine industry, and for eating; it is also the world's top producer of fishmeal. The illegal growing of coca, used to make the drug cocaine, is a major source of income in Bolivia.

LAND USE

Cropland 7%
Pasture 43%
Other (including mountains) 23%
Forest 27%

FARMING AND LAND USE

Cattle	Barren land
Fishing	Cropland
Sheep	Desert
Cotton	Forest
Fruit	Mountain region
Sugarcane	Pasture
Timber	Wetland
Vineyards	● Major conurbation
Wheat	

FALKLAND ISLANDS
(UK dependent territory)

CONTINENTAL AFRICA

Africa is the second-largest continent in the world. Its dramatic landscapes include arid deserts, humid rain forests, and the valleys of the east African rift – where humans may have first evolved. Today, there are 54 separate countries in Africa, and its people speak a rich variety of languages. The world's highest temperatures have been recorded in Africa's deserts.

4,510 miles
4,737 miles

CROSS-SECTION THROUGH AFRICA

Niger Delta | Congo Basin | Great Rift Valley | Ethiopian Highlands | Lake Victoria | Horn of Africa

W   3,230 miles   E

In the west, the Niger River flows into the Atlantic Ocean through the swampy Niger Delta. Farther east is the immense Congo Basin, where the Congo River winds its way through thick rain forests. In the east is the Great Rift Valley and the Ethiopian Highlands. The Horn of Africa is Africa's most easterly point.

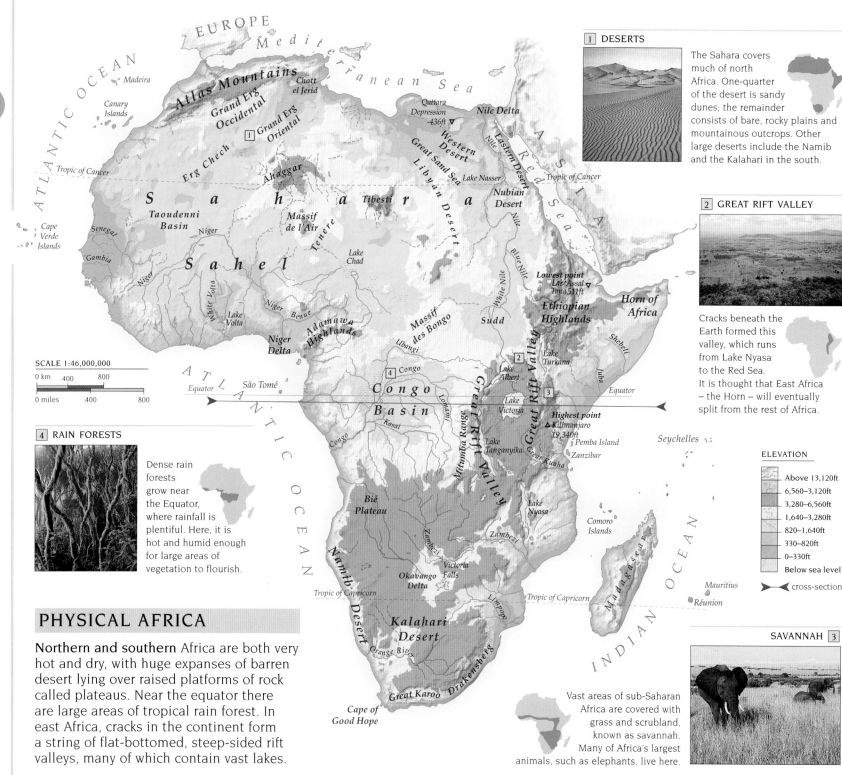

SCALE 1:46,000,000

0 km   400   800
0 miles   400   800

1 DESERTS

The Sahara covers much of north Africa. One-quarter of the desert is sandy dunes; the remainder consists of bare, rocky plains and mountainous outcrops. Other large deserts include the Namib and the Kalahari in the south.

2 GREAT RIFT VALLEY

Cracks beneath the Earth formed this valley, which runs from Lake Nyasa to the Red Sea. It is thought that East Africa – the Horn – will eventually split from the rest of Africa.

4 RAIN FORESTS

Dense rain forests grow near the Equator, where rainfall is plentiful. Here, it is hot and humid enough for large areas of vegetation to flourish.

ELEVATION

Above 13,120ft
6,560–3,120ft
3,280–6,560ft
1,640–3,280ft
820–1,640ft
330–820ft
0–330ft
Below sea level

cross-section

PHYSICAL AFRICA

Northern and southern Africa are both very hot and dry, with huge expanses of barren desert lying over raised platforms of rock called plateaus. Near the equator there are large areas of tropical rain forest. In east Africa, cracks in the continent form a string of flat-bottomed, steep-sided rift valleys, many of which contain vast lakes.

SAVANNAH 3

Vast areas of sub-Saharan Africa are covered with grass and scrubland, known as savannah. Many of Africa's largest animals, such as elephants, live here.

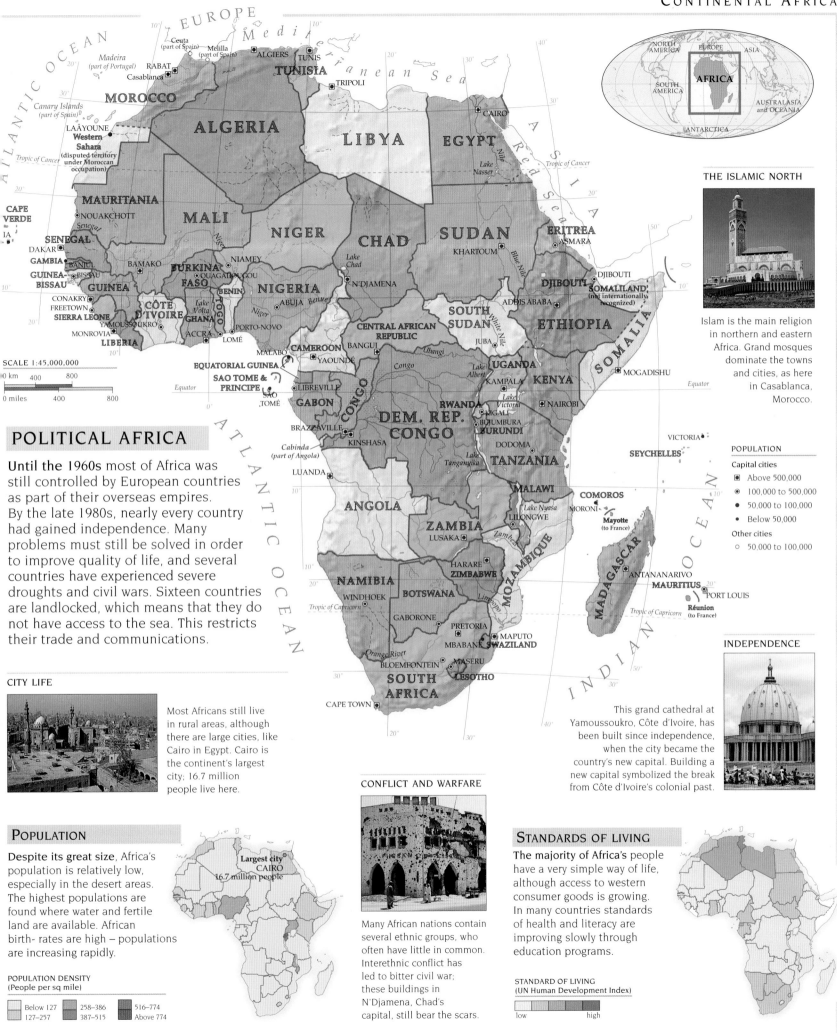

POLITICAL AFRICA

Until the 1960s most of Africa was still controlled by European countries as part of their overseas empires. By the late 1980s, nearly every country had gained independence. Many problems must still be solved in order to improve quality of life, and several countries have experienced severe droughts and civil wars. Sixteen countries are landlocked, which means that they do not have access to the sea. This restricts their trade and communications.

THE ISLAMIC NORTH

Islam is the main religion in northern and eastern Africa. Grand mosques dominate the towns and cities, as here in Casablanca, Morocco.

POPULATION

Capital cities
- ◉ Above 500,000
- ◉ 100,000 to 500,000
- ● 50,000 to 100,000
- ● Below 50,000

Other cities
- ○ 50,000 to 100,000

INDEPENDENCE

This grand cathedral at Yamoussoukro, Côte d'Ivoire, has been built since independence, when the city became the country's new capital. Building a new capital symbolized the break from Côte d'Ivoire's colonial past.

CITY LIFE

Most Africans still live in rural areas, although there are large cities, like Cairo in Egypt. Cairo is the continent's largest city; 16.7 million people live here.

POPULATION

Despite its great size, Africa's population is relatively low, especially in the desert areas. The highest populations are found where water and fertile land are available. African birth-rates are high – populations are increasing rapidly.

Largest city
CAIRO
16.7 million people

POPULATION DENSITY
(People per sq mile)

- Below 127
- 127–257
- 258–386
- 387–515
- 516–774
- Above 774

CONFLICT AND WARFARE

Many African nations contain several ethnic groups, who often have little in common. Interethnic conflict has led to bitter civil war; these buildings in N'Djamena, Chad's capital, still bear the scars.

STANDARDS OF LIVING

The majority of Africa's people have a very simple way of life, although access to western consumer goods is growing. In many countries standards of health and literacy are improving slowly through education programs.

STANDARD OF LIVING
(UN Human Development Index)

low ———— high

AFRICAN GEOGRAPHY

Africa's massive reserves of minerals, including oil, gold, copper, and diamonds, are among the largest in the world. Mining is a very important industry for many countries and has provided money for growth and development. Many different types of crops can be grown in Africa's wide range of environments. Rubber, bananas, and oil palms are grown for export in the Tropics, and east Africa is especially famous for its tea and coffee.

INDUSTRY

Most African industries are based on processing raw materials such as food crops or mineral ores. Some African countries depend on one product or crop for most of their income, but in many larger cities different industries are developing. Northern Africa, Nigeria, and South Africa have the widest range of industries.

MINERAL RESOURCES

The southern countries, in particular South Africa, have large reserves of diamonds, gold, uranium, and copper. The large copper deposits in Dem. Rep. Congo and Zambia are known as the "copper belt." Oil and gas are extracted in Algeria, Angola, Egypt, Libya, and Nigeria.

MINING

One of the world's largest uranium mines is at Rossing, Namibia. Uranium is used to fuel nuclear power plants, and is also mined in Niger and South Africa.

MINERAL RESOURCES

- Bauxite
- Copper
- Diamonds
- Iron
- Phosphates
- Gold
- Uranium
- Oil/gas field
- Coal field

OIL AND GAS

In the desert wastes of Algeria, a drilling rig searches for new sources of oil in the rich north African oilfields. There are several large oil fields in the Niger delta and North Africa.

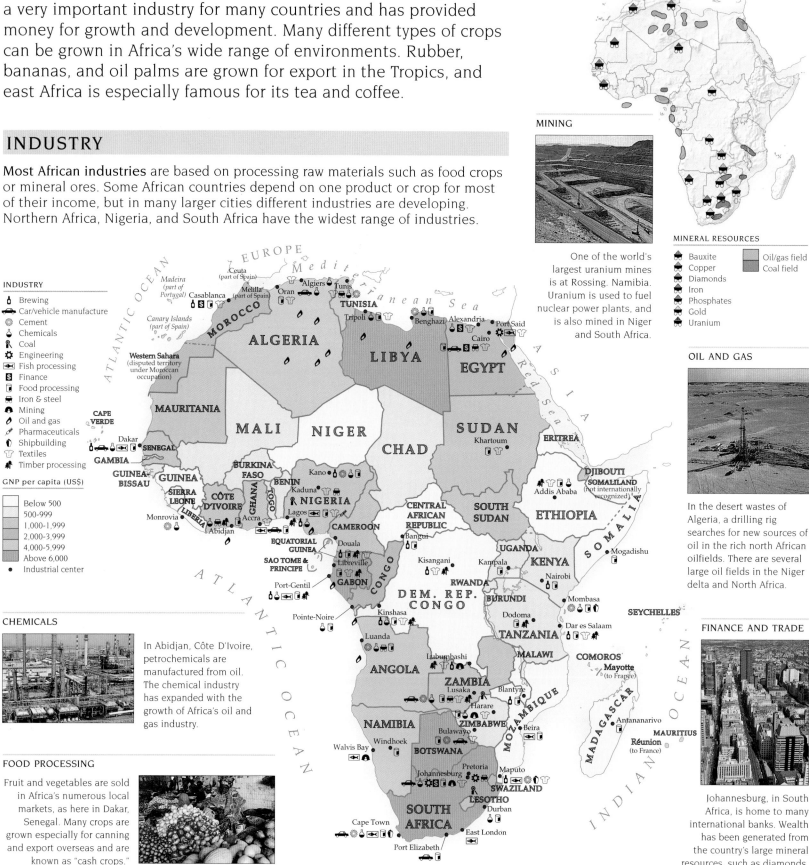

INDUSTRY

- Brewing
- Car/vehicle manufacture
- Cement
- Chemicals
- Coal
- Engineering
- Fish processing
- Finance
- Food processing
- Iron & steel
- Mining
- Oil and gas
- Pharmaceuticals
- Shipbuilding
- Textiles
- Timber processing

GNP per capita (US$)

- Below 500
- 500-999
- 1,000-1,999
- 2,000-3,999
- 4,000-5,999
- Above 6,000
- Industrial center

CHEMICALS

In Abidjan, Côte D'Ivoire, petrochemicals are manufactured from oil. The chemical industry has expanded with the growth of Africa's oil and gas industry.

FOOD PROCESSING

Fruit and vegetables are sold in Africa's numerous local markets, as here in Dakar, Senegal. Many crops are grown especially for canning and export overseas and are known as "cash crops."

FINANCE AND TRADE

Johannesburg, in South Africa, is home to many international banks. Wealth has been generated from the country's large mineral resources, such as diamonds.

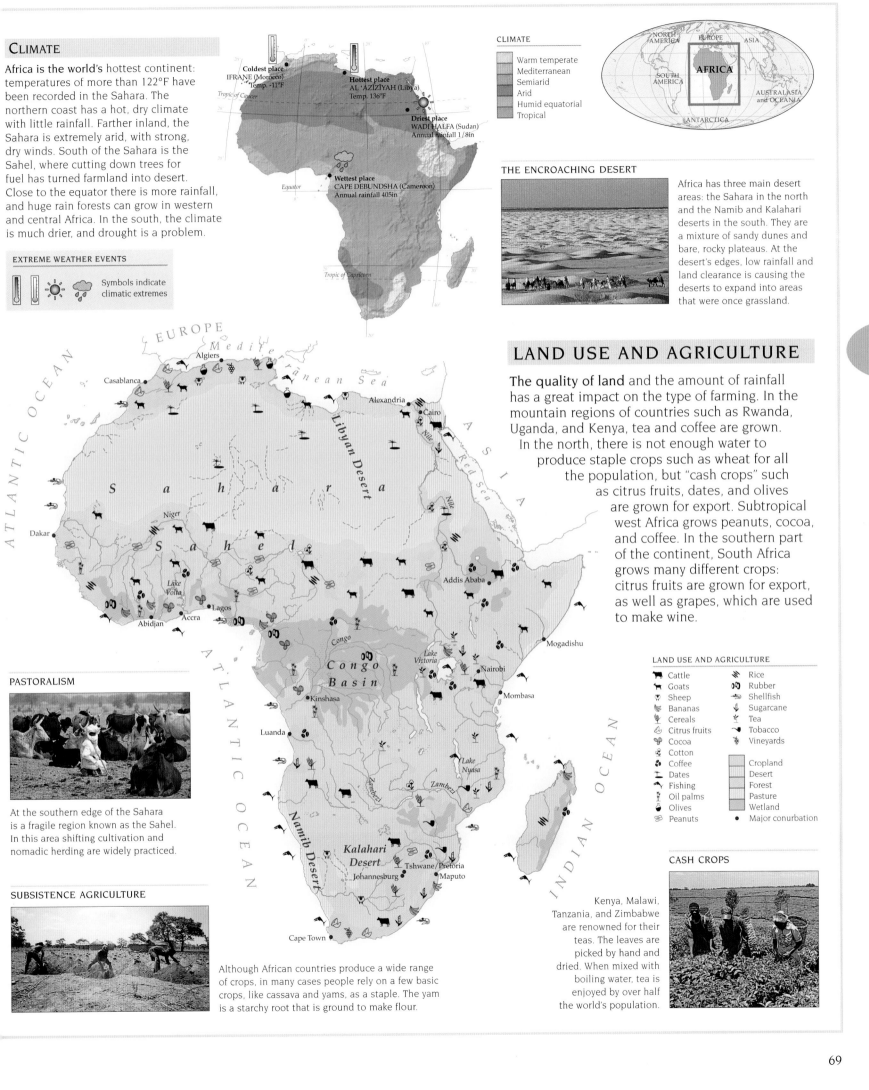

CLIMATE

Africa is the world's hottest continent: temperatures of more than 122°F have been recorded in the Sahara. The northern coast has a hot, dry climate with little rainfall. Farther inland, the Sahara is extremely arid, with strong, dry winds. South of the Sahara is the Sahel, where cutting down trees for fuel has turned farmland into desert. Close to the equator there is more rainfall, and huge rain forests can grow in western and central Africa. In the south, the climate is much drier, and drought is a problem.

EXTREME WEATHER EVENTS

Symbols indicate climatic extremes

Coldest place IFRANE (Morocco) Temp. -11°F

Hottest place AL 'AZIZIYAH (Libya) Temp. 136°F

Tropic of Cancer

Driest place WADI HALFA (Sudan) Annual rainfall 1/8in

Equator

Wettest place CAPE DEBUNDSHA (Cameroon) Annual rainfall 405in

Tropic of Capricorn

CLIMATE
- Warm temperate
- Mediterranean
- Semiarid
- Arid
- Humid equatorial
- Tropical

THE ENCROACHING DESERT

Africa has three main desert areas: the Sahara in the north and the Namib and Kalahari deserts in the south. They are a mixture of sandy dunes and bare, rocky plateaus. At the desert's edges, low rainfall and land clearance is causing the deserts to expand into areas that were once grassland.

LAND USE AND AGRICULTURE

The quality of land and the amount of rainfall has a great impact on the type of farming. In the mountain regions of countries such as Rwanda, Uganda, and Kenya, tea and coffee are grown. In the north, there is not enough water to produce staple crops such as wheat for all the population, but "cash crops" such as citrus fruits, dates, and olives are grown for export. Subtropical west Africa grows peanuts, cocoa, and coffee. In the southern part of the continent, South Africa grows many different crops: citrus fruits are grown for export, as well as grapes, which are used to make wine.

LAND USE AND AGRICULTURE
- Cattle
- Goats
- Sheep
- Bananas
- Cereals
- Citrus fruits
- Cocoa
- Cotton
- Coffee
- Dates
- Fishing
- Oil palms
- Olives
- Peanuts
- Rice
- Rubber
- Shellfish
- Sugarcane
- Tea
- Tobacco
- Vineyards
- Cropland
- Desert
- Forest
- Pasture
- Wetland
- Major conurbation

PASTORALISM

At the southern edge of the Sahara is a fragile region known as the Sahel. In this area shifting cultivation and nomadic herding are widely practiced.

SUBSISTENCE AGRICULTURE

Although African countries produce a wide range of crops, in many cases people rely on a few basic crops, like cassava and yams, as a staple. The yam is a starchy root that is ground to make flour.

CASH CROPS

Kenya, Malawi, Tanzania, and Zimbabwe are renowned for their teas. The leaves are picked by hand and dried. When mixed with boiling water, tea is enjoyed by over half the world's population.

NORTH AFRICA

ALGERIA, EGYPT, LIBYA, MOROCCO, TUNISIA.

Sandwiched between the Mediterranean and the Sahara, North Africa has a history dating back to the dawn of civilization. About 6,000 years ago, settlements were established along the banks of the Nile River. Since then, waves of settlers, including Romans, Arabs, and Turks, have brought a mix of different cultures to the area. In the 19th century, Spain, France, and Britain claimed colonies in the region, but today North Africa is independent, although Western Sahara is occupied by Morocco.

FARMING AND LAND USE

FARMING AND LAND USE
- 🐟 Fishing
- 🐐 Goats
- 🐑 Sheep
- 🍊 Citrus Fruits
- 🌳 Cork
- Cotton
- Dates
- Olives
- Vineyards
- ▢ Cropland
- ▢ Desert
- ▢ Forest
- ▢ Pasture
- • Major conurbation

Most farming in North Africa is restricted to the fertile Mediterranean coastal strip, and the banks of the Nile where it relies heavily on irrigation. In spite of these seemingly inhospitable conditions, the region is a major producer of dates, which grow in desert oases, and of cork, made from the bark of the cork oak tree. A wide variety of other crops is also grown, including grapes, olives, and cotton.

CLIMATE

Most of north Africa is desert, and the climate is harsh. Rainfall is scarce, and drought is common. Temperatures are freezing at night, scorching by day and have been known to climb to over 120°F.

January

July

whole area has below 1in rainfall

LAND USE

Forest 1%
Pasture 13%
Cropland 5%
Other (including desert) 81%

TEMPERATURE AND PRECIPITATION
- More than 95°F
- 86 to 95°F
- 77 to 86°F
- 68 to 77°F
- 59 to 68°F
- 50 to 59°F
- 41 to 50°F
- Less than 41°F
- —4— Precipitation (in)

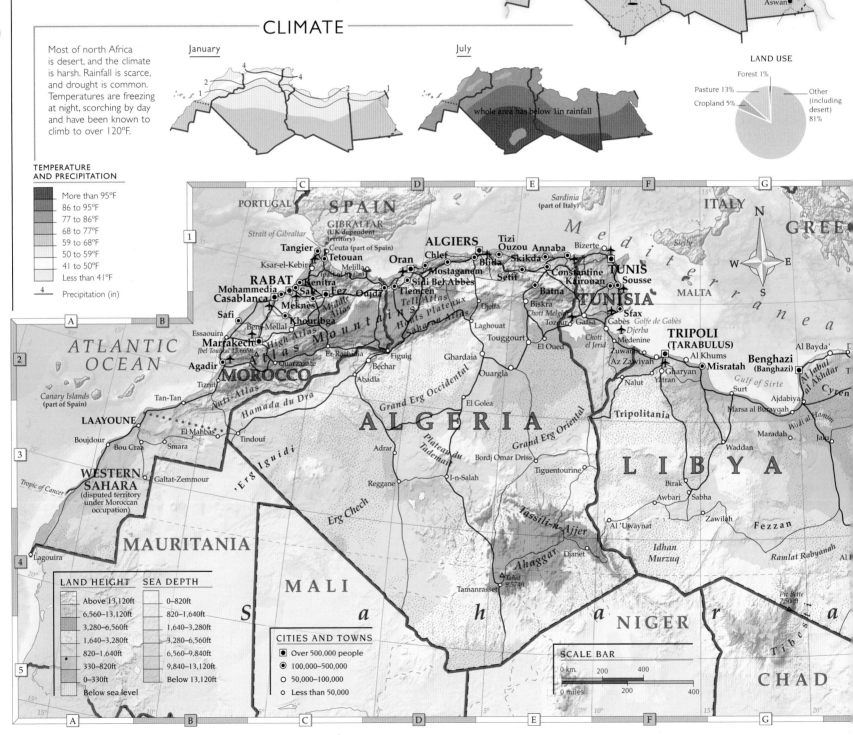

LAND HEIGHT
- Above 13,120ft
- 6,560–13,120ft
- 3,280–6,560ft
- 1,640–3,280ft
- 820–1,640ft
- 330–820ft
- 0–330ft
- Below sea level

SEA DEPTH
- 0–820ft
- 820–1,640ft
- 1,640–3,280ft
- 3,280–6,560ft
- 6,560–9,840ft
- 9,840–13,120ft
- Below 13,120ft

CITIES AND TOWNS
- ▣ Over 500,000 people
- ◉ 100,000–500,000
- ○ 50,000–100,000
- ○ Less than 50,000

SCALE BAR
0 km   200   400
0 miles   200   400

POPULATION

The majority of the population, and all of the big towns and cities, are found on the coastal plains, or along the banks of the Nile – about 99% of Egyptians live along the river. Egypt's capital, Cairo, is Africa's largest city, with over 11 million people. Western Sahara and the southern portions of Egypt, Algeria, and Libya are sparsely populated by Tuareg nomads who roam the desert.

INHABITANTS PER SQ MILE

- More than 520
- 260–520
- 130–260
- 30–130
- Less than 30

- ■ Capital city
- ● Major city

URBAN/RURAL POPULATION DIVISION

- Alexandria 2.2%
- Cairo 4.5%
- Casablanca 2%
- Rural population 46%
- Other towns and cities 45.3%

THE LANDSCAPE

The parched rocks and endless sandy expanses of the Sahara occupy much of North Africa. The only major river here is the Nile, with a delta that extends into the Mediterranean Sea. The old, eroded Atlas Mountains are the highest mountain range.

Sand dunes
Winds blowing across the Sahara cause the sand to build up into dunes which can reach heights of up to 1,411 ft.

Nile Delta (I2)
As the Nile River nears the Mediterranean, it separates into many small streams, which flow over a fertile triangle of land. Mud and rock carried by the river and deposited in the delta have formed new land.

Red Sea (J3)
The Red Sea may get its name from red algae that live on the sea floor and occasionally make the water appear red during algae blooms.

Atlas Mountains (C2)
The Atlas Mountains are made up of a number of different ranges – the Anti-Atlas, High Atlas, Middle Atlas, Tell Atlas, and Saharan Atlas. They stretch some 1,400 miles from the north of Tunisia to the Atlantic coast of Morocco.

Qattara Depression (I3)
In the northwest of Egypt is a huge desert depression 200 miles long and 75 miles wide. Its floor, part of which is 440 ft below sea level, is covered with sand, brackish ponds and salt marshes.

Nile River (I3)
The world's longest river flows 4,160 miles to the Mediterranean Sea. The system of rivers and lakes that flow into the Nile drain some 1,100,000 sq miles – about 10% of the entire African continent.

AFRICA — North Africa

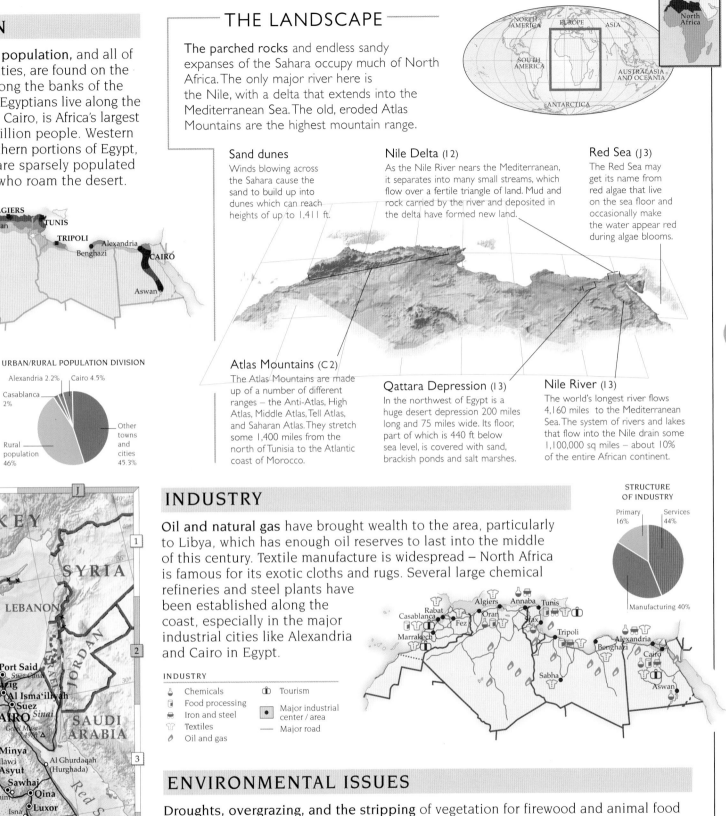

INDUSTRY

Oil and natural gas have brought wealth to the area, particularly to Libya, which has enough oil reserves to last into the middle of this century. Textile manufacture is widespread – North Africa is famous for its exotic cloths and rugs. Several large chemical refineries and steel plants have been established along the coast, especially in the major industrial cities like Alexandria and Cairo in Egypt.

STRUCTURE OF INDUSTRY

- Primary 16%
- Services 44%
- Manufacturing 40%

INDUSTRY

- Chemicals
- Food processing
- Iron and steel
- Textiles
- Oil and gas
- Tourism
- ■ Major industrial center / area
- — Major road

ENVIRONMENTAL ISSUES

Droughts, overgrazing, and the stripping of vegetation for firewood and animal food have caused the Sahara to expand northward. This has reduced the already limited amount of land available for farming. The risk of desertification is acute in many coastal areas. North Africa is very dry, and there are severe droughts periodically. Many of the larger cities like Alexandria and Cairo have very poor air quality.

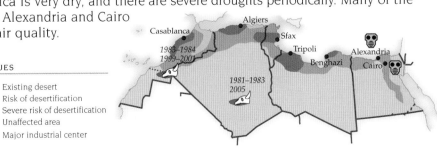

ENVIRONMENTAL ISSUES

- Drought
- Urban air pollution
- Existing desert
- Risk of desertification
- Severe risk of desertification
- Unaffected area
- ● Major industrial center

WEST AFRICA

BENIN, BURKINA FASO, CAMEROON, CENTRAL AFRICAN REPUBLIC, CHAD, CÔTE D'IVOIRE, EQUATORIAL GUINEA, GAMBIA, GHANA, GUINEA, GUINEA-BISSAU, LIBERIA, MALI, MAURITANIA, NIGER, NIGERIA, SAO TOME & PRINCIPE, SENEGAL, SIERRA LEONE, TOGO

West Africa's varied climate and agricultural and mineral wealth have provided the foundation for some of Africa's greatest civilizations, like those of the Malinke and Asante people. The area remains ethnically and culturally diverse today, as well as densely populated. Nigeria is by far the most populous country in Africa. A major outbreak of the deadly Ebola virus in the region reached epidemic proportions in 2014 and caused over 11,000 deaths.

INDUSTRY

Agricultural products still form the basis of most economies in West Africa. Food processing is widespread – oil palms and groundnuts are processed for their valuable vegetable oils. Oil and gas are found off the coast of Côte d'Ivoire and around the Niger delta, where a large chemical industry has developed.

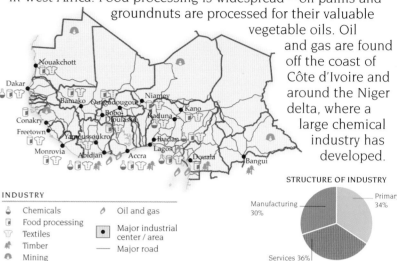

INDUSTRY

Chemicals		Oil and gas
Food processing		
Textiles		Major industrial center / area
Timber		Major road
Mining		

STRUCTURE OF INDUSTRY

Primary 34%
Manufacturing 30%
Services 36%

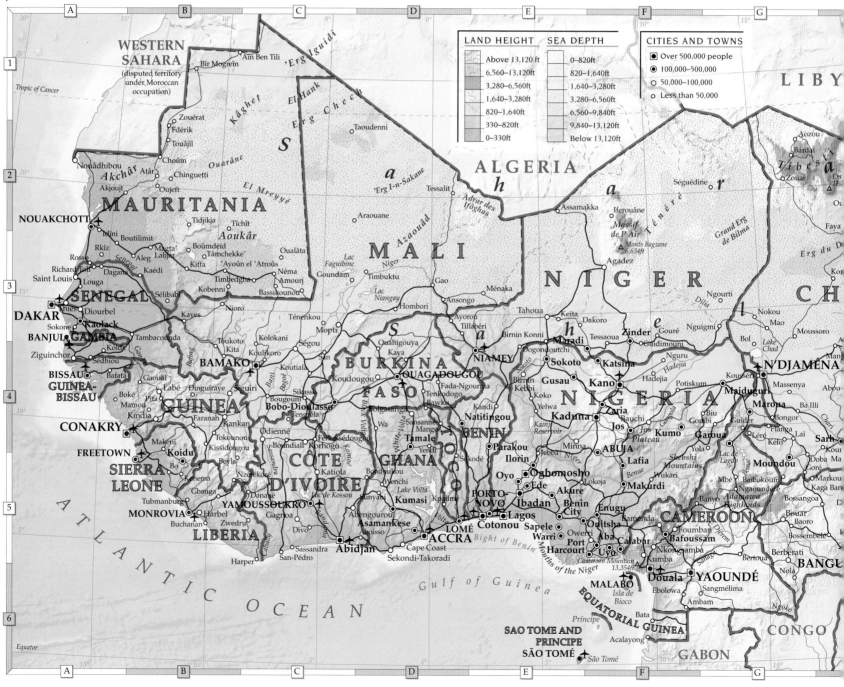

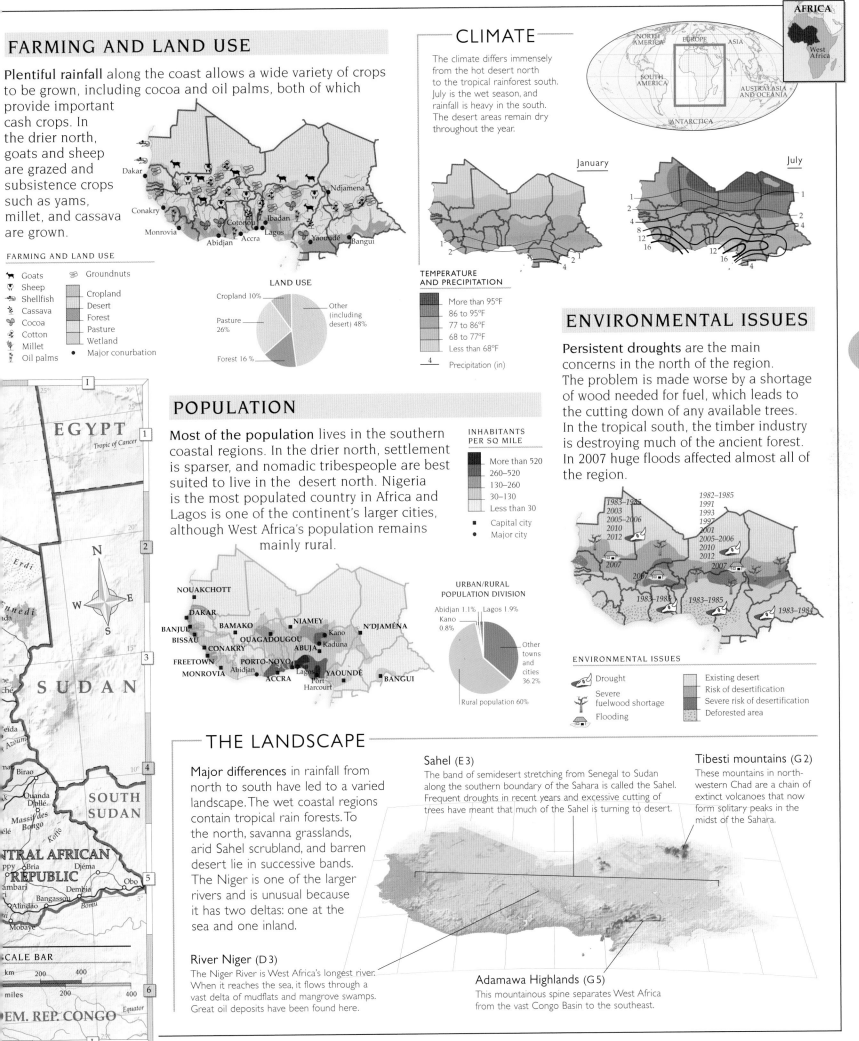

FARMING AND LAND USE

Plentiful rainfall along the coast allows a wide variety of crops to be grown, including cocoa and oil palms, both of which provide important cash crops. In the drier north, goats and sheep are grazed and subsistence crops such as yams, millet, and cassava are grown.

FARMING AND LAND USE

- Goats
- Sheep
- Shellfish
- Cassava
- Cocoa
- Cotton
- Millet
- Oil palms
- Groundnuts
- Cropland
- Desert
- Forest
- Pasture
- Wetland
- Major conurbation

LAND USE

Cropland 10%

Pasture 26%

Forest 16 %

Other (including desert) 48%

CLIMATE

The climate differs immensely from the hot desert north to the tropical rainforest south. July is the wet season, and rainfall is heavy in the south. The desert areas remain dry throughout the year.

AFRICA
West Africa

January

July

TEMPERATURE AND PRECIPITATION

- More than 95°F
- 86 to 95°F
- 77 to 86°F
- 68 to 77°F
- Less than 68°F
- 4   Precipitation (in)

ENVIRONMENTAL ISSUES

Persistent droughts are the main concerns in the north of the region. The problem is made worse by a shortage of wood needed for fuel, which leads to the cutting down of any available trees. In the tropical south, the timber industry is destroying much of the ancient forest. In 2007 huge floods affected almost all of the region.

1983–1985
2003
2005–2006
2010
2012
2007

1982–1985
1991
1993
1997
2001
2005–2006
2010
2012

1983–1985 1983–1985 1983–1984

ENVIRONMENTAL ISSUES

- Drought
- Severe fuelwood shortage
- Flooding
- Existing desert
- Risk of desertification
- Severe risk of desertification
- Deforested area

POPULATION

Most of the population lives in the southern coastal regions. In the drier north, settlement is sparser, and nomadic tribespeople are best suited to live in the desert north. Nigeria is the most populated country in Africa and Lagos is one of the continent's larger cities, although West Africa's population remains mainly rural.

INHABITANTS PER SQ MILE

- More than 520
- 260–520
- 130–260
- 30–130
- Less than 30
- Capital city
- Major city

NOUAKCHOTT
DAKAR
BANJUL
BISSAU
CONAKRY
FREETOWN
MONROVIA
BAMAKO
OUAGADOUGOU
NIAMEY
ABUJA
PORTO-NOVO
Abidjan
ACCRA
Kano
Kaduna
Lagos
Port Harcourt
YAOUNDÉ
N'DJAMÉNA
BANGUI

URBAN/RURAL POPULATION DIVISION

Abidjan 1.1%   Lagos 1.9%
Kano 0.8%

Other towns and cities 36.2%

Rural population 60%

THE LANDSCAPE

Major differences in rainfall from north to south have led to a varied landscape. The wet coastal regions contain tropical rain forests. To the north, savanna grasslands, arid Sahel scrubland, and barren desert lie in successive bands. The Niger is one of the larger rivers and is unusual because it has two deltas: one at the sea and one inland.

Sahel (E 3)
The band of semidesert stretching from Senegal to Sudan along the southern boundary of the Sahara is called the Sahel. Frequent droughts in recent years and excessive cutting of trees have meant that much of the Sahel is turning to desert.

Tibesti mountains (G 2)
These mountains in northwestern Chad are a chain of extinct volcanoes that now form solitary peaks in the midst of the Sahara.

River Niger (D 3)
The Niger River is West Africa's longest river. When it reaches the sea, it flows through a vast delta of mudflats and mangrove swamps. Great oil deposits have been found here.

Adamawa Highlands (G 5)
This mountainous spine separates West Africa from the vast Congo Basin to the southeast.

EGYPT
Tropic of Cancer

N
W   E
S

Erdi

SUDAN

SOUTH SUDAN

CENTRAL AFRICAN REPUBLIC

DEM. REP. CONGO
Equator

SCALE BAR

km   200   400
miles   200   400

EAST AFRICA

BURUNDI, DJIBOUTI, ERITREA, ETHIOPIA, KENYA, RWANDA,
SOMALIA, SOUTH SUDAN, SUDAN, TANZANIA, UGANDA

Much of East Africa is covered by long grass, scrub, and scattered trees, called savanna. This land is grazed by both domestic animals and a great variety of wild animals including lions, giraffes and elephants. The east of the region is known as the Horn of Africa, because it is shaped like an animal horn. Sudan, and the other countries there have recently been devastated by civil wars, and periods of drought and famine. In contrast, Kenya in the south is more stable but still has to battle with corruption.

FARMING AND LAND USE

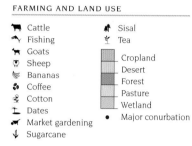

Much of the north and east is too dry for farming, but in Sudan, cotton is grown on land irrigated by the Nile River. The Lake Victoria basin and rich volcanic soils of the highlands in Kenya, Uganda, and Tanzania support staple food crops, and those grown for export, such as tea and coffee. Kenya also grows high-quality vegetables, like mangetout, and exports them by air to supermarkets abroad. Sheep, goats, and cattle are herded on the savanna.

LAND USE

Cropland 9%
Pasture 40%
Other 26%
Forest 25%

FARMING AND LAND USE

- Cattle
- Fishing
- Goats
- Sheep
- Bananas
- Coffee
- Cotton
- Dates
- Market gardening
- Sugarcane
- Sisal
- Tea
- Cropland
- Desert
- Forest
- Pasture
- Wetland
- Major conurbation

INDUSTRY

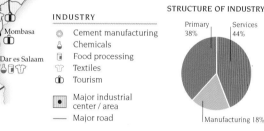

East Africa has few mineral resources, and industry is mainly based on processing raw materials. Coffee, tea, sugarcane, and sisal, are harvested and processed before being exported. Textile production is widespread, but is only on a small scale. Tourism is increasingly important in Kenya and Tanzania; each year, many thousands of people visit the wildlife reserves there.

INDUSTRY

- Cement manufacturing
- Chemicals
- Food processing
- Textiles
- Tourism
- Major industrial center / area
- Major road

STRUCTURE OF INDUSTRY

Primary 38%
Services 44%
Manufacturing 18%

THE LANDSCAPE

The south of East Africa is savanna grassland, broken by the rugged mountains — some of them active volcanoes — and large fresh and saltwater lakes that make up part of the Great Rift Valley. The Nile River has its source here, flowing through Lakes Victoria, Kyoga, and Albert as it takes much-needed water to the arid desert areas in the north.

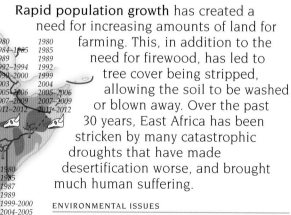

Great Rift Valley (D 6) (D 4)
The Great Rift Valley is like a deep scar running 4,300 miles from north to south through East Africa. It has been formed by the movements of two of the Earth's plates over millions of years. If these movements continue, East Africa may eventually become an island, separated by the ocean from the rest of the continent.

Sudd (B 4)
The north of Sudan is rocky desert, but in the south, the waters of the White Nile run into a swampy area called the Sudd where much of its water disperses and evaporates.

Juba River (E 5)
This river rises in the highlands of Ethiopia and flows some 750 miles southwards to the Indian Ocean. It, and the Shebeli River, which joins it about 19 miles from the coast, are the only permanent rivers in Somalia.

Lake Victoria (C 5)
Lake Victoria is Africa's largest lake and the second largest freshwater lake in the world. It lies on the equator, between Kenya, Tanzania and Uganda, and covers 26,560 sq miles. Its only outlet is the Nile River in the north.

Kilimanjaro (D 6)
This old volcano, made up of alternating layers of lava and ash, is Africa's highest mountain, rising to 19,341 ft. Although it lies only three degrees from the Equator, its peak is permanently covered with snow.

ENVIRONMENTAL ISSUES

Rapid population growth has created a need for increasing amounts of land for farming. This, in addition to the need for firewood, has led to tree cover being stripped, allowing the soil to be washed or blown away. Over the past 30 years, East Africa has been stricken by many catastrophic droughts that have made desertification worse, and brought much human suffering.

ENVIRONMENTAL ISSUES

- Drought
- Severe firewood shortage
- Flooding
- Existing desert
- Risk of desertification
- Severe risk of desertification

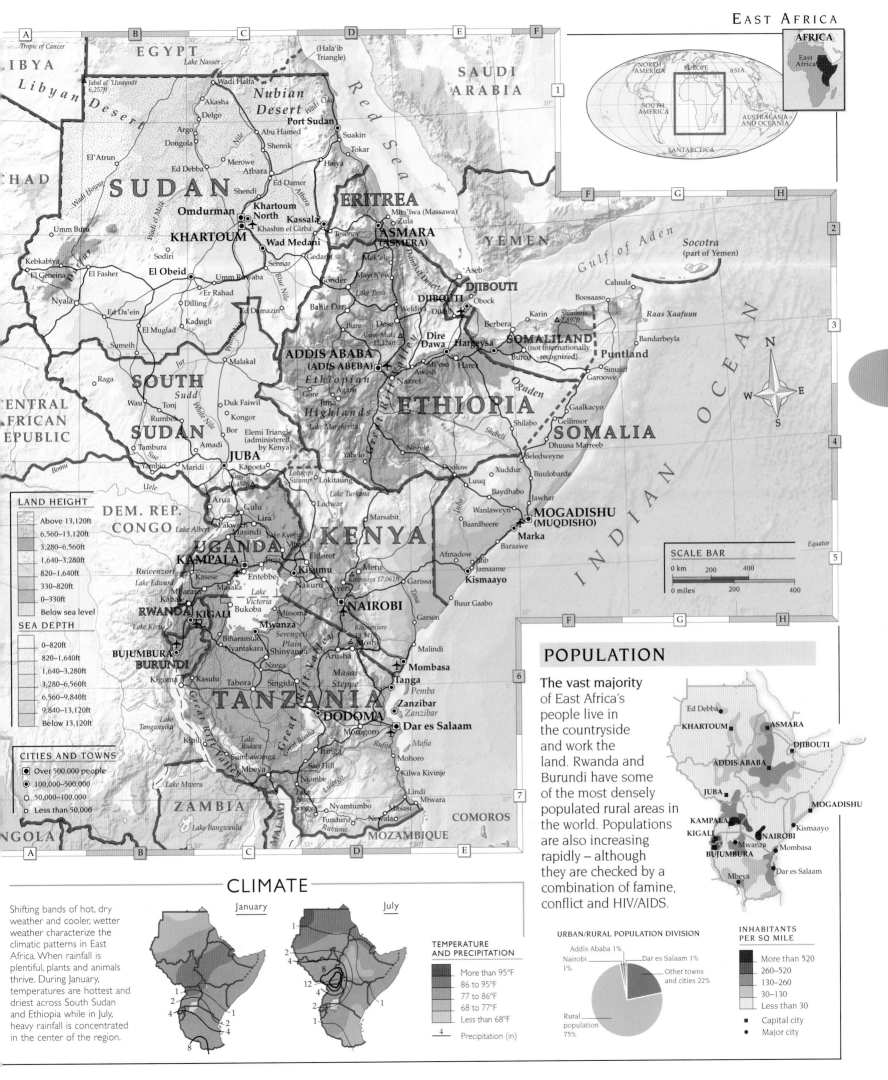

POPULATION

The vast majority of East Africa's people live in the countryside and work the land. Rwanda and Burundi have some of the most densely populated rural areas in the world. Populations are also increasing rapidly – although they are checked by a combination of famine, conflict and HIV/AIDS.

URBAN/RURAL POPULATION DIVISION

Addis Ababa 1%
Nairobi 1%
Dar es Salaam 1%
Other towns and cities 22%
Rural population 75%

INHABITANTS PER SQ MILE

- More than 520
- 260–520
- 130–260
- 30–130
- Less than 30
- ■ Capital city
- ● Major city

CLIMATE

Shifting bands of hot, dry weather and cooler, wetter weather characterize the climatic patterns in East Africa. When rainfall is plentiful, plants and animals thrive. During January, temperatures are hottest and driest across South Sudan and Ethiopia while in July, heavy rainfall is concentrated in the center of the region.

January

July

TEMPERATURE AND PRECIPITATION

- More than 95°F
- 86 to 95°F
- 77 to 86°F
- 68 to 77°F
- Less than 68°F
- 4 — Precipitation (in)

LAND HEIGHT
- Above 13,120ft
- 6,560–13,120ft
- 3,280–6,560ft
- 1,640–3,280ft
- 820–1,640ft
- 330–820ft
- 0–330ft
- Below sea level

SEA DEPTH
- 0–820ft
- 820–1,640ft
- 1,640–3,280ft
- 3,280–6,560ft
- 6,560–9,840ft
- 9,840–13,120ft
- Below 13,120ft

CITIES AND TOWNS
- ■ Over 500,000 people
- ◉ 100,000–500,000
- ○ 50,000–100,000
- ○ Less than 50,000

SCALE BAR
0 km 200 400
0 miles 200 400

SOUTHERN AFRICA

ANGOLA, BOTSWANA, COMOROS, CONGO, DEM. REP. CONGO, GABON, LESOTHO, MADAGASCAR, MALAWI, MOZAMBIQUE, NAMIBIA, SOUTH AFRICA, SWAZILAND, ZAMBIA, ZIMBABWE

Southern Africa contains the richest deposits of valuable minerals on the continent. South Africa is the wealthiest and most industrialized country in the region. Most of the surrounding countries rely on it for trade and work. Racial segregation under apartheid operated from 1948 until 1994, when South Africa held its first multiracial elections.

FARMING AND LAND USE

Most of **southern Africa's** farmers grow just enough food to feed their families, although much of the farmland is in the hands of a few wealthy landowners. In the tropical north, oil palms and rubber are grown on large commercial plantations. Fruits are cultivated in the south, and tea and coffee are important in the east. Cattle farming is widespread across the dry grasslands.

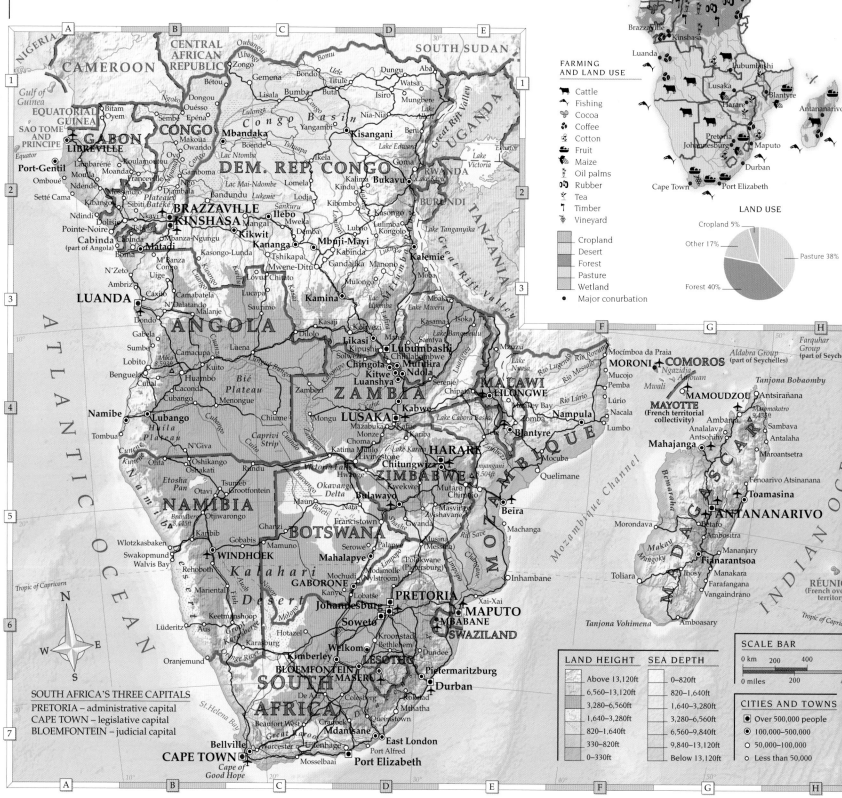

FARMING AND LAND USE

- 🐄 Cattle
- 🐟 Fishing
- 🌿 Cocoa
- ☕ Coffee
- Cotton
- 🍎 Fruit
- Maize
- 🌴 Oil palms
- Rubber
- Tea
- Timber
- 🍇 Vineyard

- Cropland
- Desert
- Forest
- Pasture
- Wetland
- • Major conurbation

LAND USE

Cropland 5%
Other 17%
Pasture 38%
Forest 40%

SOUTH AFRICA'S THREE CAPITALS
PRETORIA – administrative capital
CAPE TOWN – legislative capital
BLOEMFONTEIN – judicial capital

LAND HEIGHT

Above 13,120ft	
6,560–13,120ft	
3,280–6,560ft	
1,640–3,280ft	
820–1,640ft	
330–820ft	
0–330ft	

SEA DEPTH

0–820ft	
820–1,640ft	
1,640–3,280ft	
3,280–6,560ft	
6,560–9,840ft	
9,840–13,120ft	
Below 13,120ft	

SCALE BAR
0 km   200   400
0 miles   200

CITIES AND TOWNS
- ◉ Over 500,000 people
- ◉ 100,000–500,000
- ○ 50,000–100,000
- ○ Less than 50,000

CLIMATE

During January, temperatures are highest in the Kalahari Desert and rainfall is plentiful in the center of southern Africa. July is cooler and drier, with rainfall concentrated in the north of Dem. Rep. Congo. The Atlantic coast of Namibia receives little rain all year round.

July

TEMPERATURE AND PRECIPITATION

- More than 95°F
- 86 to 95°F
- 77 to 86°F
- 68 to 77°F
- 59 to 68°F
- Less than 59°F
- —4— Precipitation (in)

ENVIRONMENTAL ISSUES

The immense rain forests of the Congo Basin in the north remain relatively untouched, but deforestation is beginning to occur at its edges, with much more forest due to be cleared in the future. Large parts of Madagascar have also been deforested. Farther south, occasional drought and the clearing of bushlands for firewood can cause soil loss.

Congo Basin

1991–1992
1995
2005
1985
1989
1991–1992
2002, 2005, 2008
1982–1984, 1992
1997–1998, 2001
1983–1985
1992–1993
2002–2003
2000
2007
1983
1985
2001
2004
2007

ENVIRONMENTAL ISSUES

- Drought
- Severe firewood shortage
- Flooding
- Existing desert
- Risk of desertification
- Severe risk of desertification
- Deforested area
- Remaining tropical forest

INDUSTRY

Southern Africa has extraordinary mineral resources. Angola has large deposits of oil, and diamonds are found in Angola, Botswana, Namibia, and South Africa. Copper is mined in the region known as the "copper belt," that runs from Dem. Rep. Congo into Zambia. South Africa is the world's largest gold producer. Manufacturing, such as fruit canning and steel production, is most developed in South Africa.

Libreville
Kisangani
Brazzaville
Bukavu
Kinshasa
Luanda
Kolwezi
Lubumbashi
Ndola
Lusaka
Blantyre
Harare
Antananarivo
Beira
Bulawayo
Pretoria
Johannesburg
Maputo
Durban
Cape Town
Port Elizabeth

INDUSTRY

- Car manufacturing
- Chemicals
- Engineering
- Food processing
- Iron and steel
- Metal refining
- Textiles
- Oil and gas
- Mining
- Timber processing
- Tourism
- Major industrial center / area
- Major road

STRUCTURE OF INDUSTRY

Primary 10%
Services 59%
Manufacturing 31%

THE LANDSCAPE

Southern Africa stretches from just north of the equator down to the southern tip of the continent. It is an area with an extremely varied climate and geography. In the north are the tropical rain forests of the Congo Basin, while arid desert covers much of the southwest. The eastern regions are mostly grasslands, with lush vegetation found on the tropical coast of Mozambique.

Congo Basin (C1)
The Congo River is Africa's second longest river, flowing in an arc through the dense tropical forests of the Congo Basin before emptying into the Atlantic Ocean.

Namib Desert (B5)
The Namib is one of the world's driest deserts. The only water it receives is from mists that roll in from the sea. Where the desert meets the coast is known as the Skeleton Coast because of sailors who were shipwrecked and died there.

Victoria Falls (D5)
On its way to the Indian Ocean, the Zambezi River plunges over a 420 ft cliff, into a narrow chasm. The resultant spray rises up to 1,600 ft, and the thunder of the water can be heard up to 25 miles away.

Madagascar (G5)
The world's fourth largest island lies in isolation 155 miles off the east coast of southern Africa. It became separated from the African continent 135 million years ago, and its plant and animal life are unique. The rich biodiversity of the rain forests is being threatened by uncontrolled lumbering.

Okavango Delta (C5)
The Okavango River terminates in the Kalahari Desert, forming a vast, swampy inland delta.

Drakensberg (D4)
The Drakensberg are a chain of mountains that lie at the edge of a broad plateau that has tilted because of the movement of the Earth's plates. Rivers have carved through the high mountains, creating dramatic gorges and waterfalls.

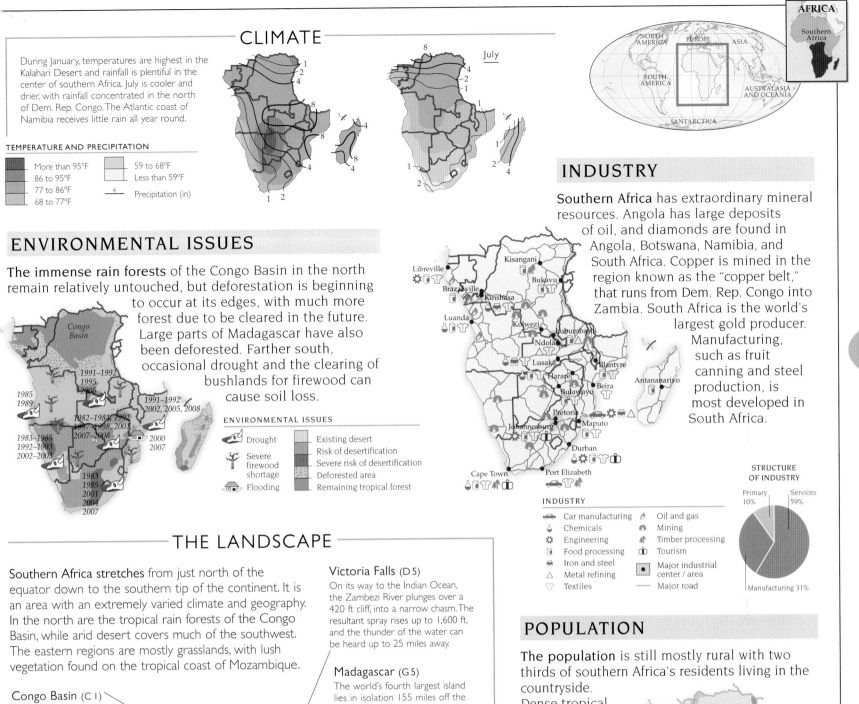

POPULATION

The population is still mostly rural with two thirds of southern Africa's residents living in the countryside. Dense tropical rain forest in the north and arid desert in the southwest have kept habitation to a bare minimum. Malawi is the most densely populated country in the region.

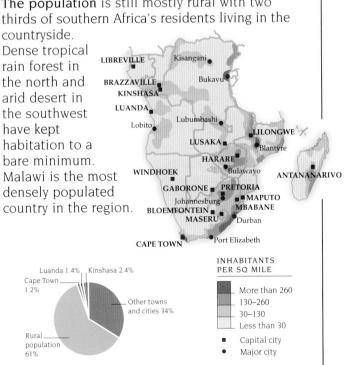

LIBREVILLE
Kisangani
BRAZZAVILLE
Bukavu
KINSHASA
LUANDA
Lobito
Lubumbashi
LILONGWE
LUSAKA
Blantyre
HARARE
WINDHOEK
Bulawayo
ANTANANARIVO
GABORONE
PRETORIA
Johannesburg
MAPUTO
BLOEMFONTEIN
MBABANE
MASERU
Durban
CAPE TOWN
Port Elizabeth

Luanda 1.4%
Kinshasa 2.4%
Cape Town 1.2%
Other towns and cities 34%
Rural population 61%

INHABITANTS PER SQ MILE

- More than 260
- 130–260
- 30–130
- Less than 30
- ■ Capital city
- ● Major city

CONTINENTAL EUROPE

Europe is the world's second smallest continent, occupying the western tip of the vast Eurasian landmass. To the north and west are old highlands, with the high peaks of the Alps in the south. Most people live on the densely populated North European Plain, which extends from southern England, through northern France, across Germany into Russia.

CROSS-SECTION THROUGH EUROPE

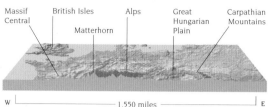

In the west, the land rises up from the Atlantic coast toward the Massif Central in France, and the high peaks of the Alps. Between the Alps and the Carpathian Mountains is the Great Hungarian Plain, where the Danube River flows on its way to the Black Sea.

PHYSICAL EUROPE

The ancient mountains of northwest Europe were scoured and smoothed by glaciers in the last Ice Age. The Alps are newer and more jagged – pushed up when Africa collided with Europe. In between is the North European Plain, where thick layers of fertile soils allow many different crops to be grown.

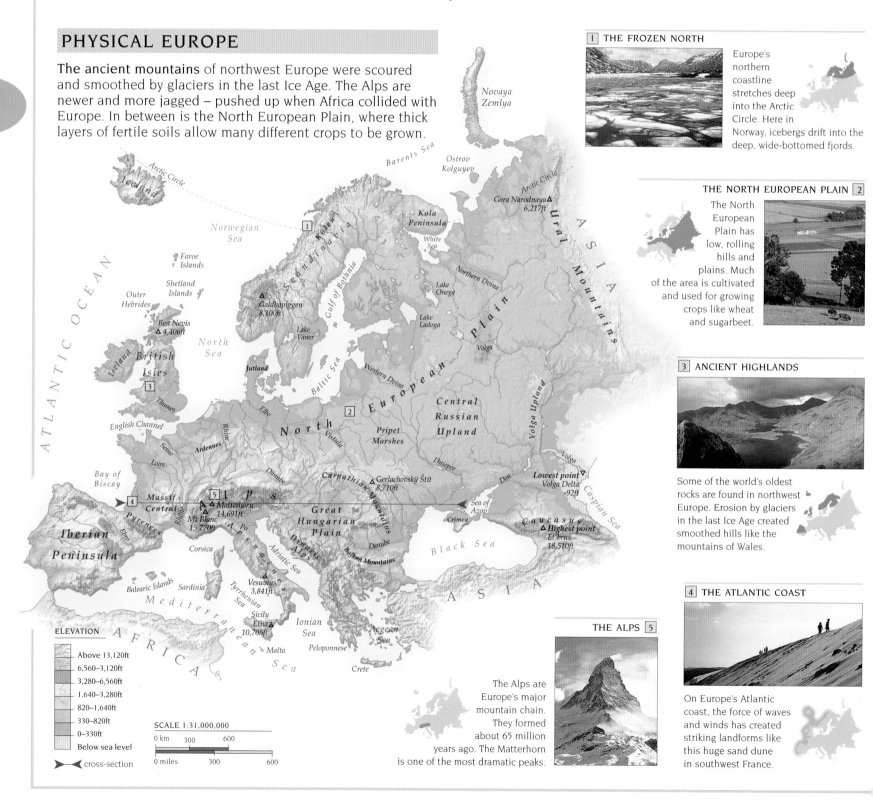

1 THE FROZEN NORTH

Europe's northern coastline stretches deep into the Arctic Circle. Here in Norway, icebergs drift into the deep, wide-bottomed fjords.

THE NORTH EUROPEAN PLAIN 2

The North European Plain has low, rolling hills and plains. Much of the area is cultivated and used for growing crops like wheat and sugarbeet.

3 ANCIENT HIGHLANDS

Some of the world's oldest rocks are found in northwest Europe. Erosion by glaciers in the last Ice Age created smoothed hills like the mountains of Wales.

THE ALPS 5

The Alps are Europe's major mountain chain. They formed about 65 million years ago. The Matterhorn is one of the most dramatic peaks.

4 THE ATLANTIC COAST

On Europe's Atlantic coast, the force of waves and winds has created striking landforms like this huge sand dune in southwest France.

ELEVATION

- Above 13,120ft
- 6,560–3,120ft
- 3,280–6,560ft
- 1,640–3,280ft
- 820–1,640ft
- 330–820ft
- 0–330ft
- Below sea level
- cross-section

SCALE 1:31,000,000

0 km   300   600

0 miles   300   600

POLITICAL EUROPE

Europe's population increased rapidly during the 18th and 19th centuries, following the Industrial Revolution. In the 20th century, Europe suffered a series of wars which redrew the political map. From 1989–1991, communist governments in eastern Europe and the former Soviet Union collapsed, as political reform swept through the countries behind the "Iron Curtain." In 2013, Croatia became the 28th country to join the European Union.

EUROPEAN UNION

- six original members, 1957
- nine further members, 1973 – 1995
- ten further members, 2004
- two further members, 2007
- one further member, 2013

REGIONAL IDENTITY

Throughout Europe, there is a growing call to recognize regional cultural identity. The Basque region, straddling southwest France and Spain, is one example.

RURAL LIFE

Away from Europe's bustling cities, traditional rural lifestyles survive. Here in the Ireland, a winter shelter is being made for cattle.

STANDARDS OF LIVING

Living standards are generally much lower in eastern Europe than in the wealthier west. Homelessness and unemployment are still common, even in the most prosperous countries.

POPULATION

Capital cities
- Above 500,000
- 100,000 to 500,000
- 50,000 to 100,000

SCALE 1:27,500,000

0 km 300 600

0 miles 300 600

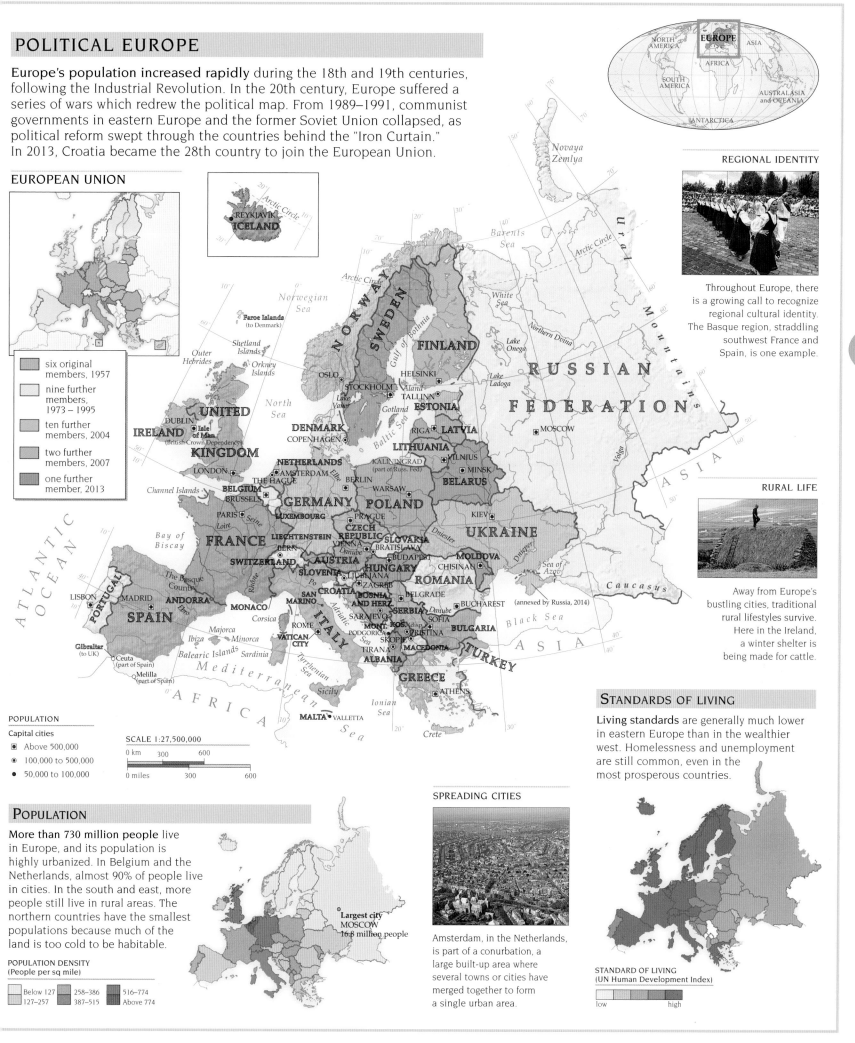

POPULATION

More than 730 million people live in Europe, and its population is highly urbanized. In Belgium and the Netherlands, almost 90% of people live in cities. In the south and east, more people still live in rural areas. The northern countries have the smallest populations because much of the land is too cold to be habitable.

POPULATION DENSITY
(People per sq mile)
- Below 127
- 127–257
- 258–386
- 387–515
- 516–774
- Above 774

SPREADING CITIES

Largest city
MOSCOW
16.8 million people

Amsterdam, in the Netherlands, is part of a conurbation, a large built-up area where several towns or cities have merged together to form a single urban area.

STANDARD OF LIVING
(UN Human Development Index)

low   high

EUROPEAN GEOGRAPHY

Europe is blessed with a temperate climate, ample mineral reserves, and good transportation links. During the 18th and 19th centuries the continent was transformed, as new methods of production made industry and farming more efficient and productive. Today, in many countries, heavy industries have been replaced by high-tech and service industries. Agriculture is still important, and many crops thrive on Europe's fertile plains.

INDUSTRY

Western Europe has some of the world's wealthiest countries. In countries such as France, Germany, and the UK, traditional industries like iron and steel-making are now being replaced by light industries, such as electronics, and services like finance and insurance. In Eastern Europe, industry was subsidized by the communist governments for years. Many factories are old-fashioned and need investment to improve their equipment and production methods.

MINERAL RESOURCES

Europe has few sizable reserves of metallic minerals; most were used up by industry during the 19th century. Oil, gas, and coal are found in large quantities – gas in the North Sea and oil in the Volga basin. Coal, although abundant, is being steadily depleted.

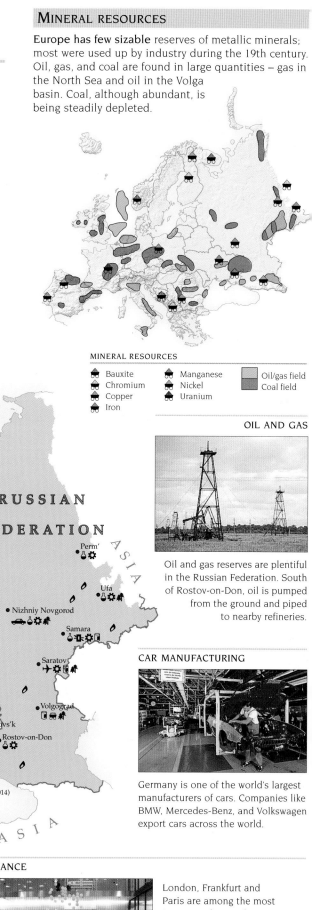

MINERAL RESOURCES

🜚 Bauxite	🜚 Manganese	⬜ Oil/gas field
🜚 Chromium	🜚 Nickel	⬛ Coal field
🜚 Copper	🜚 Uranium	
🜚 Iron		

OIL AND GAS

Oil and gas reserves are plentiful in the Russian Federation. South of Rostov-on-Don, oil is pumped from the ground and piped to nearby refineries.

CAR MANUFACTURING

Germany is one of the world's largest manufacturers of cars. Companies like BMW, Mercedes-Benz, and Volkswagen export cars across the world.

FINANCE

London, Frankfurt and Paris are among the most important financial centers in the world. Many banks and financial institutions have their headquarters here. At the London Stock Exchange, people buy and sell stocks and shares.

ECONOMIC ACTIVITY

✈ Aerospace
🚗 Vehicle manufacturing
⚗ Chemicals
⛏ Coal
✦ Defense
💻 Electronics
⚙ Engineering
S Finance
🍴 Food processing
💻 High-tech industry
🏭 Iron and steel
🜂 Oil and gas
🖨 Printing and publishing
⏚ Textiles
🌲 Timber processing

GNI per capita (US$)

⬜	Below 4,999
⬜	5,000–9,999
⬜	10,000–24,999
⬜	25,000–39,999
⬛	40,000–54,999
⬛	Above 55,000
•	Industrial center

(annexed by Russia, 2014)

CLIMATE

Europe's climate is temperate with few climatic extremes. In the far north, Europe extends into the Arctic Circle and the climate is so cold that the Baltic Sea freezes over in the winter. Toward the Atlantic coast in the west, the climate becomes wetter and warmer because of a warm ocean current, known as the Gulf Stream. Countries such as Italy and Spain that border the Mediterranean Sea have long, hot summers and low rainfall, which can sometimes lead to such problems as drought.

EXTREME WEATHER EVENTS

Symbols indicate climatic extremes

CLIMATE

- Tundra
- Subarctic
- Cool continental
- Temperate/humid
- Mediterranean
- Semiarid

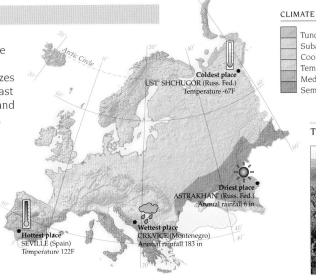

Coldest place
UST' SHCHUGOR (Russ. Fed.)
Temperature -67F

Driest place
ASTRAKHAN' (Russ. Fed.)
Annual rainfall 6 in

Hottest place
SEVILLE (Spain)
Temperature 122F

Wettest place
CRKVICE (Montenegro)
Annual rainfall 183 in

THE MEDITERRANEAN CLIMATE

The mild, warm climate around the Mediterranean Sea allows olives, citrus fruits, and grapes to thrive. Long, sunny days also help the fruits ripen. Grapes are harvested and crushed to make many different wines.

LAND USE AND AGRICULTURE

Europe's agricultural heart is the North European Plain, where fertile soils and ample rainfall allow a variety of crops to be grown. Wheat is the main grain crop, and a wide range of fruit and vegetables are also grown. Dairy and beef cattle are raised for their milk and meat throughout Europe. In the south, the Mediterranean climate is ideal for citrus fruits and olives. Forests cover much of northern Scandinavia, while sheep farming is common in the hills of the British Isles.

CROPLANDS

Many different crops are grown on the North European Plain. Sunflowers, wheat, and sugar beets – used to make sugar – are among the main crops grown there.

FISHING

The north Atlantic Ocean provides a rich marine harvest for fishermen. Today the cod, haddock and mackerel stocks have to be protected from over-fishing.

LAND USE AND AGRICULTURE

- Cattle
- Goats
- Pigs
- Reindeer
- Sheep
- Cereals
- Citrus fruits
- Fishing
- Fruit
- Olive oil
- Potatoes
- Root crops
- Shellfish
- Sunflowers
- Timber
- Vineyards

- Cropland
- Forest
- Ice cap
- Mountain region
- Pasture
- Tundra
- Wetland
- Major conurbation

DAIRY FARMING

Dairy farming is very common across northern Europe. Cows grazed on rich pastures produce milk used for making butter and cheese.

NORTHERN EUROPE

DENMARK, ESTONIA, FINLAND, ICELAND, LATVIA, LITHUANIA, NORWAY, SWEDEN

Denmark, Sweden, and Norway are together known as Scandinavia. These countries, along with the North Atlantic island of Iceland, have similar languages and cultures. Finland has a very different language and a separate identity from its Scandinavian neighbors. Estonia, Latvia, and Lithuania, known as the Baltic states, were part of the Soviet Union until 1989, when each became an independent country.

INDUSTRY

In Scandinavia, many natural resources are used in industry: timber for paper and furniture; iron ore for steel and cars; and fish and natural gas from the seas. Hydroelectric power is generated by water flowing down steep mountain slopes. The Baltic states still rely on Russia to supply their raw materials and energy.

INDUSTRY

- 🚗 Car manufacturing
- 🌢 Chemicals
- ⚙ Engineering
- 🐟 Fish processing
- ⊞ Hydroelectric power
- ⚓ Shipbuilding
- 🌲 Timber processing
- 🏛 Tourism

- ▪ Major industrial center / area
- — Major road

STRUCTURE OF INDUSTRY

Primary 4%
Services 65%
Manufacturing 31%

POPULATION

The population is distributed mainly along the warmer and flatter southern and coastal areas. Population totals and densities are low for all of the countries, and Iceland has the lowest population density in Europe, with just seven people per sq mile. Many Scandinavians have holiday homes on the islands, along the lake shores, or in coastal areas.

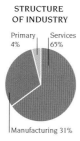

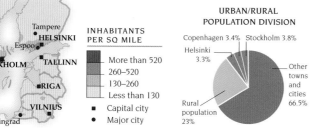

INHABITANTS PER SQ MILE

- More than 520
- 260–520
- 130–260
- Less than 130

- ▪ Capital city
- • Major city

URBAN/RURAL POPULATION DIVISION

Copenhagen 3.4% Stockholm 3.8%
Helsinki 3.3%
Other towns and cities 66.5%
Rural population 23%

FARMING AND LAND USE

Southern Denmark and Sweden are the most productive areas, with pig farming, dairy farming, and crops such as wheat, barley, and potatoes. Sheep farming is important in southern Norway and Iceland. In the Baltic states, cereals, potatoes, and sugar beets are the main crops, and cattle graze on damp pasture.

FARMING AND LAND USE

- 🐄 Cattle
- 🎣 Fishing
- 🐖 Pigs
- 🐑 Sheep
- 🌾 Cereals
- 🥔 Root crops
- 🌲 Timber

- Pasture
- Cropland
- Forest
- Ice cap
- Mountain region
- Tundra
- • Major conurbation

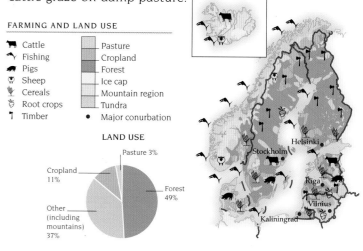

LAND USE

Pasture 3%
Cropland 11%
Forest 49%
Other (including mountains) 37%

THE LANDSCAPE

The north and west of Scandinavia is extremely rugged and mountainous, with landscapes eroded by ice. In the south of Scandinavia the land is flatter, with fertile soils deposited by glaciers. Much of Finland, Norway, and Sweden is covered by dense forests. The Baltic states are much lower, with rounded hills and many lakes and marshes.

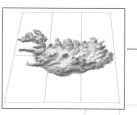

The land of ice and fire. Iceland is one of the world's most active volcanic areas. There are about 200 volcanoes on the island, along with bubbling hot springs, mud-holes, and geysers that spurt boiling water and steam high into the air.

Fjords
Norway has many fjords: deep, wide valleys carved by glaciers, drowned by seawater when the ice melted at the end of the last Ice Age.

Baltic Sea (D 7)
Ships from Finland, Sweden, and the Baltic states use the Baltic Sea as their route to the north Atlantic Ocean. In winter, much of the sea is frozen.

Glacial lakes
Finland and Sweden have many thousands of lakes. During the last Ice Age, glaciers scoured hollows that filled with water when the ice melted.

Courland Spit (D 7)
This wide sandspit runs f 62-miles along the Baltic coast of Lithuania and the Russian enclave of Kalinin It encloses a huge lagoon

ENVIRONMENTAL ISSUES

Northern Europe has been badly affected by industrial pollution from other parts of Europe. Polluted air moves north and mixes with the rain to create acid rain. This poisons forests and lakes, destroying the plants and animals living in them. Renewable energy plays a major role in this region, hydroelectric, geothermal and wind power are all exploited.

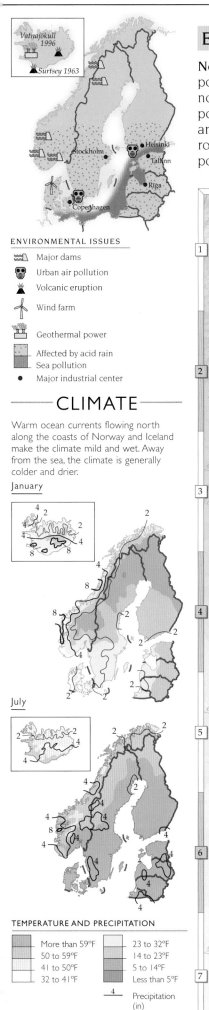

ENVIRONMENTAL ISSUES

- Major dams
- Urban air pollution
- Volcanic eruption
- Wind farm
- Geothermal power
- Affected by acid rain
  Sea pollution
- Major industrial center

CLIMATE

Warm ocean currents flowing north along the coasts of Norway and Iceland make the climate mild and wet. Away from the sea, the climate is generally colder and drier.

January

July

TEMPERATURE AND PRECIPITATION

More than 59°F	23 to 32°F
50 to 59°F	14 to 23°F
41 to 50°F	5 to 14°F
32 to 41°F	Less than 5°F

4 — Precipitation (in)

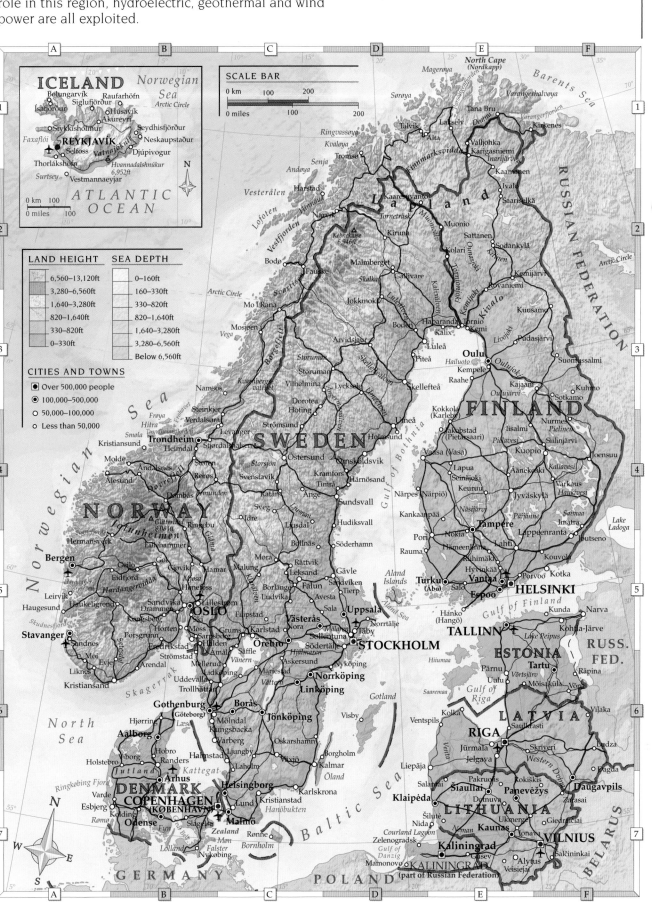

THE LOW COUNTRIES

BELGIUM, LUXEMBOURG, NETHERLANDS

Belgium, Luxembourg, and the Netherlands are called the Low Countries because most of their land is flat and low-lying. Much of the Netherlands lies below sea level, and over hundreds of years the Dutch have built dikes and dams to prevent flooding, and have pumped water off large areas of land to reclaim them from the sea. The Low Countries are Europe's most densely populated countries, but most of their people have a high living standard.

ENVIRONMENTAL ISSUES

Huge land reclamation projects in the Netherlands, such as the IJsselmeer project, have created some new land for agricultural use, and also for houses, roads, and open spaces. However, because of this work, sea-level rise is a major threat to large parts of the Netherlands.

ENVIRONMENTAL ISSUES

Urban air pollution

Built-up areas
Reclaimed land
Polluted river

- Major industrial center

CLIMATE

The Low Countries share a similar climate, with mild winters and warm summers. Only in the upland Ardennes region does rainfall increase and temperatures decrease.

January

July

TEMPERATURE AND PRECIPITATION

More than 59°F
50 to 59°F
41 to 50°F
32 to 41°F
Less than 32°F

4 — Precipitation (in)

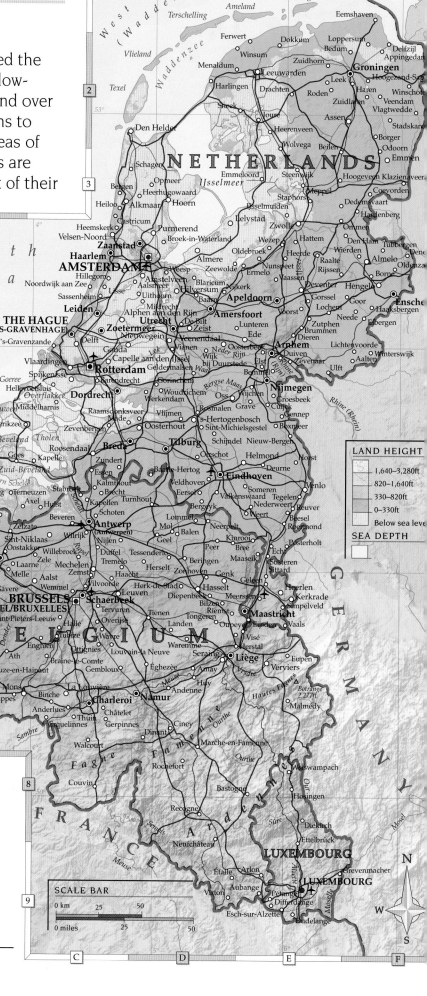

NETHERLANDS' TWO CAPITALS
AMSTERDAM - capital
THE HAGUE - seat of government

LAND HEIGHT

1,640–3,280ft
820–1,640ft
330–820ft
0–330ft
Below sea level

SEA DEPTH

CITIES AND TOWNS

- Over 500,000 people
- 100,000–500,000
- 50,000–100,000
- Less than 50,000

SCALE BAR

0 km 25 50

0 miles 25 50

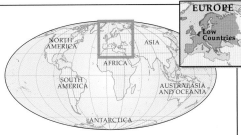

POPULATION

More than 27 million people live in the Low Countries, and nine out of every ten people live in a town or city. The largest urban area – known as the *Randstad Holland* – is in the Netherlands. It runs in an unbroken line from Rotterdam in the south, to Amsterdam in the west. Even most rural areas in the Low Countries are densely populated.

INHABITANTS PER SQ MILE

- More than 520
- 260–520
- 130–260
- 0–130
- ■ Capital city
- ● Major city

THE HAGUE
AMSTERDAM
Groningen
Randstad Holland
Utrecht
Rotterdam
Arnhem
Ghent
Antwerp
BRUSSELS
Liège
Charleroi
LUXEMBOURG

URBAN/RURAL POPULATION DIVISION

Amsterdam 2.8%   Brussels 3.9%
Rotterdam 2.3%
Rural population 8%
Other towns and cities 83%

INDUSTRY

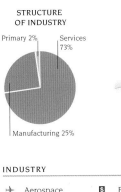

The Low Countries are an important center for the high-tech and electronics industries. Good transportation links to the rest of Europe allow them to sell their products in other countries. The built-up area stretching from Amsterdam in the Netherlands to Antwerp in Belgium has the greatest number of factories. Luxembourg is also an important banking center; many international banks have their headquarters in its capital city.

STRUCTURE OF INDUSTRY

Primary 2%   Services 73%
Manufacturing 25%

Groningen
Amsterdam
Enschede
The Hague
Utrecht
Rotterdam
Nijmegen
Breda
Tilburg
Eindhoven
Bruges
Antwerp
Ghent
Brussels
Kortrijk
Liège
Charleroi
Namur
Luxembourg

INDUSTRY

- ✈ Aerospace
- 🚗 Car manufacture
- ⚗ Chemicals
- ✿ Engineering
- 🖊 Pharmaceuticals
- 👕 Textiles
- S Finance
- 🖥 High-tech industry
- ⚓ Tourism
- ▣ Major industrial center / area
- — Major road

FARMING AND LAND USE

The Low Countries' fertile soils and flat plains provide excellent conditions for farming. The main crops grown are barley, potatoes, and flax for making linen. In the Netherlands, much farmland is used for dairy farming. The country is also famous for growing flowers, which are exported around the world. Flowers and vegetables are grown either in open fields or in enormous greenhouses, which allow production year-round.

Amsterdam
The Hague
Rotterdam
Brussels

LAND USE

Forest 16%
Pasture 26%
Cropland 29%
Other (including urban) 29%

FARMING AND LAND USE

- 🐂 Cattle
- 🐖 Pigs
- 🌾 Cereals
- ❀ Flax
- ❦ Flowers
- 🜨 Market gardening
- ♣ Sugar beet
- ▢ Pasture
- ▢ Cropland
- ▢ Forest
- ▢ Wetland
- ● Major conurbation

THE LANDSCAPE

The Low Countries are largely flat and low-lying. The ancient hills of the Ardennes, in the far southeast, are the only higher region. They rise to heights of more than 1,640 ft. Two major rivers – the Meuse and the Rhine – flow across the Low Countries to their mouths in the North Sea. At the coast, the Rhine deposits large quantities of sediment to form a delta.

Polders

In the Netherlands, land has been reclaimed from the sea since the Middle Ages by building dikes and drainage ditches. These areas of land are called polders. They are very fertile.

Rhine River (E4)

The River Rhine erodes and carries large amounts of sediment along its course. When it reaches the Netherlands it divides into three rivers. As they approach the North Sea, the rivers slow down, depositing the sediment to form a delta.

Low-lying Netherlands

Over two-thirds of the Netherlands lies at or below sea level. This makes flooding a constant threat in coastal areas.

Flanders (B6)

The plains of Flanders in western Belgium have fertile soils which were deposited by glaciers during the last Ice Age. They provide excellent land for growing crops.

Heathlands

The heathlands on the Dutch-Belgian border have thin, sandy soils. The only plants that grow well here are heathers and gorse.

Ardennes (D8)

The hills of the Ardennes were formed over 300 million years ago. They have many deep valleys, which have been eroded by rivers like the Meuse.

THE BRITISH ISLES

IRELAND, UNITED KINGDOM

The British Isles lie off the northwest coast of mainland Europe. They are made up of two large islands and more than 5,000 smaller ones. Politically, the region is divided into two countries: the United Kingdom – England, Wales, Scotland, and Northern Ireland – and Ireland. In 2014, Scotland held a referendum on independence in which 55.3% of voters elected to remain a part of the United Kingdom.

THE LANDSCAPE

Low rolling hills, high moorlands, and small fields with high hedges are all typical of the British Isles. Ireland is known as the Emerald Isle because heavy rainfall gives it a lush, green appearance. Scotland and Wales are mountainous; the rocks forming the mountains there are some of the oldest in the world.

Indented coastlines
The west coast of the British Isles faces the Atlantic Ocean, and more than 1,860 miles of open sea to the North American continent. Storms and high waves constantly batter the hard, rocky coastline, giving it a jagged outline.

Ben Nevis (C 4)
This mountain is the highest point in the British Isles. It is 4,406 ft above sea level.

The Lake District (D 5)
The Lake District National Park has England's highest peak, Scafell Pike, at 3,209 ft, its deepest lake, Wast Water (260 ft), and its largest lake, Windermere (10 miles long).

The Pennines (D 6)
The Pennines are a chain of high hills, topped by moorland. They run for more than 250 miles, and are known as the "backbone of England."

The Burren (A 6)
The Burren is a large area of limestone in the west of Ireland. Its flat surfaces are known as limestone "pavements." There are also many caves and sinkholes in the area.

The Fens (E 6)
This is the flattest area in England. Much of the land here has been reclaimed from the sea.

Rias
Rias are river valleys that have been drowned by rising sea levels. The southern coast of southwest England has many good examples.

FARMING AND LAND USE

The English lowlands and the wide, flat stretches of land in East Anglia are the agricultural heartland of the United Kingdom. The country is no longer self-sufficient in food, but wheat, potatoes and other vegetables, and fruits, are widely grown. In Ireland, and in central and southern England, dairy and beef cattle feed off grassy pastures. In the hilly and mountainous areas, sheep farming is more usual.

FARMING AND LAND USE

🐄 Cattle	Pasture
🐑 Fishing	Cropland
🐏 Sheep	Forest
🌾 Cereals	Mountain region
🐂 Market gardening	● Major conurbation
🌱 Root crops	

LAND USE

Cropland 24%
Pasture 50%
Other (including urban) 17%
Forest 9%

INDUSTRY

The United Kingdom's traditional industries, such as coal mining, steel-making, and textiles, have declined in recent years. Today, newer industries make cars, chemicals, and electronic and high-tech goods. Service industries, especially banking and insurance, have grown in importance. The country's hugely valuable North Sea oil and gas fields are expected to remain in production until around 2050.

INDUSTRY

- ✈ Aerospace
- 🚗 Car manufacturing
- 🧪 Chemicals
- ⚙ Engineering
- 👕 Textiles
- 💷 Finance
- 💻 High-tech industry
- 🏛 Tourism

- ▪ Major industrial center / area
- — Major road

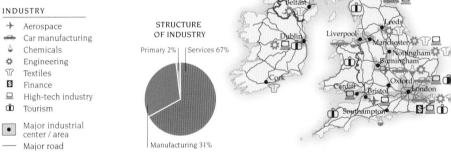

STRUCTURE OF INDUSTRY

Primary 2% | Services 67%
Manufacturing 31%

POPULATION

The United Kingdom is densely populated, with most of the people living in urban areas. The southeast is the most crowded part of the country. The Scottish Highlands are less populated today than they were 200 years ago. Ireland is still mainly rural, with many Irish people making their living from farming.

URBAN/RURAL POPULATION DIVISION

Birmingham 1.6%
London 11.4%
Glasgow 1%
Rural population 12%
Other towns and cities 74%

INHABITANTS PER SQ MILE

- More than 520
- 260–520
- 130–260
- Less than 130

- ▪ Capital city
- ● Major city

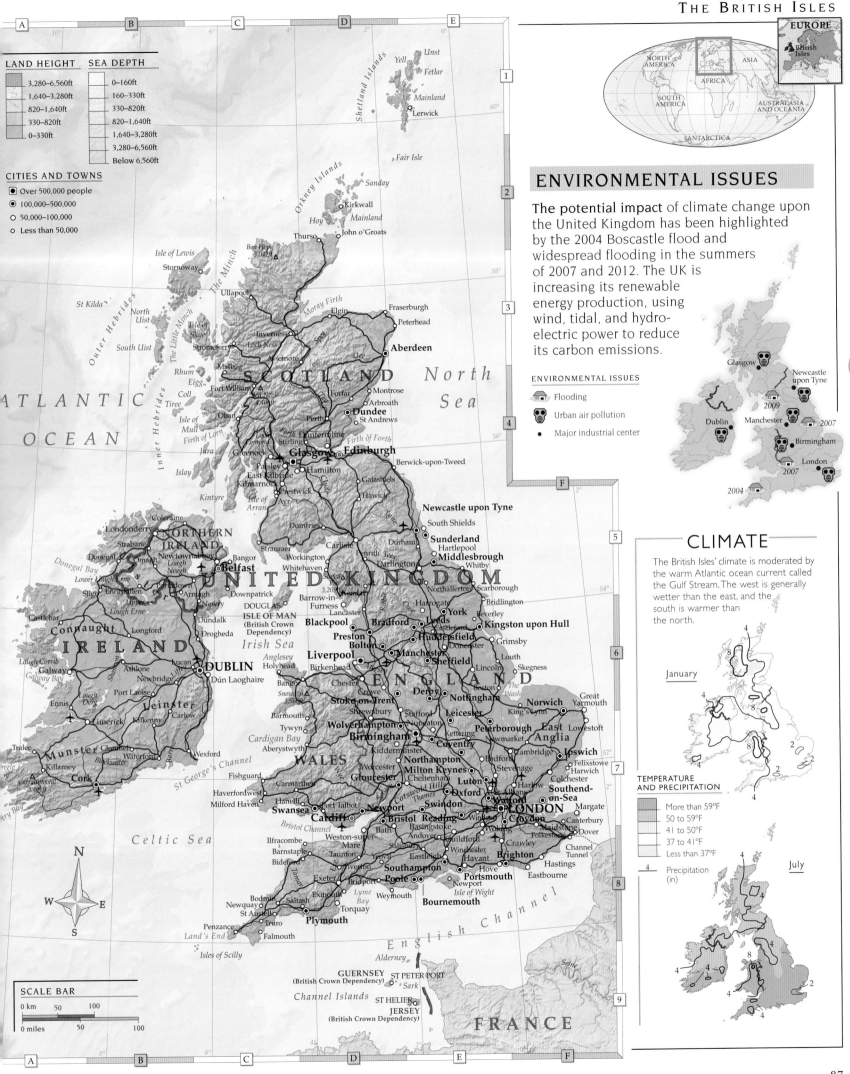

EUROPE
British Isles

ENVIRONMENTAL ISSUES

The potential impact of climate change upon the United Kingdom has been highlighted by the 2004 Boscastle flood and widespread flooding in the summers of 2007 and 2012. The UK is increasing its renewable energy production, using wind, tidal, and hydro-electric power to reduce its carbon emissions.

ENVIRONMENTAL ISSUES

- Flooding
- Urban air pollution
- Major industrial center

CLIMATE

The British Isles' climate is moderated by the warm Atlantic ocean current called the Gulf Stream. The west is generally wetter than the east, and the south is warmer than the north.

January

July

TEMPERATURE AND PRECIPITATION

- More than 59°F
- 50 to 59°F
- 41 to 50°F
- 37 to 41°F
- Less than 37°F

— 4 — Precipitation (in)

Map labels

LAND HEIGHT
- 3,280–6,560ft
- 1,640–3,280ft
- 820–1,640ft
- 330–820ft
- 0–330ft

SEA DEPTH
- 0–160ft
- 160–330ft
- 330–820ft
- 820–1,640ft
- 1,640–3,280ft
- 3,280–6,560ft
- Below 6,560ft

CITIES AND TOWNS
- ◉ Over 500,000 people
- ◎ 100,000–500,000
- ○ 50,000–100,000
- ∘ Less than 50,000

SCALE BAR
0 km   50   100
0 miles   50   100

ATLANTIC OCEAN

Shetland Islands
Yell
Unst
Fetlar
Mainland
Lerwick
Fair Isle
Orkney Islands
Sanday
Kirkwall
Hoy
Mainland
Thurso
John o'Groats

Isle of Lewis
Stornoway
St Kilda
North Uist
Outer Hebrides
South Uist
The Minch
The Little Minch
Isle of Skye
Rhum
Eigg
Coll
Tiree
Isle of Mull
Jura
Islay
Kintyre
Isle of Arran
Inner Hebrides

Ben Hope
3,042ft
Ullapool
Moray Firth
Elgin
Fraserburgh
Peterhead
Inverness
Loch Ness
Aviemore
Dee
Aberdeen
Mallaig
Stromeferry
SCOTLAND
Fort William
Ben Nevis
4,406ft
Oban
Firth of Lorn
Loch Lomond
Forfar
Montrose
Arbroath
Perth
Dundee
St Andrews
Stirling
Dunfermline
Greenock
Paisley
Glasgow
Edinburgh
Firth of Forth
East Kilbride
Hamilton
Kilmarnock
Prestwick
Clyde
Galashiels
Berwick-upon-Tweed
Ayr
Hawick
Dumfries

North Sea

Coleraine
Londonderry
Strabane
NORTHERN IRELAND
Newtownabbey
Omagh
Lough Neagh
Bangor
Belfast
Stranraer
Tweed
Newcastle upon Tyne
South Shields
Sunderland
Hartlepool
Middlesbrough
Whitby
Donegal
Donegal Bay
Lower Lough Erne
Enniskillen
Upper Lough Erne
Sligo
Armagh
Newry
Downpatrick
Dundalk
Carlisle
Workington
Whitehaven
Penrith
Durham
Darlington
Northallerton
Scarborough

UNITED KINGDOM
Barrow-in-Furness
Lancaster
Tees
Harrogate
Bridlington
Beverley
York
Castleford
Kingston upon Hull
Grimsby

Connaught
Castlebar
Longford
IRELAND
Lough Corrib
Galway
Galway Bay
Athlone
Lucan
DUBLIN
Dún Laoghaire
Newbridge
Port Laoise
Lough Derg
Ennis
Leinster
Limerick
Kilkenny
Carlow

Irish Sea
ISLE OF MAN
(British Crown Dependency)
DOUGLAS
Blackpool
Preston
Bolton
Bradford
Leeds
Huddersfield
Doncaster
Sheffield
Lincoln
Louth
Skegness
Boston
The Wash
King's Lynn
Anglesey
Holyhead
Liverpool
Birkenhead
Manchester
Bangor
Chester
Crewe
Stoke-on-Trent
Derby
Nottingham
Great Yarmouth
Norwich
ENGLAND
Snowdon
3,560ft
Shrewsbury
Stafford
Leicester
East Anglia
Lowestoft
WALES
Barmouth
Tywyn
Wolverhampton
Nuneaton
Peterborough
Newmarket
Ipswich
Cardigan Bay
Aberystwyth
Birmingham
Coventry
Kettering
Cambridge
Felixstowe
Harwich
Colchester
Kidderminster
Northampton
Bedford
Worcester
Milton Keynes
Stevenage
Harlow
Fishguard
Gloucester
Cheltenham
Luton
St Albans
Southend-on-Sea
Haverfordwest
Llanelli
Carmarthen
Wye
Oxford
Watford
Margate
Milford Haven
Swansea
Port Talbot
Newport
Swindon
Thames
LONDON
Croydon
Canterbury
Cardiff
Bristol
Reading
Woking
Maidstone
Dover
Bath
Basingstoke
Guildford
Crawley
Folkestone
Channel Tunnel
Weston-super-Mare
Andover
Winchester
Brighton
Celtic Sea
Ilfracombe
Taunton
Salisbury
Eastleigh
Havant
Hove
Hastings
Barnstaple
Yeovil
Eastbourne
Bideford
Tiverton
Southampton
Portsmouth
Newport
Bristol Channel
Exeter
Bridport
Poole
Isle of Wight
Bodmin
Exmouth
Weymouth
Bournemouth
Newquay
Saltash
Lyme Bay
St Austell
Torquay
Truro
Plymouth
Falmouth
Penzance
Land's End
Isles of Scilly

Munster
Clonmel
Blackwater
Waterford
Wexford
Tralee
Killarney
Carrauntoohil
3,406ft
Cork

St George's Channel

English Channel
Alderney
Seine
GUERNSEY
(British Crown Dependency)
ST PETER PORT
Sark
Channel Islands
ST HELIER
JERSEY
(British Crown Dependency)
FRANCE

N
W   E
S

2009
2007
2007
2004
Glasgow
Newcastle upon Tyne
Dublin
Manchester
Birmingham
London

IRELAND

IRELAND, NORTHERN IRELAND

Ireland faces the north Atlantic Ocean and is one of the remotest parts of the European Union. Since 1921 the island has been divided into two separate states: Northern Ireland, which is part of the United Kingdom, and Ireland, which has its own government in Dublin. The eastern side of the island has more people and industry. In the west, traditional ways of life based on farming remain strong and the native Irish language is still spoken by some people.

INDUSTRY

Ireland has few mineral resources, around 8% of its electricity is produced by burning peat. In the last 20 years the European Union has given money to help the Irish economy and many new factories have been set up, mainly in the area around Dublin. Hi-tech industries expanded rapidly, as a result of low set-up costs and tax benefits.

INDUSTRY

- ✈ Aerospace
- ♠ Brewing
- ♣ Chemicals
- ✿ Engineering
- ▯ Food processing
- 👕 Textiles
- ▱ Hi-tech industry
- ⊕ Tourism
- ▣ Major industrial center / area
- — Major road

POPULATION

The population of Ireland has actually fallen over the last century as a result of mass emigration, mainly to North America. The rate of people leaving the country to live abroad is still high, although one of Europe's highest birth rates and economic immigration are finally causing the population to rise again, with one person in every three being less than 20-years old.

INHABITANTS PER SQ MILE

- More than 650
- 260–650
- 130–260
- Less than 130
- ■ Capital city
- ● Major city

FARMING AND LAND USE

Potatoes were once the traditional staple food of the Irish; potatoes and cereals flourish in the drier east. The climate is too wet for many types of crop, particularly in the west, where the soils are thin and the land is mostly used for sheep grazing. In bog areas a type of soil called peat is cut from the ground and dried to be burned as fuel.

FARMING AND LAND USE

- 🐄 Cattle
- 🐑 Sheep
- 🌾 Cereals
- 🌱 Potatoes
- Cropland
- Forest
- Pasture
- ● Major conurbation

THE LANDSCAPE

Ireland's mountains are nearly all close to the sea. They form a ring of high ground – broken in only a few places – encircling a lower-lying plain which fills the central areas. Hundreds of lakes, large areas of bogland, and low, grassy hills cover this central plain. The west coast follows an extremely irregular line, with many long bays and headlands.

High cliffs (C 2)
The cliffs of Donegal are some of the highest in Europe. Slieve League has been half cut away by sea erosion, so that the cliff rises vertically, all the way up from the shore to its 2,198 ft summit.

Lakes made by glaciers
The central plain is covered with lakes of many different sizes. Most of these lakes were formed by huge blocks of ice which remained lying around as the last Ice Age came to an end, slowly melting over hundreds of years to leave sunken pits in the land surface.

Flooded river valleys (A 6)
Dingle Bay extends deep inland. Rising seas have flooded the old river valley. Bays formed when the sea floods a river valley are known as rias.

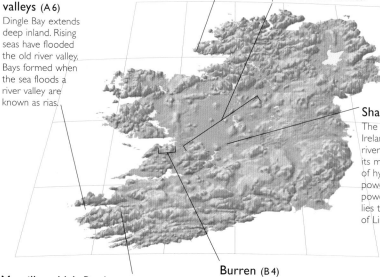

Shannon (C 4)
The Shannon is Ireland's longest river and also its main source of hydroelectric power. The main power station lies to the north of Limerick.

Macgillycuddy's Reeks (B 6)
This is the highest mountain range in Ireland. The jagged peaks and steep-sided valleys were cut from the highly resistant rocks by glacial erosion, during the last Ice Age.

Burren (B 4)
The Burren is a large plateau of limestone rock. Limestone is permeable, which means that water sinks below the surface and flows underground. The bare rock is visible at the surface in many places, where it is called a limestone pavement.

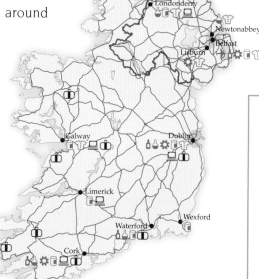

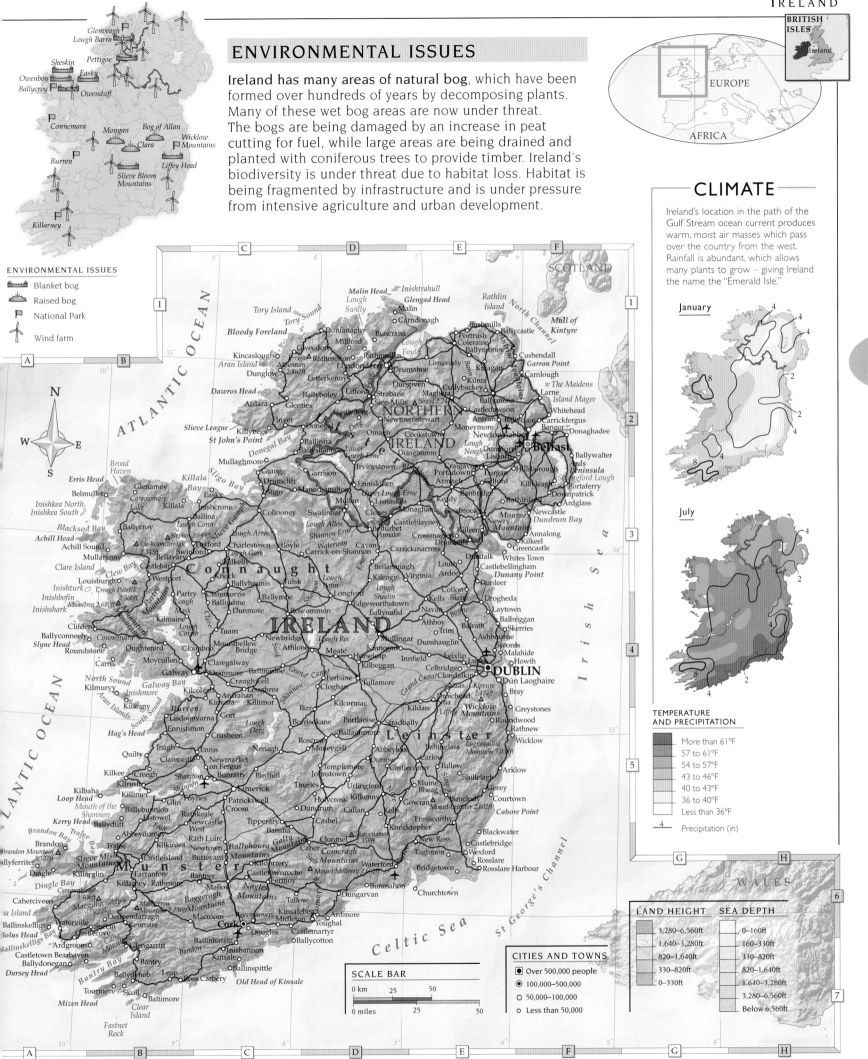

ENVIRONMENTAL ISSUES

Ireland has many areas of natural bog, which have been formed over hundreds of years by decomposing plants. Many of these wet bog areas are now under threat. The bogs are being damaged by an increase in peat cutting for fuel, while large areas are being drained and planted with coniferous trees to provide timber. Ireland's biodiversity is under threat due to habitat loss. Habitat is being fragmented by infrastructure and is under pressure from intensive agriculture and urban development.

CLIMATE

Ireland's location in the path of the Gulf Stream ocean current produces warm, moist air masses which pass over the country from the west. Rainfall is abundant, which allows many plants to grow – giving Ireland the name the "Emerald Isle."

January

July

TEMPERATURE AND PRECIPITATION

	More than 61°F
	57 to 61°F
	54 to 57°F
	43 to 46°F
	40 to 43°F
	36 to 40°F
	Less than 36°F
—4—	Precipitation (in)

ENVIRONMENTAL ISSUES

	Blanket bog
	Raised bog
	National Park
	Wind farm

CITIES AND TOWNS
- Over 500,000 people
- 100,000–500,000
- 50,000–100,000
- Less than 50,000

SCALE BAR
0 km 25 50
0 miles 25 50

LAND HEIGHT	SEA DEPTH
3,280–6,560ft	0–160ft
1,640–3,280ft	160–330ft
820–1,640ft	330–820ft
330–820ft	820–1,640ft
0–330ft	1,640–3,280ft
	3,280–6,560ft
	Below 6,560ft

SCOTLAND

Scotland occupies the northern third of Britain and has three main regions: the northern highlands and islands, the Southern Uplands and, between these two mountain areas, the central lowlands, where around three-quarters of the population live and work. Scotland was once an independent country and, after nearly 300 years of union with England, has regained its own parliament, with certain autonomous powers. In 2014, Scotland held a vote on independence and decided to remain a part of the UK.

INDUSTRY

A century ago, the area around the Clyde River was one of the great industrial regions of the world. The old heavy industries have since declined and been replaced by hi-tech and electronics industries, earning the area the name of "Silicon Glen." North Sea oil has brought many jobs and attracted new, oil-based industries such as chemicals and plastics production to the east coast.

INDUSTRY

✈	Aerospace	⬦	Oil and gas
⬧	Brewing	💻	Hi-tech industry
⬧	Chemicals	🖥	Printing and publishing
⚙	Engineering	🏛	Tourism
🐟	Fish processing		
▯	Food processing	⬛	Major industrial center / area
⏉	Textiles	—	Major road

ENVIRONMENTAL ISSUES

Over recent years dependence on coal-fired and nuclear powered electricity generation has decreased in favor of more sustainable and environmentally friendly methods.

In particular, due to its favorable landscape and climate, Scotland has seen a significant rise in the number of large-scale wind farms, although these also attract criticism from environmental groups.

Cairngorms

ENVIRONMENTAL ISSUES

- 🏭 Nuclear power station
- 🏭 Coal-fired power station
- 🌀 Wind farm
- ⚑ National Park

Loch Lomond & the Trossachs

FARMING AND LAND USE

The eastern side of Scotland has a drier climate than the west and is suitable for growing cereal crops and vegetables. Most of the mountain areas are too wet and barren for arable farming and are put to a variety of uses, which include sheep and deer farming, game-keeping, forestry, tourism, and recreation. Scottish fishermen currently land about two-thirds of all the fish caught by the UK.

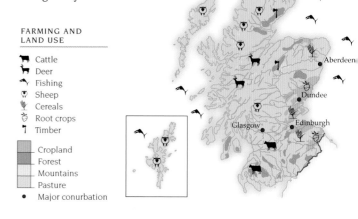

FARMING AND LAND USE

- 🐄 Cattle
- Deer
- Fishing
- 🐑 Sheep
- Cereals
- Root crops
- Timber

	Cropland
	Forest
	Mountains
	Pasture
•	Major conurbation

THE LANDSCAPE

Much of Scotland is rugged and mountainous. During the last Ice Age, around 18,000 years ago, glaciers and great sheets of ice attacked Scotland's hard, ancient rocks, leaving behind a landscape of high moorlands and steep-sided mountains separated by deep valleys, often filled by lakes known as lochs.

Glen Mor (D 3)
Glen Mor is a deep valley which runs right across Scotland. It marks a major line of rock fracture, known as a fault. Much of the fault line is filled by Loch Ness (D 3) and Loch Linnhe (C 4).

Grampians (D 4)
The Grampians are Britain's largest and highest mountain region. They include the spectacular Cairngorm range (E 3) and, to the west, Ben Nevis (D 4), the highest point in the British Isles, at 4,406 ft.

Hebrides (A 2), (B 6)
The Inner and Outer Hebrides comprise several large islands and hundreds of small ones. Many of these were formed following the last Ice Age, as the sea level rose, cutting off parts of the mountainous landscape from the mainland.

Firth of Forth (E 5)
The Firth of Forth is one of several great sea inlets, known as firths, along the Scottish coast. They include the Firths of Clyde (D 6), Tay (F 5), and Moray (E 3).

Lochs (D 5)
The many sea lochs (fjords) of the west coast were formed as the sea level rose after the last Ice Age, flooding the deep valleys that had been cut by glaciers. The sea lochs cause the coast to follow a highly irregular line.

Rannoch Moor (D 5)
Rannoch Moor is the largest wild moorland in Scotland. A great ice sheet covered the area during the last Ice Age, leaving behind a vast expanse of bleak, bare ground, pitted with small depressions.

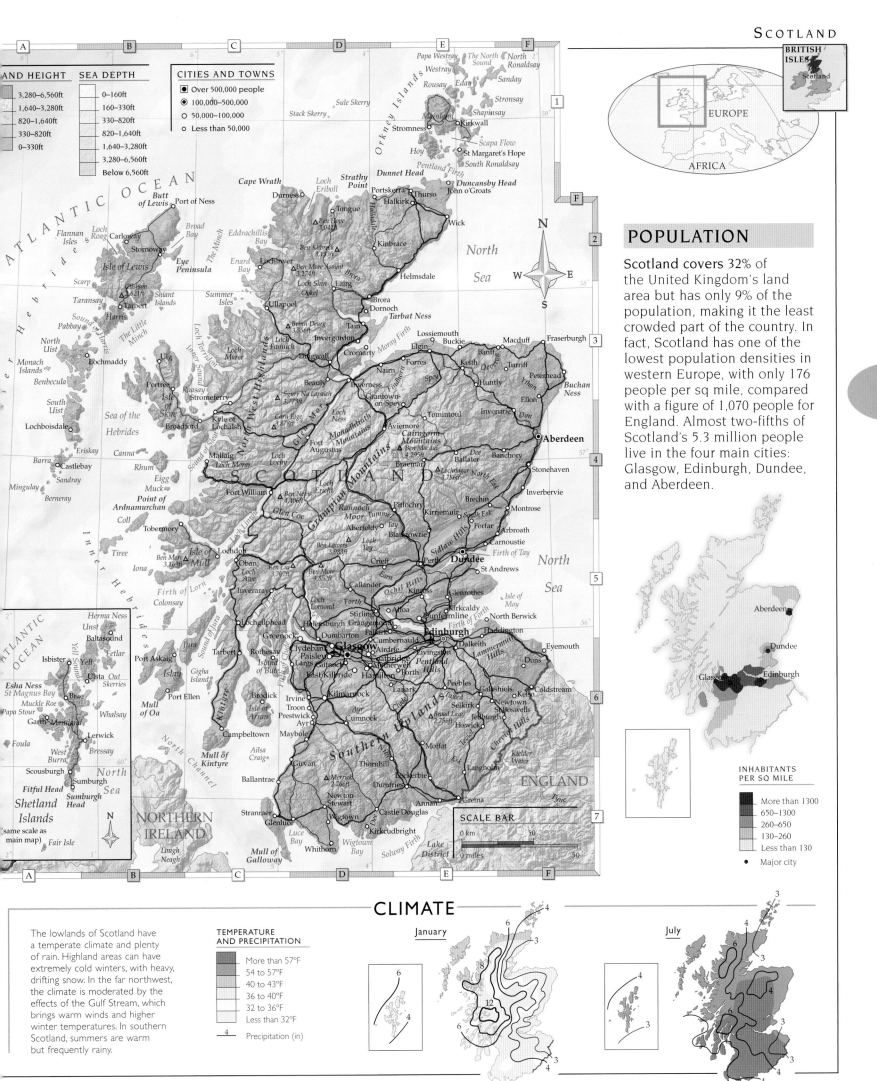

LAND HEIGHT
- 3,280–6,560ft
- 1,640–3,280ft
- 820–1,640ft
- 330–820ft
- 0–330ft

SEA DEPTH
- 0–160ft
- 160–330ft
- 330–820ft
- 820–1,640ft
- 1,640–3,280ft
- 3,280–6,560ft
- Below 6,560ft

CITIES AND TOWNS
- Over 500,000 people
- 100,000–500,000
- 50,000–100,000
- Less than 50,000

BRITISH ISLES

EUROPE

AFRICA

Scotland

POPULATION

Scotland covers 32% of the United Kingdom's land area but has only 9% of the population, making it the least crowded part of the country. In fact, Scotland has one of the lowest population densities in western Europe, with only 176 people per sq mile, compared with a figure of 1,070 people for England. Almost two-fifths of Scotland's 5.3 million people live in the four main cities: Glasgow, Edinburgh, Dundee, and Aberdeen.

INHABITANTS PER SQ MILE
- More than 1300
- 650–1300
- 260–650
- 130–260
- Less than 130
- Major city

CLIMATE

The lowlands of Scotland have a temperate climate and plenty of rain. Highland areas can have extremely cold winters, with heavy, drifting snow. In the far northwest, the climate is moderated by the effects of the Gulf Stream, which brings warm winds and higher winter temperatures. In southern Scotland, summers are warm but frequently rainy.

TEMPERATURE AND PRECIPITATION
- More than 57°F
- 54 to 57°F
- 40 to 43°F
- 36 to 40°F
- 32 to 36°F
- Less than 32°F
- —4— Precipitation (in)

January

July

NORTHERN ENGLAND & WALES

The Industrial Revolution of the 18th and 19th centuries began in northern England, exploiting rich local resources to begin a new era of mass production. Today, these industries have declined, but despite a number of difficult years, northern England is becoming more prosperous again. Similarly, south Wales was once a major coal-mining and heavy industrial area but this has largely been replaced by new service industries. The magnificent scenery throughout this region attracts many tourists and outdoor enthusiasts.

INDUSTRY

Traditional industries such as iron and steel, coal-mining and textiles have been in decline for many years. More recently, the type of industries have changed to light engineering and hi-tech industries, producing microchips and computers, together with service industries such as insurance and retailing, printing and publishing. Tourism is important; large numbers of people visit the area's stunning national parks each year.

INDUSTRY

✈ Aerospace	✎ Pharmaceuticals
🍺 Brewing	⚓ Shipbuilding
🚗 Car manufacture	👕 Textiles
Ceramics	▮ Oil refining
🍶 Chemicals	💻 Hi-tech industry
✿ Engineering	🖨 Printing and publishing
Fish processing	♿ Tourism
Food processing	◼ Major industrial
Iron & steel	center / area
△ Metal refining	— Major road

ENVIRONMENTAL ISSUES

Some of the UK's most dramatic scenery is found in this area, and national parks have long been established to protect the environment. These parks have proved so popular that in some places tourists are in danger of destroying the environment. Coal-fired power stations in the region power the large cities, but recently there has been an increase in renewable energy production.

ENVIRONMENTAL ISSUES

🏭	Coal-fired power station
🏭	Nuclear power station
〰	Hydroelectric scheme
🗼	Wind farm
⚑	National park
•	Major industrial city

FARMING AND LAND USE

The eastern lowlands have an ideal climate for arable crops, while oats and potatoes grow in the north and west. The southwest is used mainly for grazing cattle and sheep, which also graze rough in the upland areas of the Pennines and Wales. Forestry is increasingly important in mountain areas.

FARMING AND LAND USE

🐂	Cattle
🐑	Sheep
🌾	Cereals
🥕	Market gardening
🥔	Root crops
	Cropland
	Forest
	Pasture
•	Major conurbation

THE LANDSCAPE

The Pennines form the backbone of northern England. Likewise, the Cambrian Mountains, including the spectacular landscape of Snowdonia, run the length of central Wales. To the east, the Aire and Ouse rivers have cut a broad flood plain between the Pennines and the North York Moors, while in the far northwest, Cumbria's Lake District has many long, deep lakes, which were formed during the last Ice Age.

Limestone pavements
Bare "pavements" of weathered limestone are also known as karst scenery. They have a block like appearance, with deep cracks between the blocks that have been dissolved by rainwater.

Spurn Head (F4)
Spurn Head is a long sand bar (called a spit) at the mouth of the Humber estuary. It was formed by waves which deposited sand across the mouth of the bay. Constant erosion has often made Spurn Head almost inaccessible from the mainland.

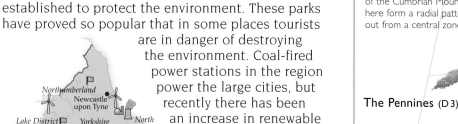

Lake District (C3)
The Lake District covers a small area of the Cumbrian Mountains. The 15 lakes here form a radial pattern, spreading out from a central zone of volcanic rock.

The Pennines (D3)

North York Moors (E3)

Snowdonia (B5)
These spectacular mountains include Snowdon, the highest point in England and Wales, at 3,560 ft. The spectacular sheer sides and jagged ridges were carved by glaciers during the last Ice Age.

Cambrian Mountains (B6)
The Cambrian range runs the whole length of the country and contains some of the oldest rocks in Britain. The rock is rich in minerals. Slate was also once mined in great quantities in northern and central areas.

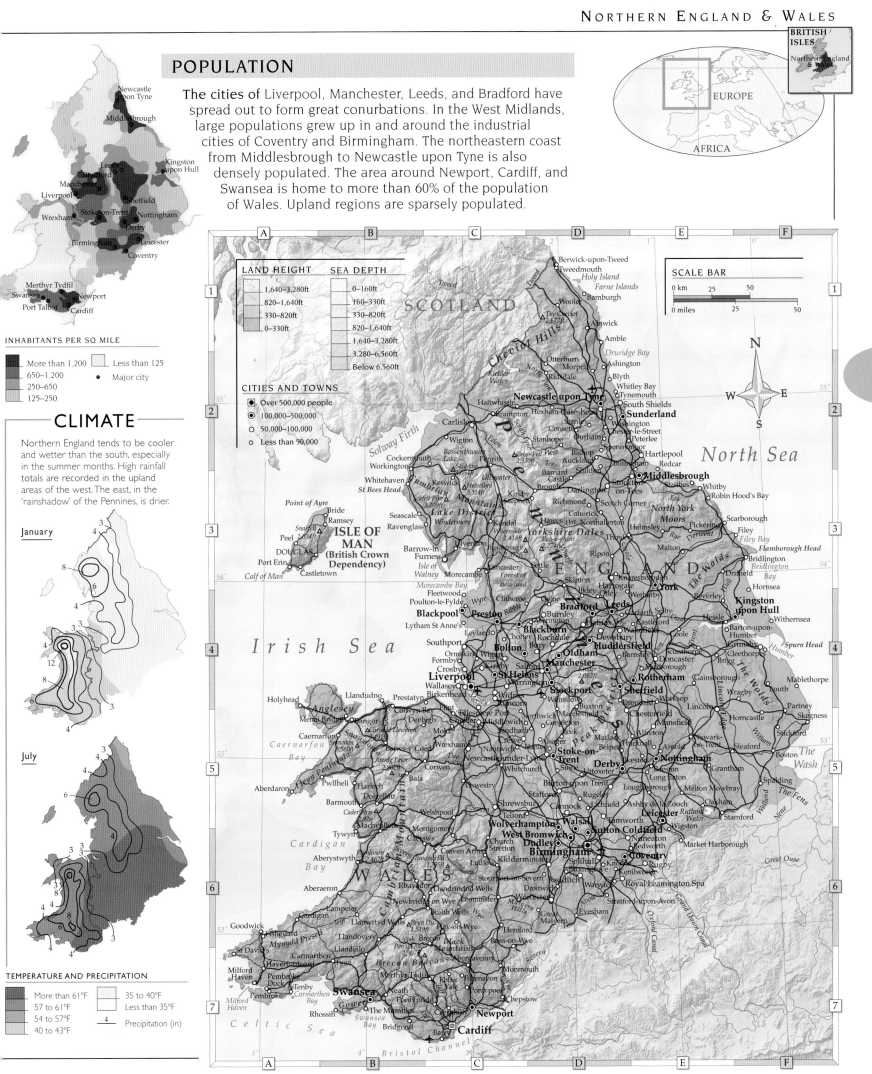

POPULATION

The cities of Liverpool, Manchester, Leeds, and Bradford have spread out to form great conurbations. In the West Midlands, large populations grew up in and around the industrial cities of Coventry and Birmingham. The northeastern coast from Middlesbrough to Newcastle upon Tyne is also densely populated. The area around Newport, Cardiff, and Swansea is home to more than 60% of the population of Wales. Upland regions are sparsely populated.

BRITISH ISLES
Northern England & Wales

EUROPE

AFRICA

INHABITANTS PER SQ MILE

More than 1,200   Less than 125
650–1,200   • Major city
250–650
125–250

CLIMATE

Northern England tends to be cooler and wetter than the south, especially in the summer months. High rainfall totals are recorded in the upland areas of the west. The east, in the 'rainshadow' of the Pennines, is drier.

January

July

TEMPERATURE AND PRECIPITATION

More than 61°F   35 to 40°F
57 to 61°F   Less than 35°F
54 to 57°F
40 to 43°F   ——4—— Precipitation (in)

LAND HEIGHT
1,640–3,280ft
820–1,640ft
330–820ft
0–330ft

SEA DEPTH
0–160ft
160–330ft
330–820ft
820–1,640ft
1,640–3,280ft
3,280–6,560ft
Below 6,560ft

CITIES AND TOWNS
● Over 500,000 people
◉ 100,000–500,000
○ 50,000–100,000
○ Less than 50,000

SCALE BAR
0 km   25   50
0 miles   25   50

SOUTHERN ENGLAND

The southern counties of England, and particularly Greater London, are the most densely populated part of the British Isles. There are more industries and more jobs here than anywhere else in the UK. In contrast, the counties of the far west and east are much less heavily populated and more rural, although towns in the eastern counties have been growing rapidly since the 1980s. Following the completion of the Channel Tunnel, the UK has had a direct rail link to Europe.

INDUSTRY

London is one of the world's top financial centers and is also a leading center for other service industries including insurance, the media, and publishing. Many car manufacturers are based in southern England, though the numbers of people employed have greatly decreased. Several cities, including Cambridge and Swindon, are centers for hi-tech industry. Thousands of tourists visit the historic and cultural centers in southern England every year.

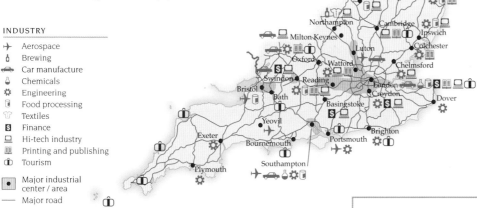

INDUSTRY

+ Aerospace
♦ Brewing
🚗 Car manufacture
♨ Chemicals
✿ Engineering
▣ Food processing
▽ Textiles
S Finance
▢ Hi-tech industry
▥ Printing and publishing
♙ Tourism

▣ Major industrial center / area
— Major road

ENVIRONMENTAL ISSUES

The large and growing population of southern England has increased pressure for the development of "green belt" land, designed to protect the countryside surrounding large cities. A perceived shortage of airport capacity in the southeast of England means that either Heathrow or Gatwick airports will be recommended for expansion over the next 15 years.

ENVIRONMENTAL ISSUES

▨ Nuclear power station
▨ "Green belt" areas
⚑ National Park
⟟ Wind farm
• Major town/city

FARMING AND LAND USE

Fertile soils and reliable rainfall mean that a wide range of crops can be grown in southern England. Large arable farms growing wheat and barley are found in the flat eastern counties, and a great variety of soft and orchard fruits and vegetables are grown in market gardens in the far southeast. Beef and dairy cattle and large flocks of sheep are grazed throughout the south.

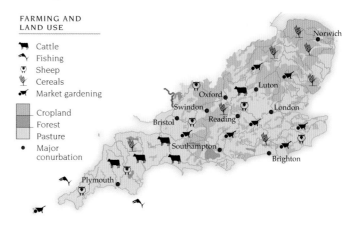

FARMING AND LAND USE

🐄 Cattle
🐟 Fishing
🐑 Sheep
🌾 Cereals
🐖 Market gardening

▨ Cropland
▨ Forest
▨ Pasture
• Major conurbation

THE LANDSCAPE

The landscape of southern England is very varied. Cornwall in the far west has craggy hills, and a jagged coastline shaped by the Atlantic Ocean. The Cotswolds and the North and South Downs are gentle hills, while toward the east, the land becomes flatter. Near the east coast, low-lying areas are occasionally prone to flooding.

Chalk hills The rounded hills of the Chilterns (F 3) are made from chalk. Because chalk is a porous rock, water quickly seeps through it, so few rivers can be seen in chalk areas.

The Broads (H 2) The Broads in Norfolk are a series of wide waterways flowing across flat meadows. The channels were cut by peat cutters and are not "natural." They then flooded, forming shallow inland lakes.

Steep cliffs The coasts of north Devon and Cornwall are battered by great waves from the Atlantic Ocean. The force of the waves weakens the rock at the foot of the cliffs, causing them to be "undercut." The top layer of rock breaks off and the cliffs recede.

Dartmoor (B 5) Dartmoor is the visible part of a great dome of granite rock. It was formed when molten rock seeped into and cooled in the Earth's crust. Because granite is so hard it erodes very slowly, so outcrops of rock known as *tors* can be seen all over Dartmoor.

Thames River (F 3) The Thames has its source close to the Cotswolds, and meanders through Oxford and London before reaching the North Sea in a wide estuary.

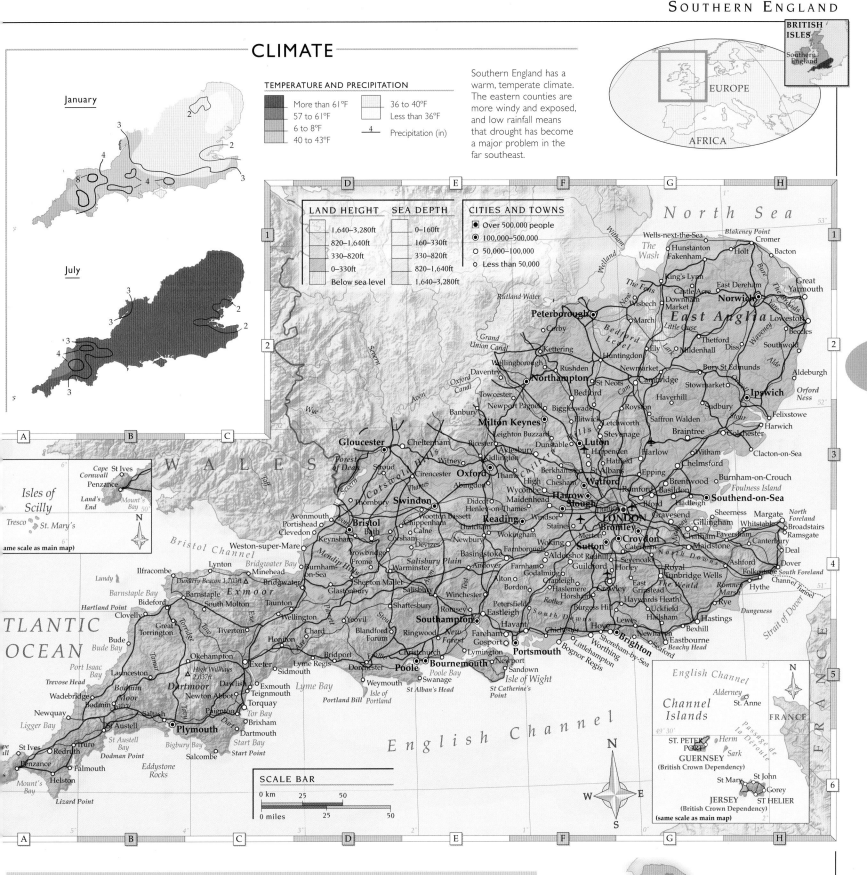

CLIMATE

January

July

TEMPERATURE AND PRECIPITATION

- More than 61°F
- 57 to 61°F
- 6 to 8°F
- 40 to 43°F
- 36 to 40°F
- Less than 36°F
- 4 — Precipitation (in)

Southern England has a warm, temperate climate. The eastern counties are more windy and exposed, and low rainfall means that drought has become a major problem in the far southeast.

BRITISH ISLES
Southern England

EUROPE

AFRICA

LAND HEIGHT
- 1,640–3,280ft
- 820–1,640ft
- 330–820ft
- 0–330ft
- Below sea level

SEA DEPTH
- 0–160ft
- 160–330ft
- 330–820ft
- 820–1,640ft
- 1,640–3,280ft

CITIES AND TOWNS
- Over 500,000 people
- 100,000–500,000
- 50,000–100,000
- Less than 50,000

North Sea

Isles of Scilly
Tresco • St. Mary's

Bristol Channel

ATLANTIC
OCEAN

English Channel

English Channel

Channel Islands
ST. PETER PORT
GUERNSEY
(British Crown Dependency)
JERSEY
ST HELIER
(British Crown Dependency)
(same scale as main map)

FRANCE

SCALE BAR
0 km   25   50
0 miles   25   50

POPULATION

Greater London and the southeastern counties are the most heavily populated areas of England. More than seven million people live in Greater London, a conurbation which extends almost to the boundary of the M25 motorway. Other large population centers are found along the south coast and close to motorways – Brighton, Southampton, Portsmouth, Oxford, Swindon, and Reading are among the biggest. Many people live a long distance from their workplaces and commute into cities by car and train.

INHABITANTS
PER SQ MILE
- More than 1300
- 650–1300
- 260–650
- 130–260
- Less than 130
- Capital city
- Major city

FRANCE

ANDORRA, FRANCE, MONACO

France has helped shape the history and culture of Europe for centuries. Today, as a founder-member of the European Union, France is an avid supporter of the eventual political and economic integration of Europe's different countries. France is Western Europe's leading farming nation and one of the world's top industrial powers. Its cultural attractions and scenery draw tourists from around the world.

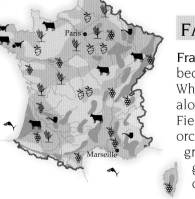

FARMING AND LAND USE

France is able to produce a variety of crops because of its rich soils and mild climate. Wheat is grown in many parts of the north, along with potatoes and other vegetables. Fields of corn and sunflowers and fruit orchards are found in the south, while grapes for the famous wine industry are grown across the country. Beef and dairy cattle are grazed on low-lying pasture.

FARMING AND LAND USE

- 🐂 Cattle
- ⚓ Fishing
- 🌾 Cereals
- 🥕 Market gardening
- 🌱 Root crops
- 🌿 Tobacco
- 🍇 Vineyards
- ▨ Pasture
- ▨ Cropland
- ▨ Forest
- ▨ Mountain region
- ▨ Wetland
- ● Major conurbation

LAND USE

- Other (including urban) 18%
- Cropland 35%
- Forest 27%
- Pasture 20%

THE LANDSCAPE

The north and west of France is made up of mainly flat, grassy plains or low hills. Wooded mountains line the country's borders in the south and east, and much of central France is taken up by the Massif Central, an enormous plateau cut by deep river valleys and scattered with extinct volcanoes. Three major rivers, the Loire, Seine, and Garonne, drain the lowland basins.

Paris Basin

The Paris Basin is a saucer-shaped hollow made up of layers of hard and soft rock, covered with very fertile soils. It runs across about 38,600 sq miles of northern France.

Alps (E 5)

The western end of the European Alpine mountain chain stretches into southeast France. The French Alps can be crossed by several passes, which give access to Italy and Switzerland.

Normandy

The coast of Normandy is lined with high chalk cliffs.

INDUSTRY

France is one of the world's top manufacturing nations, with a variety of both traditional and high-tech industries. Cars, machinery, and electronic products are exported worldwide, along with luxury goods such as perfumes, fashions, and wines. Extensive use of nuclear power has allowed France to become the world's largest net exporter of electricity.

STRUCTURE OF INDUSTRY

- Primary 3%
- Services 73%
- Manufacturing 24%

INDUSTRY

- ✈ Aerospace
- 🚗 Car manufacturing
- ⚗ Chemicals
- ⚙ Engineering
- 👕 Textiles
- 💻 High-tech industry
- 🧳 Tourism
- ▣ Major industrial center / area
- — Major road

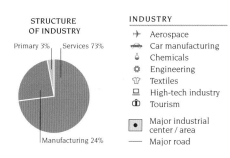

POPULATION

In the past 50 years, most people have moved from the countryside into urban areas. Paris and its suburbs, the industrial cities, and the Côte d'Azur in the southeast are the most economically developed parts of France and now have the biggest populations.

URBAN/RURAL POPULATION DIVISION

- Paris 16%
- Lyon 2.2%
- Marseille 2.2%
- Rural population 24%
- Other towns and cities 55.6%

INHABITANTS PER SQ MILE

- ▨ More than 520
- ▨ 260–520
- ▨ 130–260
- ▨ Less than 130
- ■ Capital city
- ● Major city

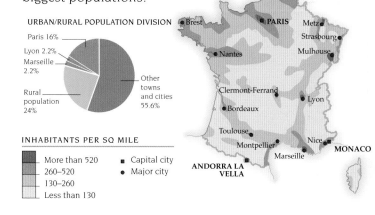

Pyrenees (C 7)

These mountains form a natural barrier between France and Spain. Several peaks reach heights of over 9,480 ft. The Pyrenees are difficult to cross, due to their height, and because they have few low passes.

Massif Central (D 5)

This vast granite plateau was formed over 200 million years ago. Volcanic activity here stopped only within the last 10,000 years, and the region's rounded hills are the worn-down remains of volcanic mountains.

Camargue (D 7)

The Camargue is an area of marshes, pastures, sand dunes, and salt flats at the mouth of the Rhône River. Rare animal and plant species are found there.

Mont Blanc (E 5)

This mountain in the French Alps is the tallest in Western Europe. It is 15,771 ft high.

ENVIRONMENTAL ISSUES

Many of France's coastal areas have been polluted by industry and tourism. A summer heatwave in 2003 severeley affected France, with temperatures of up to 104°F contributing to the deaths of an estimated 15,000 people. France's reliance on nuclear energy – over 75% of its electricity is generated by nuclear power – means that it suffers less from the pollution caused by burning fossil fuels than many other countries in Europe.

ENVIRONMENTAL ISSUES
- Nuclear power station
- Sea pollution
- Polluted rivers
- Major industrial center

CLIMATE

In winter, the coldest areas of France are the mountains of the Massif Central and the Alps. Summers are hottest on the Mediterranean coast.

TEMPERATURE AND PRECIPITATION
- More than 68°F
- 59 to 68°F
- 50 to 59°F
- 41 to 50°F
- 32 to 41°F
- 23 to 32°F
- Less than 23°F
- 4 Precipitation (in)

January

July

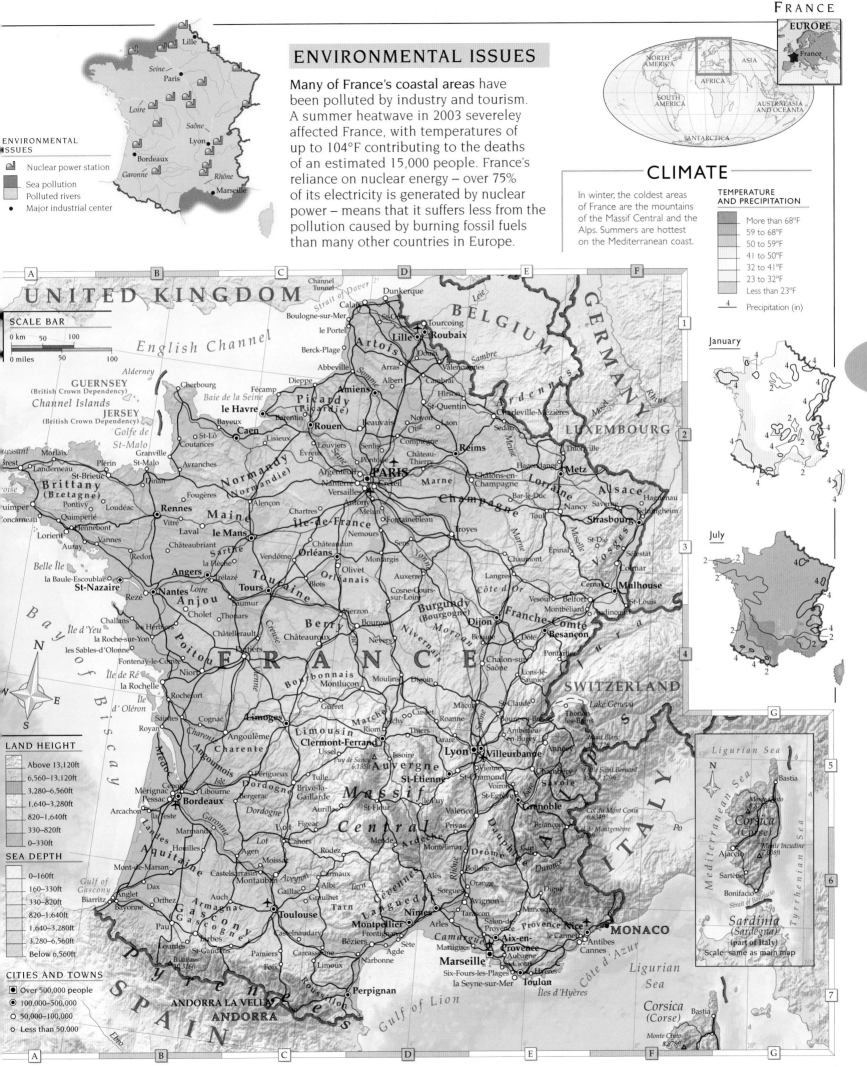

SPAIN AND PORTUGAL

PORTUGAL, SPAIN

Spain and Portugal occupy the Iberian Peninsula, which is cut off from the rest of Europe by the Pyrenees. Over the centuries, Iberia has been invaded and settled by many different peoples. The Moors, who arrived from North Africa in the 8th century, ruled much of Spain for almost 800 years, and their influence can still be seen in Spanish culture. Portugal has modernized its economy since joining the European Union, and both countries have changed their currencies to the euro.

INDUSTRY

Madrid, Barcelona, and the northern ports are Spain's industrial centers. Here, iron ore from Spanish mines is used to make steel, and factories produce cars, machinery, and chemicals. Portugal exports textiles, clothing, and footwear, along with fish, such as sardines and tuna, caught off the Atlantic coast. In both countries, tourism is very important to the economy.

STRUCTURE OF INDUSTRY

Primary 4%
Services 67%
Manufacturing 29%

INDUSTRY

✈ Aerospace	👕 Textiles
🚗 Car manufacture	⛏ Mining
💧 Chemicals	🏛 Tourism
⚙ Engineering	▥ Publishing
🖥 Fish processing	
⚓ Shipbuilding	▪ Major industrial center / area
🏭 Steel	— Major road

POPULATION

In the first half of the 20th century, most Spaniards lived in villages or small towns scattered around the country. Today, tourism and industry have drawn most of the population to the cities and coastal areas. Most Portuguese live in cities, but one third still live in rural areas along the coast or in the river valleys.

URBAN/RURAL POPULATION DIVISION

Barcelona 3%
Lisbon 1%
Madrid 6%
Other towns and cities 65%
Rural population 25%

INHABITANTS PER SQ MILE

▓ More than 520	▪ Capital city
▒ 260–520	● Major city
░ 130–260	
░ Less than 130	

FARMING AND LAND USE

Cereals, especially wheat and barley, are Iberia's chief crops. In the dry south of Spain, the land is irrigated to citrus fruits, particularly oranges, and a variety of vegetables. In both countries, olive trees and vineyards occupy large areas of land; olive oil and wine are important exports. Cork oak trees from Iberia's forests supply 80% of the world's cork.

FARMING AND LAND USE

🐟 Fishing	♦ Cork
🐑 Sheep	
🌾 Cereals	░ Pasture
🍋 Citrus fruit	░ Cropland
🐂 Market gardening	▓ Forest
🫒 Olive oil	░ Mountain region
🍇 Vineyards	● Major conurbation

LAND USE

Other 10%
Cropland 39%
Forest 33%
Pasture 18%

THE LANDSCAPE

Most of inland Spain is taken up by the Meseta, a dry, almost treeless plateau surrounded by steep mountain ranges. The only lowlands, apart from narrow strips along the Mediterranean coast, are the valleys of the Ebro, Tagus, Guadiana, and Guadalquivir Rivers. Portugal's coast is lined by wide plains. Inland, the Tagus River divides the country in two. To the north the land is hilly and wooded; to the south it is low-lying and drier.

Westward-flowing rivers
The Duero, Tagus, and Guadalquivir Rivers flow across the Meseta on their courses to the Atlantic Ocean.

Ebro River (E 2)
The Ebro River carries vital irrigation water to Spain's northeastern plains before flowing into the Mediterranean Sea.

River Duero (D 2)

Cordillera Cantábrica (C 1)
These rugged, forested mountains rise on Spain's Atlantic coast. They form the northern edge of the Meseta.

The Pyrenees (F 2)
These high mountains form a natural boundary with France.

River Tagus (B 4)

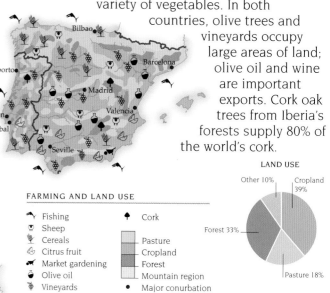

The Meseta
Much of this vast plateau of ancient rock is covered with dry, dusty high plains. It has thin soils and is mainly used to graze sheep and goats.

Sierra Morena (C 5)
The southern end of the Meseta is marked by this low range of mountains.

Guadalquivir Basin (C 5)
The Guadalquivir River has deposited layers of rich soil called alluvium on its floodplain, making this one of Spain's most fertile regions.

Mulhacén (D 5)
Mulhacén, in the snow-capped Sierra Nevada range in southern Spain, is 11,421 ft high. It is Iberia's tallest mountain.

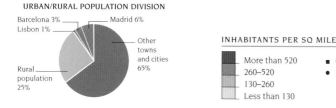

ENVIRONMENTAL ISSUES

Soil erosion – where the top layer of soil has been worn away by wind and rain – has affected much of the Iberian Peninsula. This is caused by farming, combined with drought and deforestation. In Spain, a national tree-planting program has been started to combat this problem. Industrial and tourist development along the Mediterranean coast of Spain and in the Balearic Islands has damaged natural habitats on both land and sea.

ENVIRONMENTAL ISSUES

- ⚓ Major oil spill
- 🏢 Overbuilding
- Soil degradation
- Severe soil degradation
- Polluted rivers
- Sea pollution

CLIMATE

Northern Spain is wetter and cooler than the south. On the central plateau, summers are very hot and dry, and winters often freezing. The north of Portugal is cooled by winds blowing off the Atlantic Ocean. The south is warmer, with dry, mild winters.

TEMPERATURE AND PRECIPITATION

- More than 77°F
- 68 to 77°F
- 59 to 68°F
- 50 to 59°F
- 41 to 50°F
- 32 to 41°F
- 23 to 32°F
- 14 to 23°F
- Less than 14°F

4 — Precipitation (in)

EUROPE
Spain and Portugal

January

July

LAND HEIGHT
- 6,560–13,120ft
- 3,280–6,560ft
- 1,640–3,280ft
- 820–1,640ft
- 330–820ft
- 0–330ft

SEA DEPTH
- 0–820ft
- 820–1,640ft
- 1,640–3,280ft
- 3,280–6,560ft
- 6,560–9,840ft
- 9,840–13,120ft
- Below 13,120ft

CITIES AND TOWNS
- ● Over 500,000 people
- ◉ 100,000–500,000
- ○ 50,000–100,000
- ○ Less than 50,000

SCALE BAR

0 km   50   100

0 miles   50   100

GERMANY AND THE ALPINE STATES

AUSTRIA, GERMANY, LIECHTENSTEIN, SLOVENIA, SWITZERLAND

Germany lies at the heart of Europe and is the biggest industrial power in the continent. In 1945, Germany was divided into two separate countries, East and West Germany, which were reunited in 1990. To the south, the snow-capped peaks of the Alps, Europe's highest mountains, tower over the Alpine states – Switzerland, Austria, Liechtenstein, and the former Yugoslavian state of Slovenia.

INDUSTRY

Germany is a leading manufacturer of cars, chemicals, machinery, and transportation equipment. Switzerland and Liechtenstein make high-value products such as watches and pharmaceuticals and provide services such as banking. The Alpine states are a popular tourist location year-round.

INDUSTRY

- ✈ Aerospace
- 🚗 Car manufacture
- 🧪 Chemicals
- ⚙ Engineering
- 🏭 Iron & steel
- 🚢 Shipbuilding
- 💊 Pharmaceuticals
- Ⓢ Finance
- 🖥 Hi-tech industry
- 🎡 Tourism

□ Major industrial center / area

— Major road

STRUCTURE OF INDUSTRY

Primary 1% Services 68%

Manufacturing 31%

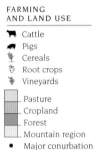
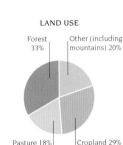

POPULATION

Western and central Germany are the most densely populated areas in this region – particularly in and around the Rhine and Ruhr valleys, where there are many industries. In the south, the steep slopes of the Alps and permanent snow cover on the higher peaks means that most large towns and cities are in scattered lowland areas.

INHABITANTS PER SQ MILE

- More than 520
- 260–520
- 130–260
- Less than 130
- ■ Capital city
- ● Major city

URBAN/RURAL POPULATION DIVISION

Hamburg 1.8% Berlin 3.5%
Vienna 1.7%

Rural population 16%

Other towns and cities 77%

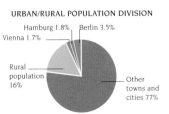

FARMING AND LAND USE

Germany produces three-quarters of its own food. Crop farming is widespread, with cereals and root crops grown in flat, fertile areas. Cattle and pig farming supplies meat and dairy products. Across the Alps, the mountains limit farming, although grapes are grown on the warmer, south-facing slopes. The rich pastures of the lower slopes are used to graze beef and dairy cattle.

FARMING AND LAND USE

- 🐄 Cattle
- 🐖 Pigs
- 🌾 Cereals
- 🌱 Root crops
- 🍇 Vineyards

Pasture
Cropland
Forest
Mountain region
● Major conurbation

LAND USE

Forest 33% Other (including mountains) 20%

Pasture 18% Cropland 29%

THE LANDSCAPE

To the north, flat plains and heathlands surround the North Sea coast. Farther south are Germany's central uplands, which are lower and older than the jagged peaks of the Alps, which began to form about 65 million years ago. From its source in the Black Forest, the Danube River flows eastward across Germany and Austria on its course to the Black Sea. The other major river, the Rhine, flows northward.

Harz mountains (C4)
These rugged, wooded mountains are much older than the Alps. They were formed over 300 million years ago.

Rhine River (B5)
The Rhine is Germany's main waterway. It is an important transportation route to and from northern ports. It twists and turns across 820 miles of Europe, from its source in southeast Switzerland, to the North Sea.

Karst region (E8)
Most of the water in this limestone region of Slovenia flows underground, through huge caves and caverns.

Danube River (B7)
The Danube is Europe's second-longest river, flowing 1,765 miles.

Lake Constance (B7)
Lake Constance covers 210 sq miles and is Germany's largest lake, although its waters are shared by Austria and Switzerland.

Alps (C8)
The Alps were formed when the African Plate collided with the Eurasian Plate, pushing up and crushing huge amounts of rock, to form mountains.

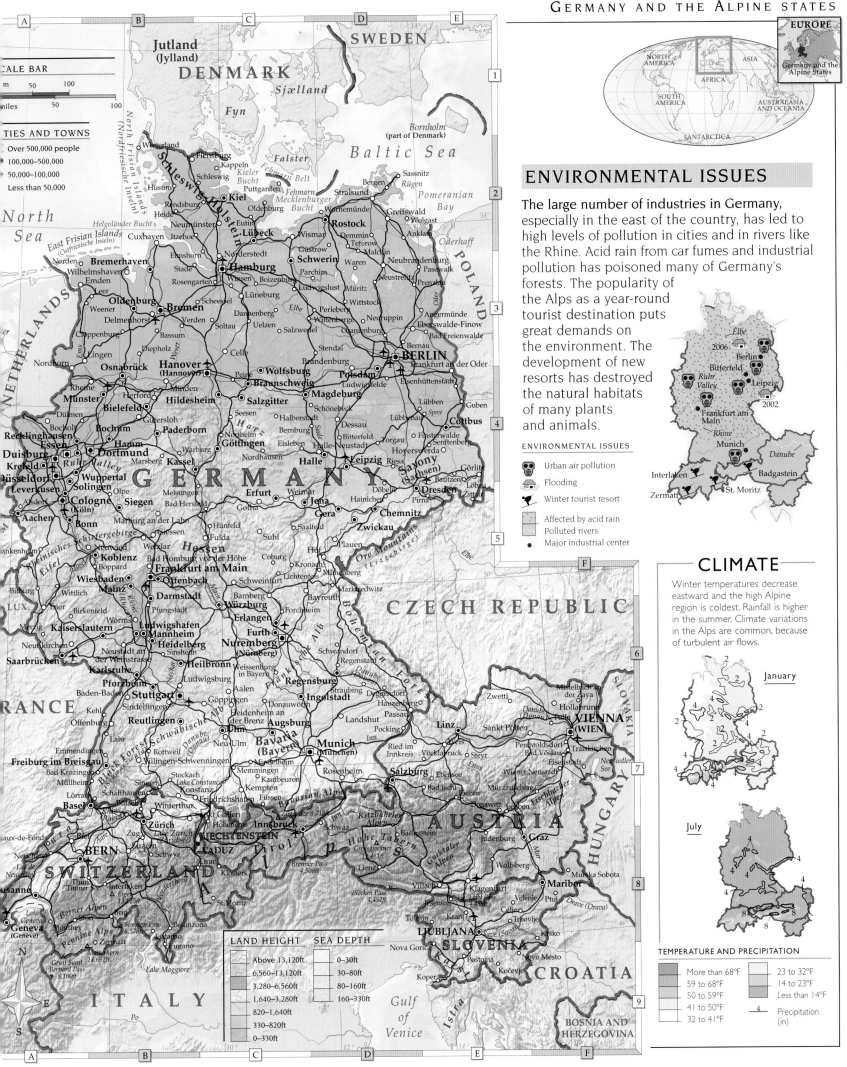

EUROPE
Germany and the Alpine States

ENVIRONMENTAL ISSUES

The large number of industries in Germany, especially in the east of the country, has led to high levels of pollution in cities and in rivers like the Rhine. Acid rain from car fumes and industrial pollution has poisoned many of Germany's forests. The popularity of the Alps as a year-round tourist destination puts great demands on the environment. The development of new resorts has destroyed the natural habitats of many plants and animals.

ENVIRONMENTAL ISSUES

- Urban air pollution
- Flooding
- Winter tourist resort
- Affected by acid rain
- Polluted rivers
- Major industrial center

CLIMATE

Winter temperatures decrease eastward and the high Alpine region is coldest. Rainfall is higher in the summer. Climate variations in the Alps are common, because of turbulent air flows.

January

July

TEMPERATURE AND PRECIPITATION

Temperature	
More than 68°F	23 to 32°F
59 to 68°F	14 to 23°F
50 to 59°F	Less than 14°F
41 to 50°F	
32 to 41°F	—4— Precipitation (in)

Map labels

SCALE BAR

CITIES AND TOWNS
- Over 500,000 people
- 100,000–500,000
- 50,000–100,000
- Less than 50,000

LAND HEIGHT
- Above 13,120ft
- 6,560–13,120ft
- 3,280–6,560ft
- 1,640–3,280ft
- 820–1,640ft
- 330–820ft
- 0–330ft

SEA DEPTH
- 0–30ft
- 30–80ft
- 80–160ft
- 160–330ft

ITALY

ITALY, SAN MARINO, VATICAN CITY

Italy has played an important role in Europe since the Romans based their mighty empire here over 2,000 years ago. The famous boot shape divides into two very different halves. Northern Italy has a varied range of industries and agriculture. Beautiful cities like Venice, Florence, and Rome draw tourists from all over the world. Southern Italy is poorer and less developed than the north, with a hotter, drier climate and less productive land.

THE LANDSCAPE

Italy is a peninsula jutting south from mainland Europe into the Mediterranean Sea. In northern and central Italy the land is mainly mountainous. Most of the flat land is in the Po Valley and along the eastern coast. Italy lies within an earthquake zone, which makes the land unstable, and there are also a number of active volcanoes.

Po Valley (C 2)
The basin of the Po River has the best soils in Italy. Rich alluvium is washed from the mountains by the river to form a wide plain.

Italian lakes
Great lakes like Garda (B3) and Como (B2) fill several south-facing valleys once occupied by glaciers.

The Dolomites (D 2)
These high mountains are part of the same range as the Alps. They were formed 65 million years ago.

The Apennines (C 4)
This mountain range forms the "backbone" of Italy, dividing the rocky west coast from the flatter, sandy east coast.

Tyrrhenian Sea (C 6)
This sea, which divides the Italian mainland from Sardinia, is gradually filling with sediment from the rivers which flow into it.

Earthquakes
The southern Apennines, as well as coastal areas of southwestern Italy, often experience earthquakes and mudslides.

Sardinia
The island of Sardinia is made from very old rocks that were thrust up to form mountains.

Sicily
Sicily is the largest island in the Mediterranean. It has a famous active volcano called Mount Etna and often experiences earthquakes.

Gulf of Taranto (F 7)
During earthquakes, great blocks of land have broken away and sunk into the sea, forming the Gulf's square shape.

FARMING AND LAND USE

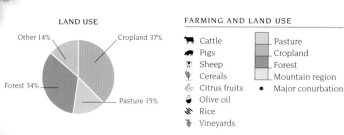

The Po Valley is a broad, flat plain in the north of Italy. It contains the most fertile land in the country, and wheat and rice are the main cereal crops grown here. Grapes for wine are grown everywhere in Italy. In much of the south, the land must be irrigated to support crops. Where there is enough water, citrus fruits, olives, and many kinds of tomatoes are grown.

LAND USE

- Other 14%
- Cropland 37%
- Forest 34%
- Pasture 15%

FARMING AND LAND USE

- Cattle
- Pigs
- Sheep
- Cereals
- Citrus fruits
- Olive oil
- Rice
- Vineyards

- Pasture
- Cropland
- Forest
- Mountain region
- Major conurbation

INDUSTRY

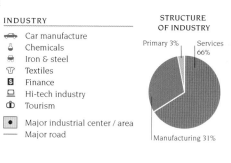

Italian industry is located mainly in the north. Design is extremely important to Italians, and they are proud of the elegant designs of their furniture, clothes, and shoes. Although many firms are small, they are very efficient. Italy has few mineral resources, so it needs to import raw materials to make cars, engines, and other high-tech products.

INDUSTRY

- Car manufacture
- Chemicals
- Iron & steel
- Textiles
- Finance
- Hi-tech industry
- Tourism
- Major industrial center / area
- Major road

STRUCTURE OF INDUSTRY

- Primary 3%
- Services 66%
- Manufacturing 31%

POPULATION

Most of Italy's population lives in the north, mainly in and around the Po Valley, which is home to over 25 million people. Most people here have a high standard of living. Southern Italy is much more rural: towns are smaller and life is often much harder.

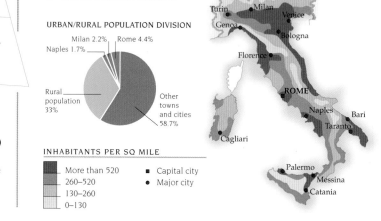

URBAN/RURAL POPULATION DIVISION

- Milan 2.2%
- Rome 4.4%
- Naples 1.7%
- Rural population 33%
- Other towns and cities 58.7%

INHABITANTS PER SQ MILE

- More than 520
- 260–520
- 130–260
- 0–130
- Capital city
- Major city

ITALY

ENVIRONMENTAL ISSUES

Sewage and chemical by-products from industry have polluted the Mediterranean and Adriatic Seas. Southern Italy is subject to natural dangers like volcanoes, earthquakes, and mudslides. Mount Etna is one of the most active volcanoes in the world.

ENVIRONMENTAL ISSUES

- ◉ Catastrophic earthquakes
- 😷 Urban air pollution
- Affected by acid rain
- Sea pollution
- Severe sea pollution
- • Major industrial center

CLIMATE

The Alpine north has cold winters, often with snow. Farther south, temperatures are higher. Sicily has Italy's highest temperatures, because of the warm African winds.

January

July

TEMPERATURE AND PRECIPITATION

- More than 77°F
- 68 to 77°F
- 59 to 68°F
- 50 to 59°F
- 41 to 50°F
- 32 to 41°F
- 23 to 32°F
- 14 to 23°F
- Less than 14°F

—4— Precipitation (in)

LAND HEIGHT
- Above 13,120ft
- 6,560–13,120ft
- 3,280–6,560ft
- 1,640–3,280ft
- 820–1,640ft
- 330–820ft
- 0–330ft

SEA DEPTH
- 0–160ft
- 160–330ft
- 330–820ft
- 820–1,640ft
- 1,640–3,280ft
- 3,280–6,560ft
- Below 6,560ft

SCALE BAR
0 km   40   80
0 miles   40   80

CITIES AND TOWNS
- ◉ Over 500,000 people
- ◉ 100,000–500,000
- ○ 50,000–100,000
- ○ Less than 50,000

CENTRAL EUROPE

CZECH REPUBLIC, HUNGARY, POLAND, SLOVAKIA

Central Europe has been invaded many times throughout history. The countries have changed shape frequently as their borders have shifted back and forth. From the end of World War Two until 1989, they were ruled by communist governments, which were supported by the Soviet Union. In 1993, the state of Czechoslovakia voted to split into two separate nations, called the Czech Republic and Slovakia.

INDUSTRY

Brown coal, or lignite, is central Europe's main fuel, and one of Poland's major exports. A variety of minerals are mined in the mountains of the Czech Republic and Slovakia. Hungary has a wide range of industries producing vehicles, metals, and chemicals, as well as textiles and electrical goods. The Czech Republic is famous for its breweries and glass-making.

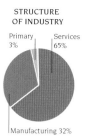

STRUCTURE
OF INDUSTRY

Primary 3%
Services 65%
Manufacturing 32%

INDUSTRY

- 🍶 Brewing
- 🚗 Car manufacturing
- 🧪 Chemicals
- ⚙ Engineering
- 📦 Food processing
- 🚆 Iron and steel
- ⛏ Coal mining
- ▣ Major industrial center / area
- — Major road

ENVIRONMENTAL ISSUES

The growth of heavy industries that took place under communist rule has caused terrible environmental pollution in some places. Hungary's oil and Poland's brown coal have a high sulfur content. Burning these fuels to produce electricity causes air pollution, and the sulfur dioxide produced combines with moisture in the air, leading to acid rain.

ENVIRONMENTAL
ISSUES

- ☁ Severe industrial pollution
- 🏠 Flooding
- 💀 Urban air pollution
- ░ Affected by acid rain
- Polluted rivers
- • Major industrial center

FARMING AND LAND USE

Central Europe's main crops are cereals such as corn, wheat and rye, along with sugar beets and potatoes. Sweet peppers grow in Hungary, helped by the warm summers and mild winters. They are used to make paprika. Grapes are also grown, to make wine. Large areas of the plains of Hungary and Poland are used for rearing pigs and cattle. Trees for timber grow in the mountains of Slovakia and the Czech Republic.

LAND USE

FARMING AND LAND USE

- 🐄 Cattle
- 🐖 Pigs
- 🌾 Cereals
- 🌱 Root crops
- 🥔 Potatoes
- 🌲 Timber
- 🍇 Vineyards

- ░ Pasture
- ▨ Cropland
- ▓ Forest
- • Major conurbation

Other 11%
Cropland 47%
Forest 29%
Pasture 13%

THE LANDSCAPE

The high Carpathian Mountains sweep across northern Slovakia. The lower Sudeten Mountains lie on the border of the Czech Republic and Poland. Together, these mountains form a barrier that divides the Great Hungarian Plain and the Danube River basin in the south from Poland and the vast rolling lowlands of the North European Plain.

Pomerania (C 2)
This is a sandy coastal area with lakes formed by glaciers. It stretches west from the River Vistula to just beyond the German border.

Vistula River (F 4)
Poland's largest river is the Vistula. It flows northward, passing through the capital, Warsaw, on its way to the Baltic Sea.

North European Plain

Hot springs
The Sudeten mountains (C5) are famous for their hot mineral springs. These occur where water heated deep within the Earth's crust finds its way to the surface along fractures in the rock.

Danube River (D 7)
The Danube River forms the border between Slovakia and Hungary for over 100 miles. It then turns south to flow across the Great Hungarian Plain.

Great Hungarian Plain (E 8)
This huge plain covers almost half of Hungary's land area. It is a mixture of farmland and steppe.

Tatra Mountains (E 6)
The Tatra Mountains are a small range at the northern end of the Carpathian Mountains. They include Gerlachovsky Stít, which is Central Europe's highest point at 8,711 ft.

POPULATION

Most people in central Europe live in low-lying areas – for example, along the Vistula River in Poland, and in the lowlands of the Czech Republic. In mountainous Slovakia, many people still live in rural towns and villages. The industrial areas and capital cities have the highest population densities.

URBAN/RURAL POPULATION DIVISION

Warsaw 2.6% Budapest 2.7%
Prague 1.7%
Rural population 34%
Other towns and cities 59%

INHABITANTS PER SQ MILE

- More than 520
- 260–520
- 130–260
- Less than 130
- ■ Capital city
- ● Major city

CLIMATE

The Carpathian Mountains are both the coldest and the wettest part of central Europe. Temperatures plunge below freezing across the whole region during winter. In summer, eastern Hungary is the hottest place.

January

July

TEMPERATURE AND PRECIPITATION

- More than 68°F
- 59 to 68°F
- 50 to 59°F
- 41 to 50°F
- 32 to 41°F
- 23 to 32°F
- Less than 23°F
- — 4 — Precipitation (in)

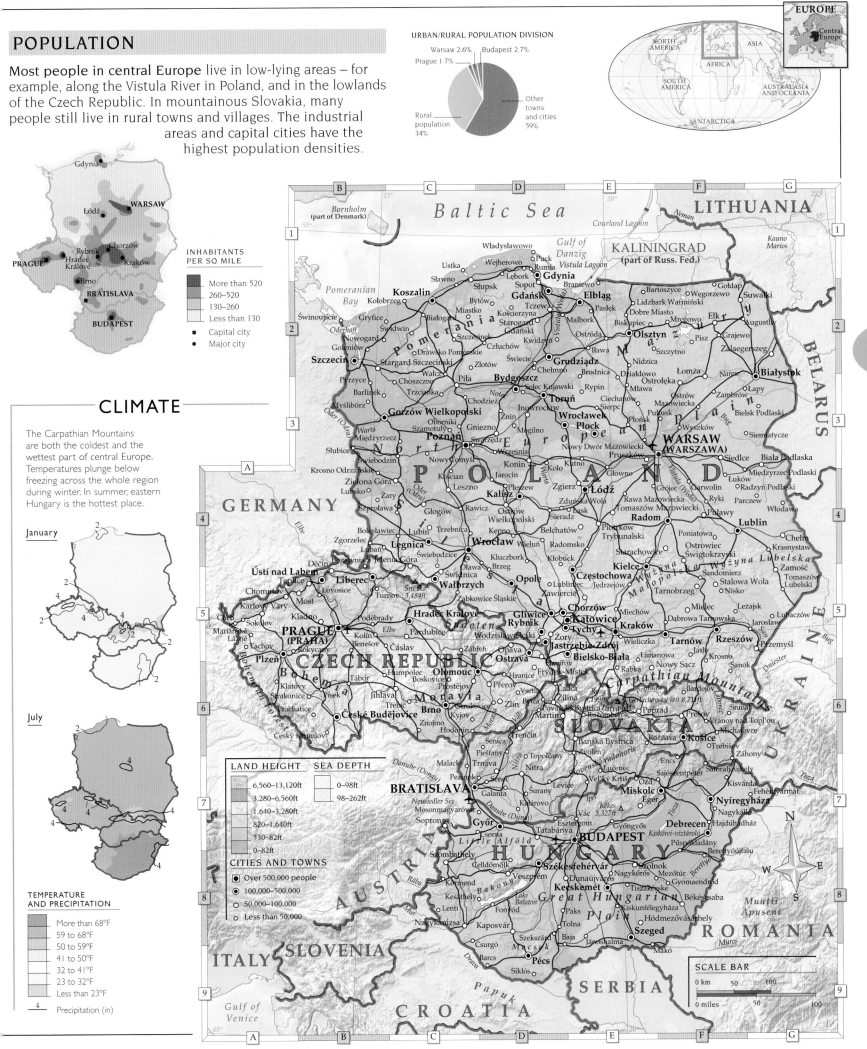

LAND HEIGHT
- 6,560–13,120ft
- 3,280–6,560ft
- 1,640–3,280ft
- 820–1,640ft
- 330–82ft
- 0–82ft

SEA DEPTH
- 0–98ft
- 98–262ft

CITIES AND TOWNS
- ◉ Over 500,000 people
- ◎ 100,000–500,000
- ○ 50,000–100,000
- · Less than 50,000

SCALE BAR
0 km   50   100
0 miles   50   100

105

SOUTHEAST EUROPE

ALBANIA, BOSNIA AND HERZEGOVINA, BULGARIA, CROATIA, GREECE, KOSOVO, MACEDONIA, MONTENEGRO, SERBIA

Southeast Europe extends inland from the coasts of the Aegean, Adriatic, and Black Seas. Ancient Greece was the birthplace of European civilization. Albania and Bulgaria were ruled by communists for over 50 years, until the early 1990s. The rest of the region was part of a communist union of states called Yugoslavia. The collapse of this union in 1991 led to a civil war, after which seven separate countries emerged.

THE LANDSCAPE

Southeast Europe is largely mountainous, with ranges running from northwest to southeast. The Dinaric Alps run parallel to the Dalmatian coast, and the Pindus Mountains continue this line into Greece. In the Aegean Sea, the drowned peaks of an old mountain chain form thousands of islands.

Earthquakes
Bulgaria, Greece, and Macedonia lie in earthquake zones. Major earthquakes have hit the Ionian Islands in 1953 and Macedonia in 1963.

Great Hungarian Plain (D 1)
The Vojvodina region of Serbia is the southern part of the Great Hungarian Plain. The plain is flat, and fertile soil enables crops like corn and wheat to be grown.

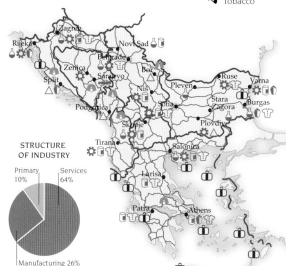

STRUCTURE OF INDUSTRY

Primary 10%
Services 64%
Manufacturing 26%

Dinaric Alps (C 2)

Balkan Mountains (F 3)
The mountains form a spur running east to west through Bulgaria and separate the two main rivers, the Danube and the Maritsa.

Dalmatian coast (B 2)
The Dalmatian coast has many long, narrow islands near the shore. These were formed as the Adriatic Sea flooded the river valleys that ran parallel to the coast.

Greek Islands

The Peloponnese (E 6)
The Peloponnese is a mountainous peninsula linked to the Greek mainland only by a narrow strip of land, only 4 miles wide, called the Isthmus of Corinth.

Greek Islands
There are two groups of Greek Islands, the Ionian Islands to the west of mainland Greece, and the more numerous islands to the east in the Aegean Sea.

FARMING AND LAND USE

Cereals like wheat, and fruits, vegetables, and grapes are grown in the fertile north of the region. The band of mountains across southeast Europe is used mainly for grazing sheep and goats. Farther south, and in coastal areas, the warm Mediterranean climate is ideal for growing grapes, olives, and tobacco.

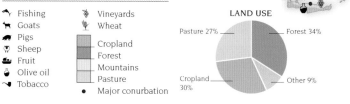

FARMING AND LAND USE

- Fishing
- Goats
- Pigs
- Sheep
- Fruit
- Olive oil
- Tobacco
- Vineyards
- Wheat
  - Cropland
  - Forest
  - Mountains
  - Pasture
- Major conurbation

LAND USE

Pasture 27%
Forest 34%
Cropland 30%
Other 9%

INDUSTRY

Mainland Greece and the many islands in the Aegean Sea are centers of a thriving tourist trade, while tourism on the Black Sea coast continues to grow. The Dalmatian coast's growing tourist industry is recovering, after the civil war in former Yugoslavia disrupted it, and other industries. Heavy industries like chemicals, engineering, and shipbuilding remain an important source of income in Bulgaria.

INDUSTRY

- Car manufacture
- Chemicals
- Engineering
- Food processing
- Metal refining
- Shipbuilding
- Textiles
- Mining
- Tourism
- Major industrial center / area
- Major road

POPULATION

Greece's population is two thirds urban; over 35% live in the capital, Athens, and in Salonica. In Bulgaria, most people live in cities. About half of Albania's and Macedonia's people are still rural. Since the civil war, the different ethnic groups in Bosnia and Herzegovina, Montenegro, Serbia, and Croatia have lived apart from one another.

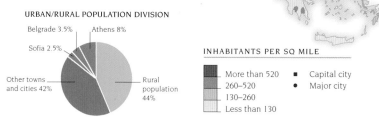

URBAN/RURAL POPULATION DIVISION

Belgrade 3.5%
Athens 8%
Sofia 2.5%
Other towns and cities 42%
Rural population 44%

INHABITANTS PER SQ MILE

- More than 520
- 260–520
- 130–260
- Less than 130
- Capital city
- Major city

CLIMATE

Southeastern Europe's climate varies from north to south. Continental climates are found in the north; winters are cold and dry, while toward the south, winters are milder and summers much hotter. Europe's wettest place is found in the mountains in Bosnia and Herzegovina.

January

July

TEMPERATURE AND PRECIPITATION

More than 77°F
68 to 77°F
59 to 68°F
50 to 59°F
41 to 50°F
32 to 41°F
23 to 32°F
Less than 23°F

4 ——— Precipitation (in)

EUROPE

Southeast Europe

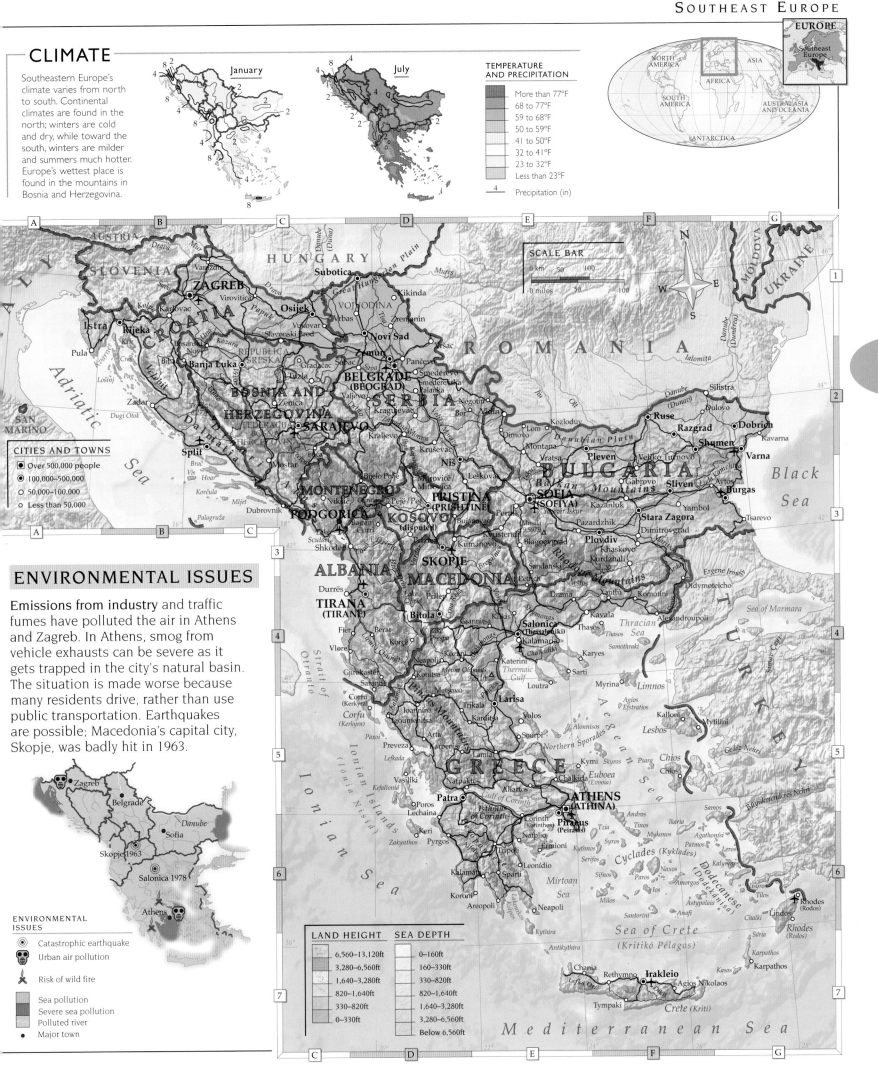

CITIES AND TOWNS

- ▪ Over 500,000 people
- ⊙ 100,000–500,000
- ○ 50,000–100,000
- ∘ Less than 50,000

ENVIRONMENTAL ISSUES

Emissions from industry and traffic fumes have polluted the air in Athens and Zagreb. In Athens, smog from vehicle exhausts can be severe as it gets trapped in the city's natural basin. The situation is made worse because many residents drive, rather than use public transportation. Earthquakes are possible; Macedonia's capital city, Skopje, was badly hit in 1963.

ENVIRONMENTAL ISSUES

- ◉ Catastrophic earthquake
- 😷 Urban air pollution
- ✖ Risk of wild fire
- Sea pollution
- Severe sea pollution
- Polluted river
- • Major town

LAND HEIGHT

- 6,560–13,120ft
- 3,280–6,560ft
- 1,640–3,280ft
- 820–1,640ft
- 330–820ft
- 0–330ft

SEA DEPTH

- 0–160ft
- 160–330ft
- 330–820ft
- 820–1,640ft
- 1,640–3,280ft
- 3,280–6,560ft
- Below 6,560ft

EASTERN EUROPE

BELARUS, MOLDOVA, ROMANIA, UKRAINE

Much of Eastern Europe, which extends north from the Danube River and the Black Sea, is covered by open grasslands called steppe. Ukraine, Moldova, and Belarus were all part of the former Soviet Union, until they became independent in 1991. Romania joined the European Union in 2007. In 2014, Russia drew international condemnation for annexing the Ukrainian territory of Crimea.

INDUSTRY

In Ukraine, most industry is based around the country's mineral reserves. The Donbass region has Europe's largest coalfield and is an important center for iron and steel production. The main industries of Belarus are chemicals, machine building, and food-processing. Romania's manufacturing industries are growing, with the help of foreign investment.

INDUSTRY

- ✈ Aerospace
- 🚗 Car manufacture
- ⚗ Chemicals
- ⚙ Engineering
- ▣ Food processing
- ⚒ Iron & steel
- 👕 Textiles
- ⛏ Coal
- ⚒ Mining
- ◔ Oil and gas
- ⛴ Tourism

▣	Major industrial center / area
—	Major road

STRUCTURE OF INDUSTRY

Primary 15%   Manufacturing 42%

Services 43%

FARMING AND LAND USE

The black soils found across much of Ukraine are very fertile and the country is a big producer of cereals, sugar beets, and sunflowers, which are grown for their oil. In Moldova and southern Romania, the warm summers are ideal for growing grapes for wine, along with sunflowers and a variety of vegetables. Cattle and pigs are farmed throughout Eastern Europe.

LAND USE

Other 11%

Forest 24%

Pasture 15%

Cropland 50%

FARMING AND LAND USE

- 🐄 Cattle
- 🐖 Pigs
- 🐑 Sheep
- Root crops
- Sunflowers
- Vineyards
- Wheat

▨	Cropland
▨	Forest
▨	Pasture
▨	Wetland
●	Major conurbation

POPULATION

Many Romanians still live in rural areas, although Bucharest, the capital, is home to six times as many people as the next largest city. In Ukraine, two-thirds of the population live in cities such as those in the Donbass industrial area. Most of Belarus's people are city dwellers. Moldova is the most rural country in Eastern Europe; over half live in the countryside.

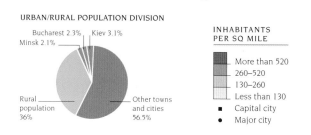

URBAN/RURAL POPULATION DIVISION

Bucharest 2.3%   Kiev 3.1%
Minsk 2.1%

Rural population 36%

Other towns and cities 56.5%

INHABITANTS PER SQ MILE

- More than 520
- 260–520
- 130–260
- Less than 130
- ■ Capital city
- ● Major city

THE LANDSCAPE

Flat or rolling grasslands, marshes, and river flood plains cover almost all of Ukraine and Belarus. The Carpathian Mountains cross the southwestern corner of Ukraine and continue in a large arc-shaped chain of high peaks at the heart of Romania. Along the southern part of this chain, the Carpathians are called the Transylvanian Alps.

Pripet Marshes (C 3)
The Pripet Marshes in Belarus and Ukraine form the largest area of marshland in Europe.

The steppes
The steppes are great, wide grasslands that are found across eastern Europe and central Asia. Over 70% of the Ukrainian landscape is steppe. Little rain falls throughout the steppes.

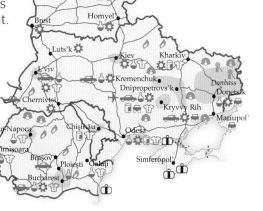

Carpathian Mountains (C 5)
The Carpathians are the largest mountain range in Eastern Europe. They are a rich source of timber and minerals.

Dnieper (E 5) and Dniester (D 5) Rivers
The Dnieper and Dniester run south and east toward the Black Sea. They flow slowly across huge areas of low-lying land.

The Crimea (F 6)
This peninsula divides the Sea of Azov from the Black Sea. The steep mountains of Kryms'ki Hory run along the southeastern coast of the Crimea.

CLIMATE

January

July

The climate is continental, with warm, dry summers and very cold, dry winters. Temperatures are higher along the fringes of the Black Sea, while the Carpathian Mountains are colder and wetter all year round.

TEMPERATURE AND PRECIPITATION

More than 68°F
59 to 68°F
50 to 59°F
41 to 50°F
32 to 41°F
23 to 32°F
Less than 23°F
4 — Precipitation (in)

Less than 2
2
Less than 2
2
4
4
2
2
2
2
4
2

ENVIRONMENTAL ISSUES

The worst nuclear accident in history happened at Chornobyl nuclear power plant in northern Ukraine in 1986. Around 70% of the nuclear fallout was received by Belarus, contaminating its farmland, forests, and water supplies. Four million Ukrainians still live in dangerously radioactive areas.

ENVIRONMENTAL ISSUES

Destroyed nuclear reactor
Levels of nuclear fallout
Very high
High
Moderate
Urban air pollution
Flooding
Polluted river
Sea pollution
Major industrial center

Minsk
Chornobyl
Kiev
Kharkiv
Dnipropetrovs'k
Donets'k
Târgu Mures
Arad
2005
Bucharest
Volganeft-139 2007

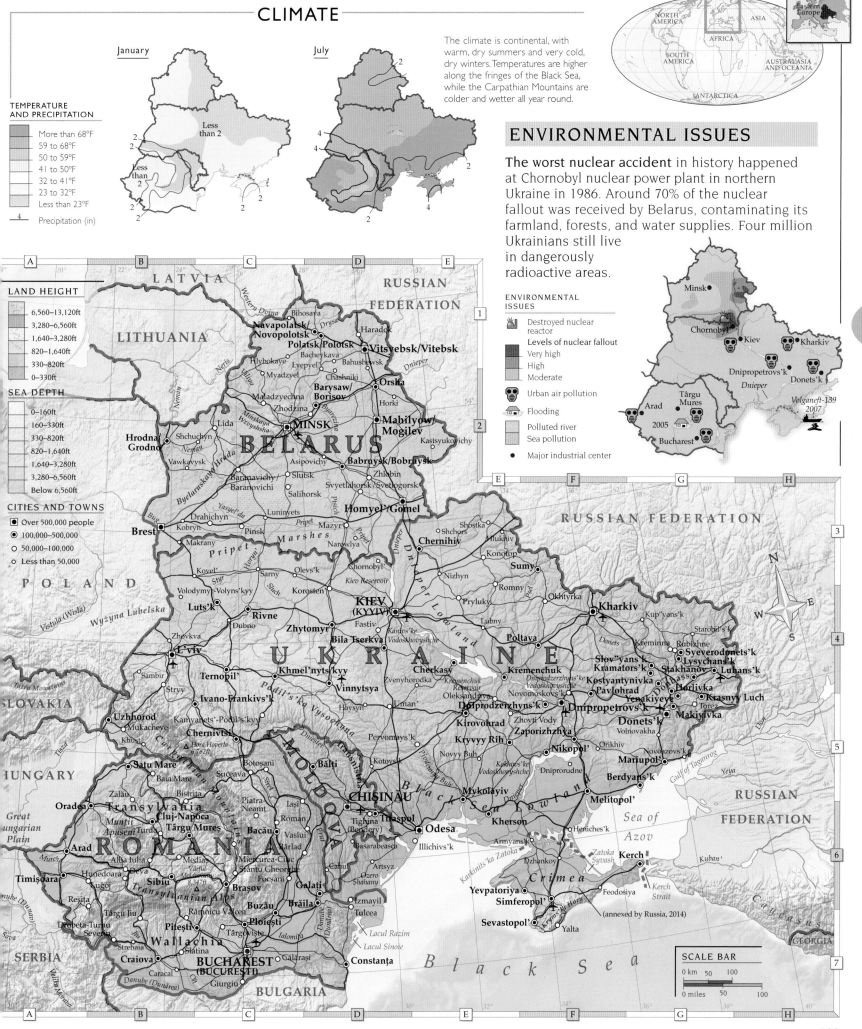

LAND HEIGHT

6,560–13,120ft
3,280–6,560ft
1,640–3,280ft
820–1,640ft
330–820ft
0–330ft

SEA DEPTH

0–160ft
160–330ft
330–820ft
820–1,640ft
1,640–3,280ft
3,280–6,560ft
Below 6,560ft

CITIES AND TOWNS

■ Over 500,000 people
● 100,000–500,000
○ 50,000–100,000
○ Less than 50,000

LATVIA
LITHUANIA
RUSSIAN FEDERATION
POLAND
SLOVAKIA
HUNGARY
SERBIA

Navapolatsk/Novopolotsk
Polatsk/Polotsk
Haradok
Vitsyebsk/Vitebsk
Bacheykava
Bahushewsk
Hlybokaye
Lyepyel'
Myadzyel
Chashniki
Orsha
Horki
Maladzyechna
Barysaw/Borisov
Zhodzina
MINSK
Mahilyow/Mogilev
Lida
Shchuchyn
Hrodna/Grodno
Vawkavysk
Asipovichy
Babruysk/Bobruysk
Kastsyukovichy
Baranavichy/Baranovichi
Slutsk
Svyetlahorsk/Svetlogorsk
Zhlobin
Salihorsk
BELARUS
Drahichyn
Kobryn
Luninyets
Pinsk
Homyel'/Gomel
Brest
Makrany
Mazyr
Narowlya
Pripet Marshes
Kovel'
Sarny
Olevs'k
Korosten
Chornobyl'
Shchors
Chernihiv
Shostka
Hlukhiv
RUSSIAN FEDERATION
Volodymyr-Volyns'kyy
Dubno
Konotop
Sumy
Luts'k
Rivne
Zhytomyr
Kiev Reservoir
Nizhyn
Romny
Pryluky
Okhtyrka
Kharkiv
Kup"yans'k
L'viv
Ternopil'
Fastiv
KIEV (KYYIV)
Bila Tserkva
Kaniv'ske Vodoskhovyshche
Lubny
Starobil's'k
Sambir
Khmel'nyts'kyy
Zhvavka
Poltava
Kreminna
Rubizhne
Syeverodonets'k
Lysychans'k
Stryy
Vinnytsya
Zvenyhorodka
Cherkasy
Kremenchuk
Slov"yans'k
Kramators'k
Stakhanov
Luhans'k
Ivano-Frankivs'k
Uman'
Kremenchuk Reservoir
Novomoskovs'k
Kostyantynivka
Pavlohrad
Horlivka
Yenakiyeve
Krasnyy Luch
Uzhhorod
Mukacheve
Khust
Kamyanets'-Podil's'kyy
Dniprodzerzhyns'k
Dnipropetrovs'k
Donets'k
Makiyivka
Torez
Chernivtsi
Hora Hoverla 6,762ft
Haysyn
Kirovohrad
Zhovti Vody
Zaporizhzhya
Volnovakha
Orikhiv
Novoazovs'k
Satu Mare
Baia Mare
Botosani
Suceava
Bălți
Kotovs'k
Pervomays'k
Novyy Buh
Kryvyy Rih
Nikopol'
Mariupol'
Zalău
Bistrita
Piatra Neamt
Iasi
Roman
Kakhovs'ke Vodoskhovyshche
Dniprorudne
Berdyans'k
Gulf of Taganrog
Yeya
Oradea
Transylvania
Cluj-Napoca
Târgu Mures
Bacău
Vaslui
CHISINAU
Tighina (Bendery)
Tiraspol'
Mykolayiv
Melitopol'
MOLDOVA
Muntii Apuseni
Turda
Alba Iulia
Medias
Sighisoara
Miercurea-Ciuc
Sfântu Gheorghe
Focsani
Bârlad
Vârful Moldoveanu 8,347ft
Basarabeasca
Odesa
Kherson
Heniches'k
Sea of Azov
RUSSIAN FEDERATION
Great Hungarian Plain
Arad
ROMANIA
Deva
Sibiu
Brasov
Galati
Buzău
Brăila
Camul
Artsyz
Illichivs'k
Armyans'k
Dzhankoy
Zatoka Syvash
Kerch
Kuban'
Timisoara
Lugoj
Hunedoara
Resita
Transylvanian Alps
Ramnicu Valcea
Ploiesti
Târgoviste
Izmayil
Tulcea
Ozero Shahany
Kankats'ka Zatoka
Crimea
Zatoka Sivash
Kerch Strait
Yevpatoriya
Simferopol'
Feodosiya
Drobeta-Turnu Severin
Târgu Jiu
Pitesti
Wallachia
Slatina
Craiova
Caracal
BUCHAREST (BUCURESTI)
Călărasi
Constanta
Lacul Razim
Lacul Sinoie
Sevastopol'
Yalta
(annexed by Russia, 2014)
GEORGIA
Strehaia
Giurgiu
Danube (Dunărea)
BULGARIA
Black Sea

SCALE BAR

0 km 50 100
0 miles 50 100

EUROPEAN RUSSIA

RUSSIAN FEDERATION

European Russia is separated from the Asiatic part of the Russian Federation by the Ural Mountains. It is home to two-thirds of the country's population. Russia was the largest and most powerful republic of the communist Soviet Union, which collapsed in 1991. New businesses were set up when communism ended, but many old state industries closed down, causing unemployment and further hardship for many people.

INDUSTRY

European Russia is rich in natural resources. Minerals are mined on the Kola Peninsula and in the Urals, while dense forests are felled and processed in many of the larger northern cities. The Volga basin is one of Europe's largest sources of oil and gas. Moscow and the cities near the Volga are centers of skilled labor for a wide range of manufacturing industries like cars, chemicals, and heavy engineering and steel production.

INDUSTRY

Car manufacturing	Oil and gas
Chemicals	Timber processing
Engineering	
Iron and steel	▣ Major industrial center/area
Textiles	— Major road
Mining	

FARMING AND LAND USE

Russia's best farmland lies within this region. Big crops of wheat, barley and oats, potatoes and sunflowers are produced in the fertile black soil that forms a thick band across the country to the south of Moscow. The far north is cold and frozen, with bare mountains and tundra making cultivation impossible. Farther south there are extensive forests, and rough pastures that are used for herding and hunting.

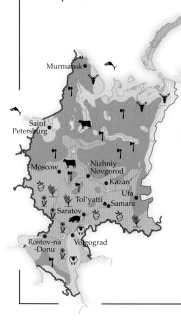

FARMING AND LAND USE

Cattle	Barren land
Fishing	Cropland
Pigs	Forest
Reindeer	Mountain region
Sheep	Pasture
Cereals	Tundra
Root crops	Wetland
Sunflowers	● Major conurbation
Timber	

POPULATION

Three-quarters of European Russia's people live in towns and cities, most in a broad band stretching south from St. Petersburg to Moscow, and eastward to the Urals. The capital, Moscow, and St. Petersburg are very crowded cities. Living conditions there are cramped, with two families often sharing one apartment. The southeast is also heavily populated. Over 12 million people live in the cities and towns that line the banks of the Volga River.

INHABITANTS PER SQ MILE

- More than 260
- 130–260
- 30–130
- Less than 30
- ■ Capital city
- ● Major city

THE LANDSCAPE

European Russia lies on the North European Plain, a huge, rolling lowland with wide river basins. The northern half of the plain, which was once covered by glaciers, has many lakes and swamps. The Volga River drains much of the plain as it flows south to the Caspian Sea. The Caucasus and Ural Mountains form natural boundaries in the south and east.

Northern European Russia (C 3)
Northern European Russia reaches into the Arctic Circle. It is a region of pine and birch forests, marshes, and tundra. There are also tens of thousands of lakes, including the biggest in Europe, Ladoga, which covers about 6,830 sq miles.

Ural Mountains (E 5)
The Ural Mountains run from north to south, stretching almost 2,500 miles.

Lake Ladoga (B 4)

Valdai Hills (A 5)
The Valdai Hills are a high, swampy region of the North European Plain. Two of Europe's biggest rivers, the Volga and the Western Dvina, have their sources here.

Caucasus (A 9)
This massive barrier of mountains stretches from the Black Sea to the Caspian Sea. It includes El'brus, the highest peak in Europe, at 18,511 feet.

Caspian Sea (C 9)

Volga River (C 7)
The Volga River flows for 2,292 miles, making it Europe's longest river and Russia's most important inland waterway. It is used for transportation and to generate hydroelectric power.

North European Plain (C 4)
The North European Plain sweeps west from the Ural Mountains, all the way to the Rhine River in Germany. In European Russia it includes a number of hill ranges, such as the Volga Uplands and the Central Russian Upland.

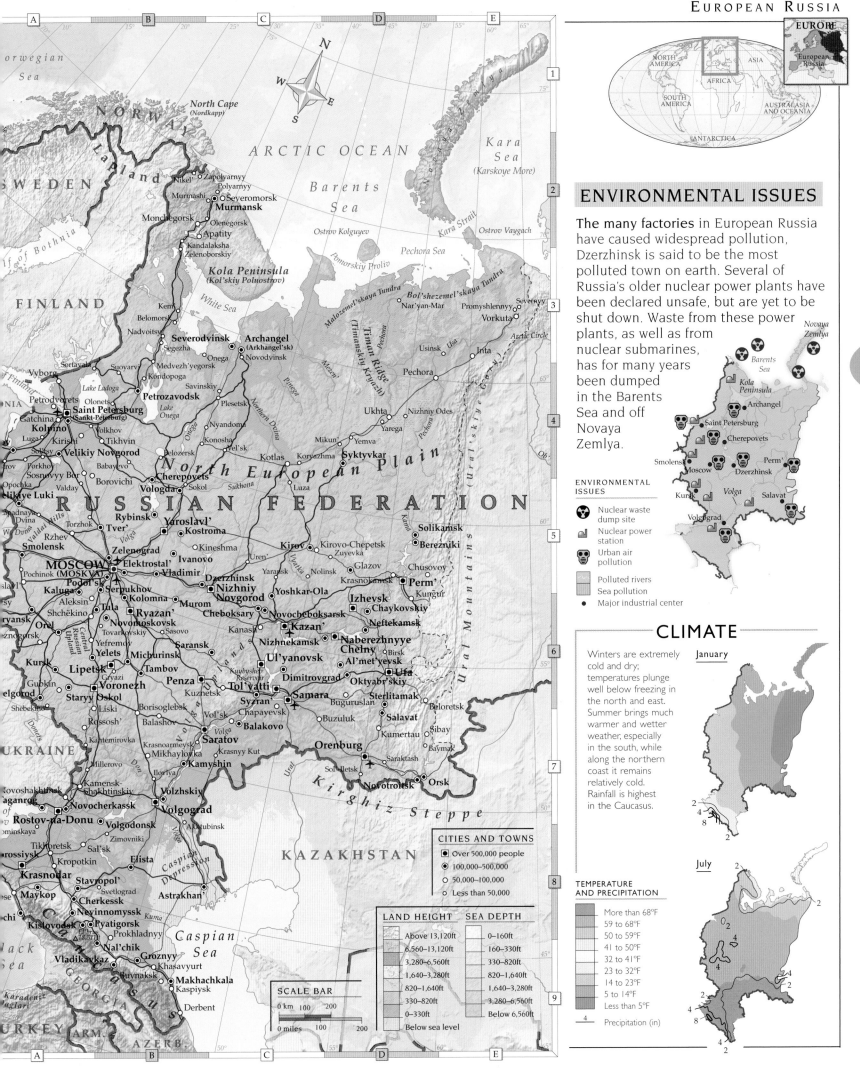

ENVIRONMENTAL ISSUES

The many factories in European Russia have caused widespread pollution, Dzerzhinsk is said to be the most polluted town on earth. Several of Russia's older nuclear power plants have been declared unsafe, but are yet to be shut down. Waste from these power plants, as well as from nuclear submarines, has for many years been dumped in the Barents Sea and off Novaya Zemlya.

ENVIRONMENTAL ISSUES

☢ Nuclear waste dump site

⌂ Nuclear power station

☻ Urban air pollution

Polluted rivers
Sea pollution

• Major industrial center

CLIMATE

Winters are extremely cold and dry; temperatures plunge well below freezing in the north and east. Summer brings much warmer and wetter weather, especially in the south, while along the northern coast it remains relatively cold. Rainfall is highest in the Caucasus.

January

July

TEMPERATURE AND PRECIPITATION

More than 68°F
59 to 68°F
50 to 59°F
41 to 50°F
32 to 41°F
23 to 32°F
14 to 23°F
5 to 14°F
Less than 5°F

—4— Precipitation (in)

CITIES AND TOWNS
■ Over 500,000 people
◉ 100,000–500,000
○ 50,000–100,000
∘ Less than 50,000

LAND HEIGHT
Above 13,120ft
6,560–13,120ft
3,280–6,560ft
1,640–3,280ft
820–1,640ft
330–820ft
0–330ft
Below sea level

SEA DEPTH
0–160ft
160–330ft
330–820ft
820–1,640ft
1,640–3,280ft
3,280–6,560ft
Below 6,560ft

SCALE BAR
0 km   100   200
0 miles   100   200

THE MEDITERRANEAN

The Mediterranean Sea separates Europe from Africa. It stretches more than 2,500 miles from east to west and is almost completely enclosed by land. Many great civilizations, including the Greek and Roman empires, grew up around the Mediterranean. It has been a crossroads of international trade routes for many centuries. More than 100 million people live in the 28 countries that border the sea, and their numbers are increased by the large crowds of tourists who regularly visit the area.

ENVIRONMENTAL ISSUES

Water pollution is widespread in the Mediterranean, especially near the large coastal resorts where raw sewage and industrial effluent is pumped out to sea, and often ends up on the beaches. Oil refining and oil spills have also increased pollution.

ENVIRONMENTAL ISSUES

🐚 Oil spill

⬜ Mild water pollution
⬛ Severe water pollution

LAND HEIGHT
- Above 13,120ft
- 6,560–13,120ft
- 3,280–6,560ft
- 1,640–3,280ft
- 820–1,640ft
- 330–820ft
- 0–330ft
- Below sea level

SEA DEPTH
- 0–820ft
- 820–1,640ft
- 1,640–3,280ft
- 3,280–6,560ft
- 6,560–9,840ft
- 9,840–13,120ft
- Below 13,120ft

CITIES AND TOWNS
- ◙ Over 500,000 people
- ● 100,000–500,000
- ◐ 50,000–100,000
- ○ Less than 50,000

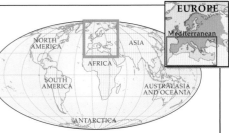

THE LANDSCAPE

The Mediterranean Sea would be an enormous lake if it were not for the Strait of Gibraltar, a narrow opening only 8 miles wide, which joins it to the Atlantic Ocean. The Mediterranean lies over the boundary of two continental plates. Where they meet, earthquakes and volcanoes are common.

Strait of Gibraltar

Sandy beaches
The Mediterranean coasts are bordered by several thousand miles of sandy beaches.

Shallow shelves
The area of water off the coast of Tunisia, and also the Adriatic Sea, are shallower than the rest of the Mediterranean.

Greek islands
Greece has thousands of islands that lie both in the Mediterranean and in the smaller Aegean Sea. Some of them are the remains of old volcanoes which have left black sand on the beaches.

Suez Canal
The Suez Canal links the Mediterranean to the Gulf of Suez and the Red Sea. Before it was built, ships had to sail around all of Africa to reach Asia.

Atlas Mountains
The rugged Atlas Mountains run through most of Morocco and Algeria. They form a barrier between the Mediterranean coast and the Sahara, which lies to the south.

TOURISM

The tourist industry in and around the Mediterranean is one of the most highly developed in the world. More than half the world's income from tourism is generated here. Resorts have grown up along the northwest coast of Africa, and in Egypt, southern Spain, France, Italy, Greece, and Turkey. Tourism brings huge economic benefits, but the ever-increasing number of visitors has also damaged the environment.

TOURISM
Major tourist destinations/resorts
Tourist center

INDUSTRY

The Mediterranean has a large fishing industry, although most of the fishing is small-scale. Tuna and sardines are caught throughout the region, and mussels are farmed off the coast of Italy. Fish canning and packing take place at most of the larger ports. Small oil and gas reserves are extracted off the coast of North Africa and near Greece, Spain, and Italy.

INDUSTRY
Fishing ports
Oil and gas
Major city

In 1974 Turkey occupied the northern part of Cyprus while Greek Cypriots remained in control of the south. Cyprus was effectively partitioned and a UN buffer zone currently divides the two areas. In 1983 the north of the island proclaimed itself the Turkish Republic of North Cyprus. It was only recognized by Turkey.

CONTINENTAL ASIA

Asia is the world's largest continent, and has the greatest range of physical extremes. Some of the highest, lowest, and coldest places on Earth are found in Asia: Mount Everest in the Himalayas is the highest, the Dead Sea in the west is the lowest, and the frozen wastes of northern Siberia are among the coldest. More people live in Asia than on any other continent – 1.3 billion of them in China, and 1.2 billion in India.

4,040 miles

6,030 miles

CROSS-SECTION THROUGH ASIA

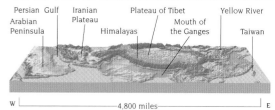

Persian Gulf Iranian Plateau of Tibet Yellow River
Arabian Plateau Mouth of
Peninsula Himalayas the Ganges Taiwan

W ——————4,800 miles———————— E

The Arabian Peninsula and the mountainous Iranian Plateau are divided by the Persian Gulf, fed by the Tigris and Euphrates Rivers. Farther east, the land begins to rise, the mountains spreading north to the Plateau of Tibet, and south to the Himalayas. The plains to the south of the Himalayas are drained by the Indus and Ganges, and to the east of the Plateau of Tibet by the Yellow River.

PHYSICAL ASIA

Northern Asia is made up of old mountains and ancient, stable plateaus. The jagged Himalayan mountains dominate the central part of the continent, along with the Plateau of Tibet, which stretches north into China. In Southeast Asia, there are many islands. Volcanoes and earthquakes are common, and some of the islands are volcanically formed.

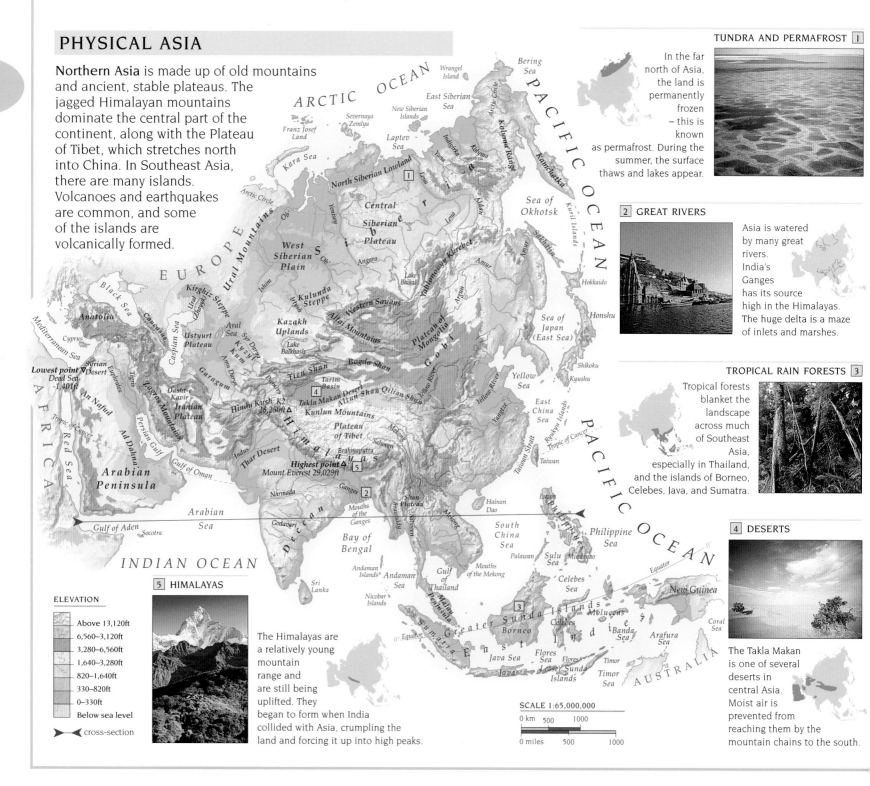

TUNDRA AND PERMAFROST 1

In the far north of Asia, the land is permanently frozen – this is known as permafrost. During the summer, the surface thaws and lakes appear.

2 GREAT RIVERS

Asia is watered by many great rivers. India's Ganges has its source high in the Himalayas. The huge delta is a maze of inlets and marshes.

TROPICAL RAIN FORESTS 3

Tropical forests blanket the landscape across much of Southeast Asia, especially in Thailand, and the islands of Borneo, Celebes, Java, and Sumatra.

4 DESERTS

The Takla Makan is one of several deserts in central Asia. Moist air is prevented from reaching them by the mountain chains to the south.

5 HIMALAYAS

ELEVATION

- Above 13,120ft
- 6,560–3,120ft
- 3,280–6,560ft
- 1,640–3,280ft
- 820–1,640ft
- 330–820ft
- 0–330ft
- Below sea level

cross-section

The Himalayas are a relatively young mountain range and are still being uplifted. They began to form when India collided with Asia, crumpling the land and forcing it up into high peaks.

SCALE 1:65,000,000

0 km 500 1000

0 miles 500 1000

POLITICAL ASIA

Asia is a continent of many contrasts: in its lands, its peoples, and its traditions. The break-up of the Soviet Union, which once stretched south from Russia to Iran, produced the new central Asian republics of Kazakhstan, Kyrgyzstan, Tajikistan, Turkmenistan, and Uzbekistan. The countries in southwest Asia are mainly Muslim, and include monarchies, republics and theocracies. India is the world's largest democracy, while China is a communist power regaining its economic influence in the world.

POPULATION

Capital cities

- Above 500,000
- 100,000 to 500,000
- 50,000 to 100,000
- Below 50,000

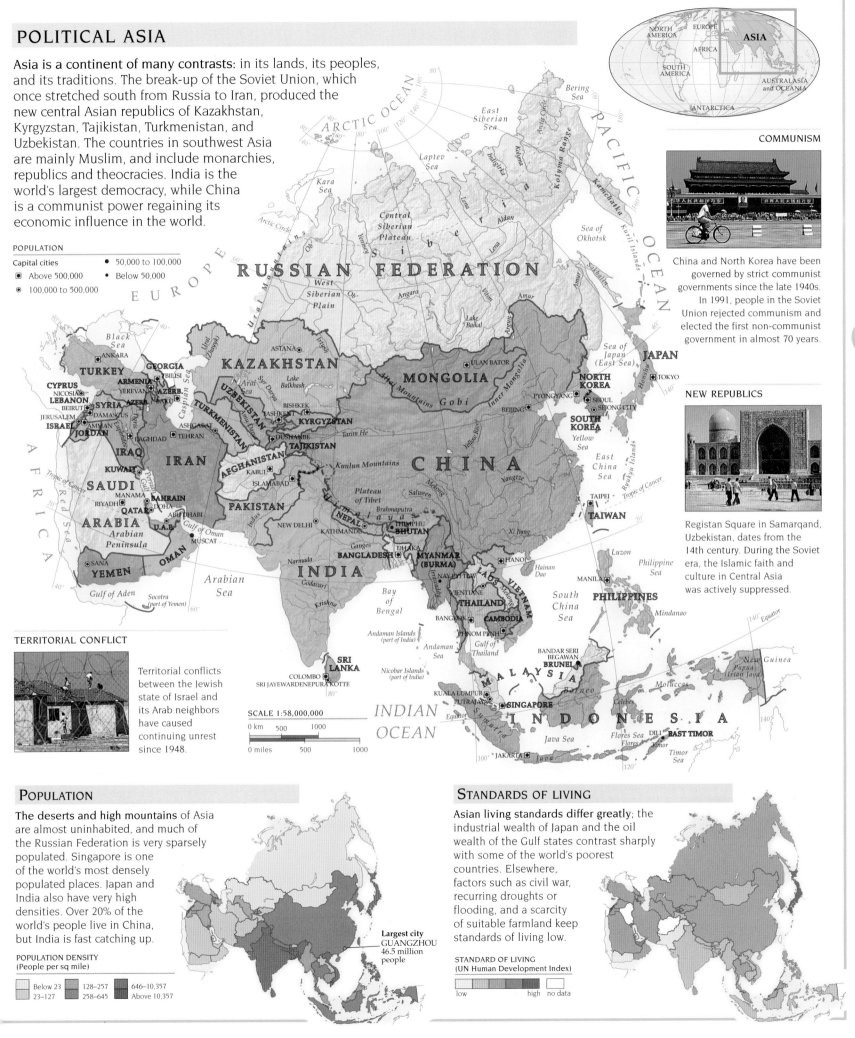

COMMUNISM

China and North Korea have been governed by strict communist governments since the late 1940s. In 1991, people in the Soviet Union rejected communism and elected the first non-communist government in almost 70 years.

NEW REPUBLICS

Registan Square in Samarqand, Uzbekistan, dates from the 14th century. During the Soviet era, the Islamic faith and culture in Central Asia was actively suppressed.

TERRITORIAL CONFLICT

Territorial conflicts between the Jewish state of Israel and its Arab neighbors have caused continuing unrest since 1948.

SCALE 1:58,000,000

0 km   500   1000

0 miles   500   1000

POPULATION

The deserts and high mountains of Asia are almost uninhabited, and much of the Russian Federation is very sparsely populated. Singapore is one of the world's most densely populated places. Japan and India also have very high densities. Over 20% of the world's people live in China, but India is fast catching up.

Largest city
GUANGZHOU
46.5 million
people

POPULATION DENSITY
(People per sq mile)

- Below 23
- 23–127
- 128–257
- 258–645
- 646–10,357
- Above 10,357

STANDARDS OF LIVING

Asian living standards differ greatly; the industrial wealth of Japan and the oil wealth of the Gulf states contrast sharply with some of the world's poorest countries. Elsewhere, factors such as civil war, recurring droughts or flooding, and a scarcity of suitable farmland keep standards of living low.

STANDARD OF LIVING
(UN Human Development Index)

low   high   no data

ASIAN GEOGRAPHY

Asia's forbidding mountain ranges, barren deserts and fertile plains have affected the way in which people settled the continent. Intensive agriculture is found in the more fertile areas, and the largest concentrations of people grew up near fertile land, and close to great rivers. Asia's mineral wealth has brought people to the more inhospitable parts of the continent; the deserts of southwest Asia for oil, and frozen Siberia for oil, gas, and minerals.

MINERAL RESOURCES

Over half of the world's oil and gas reserves are in Asia, most importantly around the Persian Gulf, and in western Siberia. Coal in Siberia and China has provided power for steel industries. Metallic minerals are also abundant: tin in Southeast Asia, and platinum and nickel in Siberia.

MINERAL RESOURCES

- Chromium
- Tin
- Nickel
- Iron
- Platinum
- Gold
- Lead
- Oil/gas field
- Coal field

INDUSTRY

Many people in Asia still rely on agriculture as a source of income, and some countries have very few industries. Heavy industry dominates eastern China and Russia, but Japan is the most industrially productive country. In recent years, booming "tiger" economies have developed in countries such as Taiwan, which border the Pacific Ocean.

OIL AND GAS

The discovery of oil in the Persian Gulf has generated enormous wealth, and produced rapid industrial and social change in countries such as Saudi Arabia, U.A.E., and Kuwait which control the oil supplies.

HI-TECH INDUSTRIES

Japan is a world-leading producer of electronic and hi-tech goods like computers, cameras, and hi-fi equipment. Taiwan, South Korea, and Singapore also produce electronic goods.

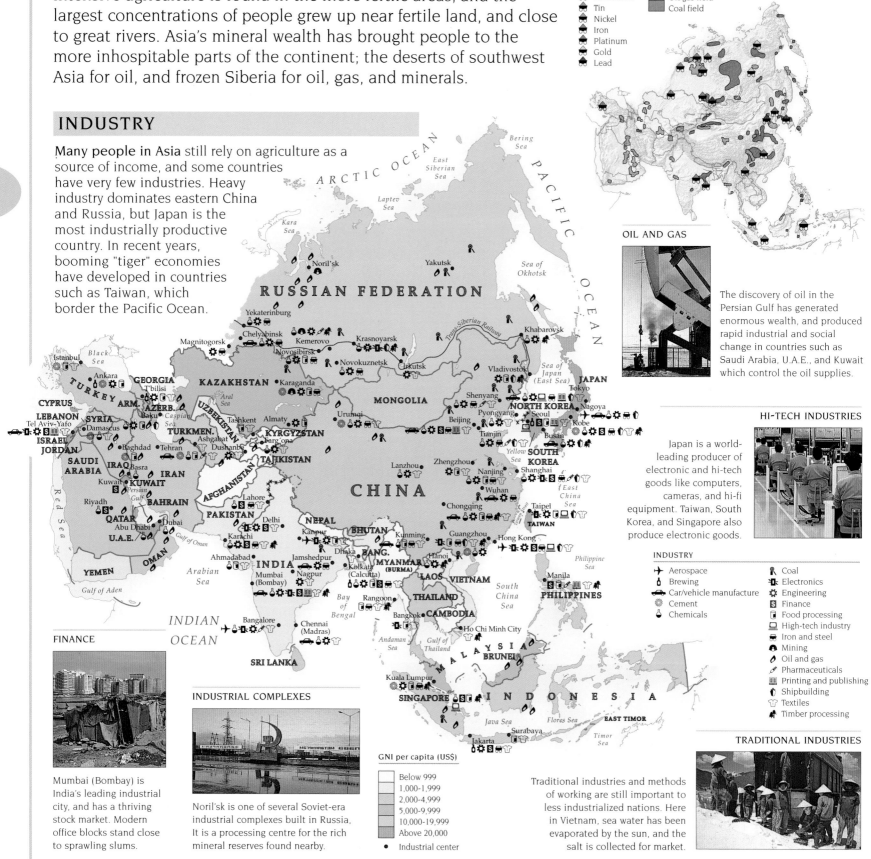

INDUSTRY

- ✈ Aerospace
- 🍺 Brewing
- 🚗 Car/vehicle manufacture
- 🏛 Cement
- ⚗ Chemicals
- ⛏ Coal
- ⚡ Electronics
- ⚙ Engineering
- $ Finance
- 🗔 Food processing
- 🖵 High-tech industry
- 🚂 Iron and steel
- ⛏ Mining
- 🛢 Oil and gas
- 💊 Pharmaceuticals
- 🖶 Printing and publishing
- 🚢 Shipbuilding
- 👕 Textiles
- 🌲 Timber processing

FINANCE

Mumbai (Bombay) is India's leading industrial city, and has a thriving stock market. Modern office blocks stand close to sprawling slums.

INDUSTRIAL COMPLEXES

Noril'sk is one of several Soviet-era industrial complexes built in Russia, It is a processing centre for the rich mineral reserves found nearby.

GNI per capita (US$)

- Below 999
- 1,000-1,999
- 2,000-4,999
- 5,000-9,999
- 10,000-19,999
- Above 20,000
- • Industrial center

TRADITIONAL INDUSTRIES

Traditional industries and methods of working are still important to less industrialized nations. Here in Vietnam, sea water has been evaporated by the sun, and the salt is collected for market.

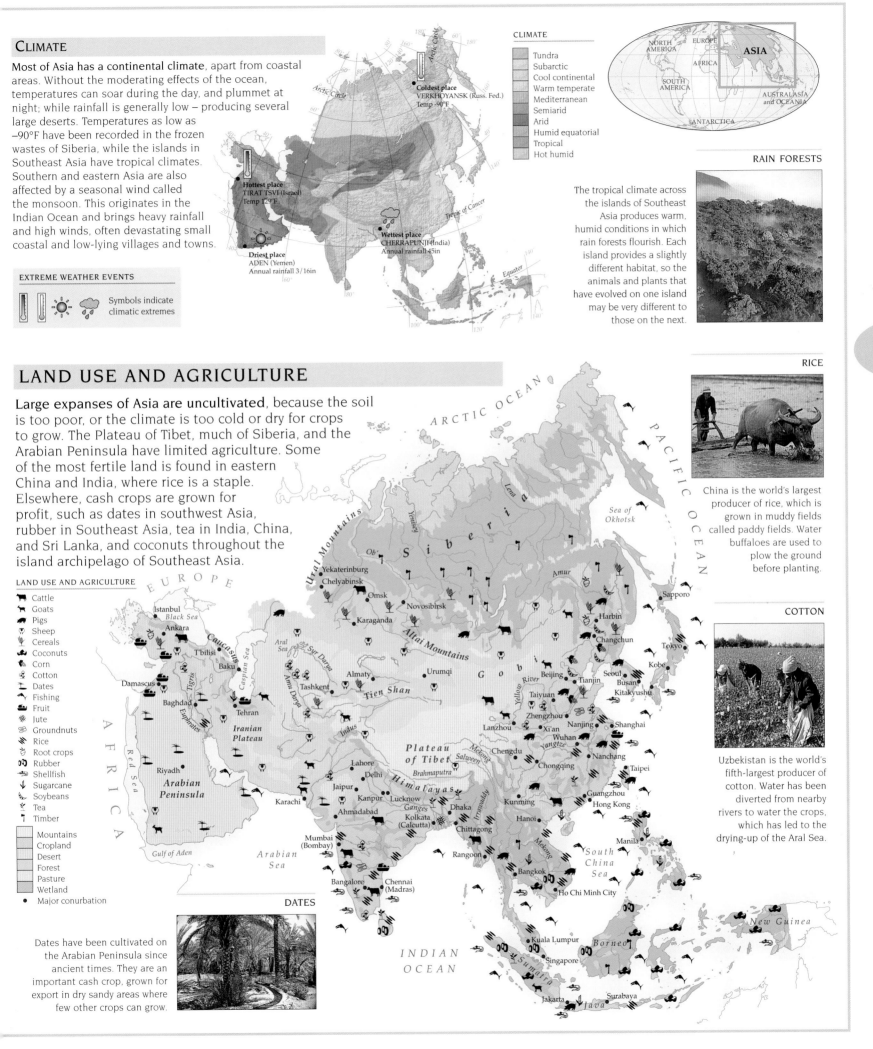

CLIMATE

Most of Asia has a continental climate, apart from coastal areas. Without the moderating effects of the ocean, temperatures can soar during the day, and plummet at night; while rainfall is generally low – producing several large deserts. Temperatures as low as –90°F have been recorded in the frozen wastes of Siberia, while the islands in Southeast Asia have tropical climates. Southern and eastern Asia are also affected by a seasonal wind called the monsoon. This originates in the Indian Ocean and brings heavy rainfall and high winds, often devastating small coastal and low-lying villages and towns.

Coldest place
VERKHOYANSK (Russ. Fed.)
Temp -90°F

Hottest place
TIRAT TSVI (Israel)
Temp 129°F

Driest place
ADEN (Yemen)
Annual rainfall 3/16in

Wettest place
CHERRAPUNJI (India)
Annual rainfall 45in

EXTREME WEATHER EVENTS
Symbols indicate climatic extremes

CLIMATE
Tundra
Subarctic
Cool continental
Warm temperate
Mediterranean
Semiarid
Arid
Humid equatorial
Tropical
Hot humid

RAIN FORESTS
The tropical climate across the islands of Southeast Asia produces warm, humid conditions in which rain forests flourish. Each island provides a slightly different habitat, so the animals and plants that have evolved on one island may be very different to those on the next.

LAND USE AND AGRICULTURE

Large expanses of Asia are uncultivated, because the soil is too poor, or the climate is too cold or dry for crops to grow. The Plateau of Tibet, much of Siberia, and the Arabian Peninsula have limited agriculture. Some of the most fertile land is found in eastern China and India, where rice is a staple. Elsewhere, cash crops are grown for profit, such as dates in southwest Asia, rubber in Southeast Asia, tea in India, China, and Sri Lanka, and coconuts throughout the island archipelago of Southeast Asia.

LAND USE AND AGRICULTURE
Cattle
Goats
Pigs
Sheep
Cereals
Coconuts
Corn
Cotton
Dates
Fishing
Fruit
Jute
Groundnuts
Rice
Root crops
Rubber
Shellfish
Sugarcane
Soybeans
Tea
Timber

Mountains
Cropland
Desert
Forest
Pasture
Wetland
Major conurbation

RICE
China is the world's largest producer of rice, which is grown in muddy fields called paddy fields. Water buffaloes are used to plow the ground before planting.

COTTON
Uzbekistan is the world's fifth-largest producer of cotton. Water has been diverted from nearby rivers to water the crops, which has led to the drying-up of the Aral Sea.

DATES
Dates have been cultivated on the Arabian Peninsula since ancient times. They are an important cash crop, grown for export in dry sandy areas where few other crops can grow.

RUSSIA AND KAZAKHSTAN

Russia lies partly in Europe but mostly in Asia. The land to the east of the Ural Mountains is called Siberia. This immense stretch of grasslands, thick, evergreen forest, and tundra is crossed by giant rivers. Vast areas of Siberia are almost untouched by human activity, yet in the industrial regions set up under communism (1922–1991), air, water, and soil are heavily polluted with harmful substances. Along with the former Soviet state of Kazakhstan, Siberia is rich in a huge variety of minerals.

INDUSTRY

The discovery of gold in the 19th century opened Siberia up to economic and industrial development. Later, vast reserves of oil, coal, and gas were found, especially in the west, which is now the main center for oil extraction. Gold and diamonds are mined in the east. In Kazakhstan, mining and other industries are growing with the help of foreign investors.

STRUCTURE OF INDUSTRY

Primary 5%
Services 60%
Manufacturing 35%

INDUSTRY

- 🚗 Car manufacture
- ⚗ Chemicals
- ⚙ Engineering
- 🚃 Iron & steel
- Textiles
- Diamonds
- Mining
- Oil and gas
- Timber manufacturing
- ■ Major industrial center / area
- — Major road

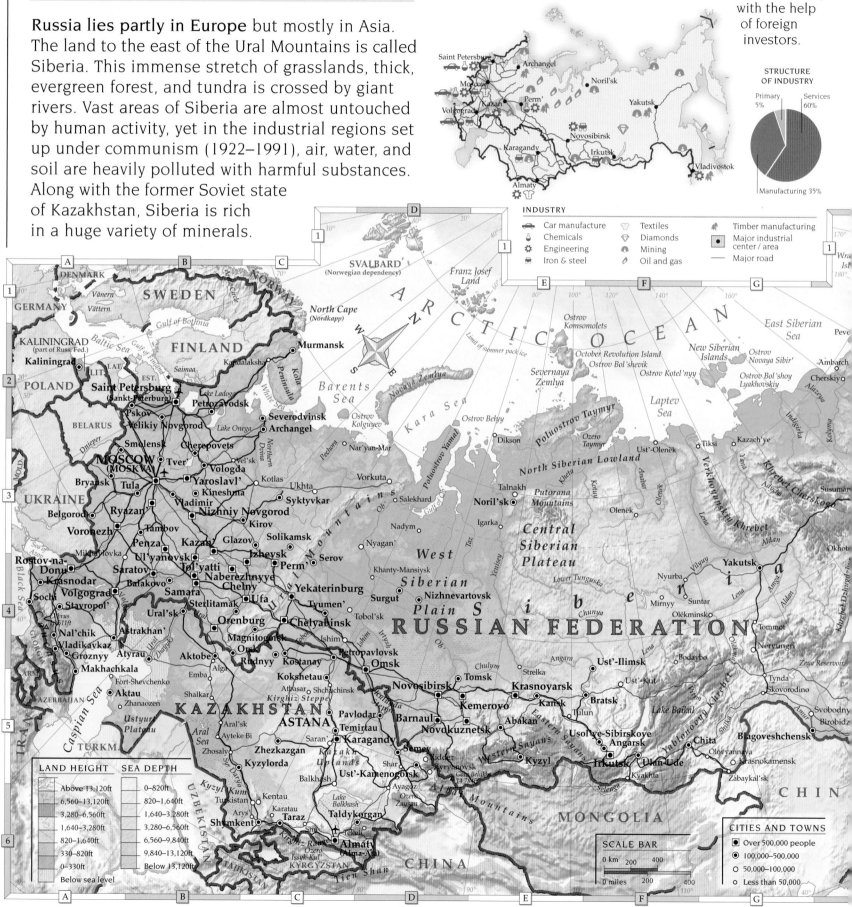

LAND HEIGHT

- Above 13,120ft
- 6,560–13,120ft
- 3,280–6,560ft
- 1,640–3,280ft
- 820–1,640ft
- 330–820ft
- 0–330ft
- Below sea level

SEA DEPTH

- 0–820ft
- 820–1,640ft
- 1,640–3,280ft
- 3,280–6,560ft
- 6,560–9,840ft
- 9,840–13,120ft
- Below 13,120ft

SCALE BAR

0 km 200 400

0 miles 200 400

CITIES AND TOWNS

- ● Over 500,000 people
- ◉ 100,000–500,000
- ○ 50,000–100,000
- ○ Less than 50,000

THE LANDSCAPE

East of the Ural Mountains lies the West Siberian Plain – the world's largest area of flat ground. The plain gradually rises to the Central Siberian Plateau and then again to highlands in the southeast. Great coniferous forests called *taiga* stretch across most of this land. The far north of Siberia extends into the Arctic Circle. Here the landscape is made up of frozen plains called tundra. Much of Kazakhstan is covered by huge rolling grasslands, or steppe. In the south are arid sandy deserts.

Tundra and *taiga*

Stubby birch trees, dwarf bushes, moss and lichen huddle close to the ground in the frozen tundra wastes of northern Russia. They lie between the permanent ice and snow of the Arctic, and the thick *taiga* forests which cover an area greater than the Amazon rain forest.

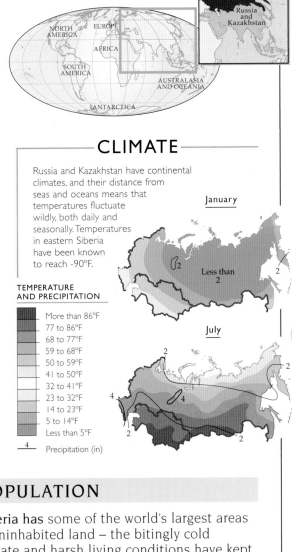

The Caspian Sea (A 5)

The Caspian Sea covers 143,243 sq miles and is the world's largest expanse of inland water. It is fed by the Volga and Ural Rivers, which flow in from the plains of the north.

West Siberian Plain (D 4)

This vast, flat expanse is covered with a network of marshes and streams. The Ob' River, which winds its way north across the plains, is frozen for up to half the year.

Lake Baikal (F 5)

Lake Baikal is the deepest lake in the world, and the largest freshwater one – it is more than 1 mile deep and covers 12,500 sq miles. It is fed by 336 rivers and contains around 20% of all the fresh water in the world.

CLIMATE

Russia and Kazakhstan have continental climates, and their distance from seas and oceans means that temperatures fluctuate wildly, both daily and seasonally. Temperatures in eastern Siberia have been known to reach -90°F.

TEMPERATURE AND PRECIPITATION

- More than 86°F
- 77 to 86°F
- 68 to 77°F
- 59 to 68°F
- 50 to 59°F
- 41 to 50°F
- 32 to 41°F
- 23 to 32°F
- 14 to 23°F
- 5 to 14°F
- Less than 5°F

— 4 — Precipitation (in)

January

July

FARMING AND LAND USE

Siberia's harsh climate has restricted farming to the south, where there are a few areas warm enough to grow cereal crops such as wheat and oats and to raise cattle on the small pockets of pasture. The rest of the region is used for hunting, herding reindeer, and forestry – the *taiga* forests contain the world's largest timber reserves. In Kazakhstan, big herds of cattle, goats, and sheep are raised for wool and meat, and wheat is cultivated in the fertile north.

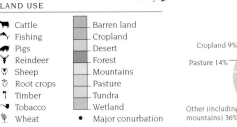

FARMING AND LAND USE

- 🐄 Cattle
- 🐟 Fishing
- 🐖 Pigs
- 🦌 Reindeer
- 🐑 Sheep
- 🥕 Root crops
- 🌲 Timber
- 🌿 Tobacco
- 🌾 Wheat

- Barren land
- Cropland
- Desert
- Forest
- Mountains
- Pasture
- Tundra
- Wetland
- ● Major conurbation

LAND USE

- Cropland 9%
- Pasture 14%
- Forest 41%
- Other (including mountains) 36%

POPULATION

Siberia has some of the world's largest areas of uninhabited land – the bitingly cold climate and harsh living conditions have kept the population small. The industrial cities in the west have the most people. Despite its huge size, Kazakhstan has only 16 million people, just over half live in urban areas.

INHABITANTS PER SQ MILE

- More than 260
- 13–260
- 30–130
- Less than 30
- ■ Capital city
- ● Major city

URBAN/RURAL POPULATION DIVISION

- Saint Petersburg 2.6%
- Novosibirsk 1%
- Moscow 6.4%
- Rural population 24%
- Other towns and cities 66%

ENVIRONMENTAL ISSUES

Decades of industrial development during the communist regime brought new industries to undeveloped parts of the region, such as Siberia. This industrial development has now led to environmental degradation on a massive scale: river, air, and land pollution in Russia is among the worst in the world.

ENVIRONMENTAL ISSUES

- 😷 Urban air pollution
- Polluted rivers
- Sea pollution
- ● Major industrial center

TURKEY AND THE CAUCASUS

ARMENIA, AZERBAIJAN, GEORGIA, TURKEY

Turkey and the Caucasus lie partly in Europe, and partly in Asia. Turkey has a long Islamic tradition, and although the country is now a secular (nonreligious) one, most. Turks are Muslims. Turkey is becoming more industrialized, although one third of its workforce is still employed in agriculture. The countries of the Caucasus were under Russian rule for 70 years, until 1991. They are home to more than 50 different ethnic groups.

INDUSTRY

Turkey has a wide range of industries, including tourism and growing trade links with Europe. Azerbaijan has large oil reserves and is able to export oil. The other states use imported fuel and hydro-electric power generated by their rushing rivers. Georgia produces industrial machinery and chemicals. Armenia's economy is recovering from the conflict with Azerbaijan.

FARMING AND LAND USE

With its warm climate and good soils, Turkey is able to produce all of its own food. Cattle and goats are kept on the central plateau. Along the Mediterranean coast, farmers grow olives, figs, grapes, and peaches. Hazelnuts are cultivated along the shores of the Black Sea. Across the Caucasus, the limited fertile land is used to grow wine grapes, tobacco, and cotton.

FARMING AND LAND USE

- Livestock
- Fishing
- Cotton
- Fruit
- Hazelnuts
- Root crops
- Tobacco
- Vineyards
- Pasture
- Cropland
- Forest
- Major conurbation

LAND USE

Other 31%
Cropland 34%
Forest 15%
Pasture 20%

INDUSTRY

- Car manufacture
- Cement manufacturing
- Chemicals
- Engineering
- Food processing
- Textiles
- Oil field
- Tourism
- Major industrial center / area
- Major road

STRUCTURE OF INDUSTRY

Primary 12%
Services 57%
Manufacturing 31%

THE LANDSCAPE

A huge semiarid plateau called Anatolia runs across the center of Turkey. It is rimmed by several mountain ranges along the Black Sea coast and the steep Taurus Mountains in the south. A narrow strip of lowland separates the Caucasus and the Lesser Caucasus mountains in the northeast.

Anatolia
Anatolia has large areas of soft limestone rock. Over a long period of time, layers of rock have been worn away by water to produce strange landscapes with caves and tall, isolated rock pinnacles.

Caucasus Mountains (H1)

Lesser Caucasus (H2)

Earthquakes
In 1988, 25,000 people were killed in an earthquake in the west of Armenia.

Between two continents
The city of Istanbul (B2) in Turkey is divided in two by a narrow channel of water called the Bosporus. One part of the city is in Europe, the other in Asia. The two parts are linked by bridges.

Taurus Mountains (D5)
The Taurus Mountains were formed around 60 to 65 million years ago. Weathering has formed caves and deep gorges.

Lake Van (H4)
Lake Van is one of the shallow salt lakes found in Anatolia. Salt lakes develop in hot, dry areas where large quantities of water evaporate, leaving behind salty deposits.

POPULATION

Over 75% of Turks live in large towns or cities, mostly in the western half of the country. The eastern and southeastern parts of Anatolia are home to the Kurdish people. The Caucasian republics became more industrialized under Russian rule, and today, two thirds of their people live in urban places.

ENVIRONMENTAL ISSUES

Turkey has built many large dams to use water from rivers – especially the Euphrates – to irrigate its farmland. Syria and Iraq, which lie downstream, have opposed the dams, because they will have less water flowing into their countries. The safety of old-style nuclear plants such as Metsamor in Armenia has caused concern.

ASIA
Turkey & the Caucasus

CLIMATE

Winters are coldest in the Caucasus Mountains and in Anatolia, while the shores of the Mediterranean and Black Seas remain mild. Summers are hottest around the edge of the Mediterranean and near Turkey's border with Syria and Iraq.

January

July

INHABITANTS PER SQ MILE

- More than 520
- 260–520
- 130–260
- Less than 130
- ■ Capital city
- ● Major city

URBAN/RURAL POPULATION DIVISION

- Istanbul 10%
- Ankara 3.7%
- Izmir 2.5%
- Other towns and cities 55.8%
- Rural population 28%

ENVIRONMENTAL ISSUES

- ◎ Earthquake zone
- 〰 Major dam
- ⌂ Unstable nuclear power station
- ☻ Urban air pollution
- ▮ Sea pollution
- ● Major industrial center

TEMPERATURE AND PRECIPITATION

- More than 86°F
- 77 to 86°F
- 68 to 77°F
- 59 to 68°F
- 50 to 59°F
- 41 to 50°F
- 32 to 41°F
- 23 to 32°F
- 14 to 23°F
- Less than 14°F
- 4 Precipitation (in)

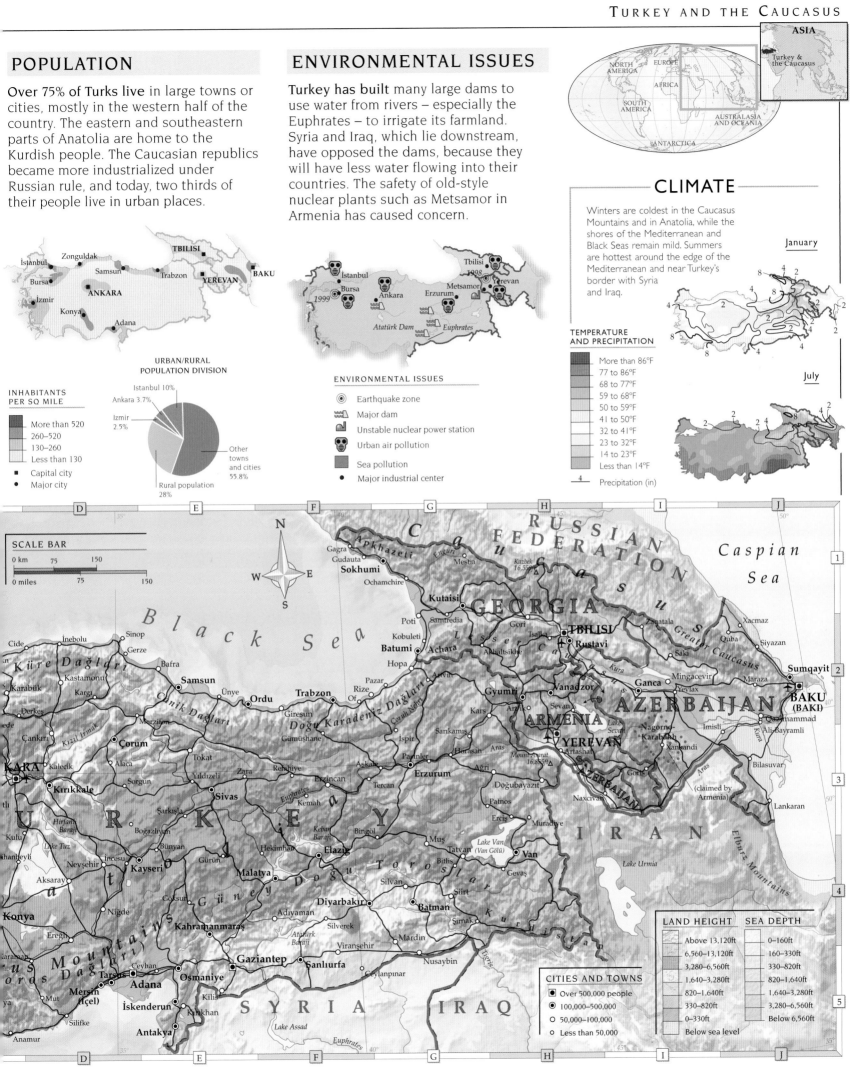

SCALE BAR
0 km 75 150
0 miles 75 150

CITIES AND TOWNS
- ■ Over 500,000 people
- ◉ 100,000–500,000
- ○ 50,000–100,000
- ∘ Less than 50,000

LAND HEIGHT	SEA DEPTH
Above 13,120ft	0–160ft
6,560–13,120ft	160–330ft
3,280–6,560ft	330–820ft
1,640–3,280ft	820–1,640ft
820–1,640ft	1,640–3,280ft
330–820ft	3,280–6,560ft
0–330ft	Below 6,560ft
Below sea level	

SOUTHWEST ASIA

BAHRAIN, IRAN, IRAQ, ISRAEL, JORDAN, KUWAIT, LEBANON, OMAN, QATAR, SAUDI ARABIA, SYRIA, UNITED ARAB EMIRATES, YEMEN

Most of southwest Asia is barren desert, yet the world's first cities originated here over 5,000 years ago. It was the birthplace of three major religions: Islam, Judaism, and Christianity. In recent years, the discovery of oil has brought great wealth to much of the region, but it has also been torn by internal conflicts and wars between neighboring countries. Most people here are Muslims, although Israel is the world's only Jewish state.

INDUSTRY

Oil has made the previously poor Arab states very wealthy. It and natural gas continue to be the main sources of income for many of the countries here. Other industries are being developed to support the region's economies when these resources run out. Iran is famous for its carpets, which are woven from wool or silk.

INDUSTRY
- ⚙ Cement manufacturing
- 🗋 Food processing
- ⚒ Iron and steel
- 🛢 Oil refining
- 👕 Textiles
- ◊ Oil and gas
- S Finance

☐ Major industrial center / area
— Major road

STRUCTURE OF INDUSTRY

Primary 10%
Services 49%
Manufacturing 41%

FARMING AND LAND USE

The best farmland is found along the Mediterranean coast and in the fertile valleys of the Tigris, Euphrates and Jordan Rivers. Wheat is the main cereal crop, and cotton, dates, and citrus and orchard fruits are grown for export. Elsewhere, modern irrigation techniques have created patches of fertile land in the desert. Dates, wheat, and coffee are cultivated in the oases and along the Persian Gulf coast.

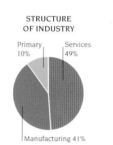

FARMING AND LAND USE
- 🐐 Goats
- 🐟 Fishing
- 🐑 Sheep
- 🍋 Citrus fruits
- ☕ Coffee
- 🌿 Cotton
- 🌾 Dates
- 🍇 Fruit
- 🌱 Tobacco
- 🌾 Wheat

- ▨ Cropland
- ▢ Desert
- ▨ Forest
- ▨ Pasture
- ▨ Wetland
- • Major conurbation

LAND USE

Forest 2%
Other (including desert) 47%
Pasture 45%
Cropland 6%

ENVIRONMENTAL ISSUES

Water shortages are common because of the hot, dry climate and the lack of rivers. Desalination plants convert seawater into freshwater, and are found along the Red Sea and Persian Gulf coasts. Lack of water also makes the risk of desertification greater. Iran has had many catastrophic earthquakes; in 2003 an earthquake in Bam killed 26,000 people.

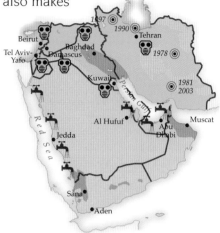

ENVIRONMENTAL ISSUES
- 🚰 Area with many desalination plants
- ◎ Catastrophic earthquake
- ☠ Urban air pollution

- ▢ Existing desert
- ▨ Risk of desertification
- ▨ Sea pollution
- • Major industrial center

THE LANDSCAPE

Great desert plateaus, both sandy and rocky, cover much of southwest Asia. On the enormous Arabian Peninsula, which covers an area almost the size of India, narrow, sandy plains along the Red Sea and south coast rise to dry mountains. In the center is a vast, high plateau that slopes gently down to the flat shores of the Persian Gulf. The mountainous areas of Iran experience frequent earthquakes.

Wadis
Valleys or riverbeds, called *wadis*, are found in the Saudi Arabian desert. They are usually dry, but after heavy rains, they are briefly filled by fast flowing rivers.

Syrian Desert (B 2)
The Syrian Desert extends from the Jordan valley in the west to the fertile plains of the Tigris and Euphrates Rivers in the east. It is mainly a rocky desert, because the sand has been swept away by winds and occasional heavy rainstorms.

Oases
Oases are areas within a desert where water is available for plants and human use. They are usually formed when a fault, or split, in the rock allows water to come to the surface. Oases can be no bigger than a few palm trees or cover several hundred sq miles.

Dead Sea (A 2)
This large lake on the border between Israel and Jordan is the lowest point on the Earth's surface – its shores lie 1,401 ft below sea level. It is also the world's saltiest body of water, and cannot sustain any life.

Ar Rub' al Khali (D 5)
The Ar Rub' al Khali desert, also known as the "Empty Quarter," is the largest uninterrupted stretch of sand on Earth. It covers some 250,000 sq miles and is one of the world's driest and most hostile deserts.

Iranian Plateau (E 3)
Central Iran is taken up by a vast, semiarid plateau, that rises steeply from the coastal lowlands bordering the Persian Gulf. It is ringed by the high Zagros and Elburz mountains.

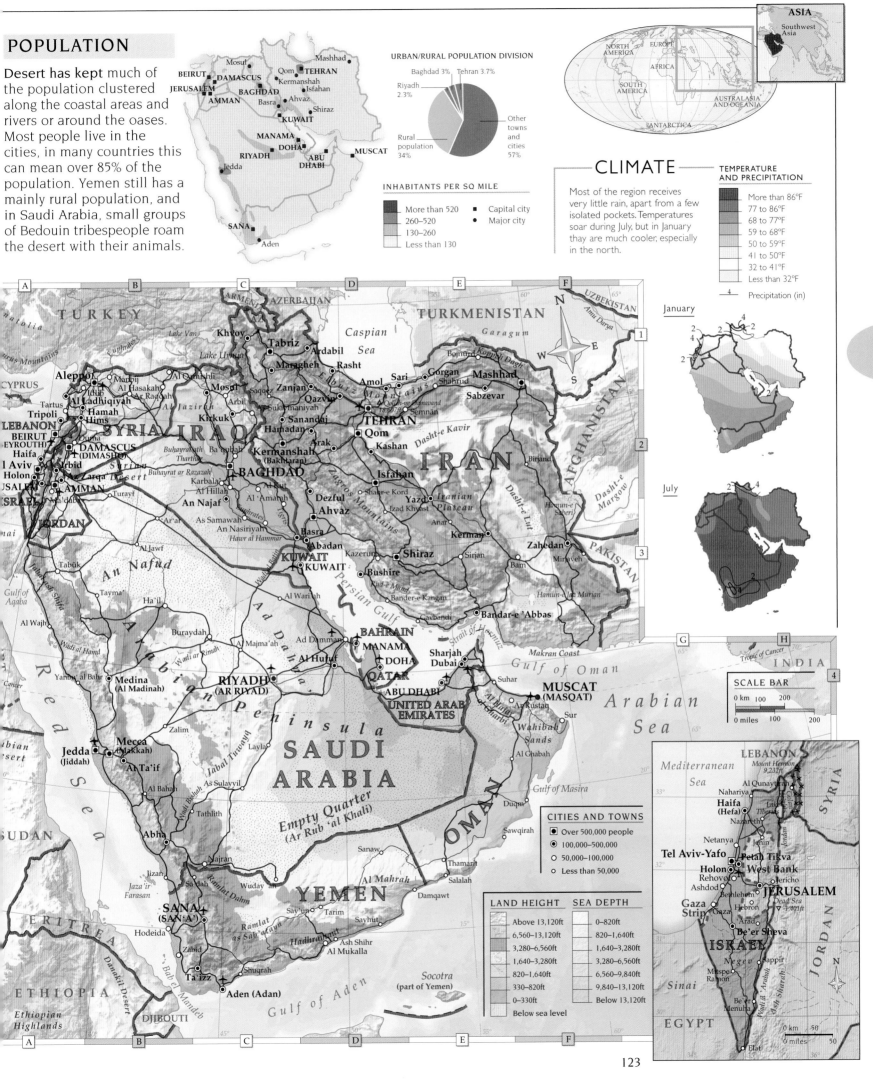

POPULATION

Desert has kept much of the population clustered along the coastal areas and rivers or around the oases. Most people live in the cities, in many countries this can mean over 85% of the population. Yemen still has a mainly rural population, and in Saudi Arabia, small groups of Bedouin tribespeople roam the desert with their animals.

URBAN/RURAL POPULATION DIVISION

- Baghdad 3%
- Tehran 3.7%
- Riyadh 2.3%
- Rural population 34%
- Other towns and cities 57%

INHABITANTS PER SQ MILE

- More than 520
- 260–520
- 130–260
- Less than 130
- ■ Capital city
- ● Major city

ASIA
Southwest Asia

CLIMATE

Most of the region receives very little rain, apart from a few isolated pockets. Temperatures soar during July, but in January they are much cooler, especially in the north.

TEMPERATURE AND PRECIPITATION

- More than 86°F
- 77 to 86°F
- 68 to 77°F
- 59 to 68°F
- 50 to 59°F
- 41 to 50°F
- 32 to 41°F
- Less than 32°F
- —4— Precipitation (in)

January

July

SCALE BAR
0 km 100 200
0 miles 100 200

CITIES AND TOWNS
- ■ Over 500,000 people
- ◉ 100,000–500,000
- ◎ 50,000–100,000
- ○ Less than 50,000

LAND HEIGHT
- Above 13,120ft
- 6,560–13,120ft
- 3,280–6,560ft
- 1,640–3,280ft
- 820–1,640ft
- 330–820ft
- 0–330ft
- Below sea level

SEA DEPTH
- 0–820ft
- 820–1,640ft
- 1,640–3,280ft
- 3,280–6,560ft
- 6,560–9,840ft
- 9,840–13,120ft
- Below 13,120ft

CENTRAL ASIA

AFGHANISTAN, KYRGYZSTAN, TAJIKISTAN, TURKMENISTAN, UZBEKISTAN

Central Asia is a land of hot, dry deserts and high, rugged mountains. It lies on the ancient Silk Road, an important trade route between China and Europe for over 400 years, until the 15th century. All of the countries here, except for Afghanistan, were part of the Soviet Union from the 1920s until 1991, when they gained independence. Since then, their people have reestablished their local languages and Islamic faith, which were restricted under Russian rule.

INDUSTRY

Fossil fuels, especially coal, natural gas, and oil, are extracted and processed throughout Central Asia. Agriculture supplies the raw materials for many industries, including food and textile processing, and the manufacture of leather goods and clothing. The region is famous for its colorful traditional carpets, hand-woven from the wool of the Karakul sheep. The Fergana Valley, southeast of Tashkent, is the main industrial area.

INDUSTRY

- ♨ Chemicals
- ✿ Engineering
- ▣ Food processing
- ⊤ Textiles
- ⋀ Mining
- ◊ Oil and gas
- ▣ Major industrial center / area
- — Major road

STRUCTURE OF INDUSTRY

Primary 39%
Manufacturing 29%
Services 32%

POPULATION

The peoples of Central Asia are mostly rural farmers, living in the river valleys and in oases. There are few large cities. A few still lead a traditional nomadic lifestyle, moving from place to place with their animals in search of new pastures. Large areas of Afghanistan, the western deserts, and the mountain regions in the east, are virtually uninhabited.

INHABITANTS PER SQ MILE

- More than 260
- 130–260
- 30–130
- Less than 30
- ■ Capital city
- ● Major city

URBAN/RURAL POPULATION DIVISION

Tashkent 3.2%
Bishkek 1.1%
Kabul 4%
Other towns and cities 22.7%
Rural population 69%

FARMING AND LAND USE

Farming is concentrated around the fertile river valleys in the east, like the Fergana Valley. A variety of cereals and fruits – including peaches, melons, and apricots – are grown. In drier areas, animal breeding is important, with goats, sheep, and cattle supplying wool, meat, and hides. Big crops of cotton, which is a major export, are produced on land irrigated by the Amu Darya River.

FARMING AND LAND USE

- 🐄 Cattle
- 🐐 Goats
- 🐑 Sheep
- ⚘ Cotton
- 🍇 Fruit
- ⚘ Opium poppies
- 🌿 Tobacco
- 🌾 Wheat
- Cropland
- Desert
- Mountains
- Pasture
- Wetland
- ● Major conurbation

LAND USE

Forest 5%
Cropland 9%
Pasture 51%
Other (including mountains and deserts) 35%

THE LANDSCAPE

Two of the world's great deserts, the Garagum and the Kyzyl Kum, cover much of the western portion of Central Asia. In the east, a belt of high mountain ranges – the Hindu Kush, the Tien Shan, and the Pamirs – tower above the land. Few rivers cross the deserts, apart from the Amu Darya, which flows from the Pamirs to the shrinking Aral Sea.

Aral Sea (D 1)
The Aral Sea was once the fourth largest lake in the world, but it has shrunk by 90% since 1960. Diversion of its water for irrigation has made the lake shallower, so its waters evaporate faster.

Garagum (D 3)
The sandy desert of the Garagum occupies over 70% of Turkmenistan. Its surface consists of wind-shaped dunes and depressions. Human settlement is limited to the desert's fringes.

Tien Shan (H 2)

Fergana Valley (G 3)
Stresses and strains in the Earth created the Fergana Valley, a deep depression encircled by high mountains. The valley's fertile soils are irrigated by water from the Syr Darya River, and underground sources.

Amu Darya river (E 3)

Hindu Kush (G 4)

Pamirs (G 4)
The Pamirs lie mainly in Tajikistan. Their highest point, at 24,590 ft, is Qullai Ismoili Somoni, previously known as Communism Peak because it was the highest peak in the former Soviet Union.

ENVIRONMENTAL ISSUES

Central Asia is a very dry area, and desertification is a constant threat, especially in Afghanistan. Severe urban and industrial air pollution is a legacy from the communist era, when heavy industries were established in the countries here. Efforts to stabilize the shrinking Aral Sea have met with some success in the northern section.

ENVIRONMENTAL ISSUES

- Urban air pollution
- Existing desert
- Risk of desertification
- Severe risk of desertification
- Polluted river
- Sea pollution
- Major industrial center

CLIMATE

Central Asia's climate is strongly inflenced by its position deep within Asia, far from the moderating effects of the oceans. Winters are cold, summers are very hot everywhere. Rainfall is virtually nonexistent all year round.

ASIA
Central Asia

January

Less than 2in precipitation

July

Less than 2in precipitation

TEMPERATURE AND PRECIPITATION

- More than 86°F
- 77 to 86°F
- 41 to 50°F
- 32 to 41°F
- Less than 32°F

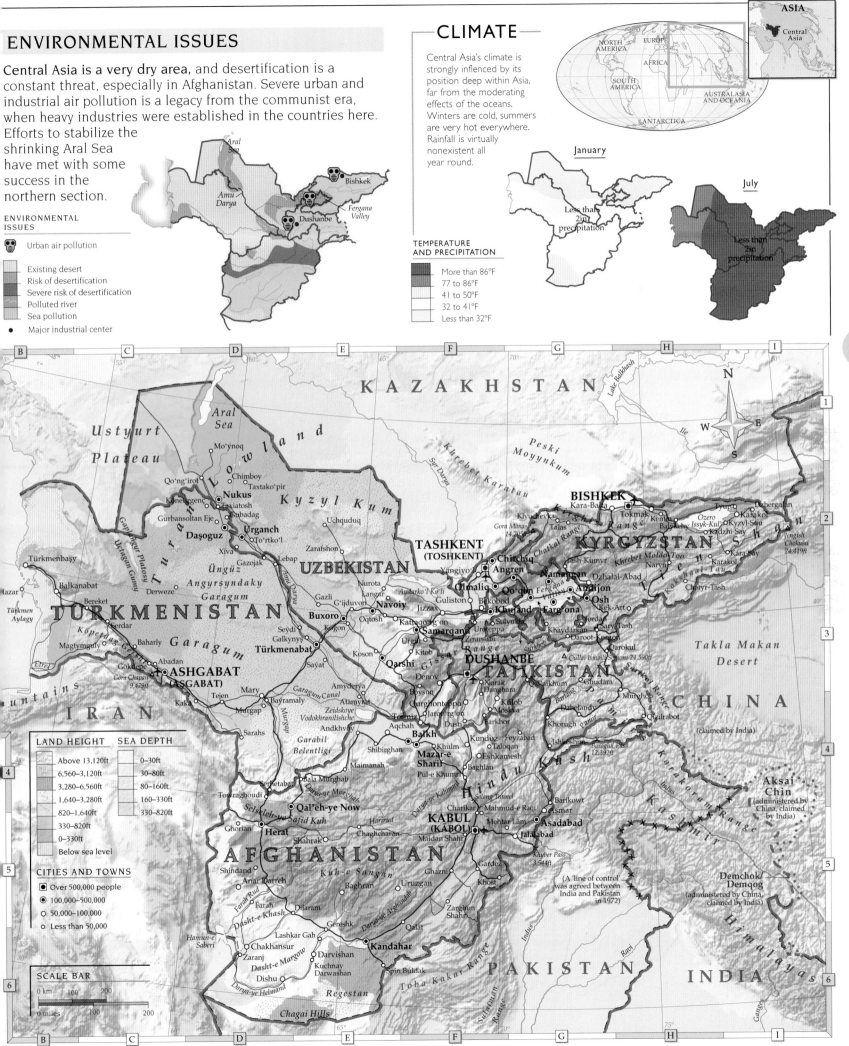

LAND HEIGHT
- Above 13,120ft
- 6,560–3,120ft
- 3,280–6,560ft
- 1,640–3,280ft
- 820–1,640ft
- 330–820ft
- 0–330ft
- Below sea level

SEA DEPTH
- 0–30ft
- 30–80ft
- 80–160ft
- 160–330ft
- 330–820ft

CITIES AND TOWNS
- Over 500,000 people
- 100,000–500,000
- 50,000–100,000
- Less than 50,000

SCALE BAR
0 km   100   200
0 miles   100   200

SOUTH ASIA

BANGLADESH, BHUTAN, INDIA, NEPAL, PAKISTAN, SRI LANKA

South Asia is a land of many contrasts. Its landscape ranges from the mighty peaks of the Himalayas in the north through vast plains and arid deserts, to tropical forests and palm-fringed beaches in the south. More than one-fifth of the world's people live here, and a long history of foreign invasions has left a mosaic of vastly different cultures, religions, and traditions and thousands of languages and dialects.

INDUSTRY

Industry has expanded in India in recent years. In the cities a variety of goods are produced and processed, including cars, airplanes, chemicals, food, and drink. Service industries such as tourism and banking are also growing. Elsewhere, small-scale cottage industries serve the needs of local people, but many products, mainly silk and cotton textiles, clothing, leather, and jewelry, are also exported.

STRUCTURE OF INDUSTRY

- Primary 23%
- Services 49%
- Manufacturing 28%

INDUSTRY

- ✈ Aerospace
- 🚗 Car manufacture
- 🧪 Chemicals
- ⚡ Electronics
- ⚙ Engineering
- 🍴 Food processing
- Iron and steel
- 👕 Textiles
- ⛏ Mining
- 💻 High-tech industry
- S Finance
- ① Tourism
- ⊡ Major industrial center / area
- — Major road

POPULATION

Most of South Asia's people live in villages scattered across the fertile river floodplains, in mountain valleys, or along the coasts, but increasing numbers are migrating to the cities in search of work. Overcrowding is a serious problem in both rural and urban areas; in many cities, thousands of people are forced to live in slums or on the streets.

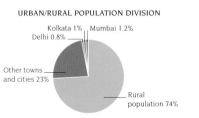

INHABITANTS PER SQ MILE

- More than 520
- 260–520
- 130–260
- Less than 130
- ■ Capital city
- • Major city

URBAN/RURAL POPULATION DIVISION

- Kolkata 1%
- Mumbai 1.2%
- Delhi 0.8%
- Other towns and cities 23%
- Rural population 74%

FARMING AND LAND USE

Over 60% of the population is involved in agriculture, but most farms are small and produce only enough food to feed one family. Grains are the staple food crops – rice in the wetter parts of the east and west, corn, and millet on the Deccan plateau, and wheat in the north. Groundnuts are widely grown as a source of cooking oil. Cash crops include tea, which is grown on plantations, and jute.

FARMING AND LAND USE

- 🐄 Cattle
- 🐟 Fishing
- 🐐 Goats
- 🌾 Cereals
- 🥜 Groundnuts
- ✳ Jute
- 〰 Rice
- 🌿 Tea
- Cropland
- Desert
- Forest
- Pasture
- Wetland
- • Major conurbation

LAND USE

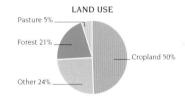

- Pasture 5%
- Forest 21%
- Cropland 50%
- Other 24%

THE LANDSCAPE

A massive, towering wall of snow-capped mountains stretches in an arc across the north, isolating South Asia from the rest of the continent. The huge floodplains and deltas of the Indus, Ganges, and Brahmaputra Rivers separate the mountains from the rest of the peninsula: a great rolling plateau, bordered on either side by coastal hills called the Eastern and Western Ghats.

Himalayas (E 2)
The Himalayas are the highest mountain system in the world. They were formed about 40 million years ago when two of the Earth's plates collided, thrusting up huge masses of land.

Mount Everest (F 3)
The northern ranges of the Himalayas average 23,000 ft in height. They include the highest point on Earth, Mount Everest on the Nepal–China border, which soars to 29,029 ft.

Thar Desert (C 3)
The border between India and Pakistan runs through the arid, sandy Thar Desert.

Western Ghats (C 5)
The Western Ghats run continuously along the Arabian Sea coast. The lower Eastern Ghats are interrupted by rivers that follow the gentle slope of the Deccan plateau and flow across broad lowlands into the Bay of Bengal. This is one of the wettest regions in the world.

Eastern Ghats (E 5)

Deccan plateau (D 5)
This giant plateau makes up most of central and southern India. Its volcanic rock has been deeply cut by rivers such as the Krishna, creating stepped valleys called *traps*.

Bangladesh (G 3)
Much of Bangladesh lies in an enormous delta formed by the Brahmaputra and Ganges Rivers. During the summer monsoon, the rivers become swollen by the torrential rains – and meltwater from the Himalayas – and the delta floods. Over the years, millions of people have drowned or been made homeless by heavy flooding.

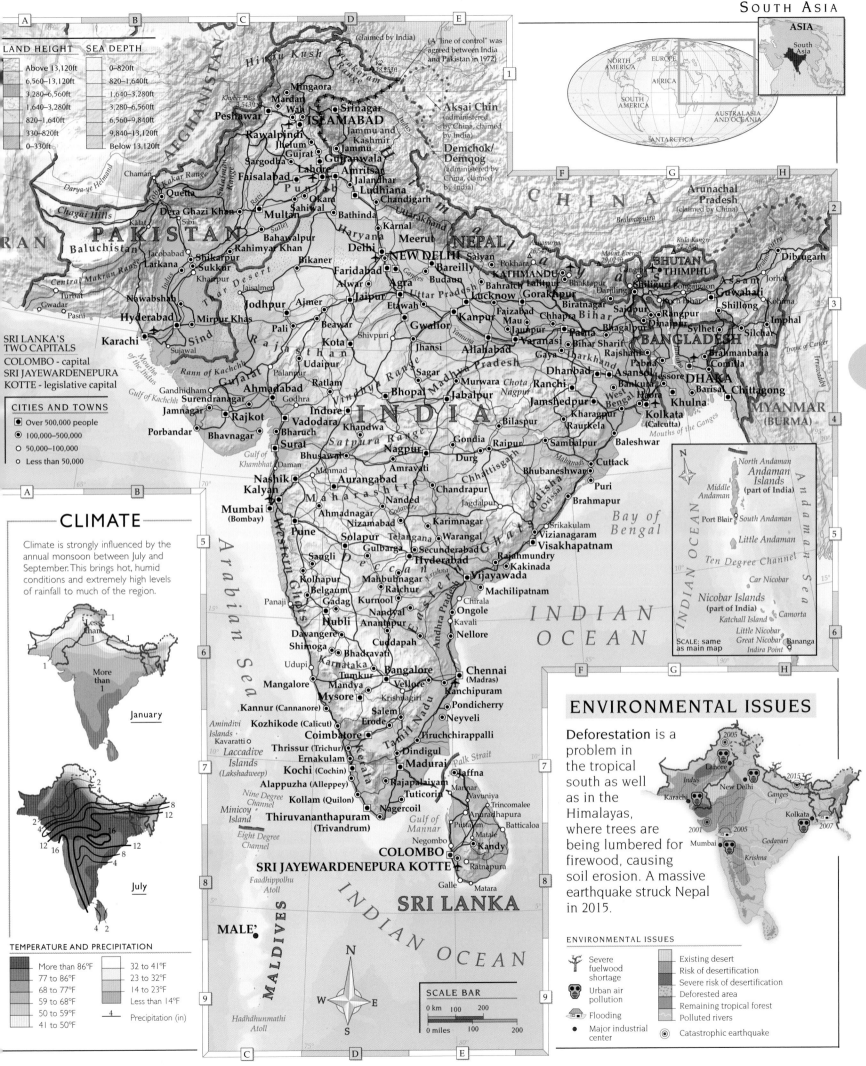

ASIA

South Asia

LAND HEIGHT
Above 13,120ft
6,560–13,120ft
3,280–6,560ft
1,640–3,280ft
820–1,640ft
330–820ft
0–330ft

SEA DEPTH
0–820ft
820–1,640ft
1,640–3,280ft
3,280–6,560ft
6,560–9,840ft
9,840–13,120ft
Below 13,120ft

SRI LANKA'S
TWO CAPITALS

COLOMBO - capital
SRI JAYEWARDENEPURA
KOTTE - legislative capital

CITIES AND TOWNS
● Over 500,000 people
◉ 100,000–500,000
○ 50,000–100,000
○ Less than 50,000

CLIMATE

Climate is strongly influenced by the
annual monsoon between July and
September. This brings hot, humid
conditions and extremely high levels
of rainfall to much of the region.

January

July

TEMPERATURE AND PRECIPITATION
More than 86°F
77 to 86°F
68 to 77°F
59 to 68°F
50 to 59°F
41 to 50°F
32 to 41°F
23 to 32°F
14 to 23°F
Less than 14°F
— 4 — Precipitation (in)

ENVIRONMENTAL ISSUES

Deforestation is a
problem in
the tropical
south as well
as in the
Himalayas,
where trees are
being lumbered for
firewood, causing
soil erosion. A massive
earthquake struck Nepal
in 2015.

ENVIRONMENTAL ISSUES
🜨 Severe fuelwood shortage
Urban air pollution
Flooding
● Major industrial center
Existing desert
Risk of desertification
Severe risk of desertification
Deforested area
Remaining tropical forest
Polluted rivers
◉ Catastrophic earthquake

SCALE BAR
0 km   100   200
0 miles   100   200

127

EAST ASIA

CHINA, MONGOLIA, TAIWAN

China is the world's fourth-largest country and its most populous – over 1.3 billion people live there. Under its communist government, which came to power in 1949, China has become a major industrial nation, but most of its people still live and work on the land as they have for thousands of years. Taiwan also has a booming economy and exports its products around the world. Mongolia is a vast, remote country with a small population, many of whom are nomads.

INDUSTRY

Chemicals, iron and steel, engineering, and textiles are the main industries in China's east coast cities, and in industrial centers like Shenyang. Shanghai, Hong Kong, and Beijing are also important financial centers. In the interior, large deposits of coal support the heavy industries in major cities such as Chengdu and Wuhan. Taiwan specializes in textiles and shoe manufacture, along with electronic goods. Mongolia's economy is mainly agricultural.

INDUSTRY

✈ Aerospace	⬡ Shipbuilding
🚗 Car manufacture	⬙ Textiles
Chemicals	Coal
Electronics	Mining
Electronic goods	$ Finance
Engineering	
Food processing	▣ Major industrial center / area
Iron & steel	— Major road

STRUCTURE OF INDUSTRY

Services 37%
Manufacturing 50%
Primary 13%

POPULATION

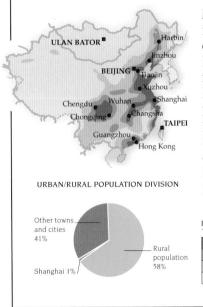

URBAN/RURAL POPULATION DIVISION

Other towns and cities 41%
Rural population 58%
Shanghai 1%

Most of China's people live in the eastern part of the country, where the climate, landscape and soils are most favorable. Chinese cities are home to over 690 million people, surpassing the rural population for the first time in 2011. Taiwan's lowlands are very densely populated. In Mongolia, one third of the people live in the countryside.

INHABITANTS PER SQ MILE

More than 520	■ Capital city
260–520	● Major city
130–260	
Less than 130	

FARMING AND LAND USE

FARMING AND LAND USE

⌐ Fishing	🌱 Tea
Pigs	Tobacco
Sheep	Wheat
Corn	
Cotton	Cropland
Fruit	Desert
Rice	Forest
Soybeans	Mountain region
Sugarcane	Pasture
	● Major conurbation

Despite its size, about 90% of China is unsuitable for farming. Either the soils and climate are poor, or the landscape is too mountainous. In the north and west, most farmers make their living by herding animals. On the fertile eastern plains, soybeans, wheat, corn, and cotton are grown. Farther south, rice becomes the main crop, and pigs are raised in large numbers.

LAND USE

Cropland 14%
Pasture 49%
Other (including mountains) 21%
Forest 16%

THE LANDSCAPE

China's landscape is divided into three areas. The vast Plateau of Tibet in the southwest is the highest and largest plateau on Earth. It contains both dry deserts and pockets of pasture surrounded by high mountains. Northwest China has dry highlands. The great plains of eastern China were formed from soils deposited by rivers like the Yellow River over thousands of years. Most of Mongolia is dry, grassland steppe and cold, arid desert.

Tien Shan mountains (B2)

The Tien Shan, or "Heavenly Mountains" reach heights of 24,419 ft. They surround fields of permanent ice and spectacular glaciers.

Gobi (E2) and Takla Makan (B3) deserts

The arid landscapes of the Gobi and Takla Makan deserts are made up of bare rock surfaces and huge areas of shifting sand dunes. They are hot in summer, but unlike most other deserts, are extremely cold in winter.

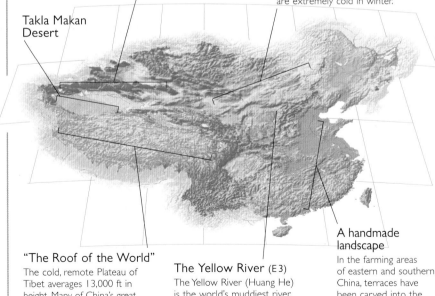

Takla Makan Desert

"The Roof of the World"

The cold, remote Plateau of Tibet averages 13,000 ft in height. Many of China's great rivers have their sources here. The world's highest human settlement, a town called Wenquan, is found in the east of the plateau. It lies 16,729 ft above sea level.

The Yellow River (E3)

The Yellow River (Huang He) is the world's muddiest river, carrying hundreds of truckloads of sediment to the sea every minute. The river has burst its banks many times throughout history, causing enormous damage and claiming millions of human lives.

A handmade landscape

In the farming areas of eastern and southern China, terraces have been carved into the hillsides to make them flat enough to grow rice and other crops. This method of farming has been used for over 7,000 years.

ENVIRONMENTAL ISSUES

China is now the world's largest emitter of greenhouse gases. Its rapid economic growth has had a huge impact upon the environment. The Yangtze and Yellow Rivers are badly polluted. Urbanization is increasing, with over 150 cities in China having populations above 1 million. The Three Gorges Dam is the largest hydroelectric project in the world.

ENVIRONMENTAL ISSUES

- Polluted river
- Sea pollution
- Major dam
- Urban air pollution
- Industrial city
- Catastrophic earthquake

CLIMATE

Two air masses control climate: one cold and dry from Siberia, and one moist and warm from the Pacific. Winters are long and cold away from the coast – especially on the Plateau of Tibet.

ASIA
East Asia

TEMPERATURE AND PRECIPITATION

- More than 86°F
- 68 to 86°F
- 50 to 68°F
- 32 to 50°F
- 14 to 32°F
- -4 to 14°F
- Less than -4°F
- ⁴ Precipitation (in)

January

July

LAND HEIGHT

- Above 13,120ft
- 6,560–13,120ft
- 3,280–6,560ft
- 1,640–3,280ft
- 820–1,640ft
- 330–820ft
- 0–330ft

SEA DEPTH

- 0–820ft
- 820–1,640ft
- 1,640–3,280ft
- 3,280–6,560ft
- 6,560–9,840ft
- 9,840–13,120ft

CITIES AND TOWNS

- ■ Over 500,000 people
- ◉ 100,000–500,000
- ○ 50,000–100,000
- · Less than 50,000

SOUTHEAST ASIA

BRUNEI, CAMBODIA, EAST TIMOR, INDONESIA, LAOS, MALAYSIA, MYANMAR (BURMA),PHILIPPINES, SINGAPORE, THAILAND, VIETNAM

Southeast Asia is made up of a mainland area and many thousands of tropical islands. The region has great natural wealth and has recently undergone rapid industrial growth. Some countries, especially Singapore and Malaysia, have become prosperous, but Laos and Cambodia remain poor, and are still recovering from years of terrible warfare.

ENVIRONMENTAL ISSUES

In Myanmar (Burma), Malaysia, and Indonesia, ancient rain forests are being cut down faster than they can grow back. On December 26th, 2004 a tsunami devastated the west of the region, it is estimated that over 225,000 people died around the Indian Ocean.

POPULATION

On the mainland, the population is concentrated in the river valleys, plateaus, or plains. Upland areas are inhabited by small groups of hill peoples. Most people still live in rural areas, but the cities are growing fast. In Indonesia and the Philippines, the population is unevenly distributed. Some islands, such as Java, are densely settled; others are barely occupied.

URBAN/RURAL POPULATION DIVISION

Bangkok 1.2% — Jakarta 1.5%
Manilla 1.8%
Rural population 37%
Other towns and cities 58.5%

INHABITANTS PER SQ MILE

- ■ More than 520
- ■ 260–520
- ■ 130–260
- Less than 130
- ■ Capital city
- • Major city

INDUSTRY

Industries based on the processing of raw materials, like metallic minerals, timber, oil and gas, and agricultural produce, are important here, but manufacturing has grown dramatically in recent years. Many foreign firms, attracted by low labor costs, have invested in the region. Malaysia and Singapore are major producers of electronic goods like disk drives for computers.

STRUCTURE OF INDUSTRY

Primary 19%
Services 45%
Manufacturing 36%

INDUSTRY

- 🧪 Chemicals
- ⚙ Engineering
- 🍴 Food processing
- 👕 Textiles
- ⛏ Mining
- 🛢 Oil and gas
- 🌲 Timber
- Ⓢ Finance
- 🖥 Hi-tech
- ⊕ Tourism
- ⊡ Major industrial center / area
- — Major road

THE LANDSCAPE

On the mainland, a belt of mountain ranges, cloaked in thick forest, runs north–south. The mountains are cut through by the wide valleys of five great rivers. On their way to the sea, these rivers have deposited sediment, forming immense, fertile flood plains and deltas. To the southeast of the mainland lies a huge arc of over 20,000 mountainous, volcanic islands.

Borneo (D7)

Borneo is the world's third-largest island, with a total area of 292,298 sq miles. Lying on the Equator and in the path of two monsoons, the island is hot and one of the wettest places on Earth. The landscape contains thickly forested central highlands and swampy lowlands.

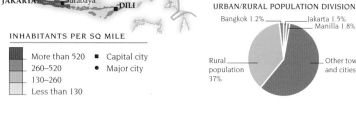

Asian Tsunami (A6)

On December 26th, 2004 the second largest earthquake ever recorded occured under the sea off the west coast of Sumatra. This triggered a huge Tsunami wave, up to 100 ft high in places, that devastated coastal communities causing the deaths of over 225,000 people in eleven countries.

Philippines (E4)

The Philippines' 7,000 islands are mountainous and volcanic with narrow coastal plains.

Irian Jaya (I7)

Irian Jaya is a province of Indonesia. Its dense rain forests are some of the last unexplored areas on Earth and are inhabited by many rare plant and animal species.

Volcanoes

Indonesia is the most active volcanic region in the world. Java alone has over 50 active volcanoes out of the country's total of more than 220.

Indonesia (C7)

Indonesia is an archipelago of 13,677 islands, scattered over almost 3,110 miles. The islands lie on the boundary between two of the Earth's tectonic plates and frequently experience earthquakes.

SCALE BAR

0 km   200   400

0 miles   200

FARMING AND LAND USE

The staple crop here is rice, which grows in low-lying flooded fields called paddies, or on terraces cut into the hillsides. Sugarcane, coconuts, bananas, and pineapples are widely grown as cash crops, and Malaysia produces 25% of the world's rubber. Freshwater and marine fish are caught in large quantities; fish is one of the main foods in this region.

FARMING AND LAND USE

- Cattle
- Fishing
- Pigs
- Shellfish
- Coconuts
- Fruit
- Rice
- Rubber
- Sugarcane
- Timber

Cropland
Forest
Pasture
Wetland
• Major conurbation

LAND USE

Pasture 4%
Cropland 21%
Other 24%
Forest 51%

ASIA
Southeast Asia

CLIMATE

Southeast Asia's climate is strongly affected by the monsoon, which brings warm, humid air and high rainfall to mainland Southeast Asia during July and to maritime southeast Asia during January.

January

July

TEMPERATURE AND PRECIPITATION

- More than 86°F
- 68 to 86°F
- 50 to 68°F
- Less than 50°F
- 4 — Precipitation (in)

LAND HEIGHT

- Above 13,120ft
- 6,560–13,120ft
- 3,280–6,560ft
- 1,640–3,280ft
- 820–1,640ft
- 330–820ft
- 0–330ft

SEA DEPTH

- 0–820ft
- 820–1,640ft
- 1,640–3,280ft
- 3,280–6,560ft
- 6,560–9,840ft
- 9,840–13,120ft
- Below 13,120ft

CITIES AND TOWNS

- Over 500,000 people
- 100,000–500,000
- 50,000–100,000
- Less than 50,000

MALAYSIA'S TWO CAPITALS
KUALA LUMPUR - capital
PUTRAJAYA - administrative capital

JAPAN AND KOREA

JAPAN, NORTH KOREA, SOUTH KOREA

Japan is a curved chain of over 4,000 islands in the Pacific Ocean. To the west, Korea juts out from northern China. Japan has few natural resources, but it has become one of the world's most successful industrial nations, due to investment in new technology and a highly efficient workforce. North Korea is a communist state with limited contact with the outside world, while South Korea is a democracy with major international trade links.

THE LANDSCAPE

Most of Japan is covered by forested mountains and hills, among which are many short, fast-flowing rivers and small lakes. Only about a quarter of the land is suitable for building and farming, and new land has been created by cutting back hillsides and reclaiming land from the sea. North and South Korea are mostly mountainous, with some coastal plains.

Hokkaido, Honshu, Shikoku, and Kyushu
Japan's four main islands were formed when two giant plates making up the Earth's crust collided, making their edges buckle upward.

T'aebaek-sanmaek (C 5)
This wooded mountain range forms the "backbone" of the Korean peninsula. It runs from north to south close to the east coast.

Tsunamis
Huge sea waves called tsunamis frequently threaten the east coast of Japan. They are set off by submarine earthquakes. The waves increase in size as they near the shore and can flood coastal areas and sink ships.

Earthquakes
In Japan, earthquakes are part of everyday life. The islands lie on a fault line, and earthquake tremors occur, on average, 5,000 times a year. Most of these are mild and may go unnoticed, but there is a constant threat of disaster.

Volcanoes
Japan's mountain ranges are studded with volcanoes, 60 of which are still active. Mount Fuji is a 12,389 ft snow-capped volcano and the highest mountain in Japan. It last erupted in 1707.

FARMING AND LAND USE

Modern farming methods allow Japan to grow much of its own food, despite a shortage of farmland. Rice is the main crop grown throughout the region. Japan has a large fishing fleet; the Japanese eat more fish than any other nation. In North Korea, farming is controlled by the government.

FARMING AND LAND USE

🐄 Cattle	🌿 Tea
🦅 Fishing	🍂 Tobacco
🐷 Pigs	▨ Cropland
🍇 Fruit	▨ Forest
〰 Rice	▨ Pasture
🌱 Soybeans	• Major conurbation

LAND USE

Pasture 1%
Cropland 16%
Other (including mountains) 18%
Forest 65%

POPULATION

Most of Japan's 128 million people live in crowded cities on the coasts of the four main islands. The Kanto Plain around Tokyo is Japan's biggest area of flat land, and the most populous part of the country. In South Korea, a quarter of the population lives in the capital, Seoul. Most North Koreans live on the coastal plains.

URBAN/RURAL POPULATION DIVISION

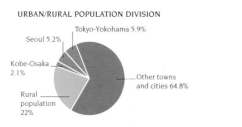

Tokyo-Yokohama 5.9%
Seoul 5.2%
Kobe-Osaka 2.1%
Rural population 22%
Other towns and cities 64.8%

INHABITANTS PER SQ MILE

▨ More than 520	■ Capital city
▨ 260–520	• Major city
▨ 130–260	
▨ Less than 130	

INDUSTRY

Japan is a world leader in high-tech electronic goods like computers, televisions and cameras, as well as cars. South Korea also has a thriving economy. It produces ships, cars, high-tech goods, shoes, and clothes for worldwide export. Both countries have to import most of their raw materials and energy. North Korea has little trade with other countries, but it is rich in minerals such as coal and silver.

STRUCTURE OF INDUSTRY

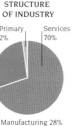

Primary 2%
Services 70%
Manufacturing 28%

INDUSTRY

🚗 Car manufacture	🅐 Mining
⚗ Chemicals	🅢 Finance
⚙ Engineering	🖥 Hi-tech
🍴 Food processing	☢ Research & Development
🔩 Iron & steel	
⚓ Shipbuilding	■ Major industrial center / area
👕 Textiles	— Major road

ASIA
Japan and Korea

ENVIRONMENTAL ISSUES

Industrial pollution from Korea and China has produced acid rain. Air pollution in cities has led to many people routinely wearing masks. Following the devastating 2011 tsunami and subsequent radiation leak at Fukushima, Japan closed all of its 22 nuclear power stations.

ENVIRONMENTAL ISSUES

- ⊙ Catastrophic earthquake
- Urban air pollution
- Affected by acid rain
- Site of nuclear accident
- ● Major industrial center

Sea of Japan / East Sea

Tohoku 2011
1999/ 2011
Tokyo
Seoul
Kobe 1995
Osaka

CLIMATE

Korea has hot summers and dry, very cold winters, especially in the north, where snow is common. In Japan, winters are less cold than on the Asian mainland; summers are hot, wet, and humid.

January

Less than 2

July

TEMPERATURE AND PRECIPITATION

More than 68°F	32 to 41°F
59 to 68°F	23 to 32°F
50 to 59°F	Less than 23°F
41 to 50°F	4 Precipitation (in)

NORTH AMERICA
EUROPE
ASIA
AFRICA
SOUTH AMERICA
AUSTRALASIA AND OCEANIA
ANTARCTICA

Kuril Islands (administered by Russian Federation, claimed by Japan)

La Pérouse Strait
Rebun-to
Rishiri-to
Wakkanai
Sea of Okhotsk
Monbetsu
Abashiri
Nemuro
Akkeshi
Nayoro
Shibetsu
Kitami
Hokkaido
Asahikawa
Takikawa
Asahi-dake 7,514ft
Obihiro
Kushiro
Ishikari-wan
Otaru
Ebetsu
Sapporo
Chitose
Horoshiri-dake 6,733ft
Iwanai
Tomakomai
Noboribetsu
Muroran
Uchiura-wan
Okushiri-to
Hakodate
Tsugaru-kaikyo

PACIFIC OCEAN

Aomori
Goshogawara
Hachinohe
Hirosaki
Kuji
Odate
Iwate
Miyako
Noshiro
Gojome
Morioka
JAPAN
Akita
Yokote
Kesennuma
Honjo
Shizugawa
Sakata
Shinjo
Furukawa
Tsuruoka
Ishinomaki
Honshu
Sendai
Yamagata
Sendai-wan
Niigata
Fukushima
Soma
Haramachi
Sado
Koriyama
Nagaoka
Inawashiro-ko
Iwaki
Sukagawa
Joetsu
Itoigawa
Utsunomiya
Hitachi
Toyama-wan
Nagano
Maebashi
Oyama
Mito
Takaoka
Shima
Kasumiga-ura
Choshi
Kanazawa
Toyama
Nagano
Kawagoe
Kanto Plain
Komatsu
Matsumoto
Hida-sanmyaku
TOKYO
Chiba
Fukui
Nakatsugawa
Kofu
Kawasaki
Tsuruga
Mount Fuji 12,388ft
Yokohama
Biwa-ko
Gifu
Shizuoka
Boso-hanto
Ogaki
Toyota
Izu-hanto
Nagoya
Okazaki
O-shima
Kyoto
Otsu
Hamamatsu
Suruga-wan
Kozu-shima
Tottori
Matsue
Yonago
Ise
Owase
Nii-jima
Miyako-jima
Mikura-jima
Oki-shoto
Dogo
Dozen
Wakasa-wan
Otsu
Tsu
Ise
Himeji
Kobe
Osaka
Nagoya
Hachijo-jima
Chugoku-sanchi
Okayama
Harima-nada
Awaji-shima
Matsue
Kurashiki
Kii-suido
Wakayama
Gotsu
Takamatsu
Hamada
Masuda
Nagato
Hiroshima
Niihama
Tokushima
Gobo
Shingu
Tanabe
Yamaguchi
Iwakuni
Matsuyama
Shikoku
Kure
Hofu
Shimonoseki
Ube
Iyo-nada
Kochi
Tosa-wan
Kitakyushu
Iki
Nakamura
Sukumo
Bungo-suido
Fukuoka
Oita
Kurume
Saga
Omuta
Kumamoto
Sasebo
Nobeoka
Nagasaki
Yatsushiro
Amakusa-nada
Kyushu
Miyazaki
Satsuma-Sendai
Miyakonojo
Koshikijima-retto
Kagoshima
Shibushi-wan

SCALE BAR

km   100   200
miles   100   200

RUSS. FED.

CHINA

Paektu-san 9,023ft
Hoeryong
Najin
Ch'ongjin
Hyesan
Kilchu
Huch'ang
Kimch'aek
Kanggye
Ch'osan
Sinp'o
Huich'on
Pukch'ong
NORTH KOREA
Namsan-ni
Sinuiju
Hamhung
Anju
East Korea Bay
Chongju
Sunch'on
Yonghung
Wonsan
Namp'o
PYONGYANG
Kosong
Sariwon
Changyon
(North and South Korea have been divided by a ceasefire agreement since 1953)
Sokcho
Haeju Kaesong Chuncheon
Ongjin
Gangneung
Liancourt Rocks (under South Korean control)
Wonju
Donghae
Incheon
SEOUL (SOUL)
Suwon
Chungju
Cheonan
Andong
SEJONG CITY
Daejeon
Pohang
SOUTH KOREA
Daegu
Gunsan
Ulsan
Namwon
Masan
Gwangju
Busan
Suncheon
Geogeum-do
Mokpo
Namhae-do
Kyushu
Kogum-do
Tsushima
Osumi-shoto
Jin-do
Korea Strait
Satsunan-shoto
Naze
Amami-gunto
Jeju Strait
Amami-o-shima
Ryukyu Islands (part of Japan)
Okinawa
Jeju-do
Naha
Senkaku-shoto
Okinawa-shoto
East China Sea
Sakishima-shoto
Ishigaki-jima
Iriomote-jima
Philippine Sea

Yellow Sea

Tumen
Yalu
Namgrim-sanmaek
Hamgyong-sanmaek
Taebaek-sanmaek
Sobaek-sanmaek

Sea of Japan / East Sea

PACIFIC OCEAN

LAND HEIGHT

	6,560–13,120ft
	3,280–6,560ft
	1,640–3,280ft
	820–1,640ft
	330–820ft
	0–330ft

SEA DEPTH

	0–820ft
	820–1,640ft
	1,640–3,280ft
	3,280–6,560ft
	6,560–9,840ft
	9,840–13,120ft
	Below 13,120ft

CITIES AND TOWNS

- ■ Over 500,000 people
- ◉ 100,000–500,000
- ○ 50,000–100,000
- ○ Less than 50,000

SOUTH KOREA'S TWO CAPITALS
SEOUL - capital
SEJONG CITY - administrative capital

AUSTRALASIA & OCEANIA

Australasia and Oceania encompasses the ancient landmass of Australia, the islands of New Zealand, and the scattering of thousands of small islands that stretch out into the Pacific Ocean. Indigenous peoples of the South Pacific, such as the Aborigines, Maoris, Polynesians, Micronesians, and Melanesians, inhabit the region. In Australia and New Zealand, they live alongside people of European origin who settled in the 18th century, and more recent arrivals from East and Southeast Asia.

PACIFIC ISLANDS

Micronesia is one of the Pacific's island nations, consisting of a group of volcanic islands, low-lying coral reefs, and lagoons. Many of the smaller Pacific islands are only a few feet above sea level.

LAND USE AND AGRICULTURE

Much of the center of Australia is a dry, barren desert and unsuitable for agriculture. At its fringes, sheep farming is practiced, and both Australia and New Zealand are massive producers of wool and lamb. The Pacific islands export many exotic fruits and crops – especially oil palms and coconut palms. Oil from the palms is processed and sold as well as the fruits themselves. Small-scale fishing is common, but larger operations are run by foreign fishing fleets, especially the Japanese, who fish for tuna in the deeper waters of the Pacific.

SHEEP FARMING

New Zealand and Australia are the world's biggest producers of wool. In New Zealand, sheep outnumber people by 12 to 1.

POPULATION

Capital cities
- ◙ Above 500,000
- ◉ 100,000 to 500,000
- ● 50,000 to 100,000
- • Below 50,000

State capitals
- ◙ Above 500,000
- ◉ 100,000 to 500,000
- ○ 50,000 to 100,000

BORDERS

- full international border
- indication of maritime country extent
- indication of maritime dependent territory extent
- state border

SCALE 1:37,250,000

0 km 300 600

0 miles 300 600

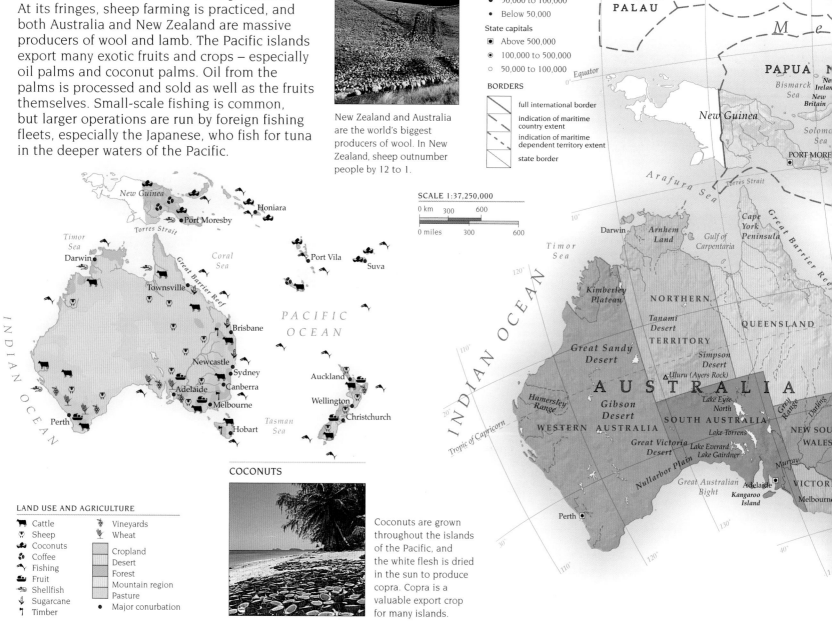

COCONUTS

Coconuts are grown throughout the islands of the Pacific, and the white flesh is dried in the sun to produce copra. Copra is a valuable export crop for many islands.

LAND USE AND AGRICULTURE

- Cattle
- Sheep
- Coconuts
- Coffee
- Fishing
- Fruit
- Shellfish
- Sugarcane
- Timber
- Vineyards
- Wheat
- Cropland
- Desert
- Forest
- Mountain region
- Pasture
- Major conurbation

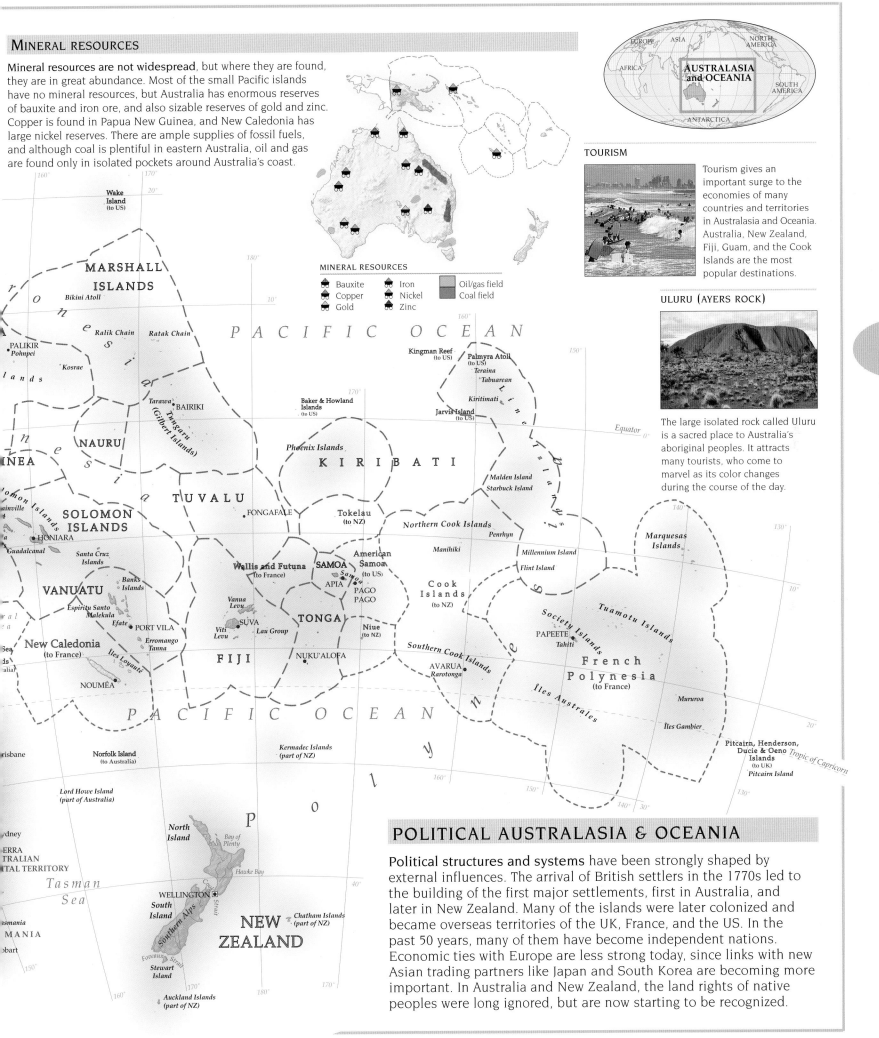

MINERAL RESOURCES

Mineral resources are not widespread, but where they are found, they are in great abundance. Most of the small Pacific islands have no mineral resources, but Australia has enormous reserves of bauxite and iron ore, and also sizable reserves of gold and zinc. Copper is found in Papua New Guinea, and New Caledonia has large nickel reserves. There are ample supplies of fossil fuels, and although coal is plentiful in eastern Australia, oil and gas are found only in isolated pockets around Australia's coast.

MINERAL RESOURCES

Bauxite	Iron		Oil/gas field
Copper	Nickel		Coal field
Gold	Zinc		

AUSTRALASIA and OCEANIA

TOURISM

Tourism gives an important surge to the economies of many countries and territories in Australasia and Oceania. Australia, New Zealand, Fiji, Guam, and the Cook Islands are the most popular destinations.

ULURU (AYERS ROCK)

The large isolated rock called Uluru is a sacred place to Australia's aboriginal peoples. It attracts many tourists, who come to marvel as its color changes during the course of the day.

POLITICAL AUSTRALASIA & OCEANIA

Political structures and systems have been strongly shaped by external influences. The arrival of British settlers in the 1770s led to the building of the first major settlements, first in Australia, and later in New Zealand. Many of the islands were later colonized and became overseas territories of the UK, France, and the US. In the past 50 years, many of them have become independent nations. Economic ties with Europe are less strong today, since links with new Asian trading partners like Japan and South Korea are becoming more important. In Australia and New Zealand, the land rights of native peoples were long ignored, but are now starting to be recognized.

AUSTRALIA

Australia is the world's sixth-largest country, and also the smallest, flattest continent, with the lowest rainfall. Most Australians are of European, mainly British, origin. However, since 1945 almost six million settlers from more than 170 countries have made Australia their home. The Aboriginal people, now only a tiny minority, were the first inhabitants. Recently, there have been several moves to restore their ancient lands.

INDUSTRY

Australia has one of the world's biggest mining industries. Bauxite, coal, copper, gold, and iron ore are mined and exported, especially to Japan. In the cities, service industries, particularly tourism, are growing fast; Australia's sunshine and dramatic scenery are attracting an increasing number of overseas visitors.

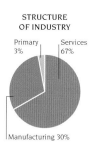

STRUCTURE
OF INDUSTRY

Primary 3%
Services 67%
Manufacturing 30%

INDUSTRY

- ♦ Brewing
- 🚗 Car manufacturing
- ⚗ Chemicals
- ▣ Electronics
- ✿ Engineering
- 🗋 Food processing
- ⚒ Coal
- ♠ Mining
- ◊ Oil and gas
- ⛴ Tourism
- ▣ Major industrial center / area
- —— Major road

POPULATION

Despite its vast size, Australia is sparsely populated. The desert outback, which covers most of the interior, is too dry and barren to support many people. About 85% of the population live in the cities and towns on the east and southeast coasts, and around Perth in the west.

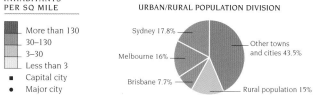

INHABITANTS
PER SQ MILE

- More than 130
- 30–130
- 3–30
- Less than 3
- ■ Capital city
- ● Major city

URBAN/RURAL POPULATION DIVISION

Sydney 17.8%
Melbourne 16%
Brisbane 7.7%
Other towns and cities 43.5%
Rural population 15%

FARMING AND LAND USE

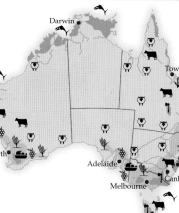

Away from the coasts, much of the land is too dry for agriculture. Fields of sugarcane grow close the east coast, and grapes for the thriving wine industry are cultivated in the south and west, along with wheat. Vast numbers of cattle and sheep are raised for their meat and wool – both of which are major exports. They are grazed in the desert, on huge farms called "stations," and in more fertile areas.

FARMING AND LAND USE

- 🐄 Cattle
- 🐑 Sheep
- ⚘ Wheat
- ⚘ Sugarcane
- 🌲 Timber
- 🍇 Vineyards
- Cropland
- Desert
- Forest
- Pasture
- ● Major conurbation

LAND USE

Cropland 6%
Other (including desert) 21%
Forest 19%
Pasture 54%

THE LANDSCAPE

Most of Australia is dry, flat, and barren; all of the wetter, fertile land is found along its coastline. Huge sun-baked deserts, fringed by semiarid plains of scrub and grassland cover most of the west and center of the country. In the east, the land rises to the highlands of the Great Dividing Range, which run the whole length of the east coast. The tropical north coast has rainforests and mangrove swamps.

Blue Mountains (G 6)

The Blue Mountains lie toward the southern end of the Great Dividing Range. They get their name from the blue haze of oil droplets given off by the eucalyptus trees covering their slopes.

Great Barrier Reef (G 2)

This spectacular coral reef, which stretches for over 1,200 miles off the coast of Queensland, is the largest living structure on Earth. The reef has built up over millions of years and its waters are home to thousands of different species of coral and marine animals.

Uluru (Ayers Rock) (D 4)

Uluru is an enormous block of red sandstone, standing almost in the middle of Australia. It is the world's biggest free-standing rock – 5.8 miles around the base, and 2,845 ft high. It is the summit of a sandstone hill that is buried beneath the sands of the desert.

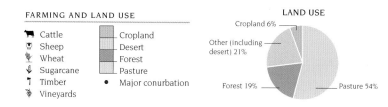

Simpson Desert (E 4)

The Simpson Desert covers around 50,000 sq miles. It contains long, parallel lines of sand dunes and is scattered with large salt pans and salt lakes, which were created when old rivers evaporated. They are now fed by the seasonal rains.

Murray River (F 5)

Together with its tributaries, the Murray River is Australia's main river system. It winds slowly westward for more than 1,562 miles from the Great Dividing Range to the Indian Ocean. It is fed by snow from mountains in the far southeast.

Great Dividing Range (H 5)

These highlands separate the desert regions from the fertile eastern plains. Rivers and streams have eroded them, creating deep valleys and gorges.

ENVIRONMENTAL ISSUES

Australia's dry climate and low rainfall make it susceptible to desertification. Between 2001 and 2007, southeast Australia experienced one of its worst droughts on record. The Murray-Darling basin, one of Australia's most productive agricultural regions, was very badly affected. During the dry season, vegetation becomes tinder-dry, and bush fires are common, burning huge tracts of land.

2001–2007

CLIMATE

Much of Australia's climate is continental, and temperatures soar during the day and fall rapidly at night. The climate is also arid and very little rain falls, apart from in the summer months when the north is affected by tropical storms.

EUROPE   ASIA   NORTH AMERICA

SOUTH AMERICA

ANTARCTICA

January

July

TEMPERATURE AND PRECIPITATION

- More than 95°F
- 86 to 95°F
- 77 to 86°F
- 68 to 77°F
- 59 to 68°F
- 50 to 59°F
- 41 to 50°F
- Less than 41°F
- —4— Precipitation (in)

ENVIRONMENTAL ISSUES

- Area at risk from bushfires
- Drought

- Existing desert
- Risk of desertification
- Severe risk of desertification

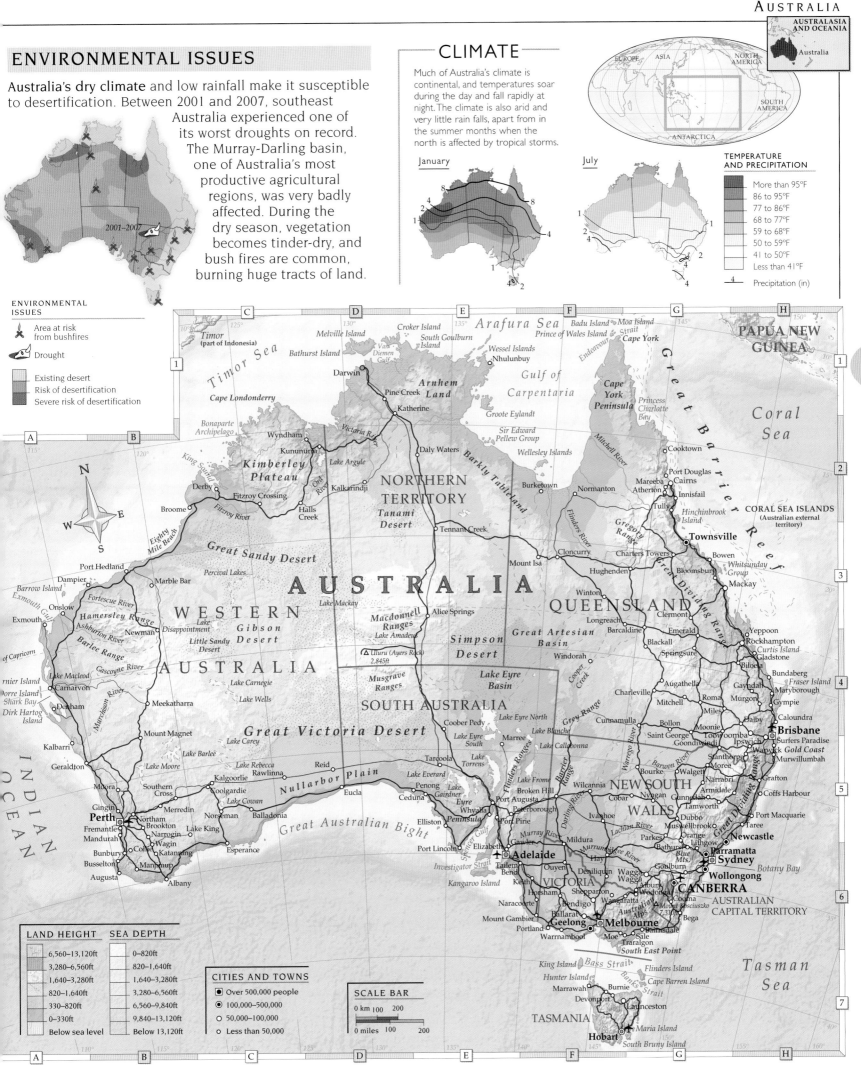

LAND HEIGHT

- 6,560–13,120ft
- 3,280–6,560ft
- 1,640–3,280ft
- 820–1,640ft
- 330–820ft
- Below sea level

SEA DEPTH

- 0–820ft
- 820–1,640ft
- 1,640–3,280ft
- 3,280–6,560ft
- 6,560–9,840ft
- 9,840–13,120ft
- Below 13,120ft

CITIES AND TOWNS

- Over 500,000 people
- 100,000–500,000
- 50,000–100,000
- Less than 50,000

SCALE BAR

0 km 100   200

0 miles 100   200

NEW ZEALAND

New Zealand is one of the most remote populated places in the world, and was one of the last places on Earth to be inhabited by people. The first people to settle on the islands were the Maori, a Polynesian people. When European settlers arrived during the 19th century, the Maori became a minority and today make up only about 8% of the population. With few people and rich natural resources, New Zealand's inhabitants have high living standards.

INDUSTRY

High-tech industries such as electronics and computing are growing in the major cities of Auckland and Wellington. Agricultural products such as meat, wool, and milk are still among New Zealand's major exports, and large pine forests supply wood for paper pulp and timber. The magnificent scenery and varied climate draw tourists from all over the world, especially for hiking and other special vacations.

STRUCTURE OF INDUSTRY

Primary 5%
Services 68%
Manufacturing 27%

INDUSTRY

Chemicals	
Electronics	
Engineering	
Fish processing	
Food processing	
Iron and steel	
Textiles	
Timber	
Tourism	

◉ Major industrial center / area
— Major road

POPULATION

Most of the population is descended from European settlers, although immigrants from Asia and the Pacific islands are increasing. About one-third of New Zealand's 4 million people live in Auckland on North Island, which also has the largest Polynesian population of any city in the Pacific. Elsewhere, the population is clustered along the coasts, where the land is lower.

URBAN/RURAL POPULATION DIVISION

Auckland 30.7%
Other towns and cities 36.8%
Wellington 9.3%
Christchurch 9.2%
Rural population 14%

INHABITANTS PER SQ MILE

More than 130	■ Capital city
30–130	● Major city
3–30	
Less than 3	

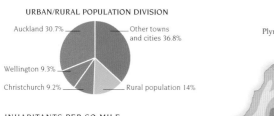

ENVIRONMENTAL ISSUES

New Zealand is one of the world's least polluted countries, largely due to its small population and lack of heavy industries. Air quality is occasionally poor in Auckland and Christchurch. Environment-friendly geothermal energy is tapped to make electricity in the volcanic region of North Island. Recently, logging companies have begun to exploit the rich forest reserves, although this has been widely opposed.

ENVIRONMENTAL ISSUES

	Geothermal power generation
	Logging activity
	Urban air pollution
●	Major industrial center
◉	Catastrophic earthquake

THE LANDSCAPE

Two large, mountainous islands form New Zealand's main land areas. A large crack or fault – the Alpine Fault, in the west of South Island – is the boundary between two plates in the Earth's crust. Land on either side of the fault tends to move, causing earthquakes. Volcanoes, many of them still active, are also found on both islands. South Island has many high peaks, several more than 10,000 ft high.

Geysers and boiling mud

Geysers occur when hot volcanic rocks come into contact with underground water. The water boils and turns to steam, forcing the water above it to burst through the Earth's surface into the air. There are many geysers and boiling mud pools in the areas around Rotorua and Taupo.

Northland (C1)

This is a tropical region in the far northwest. Many of the inlets are fringed by mangrove swamps.

Mount Taranaki (C4)

The dormant volcano of Mount Taranaki lies on New Zealand's North Island. It rises to a height of 8,262 ft.

Probable location of Alpine Fault

Lake Taupo (D3)

New Zealand's largest lake, Lake Taupo, covers 234 sq miles of North Island. It lies in the crater of an extinct volcano.

Southern Alps

New Zealand's Southern Alps stretch more than 300 miles down the backbone of South Island. They were formed by the collision of the Indo-Australian and Pacific plates. Heavy snowfalls here, brought by westerly winds, feed the Fox Glacier, which moves at a speed of 1.5–15 ft a day.

FARMING AND LAND USE

Large areas of rich, sweet grasslands have made New Zealand one of the world's top regions for rearing sheep. There are around 12 sheep for every person, grazing alongside about ten million cattle. Fruits, including strawberries, apples, oranges, peaches, and the famous kiwi, are cultivated, particularly on South Island, and exported throughout the world. Fish caught off the Pacific coast are another important source of income.

LAND USE

Other 8%
Cropland 14%
Pasture 50%
Forest 28%

FARMING AND LAND USE

- Cattle
- Fishing
- Sheep
- Fruit
- Timber
- Wheat

- Cropland
- Forest
- Mountains
- Pasture
- Major conurbation

Auckland
Hamilton
Wellington
Christchurch
Dunedin

CLIMATE

North Island has a generally warm climate that becomes tropical – hotter and more humid – toward the far north. South Island is cooler and wetter. There may be heavy snowfall in winter, particularly in the highlands, and many mountains are permanently snow-capped.

TEMPERATURE AND PRECIPITATION

- More than 59°F
- 50 to 59°F
- 41 to 50°F
- 32 to 41°F
- 23 to 32°F
- Less than 23°F
- 4 Precipitation (in)

January

July

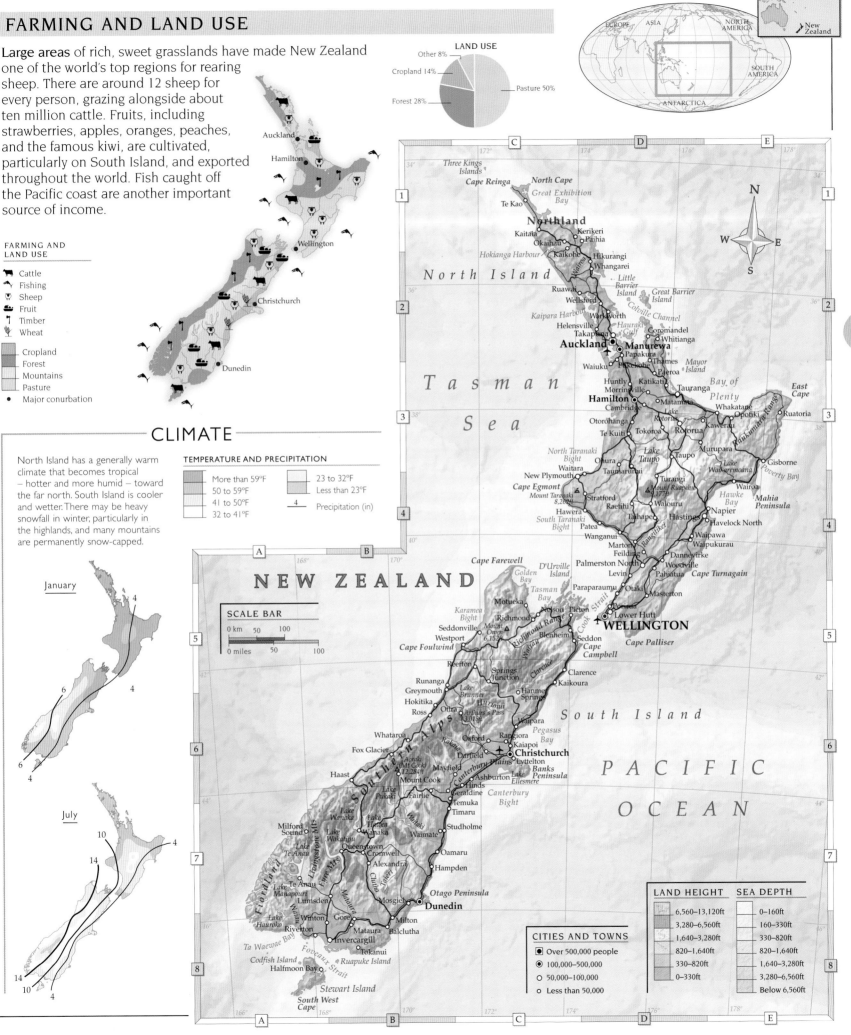

NEW ZEALAND

SCALE BAR

0 km 50 100

0 miles 50 100

North Island

Tasman Sea

South Island

PACIFIC OCEAN

LAND HEIGHT

- 6,560–13,120ft
- 3,280–6,560ft
- 1,640–3,280ft
- 820–1,640ft
- 330–820ft
- 0–330ft

SEA DEPTH

- 0–160ft
- 160–330ft
- 330–820ft
- 820–1,640ft
- 1,640–3,280ft
- 3,280–6,560ft
- Below 6,560ft

CITIES AND TOWNS

- Over 500,000 people
- 100,000–500,000
- 50,000–100,000
- Less than 50,000

SOUTHWEST PACIFIC

The many thousands of islands in the Pacific Ocean are scattered across an enormous area. The original inhabitants, the Polynesians, Melanesians, and Micronesians, settled the islands following the last Ice Age. In the 1700s Europeans arrived. They colonized all of the Pacific islands, introducing their culture, languages, and religion. Today many, though not all, of the islands have become independent. Their economies are simple, based largely on fishing and agriculture. Many are increasingly relying on their beautiful scenery and tropical climates to attract tourists and give a valuable boost to their economies.

LANDSCAPE

Most of the Pacific islands are extremely small, the largest landmass is the half of the island of New Guinea occupied by Papua New Guinea. The edges of the Indo-Australian and Pacific plates meet on the western edge of the area, leading to much volcanic and earthquake activity. Many of the islands are coral atolls, originally formed by volcanic activity, and some are no more than a few feet above sea level.

New Guinea (A 2)
A mountainous spine runs through the center of the island, separating the northern coast from the dense forests and mangroves found in the south.

Pacific Ocean
The Pacific Ocean is the Earth's oldest and deepest. Its name means peaceful, though it is far from being so; the highest wave ever recorded in open ocean – 112 ft – occurred during a hurricane in the Pacific.

Kavachi
Kavachi is an underwater volcano lying off the coast of New Georgia, in the Solomon Islands. It still erupts every few years.

Ring of Fire
The "Ring of Fire" is the term used to describe the string of volcanoes that surround the entire Pacific Ocean and erupt frequently because of intense stress and movement from within the Earth. The ring crosses the south Pacific, running between Vanuatu and New Caledonia, along the edge of the Solomon Islands, and between New Britain and New Guinea.

Sea trenches
Deep trenches mark the seafloor boundary where the Indo-Australian plate "dives" under the Pacific plate.

Coral atolls
Volcanic activity in the Pacific has led to the creation of many islands. These islands become fringed with a ring of coral. When the islands subside beneath the water once again, only the circle of coral is left, forming an atoll.

INDUSTRY

Today, the main industry for many of the Pacific islands is tourism. Food processing and small-scale textile industries are also common on many islands.

INDUSTRY
- Brewing
- Food processing
- Textiles
- Timber processing
- Mining
- Tourism
- ▣ Major industrial center
- — Major road

FARMING AND LAND USE

Most farming that takes place on the Pacific islands is at a subsistence level, and many people keep pigs and chickens. A few crops are grown for export, especially oil palms, and coconuts, which are dried in the sun to produce copra. Many islanders make their living from the rich fishing grounds of the Pacific. The thick forests of Papua New Guinea are increasingly cut down for timber.

AUSTRALASIA AND OCEANIA

LAND USE

- ⤙ Fishing
- 🍌 Bananas
- 🌿 Cocoa
- 🥥 Coconuts
- ☕ Coffee
- 🌴 Oil palms
- ⚙ Rubber
- ⑂ Timber

Cropland
Forest
Wetland
● Major conurbation

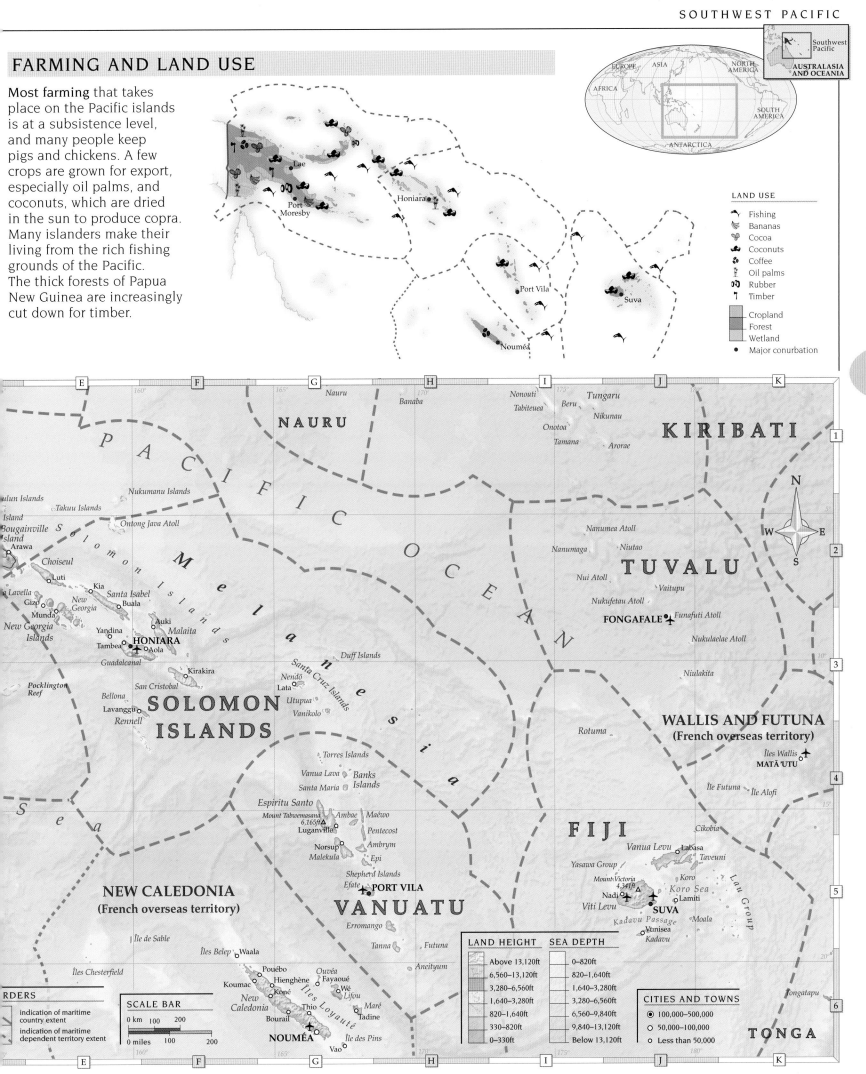

ANTARCTICA

The continent of Antarctica has no permanent human population and very few animals can survive on the frozen land, although the surrounding waters teem with fish and mammals. Even in the summer, the temperature is rarely above freezing and the sea-ice only partly melts; in winter, temperatures plummet to −112°F. The only people who live in Antarctica are teams of scientists who study the wildlife and monitor the ice for changes in the Earth's atmosphere.

THE LANDSCAPE

Frozen seas
During the cold winter months, the water surrounding Antarctica freezes, almost doubling the size of the continent.

Antarctica is the world's most southerly continent. It is also the world's coldest continent and its highest, mainly due to the great ice sheet – up to 1.25 miles thick in parts – that lies over the mountains of the Antarctic Peninsula and the plateau of East Antarctica.

Lambert Glacier (E4)
The Lambert Glacier is the world's largest series of glaciers. It is 50 miles wide at the coast and reaches more than 180 miles inland.

Transantarctic Mountains (C5)
The Transantarctic Mountains run across the continent, splitting it into East and West Antarctica.

Ice sheet
A massive sheet of ice, about 15,700 ft thick at its deepest point, covers almost the entire area of Antarctica. It contains most of the freshwater on Earth. The weight of the ice pushes the land down below sea level.

The Ross Ice Shelf (C5)
The Ross Sea is part of the Pacific Ocean. This deep bay is covered with a thick sheet of ice that floats on the ocean.

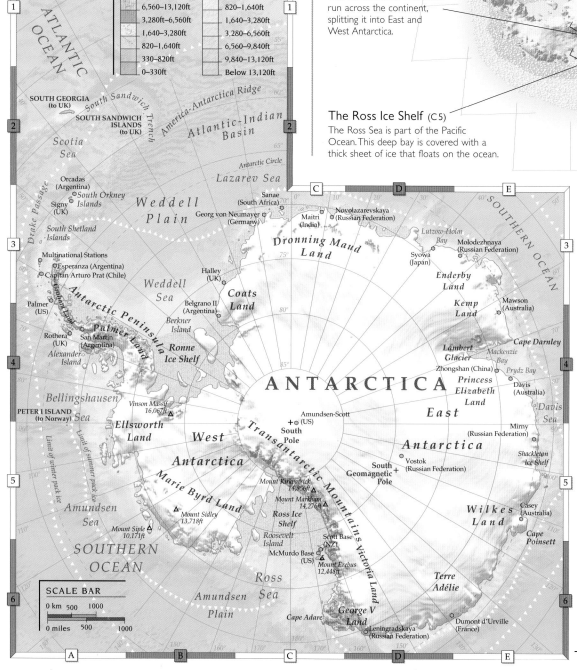

LAND HEIGHT
- Above 13,120ft
- 6,560–13,120ft
- 3,280ft–6,560ft
- 1,640–3,280ft
- 820–1,640ft
- 330–820ft
- 0–330ft

SEA DEPTH
- 0–820ft
- 820–1,640ft
- 1,640–3,280ft
- 3,280–6,560ft
- 6,560–9,840ft
- 9,840–13,120ft
- Below 13,120ft

○ Research Station
☐ Ice shelf

SCALE BAR
0 km 500 1000
0 miles 500 1000

RESOURCES

The mountains of Antarctica have rich mineral reserves. Gold, iron, and coal are found, and there is natural gas in the surrounding water. The unique and abundant marine wildlife is Antarctica's greatest resource. Colonies of penguins breed on the ice sheet, and whales, seals, and many bird and fish species thrive in the icy waters.

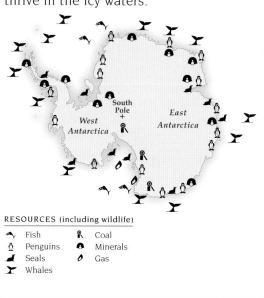

RESOURCES (including wildlife)
- Fish
- Penguins
- Seals
- Whales
- Coal
- Minerals
- Gas

THE ARCTIC

The ice-covered Arctic Ocean is encircled by the most northerly parts of Europe, North America, and Asia. Very few people live in the often-freezing conditions. Those who do, including the Sami of northern Scandinavia, the Siberian Yugyt and Nenet people, and the Canadian Inuit, were nomads who lived by hunting and herding. Some live like this today, but many have now settled in small towns.

THE LANDSCAPE

The Arctic Ocean is the smallest ocean in the world, covering a total area of 5,440,000 sq miles. The ocean is divided into two large basins, divided by three great underwater mountain ranges including the Lomonosov Ridge which is more than 9,842 ft high on average.

Lomonosov Ridge (C 4)

Arctic islands (A 4)
In the far north of Canada, there are many thousands of islands including Baffin Island and Victoria Island. Many of them are almost entirely surrounded by pack ice.

Pack ice
Much of the Arctic Ocean is permanently covered by pack ice. When the ice breaks up, it forms enormous floating ice masses called icebergs.

Greenland (A 3)
Greenland is the world's largest island. It is covered by a huge ice sheet, more than 649,960 sq miles across. The weight of the ice has pushed most of the land below sea level.

Sastrugi
Snow, blown by strong winds, can scratch deep patterns in the snow. These patterns are known as sastrugi and line up with the direction of the wind.

RESOURCES

Coal, oil, and gas are found beneath the Arctic Ocean and in Canada, Alaska, and Russia. Fears about damage to the environment and the cost of extracting these resources have restricted the quantities removed. Overfishing has reduced fish stocks to very low levels. Quotas have been put in place to allow them to revive.

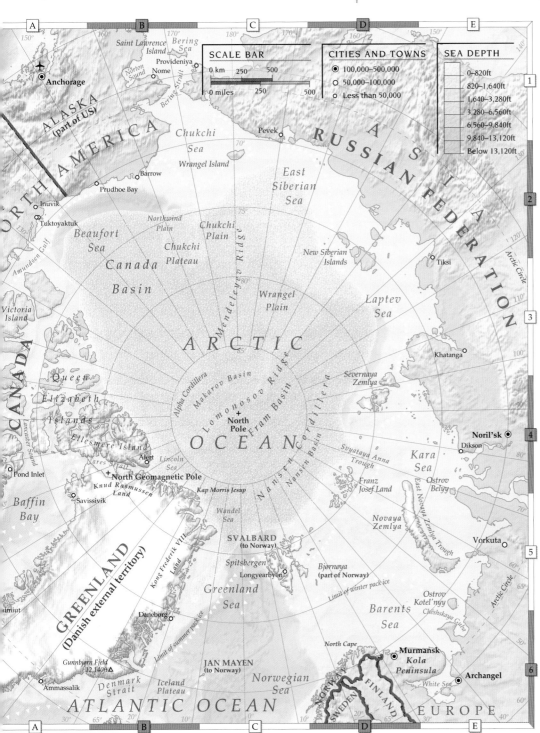

SCALE BAR
0 km 250 500
0 miles 250 500

CITIES AND TOWNS
◉ 100,000–500,000
○ 50,000–100,000
○ Less than 50,000

SEA DEPTH
0–820ft
820–1,640ft
1,640–3,280ft
3,280–6,560ft
6,560–9,840ft
9,840–13,120ft
Below 13,120ft

RESOURCES
⌐ Fish
Coal
Minerals
Oil and gas
• Major town/city

STANDARD TIME ZONES

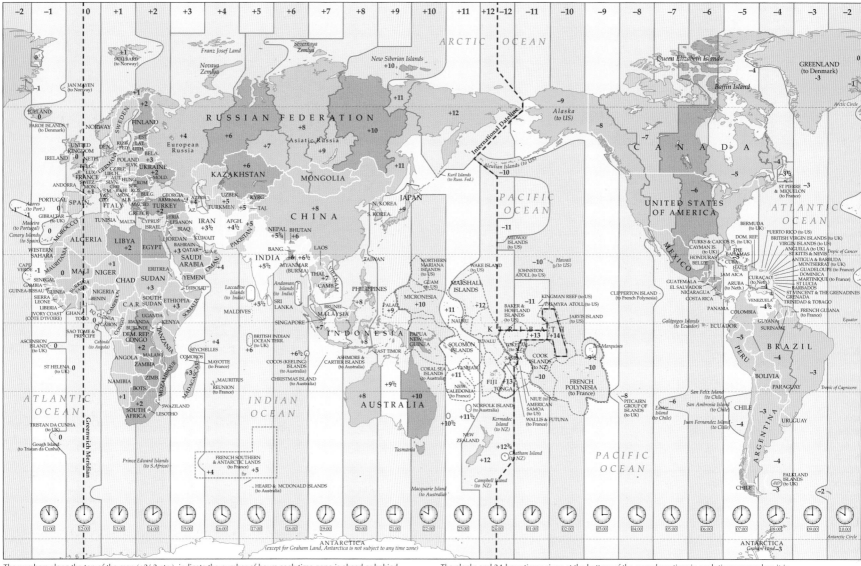

The numbers along the top of the map (+2/-2 etc.), indicate the number of hours each time zone is ahead or behind UTC (Coordinated Universal Time)

The clocks and 24-hour times given at the bottom of the map show time in each time zone when it is 12.00 hours noon UTC

TIME ZONES

The Earth is a rotating sphere, and because of this the Sun only shines on half of its surface at any one time. This means that it is morning, evening, and night time in different parts of the world (*see diagram below*). Because of these differences, each country or part of a country uses a local time. A region of Earth's surface which uses a single local time is called a time zone. There are 24 one-hour time zones around the world, arranged roughly in vertical longitudinal bands.

DAY AND NIGHT AROUND THE WORLD

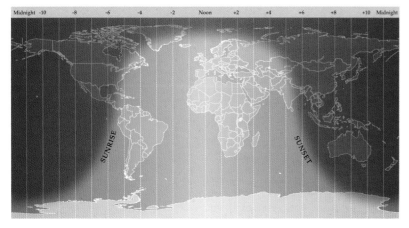

STANDARD TIME

Standard time is the official local time in a particular country or part of a country. Although time zones are arranged roughly in longitudinal bands, in many places the borders of a zone do not fall exactly along a line of longitude, as can be seen on the map, but are determined by geographical factors or by borders between countries.

Most countries have just one time zone, but some large countries (such as the US, Canada, and Russia) are split between several time zones, so standard time varies across those countries. For example, the US mainland crosses four time zones and so has four standard times, called the Eastern, Central, Mountain, and Pacific standard times. China is unusual in that just one standard time is used for the whole country, even though it extends across 60° of longitude from west to east.

COORDINATED UNIVERSAL TIME (UTC)

Coordinated Universal Time (UTC) is an international reference used to set the local time in each time zone. For example, Australian Western Standard Time (the local time in Western Australia) is set 8 hours ahead of UTC (it is UTC+8), so if it were 12.00 noon UTC in London, UK, it would be 8.00pm in Perth, Western Australia. UTC has replaced Greenwich Mean Time (GMT) because UTC is based on an atomic clock, which is more accurate and convenient than GMT. Greenwich Mean Time was determined by the Sun's position in the sky relative to the 0° line of longitude, also known as the Greenwich Meridian, which runs through Greenwich, UK.

THE INTERNATIONAL DATELINE

The International Dateline is an imaginary line from pole to pole that roughly corresponds to the 180° line of longitude. It is an arbitrary marker between calendar days. The dateline is needed because of the use of local times around the world rather than a single universal time. When moving from west to east across the dateline, travelers have to set their watches back one day. Those traveling in the opposite direction, from east to west, must add a day.

DAYLIGHT SAVING TIME

Daylight saving is a summertime adjustment to the local time in a country or region, designed to increase the hours of daylight that occur during people's normal waking hours. To follow the system, clocks are advanced by an hour on a pre-decided date in spring and reverted back in the fall. About half of the world's nations use daylight saving.

Largest Countries

Russian Federation	6,592,735 sq miles (17,075,200 sq km)
Canada	3,885,171 sq miles (9,984,670 sq km)
USA	3,794,100 sq miles (9,826,675 sq km)
China	3,705,386 sq miles (9,596,960 sq km)
Brazil	3,286,470 sq miles (8,511,965 sq km)
Australia	2,967,893 sq miles (7,686,850 sq km)
India	1,269,339 sq miles (3,287,590 sq km)
Argentina	1,068,296 sq miles (2,766,890 sq km)
Kazakhstan	1,049,150 sq miles (2,717,300 sq km)
Algeria	919,590 sq miles (2,381,740 sq km)

Smallest Countries

Vatican City	0.17 sq miles (0.44 sq km)
Monaco	0.75 sq miles (1.95 sq km)
Nauru	8.1 sq miles (21 sq km)
Tuvalu	10 sq miles (26 sq km)
San Marino	24 sq miles (61 sq km)
Liechtenstein	62 sq miles (160 sq km)
Marshall Islands	70 sq miles (181 sq km)
St. Kitts & Nevis	101 sq miles (261 sq km)
Maldives	116 sq miles (300 sq km)
Malta	122 sq miles (316 sq km)

Most Populous Countries

China	1,393,800,000
India	1,267,400,000
USA	322,600,000
Indonesia	252,800,000
Brazil	202,120,000
Pakistan	185,100,000
Nigeria	178,500,000
Bangladesh	155,500,000
Russian Federation	142,500,000
Japan	127,000,000

Least Populous Countries

Vatican City	800
Nauru	9500
Tuvalu	10,800
Palau	21,200
San Marino	32,700
Monaco	37,000
Liechtenstein	37,300
St. Kitts & Nevis	51,500
Marshall Islands	71,000
Dominica	73,400

Most Densely Populated Countries

Monaco	49,078 people per sq mile (18,949 per sq km)
Singapore	23,351 people per sq mile (9016 per sq km)
Vatican City	4957 people per sq mile (1914 per sq km)
Bahrain	4768 people per sq mile (1841 per sq km)
Maldives	3452 people per sq mile (1333 per sq km)
Malta	3237 people per sq mile (1250 per sq km)
Bangladesh	3066 people per sq mile (1184 per sq km)
Taiwan	1877 people per sq mile (725 per sq km)
Barbados	1808 people per sq mile (698 per sq km)
Mauritius	1670 people per sq mile (645 per sq km)

Most Sparsely Populated Countries

Mongolia	4 people per sq mile (2 per sq km)
Namibia	7 people per sq mile (3 per sq km)
Australia	7 people per sq mile (3 per sq km)
Suriname	8 people per sq mile (3 per sq km)
Iceland	8 people per sq mile (3 per sq km)
Botswana	9 people per sq mile (4 per sq km)
Mauritania	9 people per sq mile (4 per sq km)
Canada	9 people per sq mile (4 per sq km)
Libya	9 people per sq mile (4 per sq km)
Guyana	10 people per sq mile (4 per sq km)

Richest Countries

(GNI per capita, in US$)

Monaco	186,950
Liechtenstein	136,770
Norway	102,610
Switzerland	90,760
Qatar	86,790
Luxembourg	69,900
Australia	65,390
Sweden	61,760
Denmark	61,680
Singapore	54,040

Poorest Countries

(GNI per capita, in US$)

Burundi	260
Malawi	270
Somalia	288
Central African Republic	320
Niger	400
Liberia	410
Congo, Democratic Republic of	430
Madagascar	440
Guinea	460
Ethiopia	470

Most Widely Spoken Languages

1. Chinese (Mandarin)
2. English
3. Hindi, Hindustani, Urdu
4. Spanish
5. Russian
6. Arabic
7. Bengali
8. Portuguese
9. Malay-Indonesian
10. French

Largest Deserts

Sahara	3,450,000 sq miles (9,065,000 sq km)
Gobi	500,000 sq miles (1,295,000 sq km)
Empty Quarter (Ar Rub al Khali)	289,600 sq miles (750,000 sq km)
Great Victorian	249,800 sq miles (647,000 sq km)
Sonoran	120,000 sq miles (311,000 sq km)
Kalahari	120,000 sq miles (310,800 sq km)
Garagum	115,800 sq miles (300,000 sq km)
Takla Makan	100,400 sq miles (260,000 sq km)
Namib	52,100 sq miles (135,000 sq km)
Thar	33,670 sq miles (130,000 sq km)

NB – *Most of Antarctica is a polar desert, with only 2 inches (50 mm) of precipitation annually*

Largest Islands

Greenland	849,400 sq miles (2,200,000 sq km)
New Guinea	312,000 sq miles (808,000 sq km)
Borneo	292,222 sq miles (757,050 sq km)
Madagascar	229,300 sq miles (594,000 sq km)
Sumatra	202,300 sq miles (524,000 sq km)
Baffin Island	183,800 sq miles (476,000 sq km)
Honshu	88,800 sq miles (230,000 sq km)
Britain	88,700 sq miles (229,800 sq km)
Victoria Island	81,900 sq miles (212,000 sq km)
Ellesmere Island	75,700 sq miles (196,000 sq km)

Highest Mountains

(Height above sea level)

Everest	29,029 ft (8848 m)
K2	28,253 ft (8611 m)
Kanchenjunga I	28,210 ft (8598 m)
Makalu I	27,767 ft (8463 m)
Cho Oyu	26,907 ft (8201 m)
Dhaulagiri I	26,796 ft (8167 m)
Manaslu I	26,783 ft (8163 m)
Nanga Parbat I	26,661 ft (8126 m)
Annapurna I	26,547 ft (8091 m)
Gasherbrum I	26,471 ft (8068 m)

Deepest Ocean Features

Challenger Deep, Mariana Trench (Pacific)	35,826 ft (10,920 m)
Vityaz III Depth, Tonga Trench (Pacific)	35,704 ft (10,882 m)
Vityaz Depth, Kurile-Kamchatka Trench (Pacific)	34,588 ft (10,542 m)
Cape Johnson Deep, Philippine Trench (Pacific)	34,441 ft (10,497 m)
Kermadec Trench (Pacific)	32,964 ft (10,047 m)
Ramapo Deep, Japan Trench (Pacific)	32,758 ft (9984 m)
Milwaukee Deep, Puerto Rico Trench (Atlantic)	30,185 ft (9200 m)
Argo Deep, Torres Trench (Pacific)	30,070 ft (9165 m)
Meteor Depth, South Sandwich Trench (Atlantic)	30,000 ft (9144 m)
Planet Deep, New Britain Trench (Pacific)	29,988 ft (9140 m)

Largest Bodies of Inland Water

(Area & depth)

Caspian Sea	143,243 sq miles (371,000 sq km) 3215 ft (980 m)
Lake Superior	32,151 sq miles (83,270 sq km) 1289 ft (393 m)
Lake Victoria	26,560 sq miles (68,880 sq km) 328 ft (100 m)
Lake Huron	23,436 sq miles (60,700 sq km) 751 ft (229 m)
Lake Michigan	22,402 sq miles (58,020 sq km) 922 ft (281 m)
Lake Tanganyika	12,703 sq miles (32,900 sq km) 4700 ft (1435 m)
Great Bear Lake	12,274 sq miles (31,790 sq km) 1047 ft (319 m)
Lake Baikal	11,776 sq miles (30,500 sq km) 5712 ft (1741 m)
Great Slave Lake	10,981 sq miles (28,440 sq km) 459 ft (140 m)
Lake Erie	9915 sq miles (25,680 sq km) 197 ft (60 m)

Longest Rivers

Nile (NE Africa)	4160 miles (6695 km)
Amazon (South America)	4049 miles (6516 km)
Yangtze (China)	3915 miles (6299 km)
Mississippi/Missouri (US)	3710 miles (5969 km)
Ob'-Irtysh (Russ. Fed.)	3461 miles (5570 km)
Yellow River (China)	3395 miles (5464 km)
Congo (Central Africa)	2900 miles (4667 km)
Mekong (Southeast Asia)	2749 miles (4425 km)
Lena (Russian Federation)	2734 miles (4400 km)
Mackenzie (Canada)	2640 miles (4250 km)
Yenisey (Russian Federation)	2541 miles (4090 km)

Greatest Waterfalls

(Mean flow of water)

Boyoma (Congo)	600,400 cu. ft/sec (17,000 cu.m/sec)
Khône (Laos/Cambodia)	410,000 cu. ft/sec (11,600 cu.m/sec)
Niagara (USA/Canada)	195,000 cu. ft/sec (5500 cu.m/sec)
Grande (Uruguay)	160,000 cu. ft/sec (4500 cu.m/sec)
Paulo Afonso (Brazil)	100,000 cu. ft/sec (2800 cu.m/sec)
Urubupunga (Brazil)	97,000 cu. ft/sec (2750 cu.m/sec)
Iguaçu (Argentina/Brazil)	62,000 cu. ft/sec (1700 cu.m/sec)
Maribondo (Brazil)	53,000 cu. ft/sec (1500 cu.m/sec)
Victoria (Zimbabwe)	39,000 cu. ft/sec (1100 cu.m/sec)
Kabalega (Uganda)	42,000 cu. ft/sec (1200 cu.m/sec)
Churchill (Canada)	35,000 cu. ft/sec (1000 cu.m/sec)
Cauvery (India)	33,000 cu. ft/sec (900 cu.m/sec)

Highest Waterfalls

Angel (Venezuela)	3212 ft (979 m)
Tugela (South Africa)	3110 ft (948 m)
Utigard (Norway)	2625 ft (800 m)
Mongefossen (Norway)	2539 ft (774 m)
Mtarazi (Zimbabwe)	2500 ft (762 m)
Yosemite (USA)	2425 ft (739 m)
Ostre Mardola Foss (Norway)	2156 ft (657 m)
Tyssestrengane (Norway)	2119 ft (646 m)
*Cuquenan (Venezuela)	2001 ft (610 m)
Sutherland (New Zealand)	1903 ft (580 m)
*Kjellfossen (Norway)	1841 ft (561 m)

* *indicates that the total height is a single leap*

Country	Capital city	Land area (sq miles)	Main languages spoken	Unit of currency	Population (2014)
GENERAL FACTS					

NORTH AMERICA

Country	Capital city	Land area (sq miles)	Main languages spoken	Unit of currency	Population (2014)
Antigua & Barbuda	St John's	171	English, English patois	East Caribbean dollar	91 3(
Bahamas, The	Nassau	5 381	English, English Creole, French Creole	Bahamian dollar	400 0(
Barbados	Bridgetown	166	Bajan (Barbadian English), English	Barbados dollar	300 0(
Belize	Belmopan	8 865	English Creole, Spanish, English, Mayan, Garifuna (Carib)	Belizean dollar	300 0
Canada	Ottawa	3 885 171	English, French, Chinese, Italian, German, Ukrainian, Portuguese, Inuktitut, Cree	Canadian dollar	35 500 0
Costa Rica	San José	19 725	Spanish, English Creole, Bribri, Cabecar	Costa Rican colón	4 900 0(
Cuba	Havana	42 792	Spanish	Cuban peso	11 300 0(
Dominica	Roseau	291	French Creole, English	East Caribbean dollar	73 4(
Dominican Republic	Santo Domingo	18 810	Spanish, French Creole	Dominican Republic peso	10 500 0(
El Salvador	San Salvador	8 121	Spanish	Salvadorean colón, US $	6 400 0(
Grenada	St George's	133	English, English Creole	East Caribbean dollar	110 0(
Guatemala	Guatemala City	42 032	Quiché, Mam, Cakchiquel, Kekchí, Spanish	Quetzal	15 900 0(
Haiti	Port-au-Prince	10 712	French Creole, French	Gourde	10 500 0(
Honduras	Tegucigalpa	43 267	Spanish, Garífuna (Carib), English Creole	Lempira	8 300 0(
Jamaica	Kingston	4 243	English Creole, English	Jamaican dollar	2 800 0(
Mexico	Mexico City	744 034	Spanish, Nahuatl, Mayan, Zapotec, Mixtec, Otomi, Totonac, Tzotzil, Tzeltal	Mexican peso	123 800 0(
Nicaragua	Managua	49 985	Spanish, English Creole, Miskito	Córdoba oro	6 200 0(
Panama	Panama City	30 185	English Creole, Spanish, Amerindian languages, Chibchan languages	Balboa, US dollar	3 900 0(
St Kitts & Nevis	Basseterre	101	English, English Creole	East Caribbean dollar	51 5(
St Lucia	Castries	238	English, French Creole	East Caribbean dollar	200 0(
St Vincent & the Grenadines	Kingstown	150	English, English Creole	East Caribbean dollar	103 0(
Trinidad & Tobago	Port-of-Spain	2 037	English Creole, English, Hindi, French, Spanish	Trinidad and Tobago dollar	1 300 0(
United States	Washington D.C.	3 794 100	English, Spanish, Chinese, French, German, Tagalog, Vietnamese, Italian, Korean, Russian, Polish	US dollar	322 600 0(

SOUTH AMERICA

Country	Capital city	Land area (sq miles)	Main languages spoken	Unit of currency	Population (2014)
Argentina	Buenos Aires	1 068 296	Spanish, Italian, Amerindian languages	Argentine peso	41 800 0(
Bolivia	La Paz/Sucre	424 052	Aymara, Quechua, Spanish	Boliviano	10 800 0(
Brazil	Brasília	3 286 470	Portuguese, German, Italian, Spanish, Polish, Japanese, Amerindian languages	Real	202 000 0(
Chile	Santiago	292 183	Spanish, Amerindian languages	Chilean peso	17 800 0(
Colombia	Bogotá	439 619	Spanish, Wayuu, Páez, other Amerindian languages	Colombian peso	48 900 0(
Ecuador	Quito	109 454	Spanish, Quechua, other Amerindian languages	US dollar	16 000 0(
Guyana	Georgetown	82 978	English Creole, Hindi, Tamil, Amerindian languages, English	Guyanese dollar	800 0(
Paraguay	Asunción	157 006	Guaraní, Spanish, German	Guaraní	6 900 0(
Peru	Lima	496 095	Spanish, Quechua, Aymara	New sol	30 800 0(
Suriname	Paramaribo	63 022	Sranan (creole), Dutch, Javanese, Sarnami Hindi, Saramaccan, Chinese, Carib	Surinamese dollar	500 0(
Uruguay	Montevideo	68 021	Spanish	Uruguayan peso	3 400 0(
Venezuela	Caracas	352 051	Spanish, Amerindian languages	Bolívar fuerte	30 900 0(

AFRICA

Country	Capital city	Land area (sq miles)	Main languages spoken	Unit of currency	Population (2014)
Algeria	Algiers	919 590	Arabic, Tamazight (Kabyle, Shawia, Tamashek), French	Algerian dinar	39 900 0(
Angola	Luanda	481 226	Portuguese, Umbundu, Kimbundu, Kikongo	Readjusted kwanza	22 100 0(
Benin	Porto-Novo	43 471	Fon, Bariba, Yoruba, Adja, Houeda, Somba, French	CFA franc	10 600 0(
Botswana	Gaborone	231 743	Setswana, English, Shona, San, Khoikhoi, isiNdebele	Pula	2 000 0(
Burkina Faso	Ouagadougou	105 841	Mossi, Fulani, French, Tuareg, Dyula, Songhai	CFA franc	17 400 0(
Burundi	Bujumbura	10 742	Kirundi, French, Kiswahili	Burundian franc	10 500 0(
Cameroon	Yaoundé	183 520	Bamileke, Fang, Fulani, French, English	CFA franc	22 800 0(
Cape Verde	Praia	1 557	Portuguese Creole, Portuguese	Escudo	500 0(
Central African Republic	Bangui	240 472	Sango, Banda, Gbaya, French	CFA franc	4 700 0(
Chad	N'Djamena	495 624	French, Sara, Arabic, Maba	CFA franc	13 200 0(
Comoros	Moroni	838	Arabic, Comoran, French	Comoros franc	800 0(
Congo, Democratic Republic	Kinshasa	905 328	Kiswahili, Tshiluba, Kikongo, Lingala, French	Congolese franc	69 400 0(

POPULATION					HEALTH AND EDUCATION					ECONOMIC DEVELOPMENT			TECHNOLOGICAL DEVELOPMENT		
Population density per sq mile (2014)	Birth rate per 1 000 population (2012)	Death rate per 1 000 population (2012)	Life expectancy at birth (years; 2013–2014)		Medical doctors per 10 000 people (2004–2013)	Infant mortality (deaths per 1 000 live births; 2013)	Adult literacy rate (percentage of adults over 15; 2015)		Average calorie intake per person (2011)	GNI per person (US$; 2013)	Annual electricity consumption per person (kWh; 2012)	Annual military expenditure as percentage of GDP (2009–2014)	Mobile telephones per 1 000 population (2013)	Internet users per 1 000 population (2013)	ICT Dev. Index (IDI), compiled by the ITU (2013)
			Male	Female			Male	Female							
536	17	7	74	78	1.7	8	98.4	99.0	2 396	13 050	3 291	0.7	1 271	634	57
104	15	6	72	78	28.2	10	95.0	96.7	2 575	21 570	4 290	0.7	761	720	-
1 808	13	7	73	78	18.1	13	99.0	99.0	3 047	15 080	3 127	0.7	1 081	750	35
34	24	4	71	77	8.3	14	76.7	77.1	2 757	4 510	2 017	1.0	526	317	-
10	11	7	79	84	20.7	5	99.0	99.0	3 419	52 200	15 125	1.0	806	858	23
249	15	4	78	82	11.1	8	97.7	97.8	2 898	9 550	1 872	0.7	1 460	460	55
264	10	8	77	81	67.2	5	99.0	99.0	3 277	5 890	1 290	3.3	177	257	125
254	16	7	74	80	15.9	10	94.0	94.0	3 047	6 930	1 227	0.0	1 300	590	83
562	21	5	70	77	14.9	24	91.2	92.3	2 597	5 770	1 167	0.6	884	459	102
800	20	7	68	77	16.0	14	90.4	86.0	2 513	3 720	899	1.1	1 362	231	110
839	19	7	70	75	6.6	11	96.0	96.0	2 453	7 490	1 633	-	1 256	350	76
381	31	6	69	76	9.3	26	87.4	76.3	2 502	3 340	541	0.5	1 404	197	118
987	26	9	61	65	2.5	55	64.3	57.3	2 105	810	44	0.2	694	106	-
192	26	5	72	76	3.7	19	88.4	88.6	2 651	2 180	637	1.2	959	178	119
671	18	7	71	76	4.1	14	84.0	93.1	2 789	5 220	1 074	0.8	1 022	378	97
168	19	5	75	80	21.0	12	96.2	94.2	3 024	9 940	2 015	0.6	858	435	95
135	23	5	72	78	3.7	20	82.4	83.2	2 564	1 790	593	0.8	1 120	155	120
132	20	5	75	81	15.5	15	95.7	94.1	2 644	10 700	1 984	1.1	1 630	429	82
370	14	9	73	78	11.7	8	-	-	2 507	13 890	2 567	-	1 421	800	54
850	16	7	72	78	4.7	13	89.5	90.6	2 629	7 060	2 074	0.0	1 163	352	79
785	17	6	70	75	5.3	17	96.0	96.0	2 960	6 460	1 231	0.0	1 146	520	72
655	15	9	66	74	11.8	19	99.0	99.0	2 889	15 760	5 975	0.8	1 449	638	67
91	13	8	77	81	24.5	6	99.0	99.0	3 639	53 470	12 140	3.8	955	842	14
39	17	8	73	80	32.1	12	98.0	98.1	3 155	6 290	2 849	0.7	1 625	599	59
26	26	7	65	70	4.7	31	97.8	93.6	2 254	2 550	633	1.5	977	395	107
62	15	7	70	78	18.9	12	92.2	92.9	3 287	11 690	2 437	1.4	1 353	516	65
62	14	5	77	83	10.3	7	97.6	97.4	2 989	15 230	3 643	2.0	1 343	665	56
122	19	4	70	78	14.7	14	94.6	94.8	2 593	7 590	1 037	3.4	1 041	517	77
150	21	5	74	79	16.9	19	95.4	93.5	2 477	5 760	1 277	3.0	1 115	404	88
10	21	8	64	69	2.1	30	87.2	89.8	2 648	3 750	698	1.1	694	330	111
44	24	5	70	75	11.1	19	96.1	95.0	2 698	4 010	1 213	1.6	1 037	369	109
62	20	4	72	78	11.3	13	97.3	91.7	2 624	6 270	1 202	1.4	981	392	105
8	18	4	68	74	9.1	20	96.1	95.0	2 727	9 370	3 144	1.1	1 611	374	98
49	15	9	74	81	37.4	10	98.2	99.0	2 939	15 180	2 811	1.9	1 546	581	48
91	20	5	72	78	19.4	13	96.4	96.2	2 880	12 550	3 267	1.2	1 016	549	80
44	25	6	69	73	12.1	22	87.2	73.1	3 220	5 330	1 174	5.0	1 008	165	114
47	45	14	50	53	1.7	102	82.0	60.7	2 400	5 170	240	4.9	619	191	139
249	37	10	58	61	0.6	56	49.9	27.3	2 594	790	97	1.0	933	49	149
10	24	8	62	67	3.4	36	88.0	88.9	2 285	7 770	1 530	2.0	1 606	150	104
166	41	10	56	57	0.5	64	43.0	29.3	2 655	670	56	1.4	664	44	156
1 059	45	12	52	56	0.3	55	88.2	83.1	1 604	260	33	2.2	250	13	-
127	38	11	54	56	0.8	61	81.2	68.9	2 586	1 290	270	1.3	704	64	140
321	20	5	71	79	3.0	22	92.1	83.1	2 716	3 620	571	0.5	1 001	375	93
21	35	14	48	52	0.5	96	50.7	24.4	2 154	320	37	2.6	295	35	166
26	46	14	50	52	0.4	88	48.5	31.9	2 061	1 030	16	2.0	356	23	164
930	36	8	60	62	1.5	58	81.8	73.7	2 139	840	50	2.8	473	65	-
80	43	14	48	52	1.1	86	78.1	50.0	1 585	430	105	1.3	418	22	157

	GENERAL FACTS				
Country	Capital city	Land area (sq miles)	Main languages spoken	Unit of currency	Population (2014)
Congo	Brazzaville	132 012	Kongo, Teke, Lingala, French	CFA franc	4 600 000
Côte d'Ivoire	Yamoussoukro	124 470	Akan, French, Krou, Voltaïque	CFA franc	20 800 000
Djibouti	Djibouti	8 878	Somali, Afar, French, Arabic	Djibouti franc	900 000
Egypt	Cairo	386 560	Arabic, French, English, Berber	Egyptian pound	83 400 000
Equatorial Guinea	Malabo	10 828	Spanish, Fang, Bubi, French	CFA franc	800 000
Eritrea	Asmara	46 830	Tigrinya, English, Tigre, Afar, Arabic, Saho, Bilen, Kunama, Nara, Hadareb	Nakfa	6 500 000
Ethiopia	Addis Ababa	435 071	Amharic, Tigrinya, Galla, Sidamo, Somali, English, Arabic	Birr	96 500 000
Gabon	Libreville	103 319	Fang, French, Punu, Sira, Nzebi, Mpongwe	CFA franc	1 700 000
Gambia	Banjul	4 362	Mandinka, Fulani, Wolof, Jola, Soninke, English	Dalasi	1 900 000
Ghana	Accra	92 432	Twi, Fanti, Ewe, Ga, Adangbe, Gurma, Dagomba (Dagbani), English	Cedi	26 400 000
Guinea	Conakry	94 901	Pulaar, Malinké, Soussou, French	Guinea franc	12 000 000
Guinea-Bissau	Bissau	13 942	Portuguese Creole, Balante, Fulani, Malinké, Portuguese	CFA franc	1 700 000
Kenya	Nairobi	224 903	Kiswahili, English, Kikuyu, Luo, Kalenjin, Kamba	Kenya shilling	45 500 000
Lesotho	Maseru	11 717	English, Sesotho, isiZulu	Loti, S African rand	2 100 000
Liberia	Monrovia	42 989	Kpelle, Vai, Bassa, Kru, Grebo, Kissi, Gola, Loma, English	Liberian dollar	4 400 000
Libya	Tripoli	679 182	Arabic, Tuareg	Libyan dinar	6 300 000
Madagascar	Antananarivo	226 597	Malagasy, French, English	Ariary	23 600 000
Malawi	Lilongwe	45 733	Chewa, Lomwe, Yao, Ngoni, English	Malawi kwacha	16 800 000
Mali	Bamako	478 640	Bambara, Fulani, Senufo, Soninke, French	CFA franc	15 800 000
Mauritania	Nouakchott	397 850	Arabic, Hassaniyah Arabic, Wolof, French	Ouguiya	4 000 000
Mauritius	Port Louis	787	French Creole, Hindi, Urdu, Tamil, Chinese, English, French	Mauritian rupee	1 200 000
Morocco	Rabat	172 368	Arabic, Tamazight (Berber), French, Spanish	Moroccan dirham	33 500 000
Mozambique	Maputo	309 414	Makua, Xitsonga, Sena, Lomwe, Portuguese	New metical	26 500 000
Namibia	Windhoek	318 611	Ovambo, Kavango, English, Bergdama, German, Afrikaans	Namibian $, S African rand	2 300 000
Niger	Niamey	489 062	Hausa, Djerma, Fulani, Tuareg, Teda, French	CFA franc	18 500 000
Nigeria	Abuja	356 574	Hausa, English, Yoruba, Ibo	Naira	178 500 000
Rwanda	Kigali	10 166	Kinyarwanda, French, Kiswahili, English	Rwanda franc	12 100 000
São Tomé & Príncipe	São Tomé	386	Portuguese Creole, Portuguese	Dobra	200 000
Senegal	Dakar	75 729	Wolof, Pulaar, Serer, Diola, Mandinka, Malinké, Soninké, French	CFA franc	14 500 000
Seychelles	Victoria	176	French Creole, English, French	Seychelles rupee	91 700
Sierra Leone	Freetown	27 692	Mende, Temne, Krio, English	Leone	6 200 000
Somalia	Mogadishu	246 136	Somali, Arabic, English, Italian	Somali shilin	10 800 000
South Africa	Pretoria/Cape Town/Bloemfontein	470 886	English, isiZulu, isiXhosa, Afrikaans, Sepedi, Setswana, 5 other official languages	Rand	53 100 000
South Sudan	Juba	248 777	Arabic, Dinka, Nuer, Zande, Bari, Shilluk, Lotuko, English	South Sudan pound	11 700 000
Sudan	Khartoum	718 722	Arabic, Nubian, Beja, Fur	New Sudanese pound	38 800 000
Swaziland	Mbabane	6 702	English, siSwati, isiZulu, Xitsonga	Lilangeni	1 300 000
Tanzania	Dodoma	364 804	Kiswahili, Sukuma, Chagga, Nyamwezi, Hehe, Makonde, Yao, Sandawe, English	Tanzanian shilling	50 800 000
Togo	Lomé	21 919	Ewe, Kabye, Gurma, French	CFA franc	7 000 000
Tunisia	Tunis	63 153	Arabic, French	Tunisian dinar	11 100 000
Uganda	Kampala	91 111	Luganda, Nkole, Chiga, Lango, Acholi, Teso, Lugbara, English	Uganda shilling	38 800 000
Western Sahara (occupied by Morocco)	Laâyoune	102 676	Arabic, Hassaniyah Arabic, Tamazight (Berber), Spanish	Moroccan dirham	555 000
Zambia	Lusaka	290 509	Bemba, Tonga, Nyanja, Lozi, Lala-Bisa, Nsenga, English	New Zambian kwacha	15 000 000
Zimbabwe	Harare	150 764	Shona, isiNdebele, English	US dollar, S African rand*	14 600 000
EUROPE					
Albania	Tirana	11 097	Albanian, Greek	Lek	3 200 000
Andorra	Andorra la Vella	181	Spanish, Catalan, French, Portuguese	Euro	85 500
Austria	Vienna	32 374	German, Croatian, Slovenian, Hungarian (Magyar)	Euro	8 500 000
Belarus	Minsk	80 134	Belarussian, Russian	Belarussian rouble	9 300 000
Belgium	Brussels	11 784	Dutch, French, German	Euro	11 100 000
Bosnia & Herzegovina	Sarajevo	19 736	Bosnian, Serbian, Croatian	Marka	3 800 000
Bulgaria	Sofia	42 811	Bulgarian, Turkish, Romani	Lev	7 200 000
Croatia	Zagreb	21 825	Croatian	Kuna	4 300 000

148

* Zimbabwe dollar suspended in 2009; US dollar, South African rand, euro, UK pound, Botswanan pula, Australian dollar, Chinese yuan, Indian rupee, and Japanese yen are legal tender

POPULATION					HEALTH AND EDUCATION					ECONOMIC DEVELOPMENT			TECHNOLOGICAL DEVELOPMENT		
Population density per sq mile (2014)	Birth rate per 1 000 population (2012)	Death rate per 1 000 population (2012)	Life expectancy at birth (years; 2013–2014)		Medical doctors per 10 000 people (2004–2013)	Infant mortality (deaths per 1 000 live births; 2013)	Adult literacy rate (percentage of adults over 15; 2015)		Average calorie intake per person (2011)	GNI per person (US$; 2013)	Annual electricity consumption per person (kWh; 2012)	Annual military expenditure as percentage of GDP (2009–2014)	Mobile telephones per 1 000 population (2013)	Internet users per 1 000 population (2013)	ICT Dev. Index (IDI), compiled by the ITU (2013)
			Male	Female			Male	Female							
34	38	10	57	60	1.0	36	86.4	72.9	2 195	2 590	176	5.6	1 048	66	137
168	37	13	50	52	1.4	71	53.1	32.5	2 781	1 450	230	1.5	954	26	151
101	28	9	60	63	2.3	57	79.9	61.4	2 526	1 030	346	3.5	280	95	141
218	24	6	69	74	28.3	19	82.2	65.4	3 557	3 140	1 614	1.7	1 215	496	89
75	36	12	52	55	3.0	69	97.4	93.0	-	14 320	133	1.0	675	164	-
142	37	7	61	65	0.5	36	82.4	65.5	1 640	490	51	4.2	56	9	163
255	34	8	62	65	0.2	44	57.2	41.1	2 105	470	60	0.8	273	19	162
18	32	9	62	65	2.9	39	85.3	81.0	2 781	10 650	1 050	1.3	2 148	92	126
492	43	8	58	60	0.4	49	63.9	47.6	2 849	500	121	1.6	1 000	140	135
298	31	8	60	62	1.0	52	82.0	71.4	3 003	1 770	334	0.5	1 082	123	113
127	37	10	55	57	1.0	65	38.1	22.8	2 553	460	86	3.8	633	16	161
155	38	12	53	56	0.5	78	71.8	48.3	2 304	590	29	1.7	741	31	154
207	36	9	60	64	1.8	48	81.1	74.9	2 189	1 160	155	1.6	718	390	124
179	28	14	49	50	0.5	73	70.1	88.3	2 595	1 500	321	2.1	863	50	132
119	36	8	60	62	0.1	54	62.4	32.8	2 251	410	66	0.7	594	46	153
10	21	4	74	77	19.0	12	96.7	85.6	3 211	12 930	4 236	6.2	1 650	165	-
106	35	7	63	66	1.6	40	66.7	62.6	2 092	440	86	0.5	369	22	160
464	40	10	55	55	0.2	44	73.0	58.6	2 334	270	128	1.4	323	54	158
34	47	12	55	55	0.8	78	48.2	29.2	2 833	670	54	1.4	1 291	23	143
10	35	8	60	63	1.3	67	62.6	41.6	2 791	1 060	267	3.6	1 025	62	147
1 670	12	7	70	77	10.6	12	92.9	88.5	3 055	9 290	1 902	0.2	1 232	390	70
194	23	6	69	73	6.2	26	78.6	58.8	3 334	3 020	819	3.9	1 285	560	96
88	39	12	49	51	0.4	62	73.3	45.4	2 267	610	461	1.0	480	54	159
8	26	6	62	67	3.7	35	79.2	84.5	2 086	5 870	1 582	3.0	1 184	139	117
39	50	10	58	59	0.2	60	27.3	11.0	2 546	400	56	1.1	393	17	165
508	42	12	52	53	4.0	74	69.2	49.7	2 724	2 710	149	0.5	733	380	133
1 256	36	7	62	66	0.6	37	73.2	68.0	2 148	630	32	1.1	568	87	148
539	35	7	64	68	4.9	37	81.8	68.4	2 676	1 470	302	0.5	649	230	-
194	38	7	62	65	0.6	44	69.7	46.6	2 426	1 050	197	0.01	929	209	130
878	17	7	69	78	15.1	12	91.4	92.3	2 426	13 210	3 264	0.9	1 473	504	75
225	37	17	45	46	0.2	107	58.7	37.7	2 333	660	22	0.01	657	17	-
44	44	14	53	57	0.4	90	49.7	25.8	1 696	288	30	0.9	494	15	-
111	21	12	55	59	7.8	33	95.5	93.1	3 007	7 190	4 173	1.2	1 456	489	90
47	37	12	54	56	-	64	40.0	16.0	-	950	173	9.3	253	-	-
54	34	8	60	64	2.8	51	83.3	68.6	2 346	1 550	173	1.3	729	227	122
197	30	12	50	48	1.7	56	87.4	87.5	2 275	2 990	1 079	3.0	715	247	128
148	40	8	60	63	0.1	36	75.9	65.4	2 167	630	95	1.1	557	44	152
334	37	10	56	57	0.5	56	78.3	55.3	2 366	530	155	1.6	625	45	-
184	17	6	74	78	12.2	13	89.6	74.2	3 362	4 200	1 244	2.0	1 156	438	99
502	44	10	58	60	1.2	44	85.3	71.5	2 279	550	79	2.2	441	162	146
5	31	8	60	65	4.4	56	-	-	-	2 500	151	-	-	-	-
52	43	10	56	60	0.7	56	70.9	56.0	1 937	1 810	599	1.4	715	154	144
98	32	10	59	61	0.6	55	88.5	84.6	2 210	860	525	2.6	963	185	121
303	13	9	75	81	11.5	13	98.4	96.9	3 023	4 710	1 268	1.3	1 162	601	84
477	9	8	79	86	39.1	2	99.0	99.0	-	43 110	-	0.0	807	940	20
267	10	9	79	84	48.3	3	99.0	99.0	3 784	50 430	7 620	0.8	1 562	806	24
117	11	13	64	76	37.6	4	99.0	99.0	3 253	6 730	3 503	1.3	1 188	542	38
875	12	10	78	83	29.0	4	99.0	99.0	3 793	46 290	7 583	1.0	1 109	822	25
192	9	9	74	79	16.9	6	99.0	97.5	3 130	4 780	3 218	1.1	911	679	69
168	10	15	70	77	38.1	10	99.0	98.1	2 877	7 360	4 216	1.5	1 452	531	49
197	10	12	74	80	30.0	4	99.0	99.0	3 052	13 430	4 461	1.7	1 145	667	37

	GENERAL FACTS				
Country	Capital city	Land area (sq miles)	Main languages spoken	Unit of currency	Population (2014)
Cyprus	Nicosia	3 571	Greek, Turkish	Euro; Turkish lira in TRNC	1 200 000
Czech Republic	Prague	30 442	Czech, Slovak, Hungarian (Magyar)	Czech koruna	10 700 000
Denmark	Copenhagen	16 634	Danish	Danish krone	5 600 000
Estonia	Tallinn	17 457	Estonian, Russian	Euro	1 300 000
Finland	Helsinki	130 524	Finnish, Swedish, Sámi	Euro	5 400 000
France	Paris	211 154	French, Provençal, German, Breton, Catalan, Basque	Euro	64 600 000
Germany	Berlin	137 807	German, Turkish	Euro	82 700 000
Greece	Athens	50 543	Greek, Turkish, Macedonian, Albanian	Euro	11 100 000
Hungary	Budapest	35 910	Hungarian (Magyar)	Forint	9 900 000
Iceland	Reykjavík	39 758	Icelandic	Icelandic króna	300 000
Ireland	Dublin	27 128	English, Irish	Euro	4 700 000
Italy	Rome	116 275	Italian, German, French, Rhaeto-Romanic, Sardinian	Euro	61 100 000
Kosovo (disputed)	Pristina	4 212	Albanian, Serbian, Bosniak, Gorani, Roma, Turkish	Euro	1 900 000
Latvia	Riga	24 931	Latvian, Russian	Euro	2 000 000
Liechtenstein	Vaduz	62	German, Alemannish dialect, Italian	Swiss franc	37 300
Lithuania	Vilnius	25 167	Lithuanian, Russian	Euro	3 000 000
Luxembourg	Luxembourg-Ville	998	Luxembourgish, German, French	Euro	500 000
Macedonia	Skopje	9 779	Macedonian, Albanian, Turkish, Romani, Serbian	Macedonian denar	2 100 000
Malta	Valletta	122	Maltese, English	Euro	400 000
Moldova	Chisinau	13 063	Moldovan, Ukrainian, Russian	Moldovan leu	3 500 000
Monaco	Monaco-Ville	0.75	French, Italian, Monégasque, English	Euro	37 000
Montenegro	Podgorica	5 331	Montenegrin, Serbian, Albanian, Bosniak, Croatian	Euro	600 000
Netherlands	Amsterdam/The Hague	16 029	Dutch, Frisian	Euro	16 800 000
Norway	Oslo	125 149	Norwegian (*Bokmål* "book language" and *Nynorsk* "new Norsk"), Sámi	Norwegian krone	5 100 000
Poland	Warsaw	120 696	Polish	Zloty	38 200 000
Portugal	Lisbon	35 663	Portuguese	Euro	10 600 000
Romania	Bucharest	91 675	Romanian, Hungarian (Magyar), Romani, German	New Romanian leu	21 600 000
Russian Federation	Moscow	6 592 735	Russian, Tatar, Ukrainian, Chavash, various other national languages	Russian rouble	142 500 000
San Marino	San Marino	24	Italian	Euro	32 700
Serbia	Belgrade	29 905	Serbian, Hungarian (Magyar)	Serbian dinar	9 500 000
Slovakia	Bratislava	18 854	Slovak, Hungarian (Magyar), Czech	Euro	5 500 000
Slovenia	Ljubljana	7 825	Slovenian	Euro	2 100 000
Spain	Madrid	194 846	Spanish, Catalan, Galician, Basque	Euro	47 100 000
Sweden	Stockholm	173 686	Swedish, Finnish, Sámi	Swedish krona	9 600 000
Switzerland	Bern	15 938	German, Swiss-German, French, Italian, Romansch	Swiss franc	8 200 000
Ukraine	Kiev	233 028	Ukrainian, Russian, Tatar	Hryvna	44 900 000
United Kingdom	London	94 501	English, Welsh, Scottish Gaelic, Irish	Pound sterling	63 500 000
Vatican City	Vatican City	0.17	Italian, Latin	Euro	800

ASIA

Afghanistan	Kabul	249 935	Pashtu, Tajik, Dari, Farsi, Uzbek, Turkmen	Afghani	31 300 000
Armenia	Yerevan	11 503	Armenian, Azeri, Russian	Dram	3 000 000
Azerbaijan	Baku	33 428	Azeri, Russian	New manat	9 500 000
Bahrain	Manama	257	Arabic	Bahraini dinar	1 300 000
Bangladesh	Dhaka	55 584	Bengali, Urdu, Chakma, Marma (Magh), Garo, Khasi, Santhali, Tripuri, Mro	Taka	158 500 000
Bhutan	Thimphu	18 142	Dzongkha, Nepali, Assamese	Ngultrum	800 000
Brunei	Bandar Seri Begawan	2 227	Malay, English, Chinese	Brunei dollar	400 000
Cambodia	Phnom Penh	69 881	Khmer, French, Chinese, Vietnamese, Cham	Riel	15 400 000
China	Beijing	3 705 386	Mandarin, Wu, Cantonese, Hsiang, Min, Hakka, Kan	Renminbi (known as yuan)	1 393 800 000
East Timor	Dili	5 793	Tetum (Portuguese/Austronesian), Bahasa Indonesia, Portuguese	US dollar	1 200 000
Georgia	Tbilisi	26 904	Georgian, Russian, Azeri, Armenian, Mingrelian, Ossetian, Abkhazian	Lari	4 300 000
India	New Delhi	1 269 339	Hindi, English, Urdu, Bengali, Marathi, Telugu, Tamil, Bihari, Gujarati, Kanarese	Indian rupee	1 267 400 000

POPULATION					HEALTH AND EDUCATION					ECONOMIC DEVELOPMENT			TECHNOLOGICAL DEVELOPMENT		
Population density per sq mile (2014)	Birth rate per 1 000 population (2012)	Death rate per 1 000 population (2012)	Life expectancy at birth (years; 2013–2014)		Medical doctors per 10 000 people (2004–2013)	Infant mortality (deaths per 1 000 live births; 2013)	Adult literacy rate (percentage of adults over 15; 2015)		Average calorie intake per person (2011)	GNI per person (US$; 2013)	Annual electricity consumption per person (kWh; 2012)	Annual military expenditure as percentage of GDP (2009–2014)	Mobile telephones per 1 000 population (2013)	Internet users per 1 000 population (2013)	ICT Dev. Index (IDI), compiled by the ITU (2013)
			Male	Female			Male	Female							
337	12	6	78	82	22.9	3	99.0	99.0	2 661	25 210	3 905	2.1	964	654	51
352	11	10	75	81	36.2	3	99.0	99.0	3 292	18 950	5 712	1.0	1 277	741	41
342	11	10	77	82	34.2	3	99.0	99.0	3 363	61 680	5 708	1.4	1 271	946	1
75	11	12	69	80	32.6	3	99.0	99.0	3 214	17 690	6 323	1.9	1 597	800	21
47	11	9	77	84	29.1	2	99.0	99.0	3 285	48 820	15 192	1.2	1 716	915	8
303	12	9	78	85	31.8	4	99.0	99.0	3 524	43 460	7 104	2.2	985	819	18
614	8	11	78	83	38.1	3	99.0	99.0	3 539	47 270	6 587	1.3	1 209	840	17
220	10	10	78	83	61.7	4	99.0	96.9	3 433	22 690	5 064	2.5	1 168	599	39
277	10	13	71	79	29.6	5	99.0	99.0	2 968	13 260	3 713	0.9	1 164	726	46
8	15	6	80	84	34.8	2	99.0	99.0	3 339	46 400	56 467	0.1	1 081	966	4
176	16	6	79	83	27.2	3	99.0	99.0	3 591	43 110	5 270	0.5	1 028	782	26
539	9	9	80	85	40.9	3	99.0	99.0	3 539	35 860	4 969	1.5	1 588	585	36
451	18	7	68	72	10.8	11	95.3	90.1	-	3 940	2 676	-	845	766	-
80	11	14	67	78	28.8	7	99.0	99.0	3 293	15 280	3 246	1.0	2 284	752	33
603	10	12	80	84	13.1	8	99.0	99.0	-	136 770	-	0.0	1 041	938	-
119	11	12	66	78	41.2	4	99.0	99.0	3 463	14 900	2 928	0.8	1 513	684	40
500	12	7	78	83	28.2	2	99.0	99.0	3 568	69 900	12 216	0.5	1 486	938	10
212	11	9	73	78	26.3	6	99.0	96.8	2 923	4 870	3 516	1.2	1 062	612	60
3 237	9	7	78	82	35.0	5	93.1	95.8	3 389	20 980	4 630	0.6	1 298	689	30
269	12	12	65	73	28.6	13	99.0	99.0	2 837	2 470	1 445	0.3	1 060	488	61
49 078	7	9	86	94	71.7	3	99.0	99.0	-	186 950	-	0.0	937	907	15
111	12	9	73	77	19.8	5	99.0	98.0	3 568	7 250	5 440	1.6	1 599	568	63
1 282	11	8	79	83	28.6	3	99.0	99.0	3 147	51 060	6 436	1.2	1 137	940	7
44	13	8	79	84	37.4	2	99.0	99.0	3 484	102 610	23 101	1.4	1 163	950	6
324	11	10	72	81	22.0	4	99.0	99.0	3 485	13 240	3 629	1.8	1 491	628	44
298	9	9	77	83	38.7	3	97.1	94.4	3 456	21 260	4 355	2.1	1 130	621	43
243	10	12	70	78	23.9	10	99.0	99.0	3 363	9 060	2 157	1.3	1 056	498	58
21	12	15	62	74	43.1	9	99.0	99.0	3 358	13 850	6 232	4.2	1 528	614	42
1 391	9	10	81	86	51.3	3	99.0	99.0	-	51 470	-	-	1 170	508	
319	10	12	71	77	21.1	6	99.0	97.2	2 724	6 050	2 709	2.0	1 194	515	50
290	11	9	72	79	30.0	6	99.0	99.0	2 902	17 810	4 683	1.0	1 139	779	45
269	10	9	76	83	25.2	2	99.0	99.0	3 173	23 210	6 512	1.1	1 102	727	31
243	11	9	79	85	37.0	4	99.0	97.5	3 183	29 920	5 195	0.9	1 069	716	28
60	12	10	80	84	37.7	2	99.0	99.0	3 160	61 760	13 738	1.1	1 244	948	3
534	10	8	80	85	39.4	4	99.0	99.0	3 487	90 760	7 534	0.7	1 368	867	13
192	11	15	63	74	35.3	9	99.0	99.0	3 142	3 960	3 559	2.9	1 381	418	73
681	12	9	79	83	27.9	4	99.0	99.0	3 414	41 680	5 082	2.2	1 246	898	5
4 957	-	-	80	85	-	-	99.0	99.0	-	-	-	0.0	-	570	
124	35	8	60	62	2.3	70	52.0	24.2	2 107	690	117	6.4	707	59	155
262	14	12	71	78	26.9	14	99.0	99.0	2 809	3 800	1 627	4.1	1 124	463	74
285	18	6	68	74	34.3	30	99.0	99.0	2 952	7 350	1 893	4.7	1 076	587	64
4 768	16	2	76	78	9.1	5	96.9	93.5	-	19 700	8 349	3.8	1 659	900	27
3 066	20	6	70	72	3.6	33	64.6	58.5	2 430	1 010	272	1.2	744	65	145
44	20	7	68	69	2.6	30	73.1	55.0	-	2 330	2 052	1.0	722	299	123
197	16	4	77	81	15.0	8	97.5	94.5	2 949	31 590	8 628	2.6	1 122	645	66
225	26	6	69	75	2.2	32	84.5	70.5	2 411	950	207	1.6	1 339	60	127
386	13	7	74	77	19.4	11	98.2	94.5	3 074	6 560	3 300	2.1	887	458	86
212	36	6	66	69	0.7	46	71.5	63.4	2 083	3 580	-	2.3	574	11	-
161	14	13	71	78	42.4	12	99.0	99.0	2 731	3 570	1 969	2.7	1 150	431	78
1 103	21	8	65	68	7.0	41	81.3	60.6	2 459	1 570	687	2.4	708	151	129

	GENERAL FACTS				
Country	Capital city	Land area (sq miles)	Main languages spoken	Unit of currency	Population (2014)
Indonesia	Jakarta	740 904	Javanese, Sundanese, Madurese, Bahasa Indonesia, Dutch	Rupiah	252 800 000
Iran	Tehran	636 128	Farsi, Azeri, Luri, Gilaki, Mazanderani, Kurdish, Turkmen, Arabic, Baluchi	Iranian rial	78 500 000
Iraq	Baghdad	168 710	Arabic, Kurdish, Turkic languages, Armenian, Assyrian	New Iraqi dinar	34 800 000
Israel	Jerusalem (disputed)	8 017	Hebrew, Arabic, Yiddish, German, Russian, Polish, Romanian, Persian	Shekel	7 800 000
Japan	Tokyo	145 844	Japanese, Korean, Chinese	Yen	127 000 000
Jordan	Amman	35 628	Arabic	Jordanian dinar	7 500 000
Kazakhstan	Astana	1 049 150	Kazakh, Russian, Ukrainian, German, Uzbek, Tatar, Uighur	Tenge	16 600 000
Kuwait	Kuwait City	6 879	Arabic, English	Kuwaiti dinar	3 500 000
Kyrgyzstan	Bishkek	76 621	Kyrgyz, Russian, Uzbek, Tatar, Ukrainian	Som	5 600 000
Laos	Vientiane	91 405	Lao, Mon-Khmer, Yao, Vietnamese, Chinese, French	Kip	6 900 000
Lebanon	Beirut	4 014	Arabic, French, Armenian, Assyrian	Lebanese pound	5 000 000
Malaysia	Kuala Lumpur/Putrajaya	127 284	Bahasa Malaysia, Malay, Chinese, Tamil, English	Ringgit	30 200 000
Maldives	Male'	116	Dhivehi (Maldivian), Sinhala, Tamil, Arabic	Rufiyaa	400 000
Mongolia	Ulan Bator	603 749	Khalkha Mongolian, Kazakh, Chinese, Russian	Tugrik (tögrög)	2 900 000
Myanmar (Burma)	Nay Pyi Taw	265 375	Burmese (Myanmar), Shan, Karen, Rakhine, Chin, Yangbye, Kachin, Mon	Kyat	53 700 000
Nepal	Kathmandu	54 349	Nepali, Maithili, Bhojpuri	Nepalese rupee	28 100 000
North Korea	Pyongyang	46 528	Korean	North Korean won	25 000 000
Oman	Muscat	82 010	Arabic, Baluchi, Farsi, Hindi, Punjabi	Omani rial	3 900 000
Pakistan	Islamabad	310 321	Punjabi, Sindhi, Pashtu, Urdu, Baluchi, Brahui	Pakistani rupee	185 100 000
Philippines	Manila	115 800	Filipino, English, Tagalog, Cebuano, Ilocano, Hiligaynon, many other local languages	Philippine peso	100 100 000
Qatar	Doha	4 415	Arabic	Qatar riyal	2 300 000
Saudi Arabia	Riyadh	756 785	Arabic	Saudi riyal	29 400 000
Singapore	Singapore	267	Mandarin, Malay, Tamil, English	Singapore dollar	5 500 000
South Korea	Seoul/Sejong City	38 013	Korean	South Korean won	49 500 000
Sri Lanka	Colombo/Sri Jayewardenepura Kotte	25 325	Sinhala, Tamil, Sinhala-Tamil, English	Sri Lanka rupee	21 400 000
Syria	Damascus	71 480	Arabic, French, Kurdish, Armenian, Circassian, Turkic languages, Assyrian, Aramaic	Syrian pound	22 000 000
Taiwan	Taipei	13 888	Amoy Chinese, Mandarin Chinese, Hakka Chinese	Taiwan dollar	23 400 000
Tajikistan	Dushanbe	55 237	Tajik, Uzbek, Russian	Somoni	8 400 000
Thailand	Bangkok	198 404	Thai, Chinese, Malay, Khmer, Mon, Karen, Miao	Baht	67 200 000
Turkey	Ankara	301 304	Turkish, Kurdish, Arabic, Circassian, Armenian, Greek, Georgian, Ladino	Turkish lira	75 800 000
Turkmenistan	Ashgabat	188 407	Turkmen, Uzbek, Russian, Kazakh, Tatar	New manat	5 300 000
United Arab Emirates	Abu Dhabi	31 992	Arabic, Farsi, Indian and Pakistani languages, English	UAE dirham	9 400 000
Uzbekistan	Tashkent	172 696	Uzbek, Russian, Tajik, Kazakh	Som	29 300 000
Vietnam	Hanoi	127 210	Vietnamese, Chinese, Thai, Khmer, Muong, Nung, Miao, Yao, Jarai	Dông	92 500 000
Yemen	Sana	203 796	Arabic	Yemeni rial	25 000 000

AUSTRALASIA & OCEANIA

Australia	Canberra	2 967 893	English, Italian, Cantonese, Greek, Arabic, Vietnamese, Aboriginal languages	Australian dollar	23 600 000
Fiji	Suva	7 052	Fijian, English, Hindi, Urdu, Tamil, Telugu	Fiji dollar	900 000
Kiribati	Bairiki (Tarawa Atoll)	313	English, Kiribati	Australian dollar	104 000
Marshall Islands	Majuro	70	Marshallese, English, Japanese, German	US dollar	71 000
Micronesia	Palikir (Pohnpei Island)	271	Trukese, Pohnpeian, Kosraean, Yapese, English	US dollar	106 000
Nauru	None	8.1	Nauruan, Kiribati, Chinese, Tuvaluan, English	Australian dollar	9 500
New Zealand	Wellington	103 710	English, Maori	New Zealand dollar	4 600 000
Palau	Ngerulmud	177	Palauan, English, Japanese, Angaur, Tobi, Sonsorolese	US dollar	21 200
Papua New Guinea	Port Moresby	178 656	Pidgin English, Papuan, English, Motu, around 800 native languages	Kina	7 500 000
Samoa	Apia	1 136	Samoan, English	Tala	200 000
Solomon Islands	Honiara	10 982	English, Pidgin English, Melanesian Pidgin, around 120 native languages	Solomon Islands dollar	600 000
Tonga	Nuku'alofa	289	English, Tongan	Pa'anga (Tongan dollar)	106 000
Tuvalu	Fongafale (Funafuti Atoll)	10	Tuvaluan, Kiribati, English	Australian $, Tuvaluan $	10 800
Vanuatu	Port Vila	4 709	Bislama (Melanesian pidgin), English, French, other indigenous languages	Vatu	300 000

POPULATION					HEALTH AND EDUCATION					ECONOMIC DEVELOPMENT			TECHNOLOGICAL DEVELOPMENT		
Population density per sq mile (2014)	Birth rate per 1 000 population (2012)	Death rate per 1 000 population (2012)	Life expectancy at birth (years; 2013–2014)		Medical doctors per 10 000 people (2004–2013)	Infant mortality (deaths per 1 000 live births; 2013)	Adult literacy rate (percentage of adults over 15; 2015)		Average calorie intake per person (2011)	GNI per person (US$; 2013)	Annual electricity consumption per person (kWh; 2012)	Annual military expenditure as percentage of GDP (2009–2014)	Mobile telephones per 1 000 population (2013)	Internet users per 1 000 population (2013)	ICT Dev. Index (IDI), compiled by the ITU (2013)
			Male	Female			Male	Female							
365	19	6	69	73	2.0	24	96.3	91.5	2 713	3 580	684	0.9	1 254	158	106
124	19	5	72	76	8.9	14	91.2	82.5	3 058	5 780	2 584	2.1	842	314	94
207	32	5	66	73	6.1	28	85.7	73.7	2 489	6 720	1 332	3.4	961	92	-
995	21	5	80	84	33.5	3	99.0	99.0	3 619	33 930	6 893	5.6	1 228	708	29
873	8	9	80	87	23.0	2	99.0	99.0	2 719	46 330	7 287	1.0	1 176	863	11
218	28	4	72	76	25.6	16	97.7	92.9	3 149	4 950	2 138	3.6	1 418	442	87
16	21	10	61	72	35.8	15	99.0	99.0	3 107	11 550	4 896	1.2	1 847	540	53
508	21	2	74	76	17.9	8	96.5	95.8	3 471	45 130	17 242	3.3	1 903	755	-
73	27	7	63	72	19.6	22	99.0	99.0	2 828	1 210	1 841	3.2	1 214	234	108
78	27	7	67	70	1.8	54	87.1	72.8	2 356	1 450	449	0.2	681	125	134
1 267	13	5	78	82	32.0	8	96.0	91.8	3 181	9 870	3 009	4.4	806	705	62
238	18	5	73	77	12.0	7	96.2	93.2	2 855	10 430	4 046	1.5	1 447	670	71
3 452	22	4	77	79	14.2	8	99.0	99.0	2 722	5 600	890	4.0	1 812	441	85
5	23	7	64	72	27.6	26	98.2	99.0	2 463	3 770	1 502	1.1	1 242	177	92
212	17	8	63	67	6.1	40	95.2	91.2	2 528	578	159	4.3	128	12	150
531	22	7	67	70	2.1	32	76.4	53.1	2 580	730	104	1.4	768	133	131
539	14	9	66	73	32.9	22	99.0	99.0	2 103	555	639	22.3	97	-	-
47	21	3	75	79	22.2	10	93.6	85.6	-	25 150	7 020	11.6	1 546	664	52
622	26	7	66	68	8.3	69	69.5	45.8	2 428	1 360	427	3.5	701	109	142
870	25	6	65	72	11.5	24	95.8	96.8	2 608	3 270	635	1.3	1 045	370	103
541	11	1	78	80	77.4	7	97.4	96.8	-	86 790	16 069	1.5	1 526	853	34
36	20	3	74	78	9.4	13	97.0	91.1	3 122	26 260	8 070	9.0	1 842	605	47
23 351	10	4	80	85	19.2	2	99.0	95.0	-	54 040	8 303	3.3	1 559	730	16
1 298	10	5	78	85	21.4	3	99.0	99.0	3 329	25 920	9 926	2.6	1 110	848	2
857	18	7	71	77	6.8	8	93.6	91.7	2 488	3 170	480	2.7	955	219	116
311	24	6	72	78	15.0	12	91.7	81.0	3 106	1 850	1 218	4.2	561	262	112
1 877	9	7	77	83	19.0	4	99.0	97.0	2 959	20 690	9 628	2.0	1 275	800	-
153	33	6	64	71	19.0	41	99.0	99.0	2 101	990	2 031	1.1	918	160	-
342	11	8	71	78	3.9	11	96.6	96.7	2 757	5 340	2 230	1.5	1 401	289	81
254	17	6	72	79	17.1	16	98.4	91.8	3 680	10 970	2 645	2.3	930	463	68
28	22	9	61	70	23.9	47	99.0	99.0	2 883	6 880	2 259	1.6	1 169	96	-
290	15	1	76	78	19.3	7	93.1	95.8	3 215	38 360	11 517	5.0	1 719	880	32
168	22	6	65	72	23.8	37	99.0	99.0	2 675	1 880	1 609	3.5	743	382	115
736	16	6	71	81	11.6	19	96.3	92.8	2 703	1 740	1 207	2.2	1 309	439	101
114	32	7	62	65	2.0	40	85.1	55.0	2 185	1 330	150	3.9	690	200	138
8	13	6	80	85	32.7	3	99.0	99.0	3 265	65 390	9 721	1.6	1 068	830	12
127	21	7	67	73	4.3	20	95.9	92.9	2 930	4 370	864	1.4	1 056	371	91
381	23	8	66	72	3.8	45	99.0	99.0	3 022	2 620	237	0.0	166	115	-
1 015	28	7	70	75	4.4	31	93.6	93.7	-	4 310	-	0.0	70	117	-
391	24	6	68	70	1.8	30	91.0	88.0	-	3 280	-	0.0	303	278	-
1 171	27	4	62	70	7.1	30	-	-	-	3 433	2 479	0.0	678	540	-
44	14	6	79	83	27.4	5	99.0	99.0	3 170	35 550	8 956	1.0	1 058	828	19
109	11	6	69	76	13.8	15	99.0	99.0	-	10 970	-	0.0	858	310	-
44	29	8	60	65	0.5	47	65.6	62.8	2 193	2 010	433	0.6	410	65	-
184	27	5	70	77	4.8	16	99.0	99.0	2 872	3 970	452	0.0	914	153	-
54	32	5	66	69	2.2	25	83.7	69.0	2 473	1 600	132	0.0	576	80	136
383	26	7	70	76	5.6	10	99.0	99.0	-	4 490	421	0.9	546	350	-
1075	23	9	64	68	10.9	24	-	-	-	5 840	-	0.0	344	370	-
65	27	5	70	74	1.2	15	86.6	83.8	2 820	3 130	164	0.0	503	113	-

GLOSSARY

This glossary defines certain geographical and technical terms used in this Atlas.

Acid rain Rain, sleet, snow, or mist that has absorbed waste gases from fossil-fueled power stations and vehicle exhausts, becoming acidic and poisonous.

Alluvium Material deposited by a river, such as silt, sand, and mud.

Archipelago A group, or chain, of islands.

Atoll A circular or horseshoe-shaped coral reef enclosing a shallow area of water (lagoon).

Aquifer A body of rock that can absorb water. It may be a source of water for wells or springs.

Bar, coastal An offshore strip of sand or shingle, either above or below the water.

Biodiversity The quantity of different animal or plant species in a given area.

Birthrate The number of live births per 1,000 individuals annually within a population.

Cash crop Agricultural produce grown for sale, often for foreign export, rather than to be consumed within the country or area in which it was grown.

Climate The long-term trends in weather conditions for an area.

Coniferous forest A type of forest containing trees or shrubs, like pines and firs, that have needles instead of leaves. They are found in temperate zones.

Continental plates The huge interlocking plates that make up the Earth's surface. A plate boundary is an area where two plates meet, and is the point at which earthquakes occur most frequently.

Conurbation A large urban area created by the merging of several towns.

Coral reef An underwater barrier created by colonies of coral polyps. The polyps secrete a protective skeleton of calcium carbonate, and reefs develop as live polyps build on the skeletons of dead generations.

Core The layers of liquid rock and solid iron at the center of the Earth.

Crust The hard, thin outer shell of the Earth. The crust floats on the mantle, which is softer, but more dense.

Deciduous forest A type of broadleaf forest found in temperate regions.

Deforestation Cutting down trees or forest for timber or farmland. It can lead to soil erosion, flooding, and landslides.

Delta A low-lying, fan-shaped area at a river mouth, formed by the deposition of successive layers of sediment. Slowing as it enters the sea, a river deposits sediment and may, as a result, split into many smaller channels called distributaries.

Deposition The laying down of material broken down by erosion or weathering and transported by the wind, water, or gravity.

Desertification The spread of desert conditions into a region that was not previously a desert.

Drainage basin The land drained by a river and its tributaries.

Drought A long period of continuously low rainfall.

Earthquake A trembling or shaking of the ground caused by the sudden movement of rocks in the Earth's crust – and sometimes deeper than the crust. Earthquakes occur most frequently along continental plate boundaries.

Economy The organization of a country's finances, exports, imports, industry, agriculture, and services.

Ecosytem A community of species dependent on each other and on the habitat in which they live.

Equator The 0° line of latitude. Equatorial climates are hot and there is plenty of rain.

Erosion The wearing down of the land surface by running water, waves, moving ice, wind, and weather.

Estuary The mouth of a river, where the saltwater from the sea meets the freshwater of the river.

Fault A crack or fracture in the Earth along which there has been movement of the rock masses relative to one another.

Fjord A coastal valley that was sculpted by glacial action.

Floodplain The broad, flat part of a river valley, next to the river itself, formed by sediment deposited during flooding.

Geyser A fountain of hot water or steam that erupts periodically as a result of underground streams coming into contact with hot rocks.

GDP Gross Domestic Product. The total value of goods and services produced by a country, excluding income from foreign countries.

GIS Geographic Information System. A computerized system for the collection, storage, and retrieval of geographic data.

Glacier A huge mass of ice made up of compacted and frozen snow, that moves slowly, eroding and depositing rock.

Glaciation The molding of the land by a glacier or ice sheet.

GNI Gross National Income. The total value of goods and services produced by a country.

Groundwater Water that has seeped into the pores, cavities, and cracks of rocks or into soil and water held in an aquifer or permeable rock.

Gully A deep, narrow chasm eroded in the landscape by a fast-flowing stream.

Heavy industry Industry that uses large amounts of energy and raw materials to produce heavy goods, such as machinery, ships, or locomotives.

Humidity The moisture content of the air.

Hurricane A violent tropical storm, also known as a cyclone in the Indian Ocean and a typhoon in the Pacific Ocean.

Hydroelectric power Energy produced by harnessing the rapid movement of water down steep mountain slopes to drive turbines to generate electricity.

Ice Age Periods of time in the past when much of the Earth's surface was covered by massive ice sheets. The most recent Ice Age began two million years ago and ended 10,000 years ago.

Iceberg A floating mass of ice that has broken off from a glacier or ice sheet.

Ice sheet A massive area of ice, thousands of feet thick.

Irrigation The artificial supply of water to dry areas – mainly for agricultural use. Water is carried or pumped to the area through pipes or ditches.

Lagoon A shallow stretch of coastal saltwater behind a partial barrier such as a sandbank or coral reef.

Latitude The distance north or south of the equator, measured in degrees, and shown on a globe as imaginary circles running around the Earth parallel to the equator.

Lava The molten rock, magma, that erupts onto the Earth's surface through a volcano, or through a fault or crack in the Earth's crust. Lava refers to the rock both in its liquid and its later, solidified form.

Load The material that is carried by a river or stream.

Longitude The distance, measured in degrees, east or west of the Prime Meridian.

Limestone A type of rock, formed by sediment, through which water can pass.

Magma Underground, molten rock, that is very hot and highly charged with gas. It originates in the Earth's lower crust or mantle.

Mantle The layer of the Earth's interior between the crust and the core. It is about 1,800 miles thick.

Map projection A mathematical formula that is used to show the curved surface of the Earth on a flat map.

Market gardening The intensive growing of fruit and vegetables close to large local markets.

Meander A looplike bend in a river. As a river nears the sea, it tends to wind more and more. The bigger the river and the shallower its slope, the more likely it is that meanders will form.

Mediterranean climate A temperate climate of hot, dry summers and warm, damp winters.

Meltwater Water that has melted from glaciers or ice sheets.

Mestizo A person of mixed native American and European origin.

Mineral A chemical compound that occurs naturally in the Earth.

Monsoon Winds that change direction according to the seasons. They are most common in South and East Asia, where they blow from the southwest in summer, bringing heavy rainfall, and the northeast in winter.

Moraine Sand and gravel that have been deposited by a glacier or ice sheet.

Nomads (nomadic) Wandering communities who move around in search of suitable pasture for their herds of animals.

Oasis A fertile area in a desert, usually watered by an underground aquifer.

Pack ice Ice masses more than 10 ft thick that form on the sea surface and are not attached to a landmass.

Pacific Rim The name given to the economically dynamic countries bordering the Pacific Ocean.

Peat Decomposed vegetation found in bogs. It can be dried and used as fuel.

Per capita A latin term meaning "for each person."

Plantation A large farm on which only one crop is usually grown, e.g. bananas or coffee.

Plain A flat, level region of land, often relatively low-lying.

Plateau A large area of high, flat land. When surrounded by steep slopes it is called a tableland.

Peninsula A thin strip of land surrounded on three of its sides by water. Large examples include Italy, Florida, and Korea.

Permafrost Permanently frozen ground, in which temperatures have remained below 32°F for more than two years.

Precipitation The fall of moisture from the atmosphere onto the surface of the Earth, as dew, hail, rain, sleet, or snow.

Prairie A Spanish-American term for grassy plains, with few or no trees.

Prime Meridian 0° longitude. Also known as the Greenwich Meridian because it runs through Greenwich in England.

Rain forest Dense forests in tropical zones with high rainfall, temperature, and humidity.

Rain shadow An area downwind from high terrain that has little or no rainfall because it has fallen upon the high relief.

Remote-sensing A way of obtaining information about the environment by using unmanned equipment, such as a satellite, that relays the information to a point where it is collected.

Ria A flooded V-shaped river valley or estuary flooded by a rise in sea level or sinking land.

Rift valley A long, narrow depression in the Earth's crust, formed by the sinking of rocks between two faults.

Savanna Open grassland, where an annual dry season prevents the growth of most trees. They lie between the tropical rain forest and hot desert regions.

Scale The relationship between distance on a map and on the Earth's surface.

Sediment Grains of rock transported and deposited by rivers, sea, ice, or wind.

Semiarid Areas between deserts and better-watered areas, where there is sufficient moisture to support a little more vegetation than in a true desert.

Service industry An industry that supplies services, such as banking, rather than producing manufactured goods.

Shanty town An area in or around a city where people live in temporary shacks, usually without basic facilities such as running water.

Silt Small particles, finer than sand, often carried by water and deposited on riverbanks, at river mouths, and harbors.

Soil A thin layer of rock particles mixed with the remains of dead organisms. Soil occurs naturally on the surface of the Earth and provides a medium for plants to grow.

Soil erosion The wearing away of soil more quickly than it is replaced by natural processes. Overgrazing and the clearing of land for farming speeds up the process.

Sorghum A type of grass found in South America, similar to sugarcane.

Spit A narrow bank of pebbles or sand extending out from the seashore. Spits are made out of material transported along the coast by currents, wind, and waves.

Staple crop The main food crop grown in a region, for example, rice in Southeast Asia.

Steppe Large areas of dry grassland in the Northern Hemisphere – particularly found in southeast Europe and central Asia.

Subsistence farming A method of farming in which enough food is produced to feed farmers and their families but not providing any extra to generate an income.

Taiga A Russian name given to the belt of coniferous forest found in Russia, which borders tundra in the north and mixed forests and grasslands in the south.

Temperate The mild, variable climate found in areas between the tropics and cold polar regions.

Terrace Steps cut into steep slopes to create flat surfaces for cultivating crops.

Tropics An area between the equator and the Tropic of Cancer and Tropic of Capricorn that has heavy rainfall and high temperatures, and lacks any clear seasonal variation.

Tundra The land area lying in the very cold northern regions of Europe, Asia, and Canada, where winters are long and cold and the ground beneath the surface is permanently frozen.

U-shaped valley A river valley that has been deepened and widened by a glacier. They are flat-bottomed and steep-sided, and usually much deeper than river valleys.

V-shaped valley A typical valley eroded by a river in its upper course.

Volcano An opening or vent in the Earth's crust where magma erupts. Volcanos are caused by the movement of the Earth's plates. When the plates collide or spread apart, magma is forced to the surface, at or near the place where the plates meet.

Watershed The dividing line between one drainage basin and another.

INDEX

◈ Administrative region   ◆ Country   ● Country capital   ◇ Dependent territory   ○ Dependent territory capital   ▲ Mountain range   ▲ Mountain   ☆ Volcano   ◈ River   ⬡ Lake   ⬡ Reservoir

155

B

BROOKS RANGE

Beaverton 49 B3 Oregon, NW USA
Beawar 127 D3 N India
Beccles 95 H2 E England, United Kingdom
Béchar 70 D2 W Algeria
Beckley 39 G2 West Virginia, NE USA
Bedford 95 F2 E England, United Kingdom
Bedford 40 D7 Indiana, N USA
Bedford Level 95 F2 *physical region* E England, United Kingdom
Bedum 84 F2 NE Netherlands
Bedworth 93 D6 C England, United Kingdom
Be'er Menuha 123 H7 S Israel
Beernem 84 B6 NW Belgium
Be'er Sheva 123 G6 S Israel
Beesel 84 E6 SE Netherlands
Beeston 93 E5 C England, United Kingdom
Beeville 44 G5 Texas, SW USA
Bega 137 G6 New South Wales, SE Australia
Beihai 129 F6 S China
Beijing 129 F3 ● E China
Beilen 84 E3 NE Netherlands
Beinn Dearg 91 D3 ▲ N Scotland, United Kingdom
Beira 76 E5 C Mozambique
Beirut 123 A2 ● W Lebanon
Beja 99 B5 SE Portugal
Béjar 99 C3 N Spain
Békéscsaba 105 F8 SE Hungary
Bekobod 125 F3 E Uzbekistan
Belarus 109 C2 ◆ *republic* E Europe
Bełchatów 105 E4 C Poland
Belcher Islands 35 C2 *island group* Nunavut, SE Canada
Beledweyne 75 F4 C Somalia
Belém 63 G3 N Brazil
Belén 55 D5 SW Nicaragua
Belen 44 D2 New Mexico, SW USA
Belep, Îles 141 F6 *island group* W New Caledonia
Belfast 89 F2 *National region capital,* E Northern Ireland, United Kingdom
Belfield 43 A2 North Dakota, N USA
Belfort 97 F3 E France
Belgaum 127 D6 W India
Belgium 84 B7 ◆ *monarchy* NW Europe
Belgorod 111 A6 W Russian Federation
Belgrade 107 D2 ● N Serbia
Belgrano II 142 B4 *Argentinian research station* Antarctica
Belitung, Pulau 131 C7 *island* W Indonesia
Belize 55 B2 ◆ *commonwealth republic* Central America
Belize 55 B1 ≈ Belize/Guatemala
Belize City 55 C1 NE Belize
Belkofski 50 C3 Alaska, USA
Bellananagh 89 D3 N Ireland
Bellavary 89 B3 NW Ireland
Belle Île 97 A3 *island* NW France
Belle Isle, Strait of 35 G3 *strait* Newfoundland and Labrador, E Canada
Belleville 40 B7 Illinois, N USA
Bellevue 43 D5 Nebraska, C USA
Bellevue 49 B2 Washington, NW USA
Bellingham 49 B1 Washington, NW USA
Bellingshausen Sea 142 A4 *sea* Antarctica
Bellinzona 101 B8 S Switzerland
Bello 63 B2 W Colombia
Bellona 141 E3 *island* S Solomon Islands
Belville 76 C7 SW South Africa
Belmopan 55 B2 ● C Belize
Belmullet 89 B3 W Ireland
Belo Horizonte 63 G7 SE Brazil
Belomorsk 111 B3 NW Russian Federation
Beloretsk 111 D6 W Russian Federation
Belorussia *see* Belarus
Belozersk 111 B4 NW Russian Federation
Belper 93 D5 C England, United Kingdom
Belton 44 H4 Texas, SW USA
Belturbet 89 D3 N Ireland
Belukha, Gora 118 D5 ▲ Kazakhstan/Russian Federation
Belyy, Ostrov 118 D2 *island* N Russian Federation
Bemaraha 76 G5 ⛰ W Madagascar
Bemidji 43 E2 Minnesota, N USA
Bemmel 84 E4 SE Netherlands
Benavente 99 C2 N Spain
Benbecula 91 A3 *island* NW Scotland, United Kingdom
Bend 49 B4 Oregon, NW USA
Bendery *see* Tighina
Bendigo 137 F6 Victoria, SE Australia
Benešov 105 B5 W Czech Republic
Benevento 103 D6 S Italy
Bengbu 129 G4 E China
Benghazi 70 G2 NE Libya
Bengkulu 131 B7 Sumatra, W Indonesia
Benguela 76 B4 W Angola
Ben Hope 91 D2 ▲ N Scotland, United Kingdom
Beni 76 D1 NE Dem. Rep. Congo
Benidorm 99 F4 SE Spain
Beni-Mellal 70 C2 C Morocco
Benin 72 D4 ◆ *republic* W Africa
Benin, Bight of 72 E5 *gulf* W Africa
Benin City 72 E5 SW Nigeria
Beni, Río 65 A2 ≈ N Bolivia
Ben Klibreck 91 C2 ▲ N Scotland, United Kingdom
Ben Lawers 91 D5 ▲ C Scotland, United Kingdom
Ben Lui 91 C5 ▲ C Scotland, United Kingdom
Ben Macdui 91 E4 ▲ C Scotland, United Kingdom
Ben More 91 B5 ▲ W Scotland, United Kingdom
Ben More 91 D5 ▲ C Scotland, United Kingdom
Ben More Assynt 91 D2 ▲ N Scotland, United Kingdom
Ben Nevis 91 C4 ▲ N Scotland, United Kingdom
Benson 44 C3 Arizona, SW USA
Benton 39 B4 Arkansas, C USA
Benton Harbor 40 D5 Michigan, N USA
Benue 72 F5 ≈ Cameroon/Nigeria
Beograd *see* Belgrade
Berat 107 D4 C Albania
Berau, Teluk 131 H7 *bay* Papua, E Indonesia
Berbera 75 F3 NW Somalia
Berbérati 72 G5 SW Central African Republic
Berck-Plage 97 D1 N France
Berdyans'k 109 G6 SE Ukraine
Bereket 125 C3 W Turkmenistan
Berettyó 105 F8 ≈ Hungary/Romania
Berettyóújfalu 105 F7 E Hungary
Berezniki 111 D5 NW Russian Federation
Berga 99 G2 NE Spain
Bergamo 103 B2 N Italy
Bergen 101 D2 NE Germany
Bergen 84 C3 NW Netherlands
Bergen 83 A5 S Norway
Bergerac 97 C5 SW France
Bergeyk 84 D6 S Netherlands
Bergse Maas 84 D5 ≈ S Netherlands
Beringen 84 D6 NE Belgium
Bering Sea 50 B1 *sea* N Pacific Ocean
Bering Strait 50 D1 *strait* Bering Sea/Chukchi Sea
Berja 99 E6 S Spain
Berkeley 49 B7 California, W USA
Berkhamsted 95 F3 SE England, United Kingdom
Berkner Island 142 B4 *island* Antarctica
Berlin 101 D3 ● NE Germany
Berlin 37 F3 New Hampshire, NE USA
Bermejo, Río 65 B3 ≈ N Argentina
Bermeo 99 E1 N Spain
Bermuda 26 *UK* ◇ NW Atlantic Ocean
Bern 101 A8 ● W Switzerland
Bernau 101 D3 NE Germany
Bernburg 101 D4 C Germany
Berner Alpen 101 A8 ⛰ SW Switzerland
Berneray 91 A4 *island* NW Scotland, United Kingdom
Bernier Island 137 A4 *island* Western Australia
Berry 97 D3 *cultural region* C France
Berry Islands 57 C1 *island group* N Bahamas
Bertoua 72 G5 E Cameroon
Berwick-upon-Tweed 93 D1 N England, United Kingdom
Besançon 97 E4 E France
Bessbrook 89 E3 S Northern Ireland, United Kingdom
Betafo 76 G5 C Madagascar
Betanzos 99 B1 NW Spain
Bethlehem 76 D6 C South Africa
Bethlehem 37 D5 Pennsylvania, NE USA
Bethlehem 123 H6 C West Bank
Béticos, Sistemas 99 D5 ⛰ S Spain
Bétou 76 C1 N Congo
Bette, Picco 70 G4 ▲ S Libya
Betws-y-Coed 93 B5 N Wales, United Kingdom
Beulah 40 D3 Michigan, N USA
Beveren 84 C6 N Belgium
Beverley 93 F4 E England, United Kingdom
Bexhill 95 G4 SE England, United Kingdom
Beyla 72 C4 SE Guinea
Beyrouth *see* Beirut
Beyşehir Gölü 120 B4 ◎ C Turkey
Béziers 97 D6 S France
Bhadravati 127 D6 SW India
Bhagalpur 127 F3 NE India
Bhaktapur 127 F3 C Nepal
Bharuch 127 C4 W India
Bhavnagar 127 C4 W India
Bhopal 127 D4 C India
Bhubaneshwar 127 F4 E India
Bhusawal 127 D4 C India
Bhutan 127 G3 ◆ *monarchy* S Asia
Biak, Pulau 131 H6 *island* E Indonesia
Biała Podlaska 105 G3 E Poland
Białogard 105 C2 NW Poland
Białystok 105 G2 NE Poland
Biarritz 97 B6 SW France
Bicester 95 E3 C England, United Kingdom
Biddeford 37 F3 Maine, NE USA
Bideford 95 B4 SW England, United Kingdom
Biel 101 A8 W Switzerland
Bielefeld 101 B4 NW Germany
Bielsko-Biała 105 E5 S Poland
Bielsk Podlaski 105 G3 E Poland
Biên Hoa 131 C4 S Vietnam
Bienville, Lac 35 D3 ◎ Québec, C Canada
Bié Plateau 76 C4 *plateau* C Angola
Big Bend National Park 44 E5 *national park* Texas, S USA
Bigbury Bay 95 B6 *bay* SW England, United Kingdom
Big Cypress Swamp 39 G8 *wetland* Florida, SE USA
Biggleswade 95 F2 C England, United Kingdom
Bighorn Mountains 47 E3 ⛰ Wyoming, C USA
Bighorn River 47 E3 ≈ Montana/Wyoming, NW USA
Big Sioux River 43 D4 ≈ Iowa/South Dakota, N USA
Big Smoky Valley 47 B6 *valley* Nevada, W USA
Big Spring 44 F3 Texas, SW USA
Bihać 107 B2 NW Bosnia and Herz.
Bihar 127 F3 *cultural region* N India Asia
Biharamulo 75 C6 NW Tanzania
Bihar Sharif 127 F3 NE India
Bihosava 109 C1 NW Belarus
Bijelo Polje 107 D3 E Montenegro
Bikaner 127 D3 NW India
Bikin 118 H5 SE Russian Federation
Bilaspur 127 E4 C India
Biläsuvar 121 I3 SE Azerbaijan
Bila Tserkva 109 D4 N Ukraine
Bilauktaung Range 131 B4 ⛰ Myanmar (Burma)/Thailand
Bilbao 99 E1 N Spain
Bilecik 120 B3 NW Turkey
Billingham 93 E2 N England, United Kingdom
Billings 47 E2 Montana, NW USA
Bilma, Grand Erg de 72 G2 *desert* NE Niger
Biloela 137 H4 Queensland, E Australia
Biloxi 39 C6 Mississippi, S USA
Biltine 72 H3 E Chad
Bilzen 84 D6 NE Belgium
Bimini Islands 57 C1 *island group* W Bahamas
Binche 84 C7 S Belgium
Binghamton 37 D4 New York, NE USA
Bingöl 121 F3 E Turkey
Bintulu 131 D6 C Malaysia
Binzhou 129 G3 E China
Bío Bío, Río 65 A6 ≈ C Chile
Bioco, Isla de 72 F6 *island* NW Equatorial Guinea
Birak 70 F3 C Libya
Birao 72 I4 NE Central African Republic
Biratnagar 127 F3 SE Nepal
Birdhill 89 C5 S Ireland
Birhar Sharif 127 F3 N India
Birjand 123 F2 E Iran
Birkenfeld 101 A6 SW Germany
Birkenhead 93 C4 NW England, United Kingdom
Birmingham 93 D6 C England, United Kingdom
Birmingham 39 D4 Alabama, S USA
Bir Mogreïn 72 B1 N Mauritania
Birnin Kebbi 72 E4 NW Nigeria
Birnin Konni 72 E3 SW Niger
Birobidzhan 118 H5 SE Russian Federation
Birr 89 D4 C Ireland
Birsk 111 D6 W Russian Federation
Birżebbuġa 112 B6 SE Malta
Bisbee 44 C4 Arizona, SW USA
Biscay, Bay of 97 B4 *bay* France/Spain
Bishah, Wadi 123 B5 *dry watercourse* C Saudi Arabia
Bishkek 125 H2 ● N Kyrgyzstan
Bishop 49 C7 California, W USA
Bishop Auckland 93 D2 N England, United Kingdom
Biskra 70 E1 NE Algeria
Biskupiec 105 F2 NE Poland
Bislig 131 G5 S Philippines
Bismarck 43 B2 *state capital* North Dakota, N USA
Bismarck Archipelago 141 B1 *island group* NE Papua New Guinea
Bismarck Sea 141 B1 *sea* W Pacific Ocean
Bissau 72 A4 ● W Guinea-Bissau
Bistriţa 109 B6 N Romania
Bitam 76 A1 N Gabon
Bitburg 101 A5 SW Germany
Bitlis 121 G4 SE Turkey
Bitola 107 D4 S Macedonia
Bitonto 103 E6 SE Italy
Bitterfeld 101 D4 E Germany
Bitterroot Range 47 C2 ⛰ Idaho/Montana, NW USA
Biu 72 G4 E Nigeria
Biwa-ko 133 E6 ◎ Honshu, SW Japan
Bizerte 70 F1 N Tunisia
Bjørnøya 143 D5 *island* N Norway
Blackall 137 G4 Queensland, E Australia
Blackburn 93 C4 NW England, United Kingdom
Black Drin 107 D3 ≈ Albania/Macedonia
Blackfoot 47 D4 Idaho, NW USA
Black Forest 101 B7 ⛰ SW Germany
Black Hills 43 A4 ⛰ South Dakota/Wyoming, N USA
Black Mountain 47 D5 ▲ Colorado, C USA
Black Mountains 93 C6 ⛰ SE Wales, United Kingdom
Blackpool 93 C4 NW England, United Kingdom
Black Range 44 D3 ⛰ New Mexico, SW USA
Black River 131 B2 ≈ China/Vietnam
Black Rock Desert 47 A4 *desert* Nevada, W USA
Black Sea 78 *sea* Asia/Europe
Black Sea Lowland 109 E6 *depression* SE Europe
Blacksod Bay 89 A3 *inlet* W Ireland
Black Volta 72 D4 ≈ W Africa
Blackwater 89 E6 SE Ireland
Blackwater 89 D6 ≈ S Ireland
Blackwater 89 E2 ≈ Ireland/Northern Ireland, United Kingdom
Blaenavon 93 C7 SE Wales, United Kingdom
Blagoevgrad 107 E3 W Bulgaria
Blagoveshchensk 118 H5 SE Russian Federation
Blairgowrie 91 E5 C Scotland, United Kingdom
Blakeney Point 95 G1 *headland* E England, United Kingdom
Blanca, Bahía 65 B6 *bay* E Argentina
Blanca, Costa 99 F5 *physical region* SE Spain
Blanche, Lake 137 F4 ◎ South Australia
Blanc, Mont 97 F5 ▲ France/Italy
Blanco, Cape 49 A4 *headland* Oregon, NW USA
Blandford Forum 95 D5 S England, United Kingdom
Blanes 99 H2 NE Spain
Blankenberge 84 B5 NW Belgium
Blankenheim 101 A5 W Germany
Blanquilla, Isla 57 I7 *island* N Venezuela
Blantyre 76 E4 S Malawi
Blaricum 84 D4 C Netherlands
Blenheim 139 C5 South Island, New Zealand
Blida 70 D1 N Algeria
Bloemfontein 76 D6 ● C South Africa
Blois 97 C3 C France
Bloody Foreland 89 C1 *headland* NW Ireland
Bloomfield 44 C1 New Mexico, SW USA
Bloomington 40 B6 Illinois, N USA
Bloomington 40 D7 Indiana, N USA
Bloomington 43 E3 Minnesota, N USA
Bloomsburg 37 D5 Pennsylvania, NE USA
Bloomsbury 137 G3 Queensland, NE Australia
Bluefield 39 G2 West Virginia, NE USA
Bluefields 55 E4 SE Nicaragua
Blue Mountains 137 G6 ⛰ New South Wales, SE Australia
Blue Mountains 49 C3 ⛰ Oregon/Washington, NW USA
Blue Nile 75 C3 ≈ Ethiopia/Sudan
Bluff 47 D6 Utah, W USA
Blumenau 63 F8 S Brazil
Blyth 93 D2 N England, United Kingdom
Blythe 49 E9 California, W USA
Blytheville 39 C3 Arkansas, C USA
Bo 72 B5 S Sierra Leone
Boaco 55 D4 S Nicaragua
Boa Vista 63 E3 NW Brazil
Bobaomby, Tanjona 76 G4 *headland* N Madagascar
Bobo-Dioulasso 72 C4 SW Burkina Faso
Bobruysk *see* Babruysk
Boca Raton 39 G8 Florida, SE USA
Bocay 55 D3 N Nicaragua
Bocholt 101 A4 W Germany
Bochum 101 A4 W Germany
Bodaybo 118 F4 E Russian Federation
Boden 83 D3 N Sweden
Bodmin 95 B5 SW England, United Kingdom
Bodmin Moor 95 B5 *moorland* SW England, United Kingdom
Bodø 83 C2 C Norway
Bodrum 120 A4 SW Turkey
Boende 76 C2 C Dem. Rep. Congo
Bofin, Lough 89 D3 ◎ N Ireland
Bogalusa 39 C6 Louisiana, S USA
Bogatynia 105 B4 SW Poland
Boğazlıyan 121 D3 C Turkey
Boggeragh Mountains 89 C6 ⛰ S Ireland
Bogia 141 B1 N Papua New Guinea
Bognor Regis 95 F5 SE England, United Kingdom
Bogor 131 C8 Java, C Indonesia
Bogotá 63 B2 ● C Colombia
Bo Hai 129 G3 *gulf* NE China
Bohemia 105 B6 *cultural region* W Czech Republic
Bohemian Forest 101 D6 ⛰ C Europe
Bohol Sea 131 F5 *sea* S Philippines
Bohoro Shan 129 B2 ⛰ NW China
Boise 47 B3 *state capital* Idaho, NW USA
Boise City 43 A7 Oklahoma, C USA
Boizenburg 101 C3 N Germany
Bojnürd 123 E1 N Iran
Boké 72 B5 W Guinea
Bol 72 G3 W Chad
Bolesławiec 105 C4 SW Poland
Bolgatanga 72 D4 N Ghana
Bolivia 65 A2 ◆ *republic* W South America
Bollene 97 E6 SE France
Bollnäs 83 C5 C Sweden
Bollon 137 G4 Queensland, C Australia
Bologna 103 C3 N Italy
Bol'shevik, Ostrov 118 F2 *island* Severnaya Zemlya, N Russian Federation
Bol'shezemel'skaya Tundra 111 E3 *physical region* NW Russian Federation
Bol'shoy Lyakhovskiy, Ostrov 118 G2 *island* NE Russian Federation
Bolton 93 C4 NW England, United Kingdom
Bolu 121 C2 NW Turkey
Bolungarvík 83 A1 NW Iceland
Bolus Head 89 A6 *headland* SW Ireland
Bolzano 103 C1 N Italy
Boma 76 B3 W Dem. Rep. Congo
Bombay *see* Mumbai
Bomu 76 C1 ≈ Central African Republic/Dem. Rep. Congo
Bonaire 57 H7 *Dutch* ◇ S Caribbean Sea
Bonanza 55 E3 NE Nicaragua
Bonaparte Archipelago 137 B2 *island group* Western Australia
Bon, Cap 112 E4 *headland* N Tunisia
Bondo 76 C1 N Dem. Rep. Congo
Bondoukou 72 D5 E Côte d'Ivoire
Bone, Teluk 131 F7 *bay* Celebes, C Indonesia
Bongaigaon 127 G3 NE India
Bongo, Massif des 72 H4 ⛰ NE Central African Republic
Bongor 72 G4 SW Chad
Bonifacio 97 G6 Corsica, France
Bonifacio, Strait of 103 A5 *strait* C Mediterranean Sea
Bonin Trench 15 *undersea feature* NW Pacific Ocean
Bonn 101 A5 W Germany
Boonville 37 D3 New York, NE USA
Boosaaso 75 F3 N Somalia
Boothia, Gulf of 33 H3 *gulf* Nunavut, NE Canada
Boothia Peninsula 33 H3 *peninsula* Nunavut, NE Canada
Boppard 101 B5 W Germany
Boquete 55 F6 W Panama
Boquillas 53 D2 NE Mexico
Bor 107 D2 E Serbia
Bor 75 C4 C South Sudan
Borah Peak 47 B3 ▲ Idaho, NW USA
Borås 83 C6 S Sweden
Bordeaux 97 B5 SW France
Bordj Omar Driss 70 E3 E Algeria
Bordon 95 F4 S England, United Kingdom
Borgefjelt 83 C3 ⛰ C Norway
Borger 84 F2 NE Netherlands
Borger 44 F2 Texas, SW USA
Borgholm 83 C6 S Sweden
Borisoglebsk 111 B6 W Russian Federation
Borisov *see* Barysaw
Borlänge 83 C5 C Sweden
Borne 84 F4 E Netherlands
Borneo 131 D7 *island* Brunei/Indonesia/Malaysia
Bornholm 83 C7 *island* E Denmark
Borovichi 111 A4 W Russian Federation
Borriana 99 F3 E Spain
Borrisokane 89 C5 S Ireland
Bosanski Novi 107 B1 Republika Srpska, NW Bosnia and Herzegovina
Boskovice 105 C6 SE Czech Republic
Bosna 107 C2 ≈ N Bosnia and Herzegovina
Bosna I Hercegovina, Federacija 107 C2 *republic* Bosnia and Herzegovina
Bosnia and Herzegovina 107 C2 ◆ *republic* SE Europe
Boso-hanto 133 G6 *peninsula* S Japan
Bosporus 120 B2 *strait* NW Turkey
Bossangoa 72 H5 C Central African Republic
Bossembélé 72 H5 C Central African Republic
Bossier City 39 B5 Louisiana, S USA
Bosten Hu 129 C3 ◎ NW China
Boston 93 F5 E England, United Kingdom
Boston 37 F4 *state capital* Massachusetts, NE USA
Boston Mountains 39 B3 ⛰ Arkansas, C USA
Botany Bay 137 H6 *inlet* New South Wales, SE Australia
Boteti 76 C5 ≈ N Botswana
Bothnia, Gulf of 83 D4 *gulf* N Baltic Sea
Botoşani 109 C5 NE Romania
Botrange 84 E7 ▲ E Belgium
Botswana 76 C5 ◆ *republic* S Africa
Bouar 72 G5 W Central African Republic
Bou Craa 70 B3 NW Western Sahara
Bougainville Island 141 D2 *island* NE Papua New Guinea
Bougaroun, Cap 112 D4 *headland* NE Algeria
Bougouni 72 C4 SW Mali
Boujdour 70 A3 W Western Sahara
Boulder 47 F5 Colorado, C USA
Boulder 47 D2 Montana, NW USA
Boulogne-sur-Mer 97 D1 N France
Boûmdeïd 72 B3 S Mauritania
Boundiali 72 C4 N Côte d'Ivoire
Bountiful 47 D5 Utah, W USA
Bourail 141 G6 C New Caledonia
Bourbonnais 97 D4 *cultural region* C France
Bourg-en-Bresse 97 E4 E France
Bourges 97 D4 C France
Bourgogne *see* Burgundy
Bourke 137 G5 New South Wales, SE Australia
Bournemouth 95 E5 S England, United Kingdom
Boutilimit 72 A3 SW Mauritania
Bowen 137 G3 Queensland, NE Australia
Bowland, Forest of 93 C3 *forest* N England, United Kingdom
Bowling Green 39 E3 Kentucky, S USA
Bowling Green 40 E5 Ohio, N USA
Bowman 43 A2 North Dakota, N USA
Boxmeer 84 E5 SE Netherlands
Boyle 89 C3 C Ireland
Boyne 89 E4 ≈ E Ireland
Boysun 125 F3 S Uzbekistan
Bozeman 47 D3 Montana, NW USA
Bozüyük 120 B3 NW Turkey
Brač 107 B3 *island* S Croatia
Brades 57 J5 ○ Montserrat
Bradford 93 D4 N England, United Kingdom
Bradford 37 B4 Pennsylvania, NE USA
Brady 44 G4 Texas, SW USA
Brae 91 A6 NE Scotland, United Kingdom
Braemar 91 E4 NE Scotland, United Kingdom
Braga 99 B2 NW Portugal
Bragança 99 C2 NE Portugal
Brahmanbaria 127 G3 E Bangladesh
Brahmapur 127 F5 E India
Brahmaputra 127 H3 ≈ S Asia
Brăila 109 D7 E Romania
Braine-le-Comte 84 C7 SW Belgium
Brainerd 43 E2 Minnesota, N USA
Braintree 95 G3 SE England, United Kingdom
Brampton 35 D6 Ontario, S Canada
Brampton 93 C2 NW England, United Kingdom
Brandberg 76 B5 ▲ NW Namibia
Brandenburg 101 D3 NE Germany
Brandon 33 H7 Manitoba, S Canada
Brandon 89 A6 SW Ireland
Brandon Bay 89 A6 *bay* SW Ireland
Brandon Mountain 89 A6 ▲ SW Ireland
Braniewo 105 E2 NE Poland
Brasília 63 G6 ● C Brazil
Braşov 109 C6 C Romania
Bratislava 105 D7 ● W Slovakia
Bratsk 118 F5 C Russian Federation
Braunschweig 101 C4 N Germany
Brava, Costa 99 H2 *coastal region* NE Spain
Bravo, Río 53 D2 ≈ Mexico/USA North America
Brawley 49 D9 California, W USA
Bray 89 E4 E Ireland
Brazil 63 C4 ◆ *federal republic* South America
Brazil Basin 14 *undersea feature* W Atlantic Ocean
Brazilian Highlands 63 G6 ⛰ E Brazil
Brazos River 44 H4 ≈ Texas, SW USA
Brazzaville 76 B2 ● S Congo
Brechin 91 E4 E Scotland, United Kingdom
Brecht 84 C5 N Belgium
Brecon 93 C6 E Wales, United Kingdom
Brecon Beacons 93 B7 ⛰ S Wales, United Kingdom
Breda 84 D5 S Netherlands
Bree 84 D6 NE Belgium
Bregalnica 107 E3 ≈ E Macedonia
Bremen 101 B3 NW Germany
Bremerhaven 101 B3 NW Germany
Bremerton 49 B2 Washington, NW USA
Brenham 44 H4 Texas, SW USA
Brenner Pass 101 C8 *pass* Austria/Italy
Brentwood 95 G3 E England, United Kingdom
Brescia 103 C2 N Italy
Bressanone 103 C1 N Italy
Bressay 91 B6 *island* NE Scotland, United Kingdom
Brest 109 B3 SW Belarus
Brest 97 A2 NW France
Bretagne *see* Brittany
Brewton 39 D6 Alabama, S USA
Bria 72 H5 C Central African Republic
Briançon 97 F5 SE France
Bride 93 B3 N Isle of Man
Bridgend 93 B7 S Wales, United Kingdom
Bridgeport 49 C6 California, W USA
Bridgeport 37 E5 Connecticut, NE USA
Bridgetown 57 K6 ● SW Barbados
Bridgetown 89 E6 SE Ireland
Bridgwater 95 D4 SW England, United Kingdom
Bridgwater Bay 95 C4 *bay* SW England, United Kingdom
Bridlington 93 F3 E England, United Kingdom
Bridlington Bay 93 F3 *bay* E England, United Kingdom
Bridport 95 D5 S England, United Kingdom
Brig 101 B8 SW Switzerland
Brigg 93 E4 N England, United Kingdom
Brigham City 47 D4 Utah, W USA
Brighton 95 F5 SE England, United Kingdom
Brighton 47 F5 Colorado, C USA
Brindisi 103 F6 SE Italy
Brisbane 137 H4 *state capital* Queensland, E Australia
Bristol 95 D4 SW England, United Kingdom
Bristol 37 E4 Connecticut, NE USA
Bristol 39 F3 Virginia, NE USA North America
Bristol Bay 50 C2 *bay* Alaska, USA
Bristol Channel 95 C4 *inlet* England/Wales, United Kingdom
British Columbia 33 E5 ⬖ *province* SW Canada
British Indian Ocean Territory 27 *UK* ◇ C Indian Ocean
British Isles 78 *island group* NW Europe
British Virgin Islands 57 I4 *UK* ◇ E West Indies
Brittany 97 B2 *cultural region* NW France Europe
Brive-la-Gaillarde 97 C5 C France
Brixham 95 C5 SW England, United Kingdom
Brno 105 C6 SE Czech Republic
Broad Bay 91 C2 *bay* NW Scotland, United Kingdom
Broadford 91 C4 N Scotland, United Kingdom
Broad Haven 89 B2 *inlet* NW Ireland
Broad Law 91 E6 ▲ S Scotland, United Kingdom
Broadstairs 95 H4 SE England, United Kingdom
Broads, The 95 H2 *wetland* E England, United Kingdom
Brockton 37 F4 Massachusetts, NE USA
Brodeur Peninsula 33 H3 *peninsula* Baffin Island, Nunavut, NE Canada
Brodick 91 C6 W Scotland, United Kingdom
Brodnica 105 E2 C Poland
Broek-in-Waterland 84 D3 C Netherlands
Broken Hill 137 F5 New South Wales, SE Australia
Bromley 95 F4 SE England, United Kingdom
Bromsgrove 93 D6 W England, United Kingdom
Brookhaven 39 C5 Mississippi, S USA
Brookings 43 D3 South Dakota, N USA
Brooks Range 50 E2 ⛰ Alaska, USA

⬖ Administrative region ◆ Country ● Country capital ◇ Dependent territory ○ Dependent territory capital ⛰ Mountain range ▲ Mountain ☼ Volcano ≈ River ◎ Lake ⊡ Reservoir

◆ Administrative region　◆ Country　● Country capital　◇ Dependent territory　○ Dependent territory capital　▲ Mountain range　▲ Mountain　☒ Volcano　∿ River　◉ Lake　☒ Reservoir

D

◆ Administrative region ◆ Country ● Country capital ◇ Dependent territory ○ Dependent territory capital ▲ Mountain range ▲ Mountain ⚐ Volcano ⚐ River ☉ Lake ☒ Reservoir

159

DARFUR

Darfur 75 B3 *cultural region* W Sudan
Darhan 129 E2 N Mongolia
Darien, Gulf of 63 B2 *gulf* S Caribbean Sea
Darién, Serranía del 55 I6 ⛰ Colombia/Panama
Darjiling 127 G3 NE India
Darling River 137 F5 ≈ New South Wales, SE Australia
Darlington 93 D3 N England, United Kingdom
Darmstadt 101 B5 SW Germany
Darnah 70 H2 NE Libya
Darnley, Cape 142 E4 *cape* Antarctica
Daroca 99 E3 NE Spain
Daroot-Korgon 125 G3 SW Kyrgyzstan
Dart 95 C5 ≈ SW England, United Kingdom
Dartmoor 95 B5 *moorland* SW England, United Kingdom
Dartmouth 35 G5 Nova Scotia, SE Canada
Dartmouth 95 C5 SW England, United Kingdom
Daru 141 A3 SW Papua New Guinea
Darvishan 125 E6 S Afghanistan
Darwin 137 D1 *territory capital* Northern Territory, N Australia
Darwin, Isla 63 A6 *island* Galápagos Islands, Ecuador
Daşoguz 125 D2 N Turkmenistan
Datong 129 F3 C China
Daugavpils 83 F7 SE Latvia
Dauphiné 97 E6 *cultural region* E France
Davangere 127 D6 W India
Davao 131 F5 S Philippines
Davao Gulf 131 G5 *gulf* S Philippines
Davenport 43 F5 Iowa, C USA
Daventry 95 E2 C England, United Kingdom
David 55 F7 W Panama
Davis 142 E4 *Australian research station* Antarctica
Davis Sea 142 E4 *sea* Antarctica
Davis Strait 33 J2 *strait* Baffin Bay/Labrador Sea
Dawei 131 B4 S Myanmar (Burma)
Dawlish 95 C5 SW England, United Kingdom
Dawros Head 89 C2 *headland* N Ireland
Dax 97 B6 SW France
Dayton 40 E6 Ohio, N USA
Daytona Beach 39 G7 Florida, SE USA
De Aar 76 C7 C South Africa
Dead Sea 123 H6 *salt lake* Israel/Jordan
Deal 95 H4 SE England, United Kingdom
Dean, Forest of 95 D3 *forest* C England, United Kingdom
Deán Funes 65 B5 C Argentina
Death Valley 49 D7 *valley* California, W USA
Deatnu 83 E1 ≈ Finland/Norway
De Bilt 84 D4 C Netherlands
Debrecen 105 F7 E Hungary
Decatur 39 D4 Alabama, S USA
Decatur 40 B6 Illinois, N USA
Deccan 127 D5 *plateau* C India
Děčín 105 B5 NW Czech Republic
Dedemsvaart 84 E3 E Netherlands
Dee 91 E4 ≈ NE Scotland, United Kingdom
Dee 93 F2 ≈ England/Wales, United Kingdom
Dee 93 C5 ≈ S Scotland, United Kingdom
Deering 50 D1 Alaska, USA
Deggendorf 101 D6 SE Germany
Değirmenlik 112 D6 N Cyprus
Deinze 84 B6 NW Belgium
Dékoa 72 H5 C Central African Republic
De Land 39 G7 Florida, SE USA
Delano 49 C8 California, W USA
Delaware 40 E6 Ohio, N USA
Delaware 37 D6 ◈ *state* NE USA
Delaware Bay 37 D6 *bay* NE USA
Delft 84 C4 W Netherlands
Delfzijl 84 F2 NE Netherlands
Delgo 75 C1 N Sudan
Delhi 127 D3 N India
Delicias 53 D2 N Mexico
Delmenhorst 101 B3 NW Germany
Del Rio 44 F5 Texas, SW USA
Delta 47 C5 Utah, W USA
Deltona 39 G7 Florida, SE USA
Demba 76 C2 C Dem. Rep. Congo
Dembia 72 I5 SE Central African Republic
Demchok 129 A4 *disputed region* China/India
Deming 44 D3 New Mexico, SW USA
Demmin 101 D2 NE Germany
Demopolis 39 D5 Alabama, S USA
Demqog *see* Demchok
Denali *see* McKinley, Mount
Denbigh 93 B5 NE Wales, United Kingdom
Dender 84 B7 ≈ W Belgium
Denekamp 84 F3 E Netherlands
Denham 137 A4 Western Australia
Den Ham 84 F3 E Netherlands
Den Helder 84 C2 NW Netherlands
Dénia 99 F4 E Spain
Deniliquin 137 F6 New South Wales, SE Australia
Denison 43 D5 Iowa, C USA
Denison 44 H2 Texas, SW USA
Denizli 120 B4 SW Turkey
Denmark 83 B7 ◆ *monarchy* N Europe
Denov 125 F3 S Uzbekistan
Denpasar 131 E8 Bali, C Indonesia
Denton 44 H3 Texas, SW USA
D'Entrecasteaux Islands 141 C3 *island group* SE Papua New Guinea
Denver 47 F5 *state capital* Colorado, C USA
De Queen 39 A4 Arkansas, C USA
Dera Ghazi Khan 127 C2 C Pakistan
Derbent 111 B9 SW Russian Federation
Derby 137 C2 Western Australia
Derby 93 D5 C England, United Kingdom
Derg 89 D2 ≈ Ireland/Northern Ireland, United Kingdom
Derg, Lough 89 C5 ◎ W Ireland
De Ridder 39 B6 Louisiana, S USA
Déroute, Passage de la 95 G5 *strait* Channel Islands/France
Derreendarragh 89 B6 SW Ireland
Derwent 93 E3 ≈ N England, United Kingdom
Derweze 125 C3 C Turkmenistan
Deschutes River 49 B3 ≈ Oregon, NW USA
Dese 75 E3 N Ethiopia
Deseado, Río 65 B8 ≈ S Argentina
Des Moines 43 E5 *state capital* Iowa, C USA
Desna 111 A6 ≈ Russian Federation/Ukraine
Dessau 101 D4 E Germany
Detroit 40 E5 Michigan, N USA
Detroit Lakes 43 D2 Minnesota, N USA
Deurne 84 E5 SE Netherlands
Deva 109 B6 W Romania
Deventer 84 E4 E Netherlands
Deveron 91 E3 ≈ NE Scotland, United Kingdom
Devils Lake 43 C2 North Dakota, N USA
Devizes 95 E4 S England, United Kingdom
Devon Island 33 H2 *island* Parry Islands, Nunavut, NE Canada
Devonport 137 F7 Tasmania, SE Australia
Devrek 121 C2 N Turkey
Dewsbury 93 D4 N England, United Kingdom
Dexter 43 G7 Missouri, C USA
Dezful 123 D2 SW Iran
Dezhou 129 G3 E China
Dhaka 127 G4 ● C Bangladesh
Dhanbad 127 F4 NE India
Dhekelia Sovereign Air Base 112 D6 *UK air base* SE Cyprus
Dhuusa Marreeb 75 F4 C Somalia
Diamantina, Chapada 63 H5 ⛰ E Brazil
Dibrugarh 127 H3 NE India
Dickinson 43 B2 North Dakota, N USA
Didcot 95 E3 C England, United Kingdom
Didymoteicho 107 F4 NE Greece
Diekirch 84 E8 C Luxembourg
Diepenbeek 84 D6 NE Belgium
Diepholz 101 B3 NW Germany
Dieppe 97 C1 N France
Dieren 84 E4 E Netherlands
Differdange 84 E9 SW Luxembourg
Digne 97 E6 SE France
Digoin 97 E4 C France
Digul, Sungai 131 I7 ≈ Papua, E Indonesia
Dijon 97 E4 C France
Dikhil 75 E3 SW Djibouti
Dikson 118 E2 N Russian Federation
Dikti 107 F7 ⛰ Crete, Greece
Dilaram 125 E5 SW Afghanistan
Dili 131 F8 ● C East Timor
Dilia 72 G3 ≈ SE Niger
Dilling 75 C3 C Sudan
Dillon 47 C3 Montana, NW USA
Dilolo 76 C3 S Dem. Rep. Congo
Dimashq *see* Damascus
Dimitrovgrad 107 F3 S Bulgaria
Dimitrovgrad 111 C6 W Russian Federation
Dimovo 107 E2 NW Bulgaria
Dinajpur 127 G3 NW Bangladesh
Dinan 97 B3 NW France
Dinant 84 D8 S Belgium
Dinar 120 B4 SW Turkey
Dinaric Alps 107 C2 ⛰ Bosnia and Herzegovina/Croatia
Dindigul 127 D7 SE India
Dingle 89 A6 SW Ireland
Dingle Bay 89 A6 *bay* SW Ireland
Dinguiraye 72 B4 N Guinea
Dingwall 91 D3 N Scotland, United Kingdom
Diourbel 72 A3 W Senegal
Dire Dawa 75 E3 E Ethiopia
Dirk Hartog Island 137 A4 *island* Western Australia
Disappointment, Lake 137 B3 *salt lake* Western Australia
Dishu 125 D6 S Afghanistan
Diss 95 H2 E England, United Kingdom
Divinópolis 63 G7 SE Brazil
Divo 72 C5 S Côte d'Ivoire
Diyarbakır 121 F4 SE Turkey
Djambala 76 B2 C Congo
Djanet 70 E4 SE Algeria
Djelfa 70 E1 N Algeria
Djéma 72 I5 E Central African Republic
Djerba 70 F2 *island* E Tunisia
Djérem 72 G5 ≈ C Cameroon
Djibouti 75 E3 ● E Djibouti
Djibouti 75 E3 ◆ *republic* E Africa
Djourab, Erg du 72 H3 *desert* N Chad
Djúpivogur 83 B1 SE Iceland
Dnieper 79 E3 ≈ E Europe
Dnieper Lowland 109 E4 *lowlands* Belarus/Ukraine
Dniester 109 D5 ≈ Moldova/Ukraine
Dniprodzerzhyns'k 109 F5 E Ukraine
Dniprodzerzhyns'ke Vodoskhovyshche 109 F5 ⊠ C Ukraine
Dnipropetrovs'k 109 F5 E Ukraine
Dniprorudne 109 F5 SE Ukraine
Doba 72 G4 S Chad
Döbeln 101 D4 E Germany
Doberai Peninsula 131 G7 *peninsula* E Indonesia
Dobre Miasto 105 E2 NE Poland
Dobrich 107 G2 NE Bulgaria
Dodecanese 107 F6 *island group* SE Greece
Dodekánisa *see* Dodecanese
Dodge City 43 C7 Kansas, C USA
Dodman Point 95 B6 *headland* SW England, United Kingdom
Dodoma 75 D6 ● C Tanzania
Dogai Coring 129 C4 ◎ W China
Dogo 133 D6 *island* Oki-shoto, SW Japan
Dogondoutchi 72 E3 SW Niger
Doğubayazıt 121 H3 E Turkey
Doğu Karadeniz Dağları 121 F2 ⛰ NE Turkey
Doha 123 D4 ● C Qatar
Dokkum 84 E2 N Netherlands
Dôle 97 E4 E France
Dolgellau 93 B5 NW Wales, United Kingdom
Dolisie 76 B2 S Congo
Dolomites 103 C2 ⛰ NE Italy
Dolores 65 C6 E Argentina
Dolores 55 B2 N Guatemala
Dolores 65 C5 SW Uruguay
Dolores Hidalgo 53 E4 C Mexico
Dombås 83 B4 S Norway
Domeyko 65 A4 N Chile
Dominica 57 K5 ◆ *republic* E West Indies
Dominican Republic 57 F5 ◆ *republic* C West Indies
Don 111 B7 ≈ SW Russian Federation
Don 91 F4 ≈ NE Scotland, United Kingdom
Don 93 E4 ≈ N England, United Kingdom
Donaghadee 89 F2 E Northern Ireland, United Kingdom
Donau *see* Danube
Donauwörth 101 C6 S Germany
Donawitz 101 E7 SE Austria
Donbass 109 G5 *industrial region* Russian Federation/Ukraine
Don Benito 99 C4 W Spain
Doncaster 93 E4 N England, United Kingdom
Dondo 76 B3 NW Angola
Donegal 89 D2 NW Ireland
Donegal Bay 89 C2 *bay* NW Ireland
Donets 111 A7 ≈ Russian Federation/Ukraine
Donets'k 109 G5 E Ukraine
Dongfang 129 F6 S China
Donghae 133 C5 NE South Korea
Dongola 75 C1 N Sudan
Dongou 76 B1 NE Congo
Dongting Hu 129 F5 ◎ S China
Donostia 99 E1 N Spain (see also San Sebastián)
Doolow 75 E4 E Ethiopia
Door Peninsula 40 C3 *peninsula* Wisconsin, N USA
Dorchester 95 D5 S England, United Kingdom
Dordogne 97 C5 *cultural region* SW France Europe
Dordogne 97 C5 ≈ W France
Dordrecht 84 C5 SW Netherlands
Dornoch 91 D3 N Scotland, United Kingdom
Dorotea 83 C3 N Sweden
Dorre Island 137 A4 *island* Western Australia
Dortmund 101 B4 W Germany
Dos Hermanas 99 C5 SW Spain
Dothan 39 E6 Alabama, S USA
Dotnuva 83 E7 C Lithuania
Douai 97 D1 N France
Douala 72 F5 W Cameroon
Douglas 89 C6 S Ireland
Douglas 93 B3 ○ E Isle of Man
Douglas 44 C4 Arizona, SW USA
Douglas 39 F5 Georgia, SE USA
Douglas 47 F4 Wyoming, C USA
Douro 99 B3 ≈ Portugal/Spain
Dover 95 H4 SE England, United Kingdom
Dover 37 D6 *state capital* Delaware, NE USA
Dover, Strait of 97 D1 *strait* England, United Kingdom/France
Dovrefjell 83 B4 *plateau* S Norway
Downham Market 95 G2 E England, United Kingdom
Downpatrick 89 F3 SE Northern Ireland, United Kingdom
Dozen 133 D6 *island* Oki-shoto, SW Japan
Drachten 84 E2 N Netherlands
Dra, Hamada du 70 C2 *plateau* W Algeria
Drahichyn 109 C3 SW Belarus
Drakensberg 76 D7 ⛰ Lesotho/South Africa
Drake Passage 65 B9 *passage* Atlantic Ocean/Pacific Ocean
Dráma 107 E4 NE Greece
Drammen 83 B5 S Norway
Drau *see* Drava
Drava 105 C9 ≈ C Europe
Drave *see* Drava
Drawsko Pomorskie 105 C2 NW Poland
Dresden 101 D5 E Germany
Driffield 93 E3 E England, United Kingdom
Drina 107 D2 ≈ Bosnia and Herzegovina/Serbia
Drinit, Lumi 107 D3 ≈ NW Albania
Drobeta-Turnu Severin 109 B7 SW Romania
Drogheda 89 E4 NE Ireland
Droichead Nua 89 E4 E Ireland
Droitwich 93 D6 W England, United Kingdom
Drôme 97 E6 *cultural region* SE France Europe
Dronfield 93 D4 C England, United Kingdom
Dronning Maud Land 142 C3 *physical region* Antarctica
Drumahoe 89 D2 NW Northern Ireland, United Kingdom
Drumbilla 89 E3 NE Ireland
Drumcliff 89 C3 N Ireland
Drummondville 35 E5 Québec, SE Canada
Druridge Bay 93 D2 *bay* N England, United Kingdom
Dryden 35 A4 Ontario, C Canada
Dryden 44 F4 Texas, SW USA
Drysa 109 D1 ≈ N Belarus
Duarte, Pico 57 G4 ▲ C Dominican Republic
Dubai 123 E4 NE United Arab Emirates
Dubawnt 33 G5 ≈ Nunavut, NW Canada
Dubbo 137 G5 New South Wales, SE Australia
Dublin 89 E4 ● E Ireland
Dublin 39 F5 Georgia, SE USA
Dubno 109 C4 NW Ukraine
Dubois 47 D3 Idaho, NW USA
Du Bois 37 B5 Pennsylvania, NE USA
Dubrovnik 107 C3 SE Croatia
Dubuque 43 F4 Iowa, C USA
Duchesne 47 D5 Utah, W USA
Dudelange 84 E9 S Luxembourg
Dudley 93 D6 C England, United Kingdom
Duero 92 D2 ≈ Portugal/Spain
Duffel 84 C6 C Belgium
Duff Islands 141 G3 *island group* E Solomon Islands
Dugi Otok 107 B2 *island* W Croatia
Duisburg 101 A4 W Germany
Duiven 84 E4 E Netherlands
Duk Faiwil 75 C4 E South Sudan
Dulan 129 D4 C China
Dulce 44 D1 New Mexico, SW USA
Dulce, Golfo 55 F7 *gulf* S Costa Rica
Dülmen 101 B4 W Germany
Dulovo 107 F2 NE Bulgaria
Duluth 43 F2 Minnesota, N USA
Duma 123 A2 SW Syria
Dumas 44 F2 Texas, SW USA
Dumbarton 91 D5 W Scotland, United Kingdom
Dumfries 91 E7 S Scotland, United Kingdom
Dumont d'Urville 142 E6 *French research station* Antarctica
Dumyat 70 I2 N Egypt
Duna *see* Danube
Dunaj *see* Danube
Dunany Point 89 E3 *headland* NE Ireland
Dunărea *see* Danube
Dunaújváros 105 E8 C Hungary
Dunav *see* Danube
Duncan 44 C3 Arizona, SW USA
Duncan 43 C8 Oklahoma, C USA
Duncansby Head 91 E2 *headland* N Scotland, United Kingdom
Dundalk 89 E3 NE Ireland
Dundee 76 D6 E South Africa
Dundee 91 E5 E Scotland, United Kingdom
Dundrum 89 C5 S Ireland
Dundrum Bay 89 F3 *inlet* NW Irish Sea
Dunedin 139 B7 South Island, New Zealand
Dunfanaghy 89 D1 NW Ireland
Dunfermline 91 E5 C Scotland, United Kingdom
Dungannon 89 E2 C Northern Ireland, United Kingdom
Dungarvan 89 D6 S Ireland
Dungeness 95 H4 *headland* SE England, United Kingdom
Dungiven 89 E2 N Northern Ireland, United Kingdom
Dunglow 89 C2 NW Ireland
Dungu 76 D1 NE Dem. Rep. Congo
Dunkerque 97 D1 N France
Dunkery Beacon 95 B4 ▲ SW England, United Kingdom
Dunkirk 37 B4 New York, NE USA
Dún Laoghaire 89 E4 E Ireland
Dunleer 89 E3 NE Ireland
Dunmore 89 C4 W Ireland
Dunmurry 89 F2 E Northern Ireland, United Kingdom
Dunnet Head 91 D2 *headland* N Scotland, United Kingdom
Dunning 43 C5 Nebraska, C USA
Duns 91 F6 SE Scotland, United Kingdom
Dunseith 43 C1 North Dakota, N USA
Dunshaughlin 89 E4 E Ireland
Dunstable 95 F3 E England, United Kingdom
Duqm 123 F5 E Oman
Durance 97 E6 ≈ SE France
Durango 53 D4 W Mexico
Durango 47 E6 Colorado, C USA
Durant 43 D9 Oklahoma, C USA
Durban 76 D7 E South Africa
Durg 127 E4 C India
Durham 93 D2 N England, United Kingdom
Durham 39 H3 North Carolina, SE USA
Durness 91 D2 N Scotland, United Kingdom
Durrës 107 C4 W Albania
Durrow 89 D5 C Ireland
Dursey Head 89 A7 *headland* S Ireland
D'Urville Island 139 C4 *island* C New Zealand
Dushanbe 125 F3 ● W Tajikistan
Düsseldorf 101 A4 W Germany
Dusti 125 F4 SW Tajikistan
Dutch Harbor 50 B2 Unalaska Island, Alaska, USA
Dyersburg 39 C3 Tennessee, S USA
Dzerzhinsk 111 B5 W Russian Federation
Dzhalal-Abad 125 G3 W Kyrgyzstan
Dzhankoy 109 F6 S Ukraine
Dzhelandy 125 G4 SE Tajikistan
Dzhergalan 125 I2 NE Kyrgyzstan
Dzhugdzhur, Khrebet 118 H4 ⛰ E Russian Federation
Działdowo 105 E3 C Poland

E

Eagar 44 C2 Arizona, SW USA
Eagle Pass 44 F5 Texas, SW USA
Earn 91 D5 ≈ N Scotland, United Kingdom
Easky 89 C3 N Ireland
East Anglia 95 G2 *physical region* E England, United Kingdom
East Antarctica 142 D4 *physical region* Antarctica
Eastbourne 95 G5 SE England, United Kingdom
East Cape 139 E3 *headland* North Island, New Zealand
East China Sea 114 *sea* W Pacific Ocean
East Dereham 95 G1 E England, United Kingdom
Easter Island 141 D5 *island* Chile, E Pacific Ocean
Eastern Ghats 127 E5 ⛰ SE India
Eastern Sayans 118 E5 ⛰ Mongolia/Russian Federation
East Falkland 65 C9 *island* E Falkland Islands
East Frisian Islands 101 A2 *island group* NW Germany
East Grand Forks 43 D2 Minnesota, N USA
East Grinstead 95 G4 SE England, United Kingdom
East Kilbride 91 D6 S Scotland, United Kingdom
East Korea Bay 133 B5 *bay* E North Korea
Eastleigh 95 E4 S England, United Kingdom
East Liverpool 40 F6 Ohio, N USA
East London 76 D7 S South Africa
Eastmain 35 D4 ≈ Québec, C Canada
East Novaya Zemlya Trough 143 E5 *undersea feature* W Kara Sea
East Pacific Rise 14 *undersea feature* E Pacific Ocean
East Saint Louis 40 A7 Illinois, N USA
East Sea *see* Japan, Sea of
East Siberian Sea 143 C2 *sea* Arctic Ocean
East Timor 131 F8 ◆ *republic* SE Asia
Eau Claire 40 A3 Wisconsin, N USA
Ebbw Vale 93 C7 SE Wales, United Kingdom
Ebensee 101 E7 N Austria
Eberswalde-Finow 101 D3 E Germany
Ebetsu 133 F2 NE Japan
Ebolowa 72 F6 S Cameroon
Ebro 99 E2 ≈ NE Spain
Echo Bay 33 G4 Northwest Territories, NW Canada
Echt 84 E6 SE Netherlands
Ecija 99 C5 SW Spain
Ecuador 63 B3 ◆ *republic* NW South America
Eday 91 E1 *island* NE Scotland, United Kingdom
Ed Da'ein 75 B3 W Sudan
Ed Damazin 75 C2 S Sudan
Ed Damer 75 C2 NE Sudan
Ed Debba 75 C2 N Sudan
Eddrachillis Bay 91 C2 *bay* NW Scotland, United Kingdom
Eddystone Rocks 95 B6 *rocks* SW England, United Kingdom
Ede 84 E4 C Netherlands
Ede 72 E5 SW Nigeria
Eden 44 G4 Texas, SW USA
Eden 93 C2 ≈ NW England, United Kingdom
Edgeley 43 C2 North Dakota, N USA
Edgeworthstown 89 D4 C Ireland
Edinburg 44 G6 Texas, SW USA
Edinburgh 91 E5 *National region capital,* S Scotland, United Kingdom
Edirne 120 A2 NW Turkey
Edison 37 E5 New Jersey, NE USA
Edmonds 49 B2 Washington, NW USA
Edmonton 33 G6 *province capital* Alberta, SW Canada
Edmundston 35 F5 New Brunswick, SE Canada
Edolo 103 C2 N Italy
Edremit 120 A3 NW Turkey
Edward, Lake 76 D2 ◎ Dem. Rep. Congo/Uganda
Edwards Plateau 44 F4 *plain* Texas, SW USA
Edzo 33 F5 Northwest Territories, NW Canada
Eeklo 84 B6 NW Belgium
Eemshaven 84 F1 NE Netherlands
Eersel 84 D5 S Netherlands
Efate 141 H5 *island* C Vanuatu
Effingham 40 C7 Illinois, N USA
Efstrátios, Ágios 107 F5 *island* E Greece
Egadi Is. 103 B8 *island group* S Italy
Eger 105 E7 NE Hungary
Éghezèe 84 D7 C Belgium
Egmont, Mount *see* Taranaki, Mount
Egmont, Cape 139 C4 *cape* North Island, New Zealand
Egypt 70 I4 ◆ *republic* NE Africa
Eibar 99 E1 N Spain
Eibergen 84 F4 E Netherlands
Eidfjord 83 A5 S Norway
Eifel 101 A5 *plateau* W Germany
Eiger 101 B8 ▲ C Switzerland
Eigg 91 B4 *island* W Scotland, United Kingdom
Eight Degree Channel 127 C8 *channel* India/Maldives
Eighty Mile Beach 137 B3 *beach* Western Australia
Eijsden 84 E7 SE Netherlands
Eindhoven 84 D5 S Netherlands
Eisenhüttenstadt 101 E4 E Germany
Eisenstadt 101 F7 E Austria
Eisleben 101 C4 C Germany
Eivissa *see* Ibiza
Ejea de los Caballeros 99 E2 NE Spain
Elat 123 G7 S Israel
El'Atrun 75 B2 NW Sudan
Elâzığ 121 F3 E Turkey
Elba 103 B4 *island* Archipelago Toscano, C Italy
Elbe 101 C3 ≈ Czech Republic/Germany
Elbert, Mount 47 E5 ▲ Colorado, C USA
Elbląg 105 E2 NE Poland
El'brus 111 A8 ▲ SW Russian Federation
El Burgo de Osma 99 E2 C Spain
Elburz Mountains 123 D2 ⛰ N Iran
El Cajon 49 D9 California, W USA
El Calafate 65 A8 S Argentina
El Campo 44 H5 Texas, SW USA
El Centro 49 D9 California, W USA
Elche 99 F5 E Spain
El Chichónal, Volcán 53 G5 🌋 SE Mexico
Elda 99 F4 E Spain
Eldorado 65 D4 NE Argentina
El Dorado 53 C4 C Mexico
El Dorado 39 B4 Arkansas, C USA
El Dorado 43 D7 Kansas, C USA
Eldoret 75 D5 W Kenya
Elektrostal' 111 B5 W Russian Federation
Elemi Triangle 75 C4 *disputed region* Kenya/Sudan
Elephant Butte Reservoir 44 D3 ⊠ New Mexico, SW USA
Eleuthera Island 57 D1 *island* N Bahamas
El Fasher 75 B3 W Sudan
El Geneina 75 A3 W Sudan
Elgin 91 E3 NE Scotland, United Kingdom
Elgin 40 C5 Illinois, N USA
El Golea 70 D2 C Algeria
El Ḩank 72 C1 *cliff* N Mauritania
Elida 44 E3 New Mexico, SW USA
Elista 111 B8 SW Russian Federation
Elizabeth 137 E6 South Australia
Elizabeth City 39 I3 North Carolina, SE USA
Elizabethtown 39 E2 Kentucky, S USA
Ełk 105 F2 NE Poland
Elk City 43 C8 Oklahoma, C USA
Elkhart 40 D5 Indiana, N USA
Elk River 43 E3 Minnesota, N USA
Ellef Ringnes Island 33 G2 *island* Nunavut, N Canada
Ellensburg 49 C2 Washington, NW USA
Ellesmere Island 33 H1 *island* Queen Elizabeth Islands, Nunavut, N Canada
Ellesmere, Lake 139 C6 ◎ South Island, New Zealand
Ellesmere Port 93 C4 C England, United Kingdom
Elliston 137 E5 South Australia
Ellon 91 F3 NE Scotland, United Kingdom
Ellsworth 37 G2 Maine, NE USA
Ellsworth Land 142 A5 *physical region* Antarctica
El Mahbas 70 B3 SW Western Sahara
Elmira 37 C4 New York, NE USA
El Mreyyé 72 C2 *desert* E Mauritania
Elmshorn 101 C2 N Germany
El Muglad 75 B3 C Sudan
El Obeid 75 C3 C Sudan
El Oued 70 E2 NE Algeria
Eloy 44 B3 Arizona, SW USA
El Paso 44 D4 Texas, SW USA
El Porvenir 55 H6 N Panama
El Progreso 55 C3 NW Honduras
El Puerto de Santa María 99 C6 SW Spain
El Rama 55 E4 SE Nicaragua
El Real 55 I6 SE Panama
El Reno 43 C8 Oklahoma, C USA
El Salvador 55 B4 ◆ *republic* Central America
El Sáuz 53 C2 N Mexico
Elst 84 E4 E Netherlands
El Sueco 53 C2 N Mexico
El Tigre 63 D2 Colombia
Elvas 99 B4 C Portugal
El Vendrell 99 G3 NE Spain
Elwell, Lake 47 D1 ⊠ Montana, NW USA
Elx *see* Elche
Ely 95 G2 E England, United Kingdom
Ely 47 C5 Nevada, W USA
Ely 93 C7 ≈ SE Wales, United Kingdom
El Yunque 51 ▲ E Puerto Rico
Emba 118 B5 W Kazakhstan
Emden 101 B3 NW Germany
Emerald 137 G4 Queensland, E Australia
Emeti 141 A2 SW Papua New Guinea
Emi Koussi 72 H2 ▲ N Chad

◈ Administrative region ◆ Country ● Country capital ◇ Dependent territory ○ Dependent territory capital ⛰ Mountain range ▲ Mountain 🌋 Volcano ≈ River ◎ Lake ⊠ Reservoir

F

G

◆ Administrative region   ◆ Country   ● Country capital   ◇ Dependent territory   ○ Dependent territory capital   ▲ Mountain range   ▲ Mountain   ☒ Volcano   ◢ River   ◎ Lake   ☒ Reservoir

161

◆ Administrative region ● Country ● Country capital ◇ Dependent territory ○ Dependent territory capital ▲ Mountain range ▲ Mountain ♨ Volcano ♨ River ◎ Lake ▣ Reservoir

◆ Administrative region   ◆ Country   ● Country capital   ◇ Dependent territory   ○ Dependent territory capital   ▲▲ Mountain range   ▲ Mountain   ☀ Volcano   ⊿ River   ◎ Lake   ⊠ Reservoir

L

◆ Administrative region   ◆ Country   ○ Country capital   ◇ Dependent territory   ○ Dependent territory capital   ▲ Mountain range   ▲ Mountain   ☒ Volcano   ⤳ River   ☉ Lake   ☒ Reservoir

165

LICHFIELD

Lichfield *93 D5* C England, United Kingdom
Lichtenfels *101 C5* SE Germany
Lichtenvoorde *84 F4* E Netherlands
Lichuan *129 F4* C China
Lida *109 C2* W Belarus
Lidköping *83 C6* S Sweden
Lidzbark Warmiński *105 E2* N Poland
Liechtenstein *101 C8* ◆ *monarchy* C Europe
Liège *84 D7* E Belgium
Lienz *101 D8* W Austria
Liepāja *83 E6* W Latvia
Liezen *101 E7* C Austria
Liffey *89 E5* 〜 E Ireland
Lifford *89 D2* NW Ireland
Lifou *141 G6 island* Îles Loyauté, E New Caledonia
Ligger Bay *95 A5 bay* SW England, United Kingdom
Lighthouse Reef *55 C1 reef* E Belize
Ligure, Appennino *103 B2* ▲▲ NW Italy
Ligurian Sea *103 A3 sea* N Mediterranean Sea
Lihir Group *141 D1 island group* NE Papua New Guinea
Lihue *51 B1* Kaua'i, Hawaii, USA
Likasi *76 D3* SE Dem. Rep. Congo
Liknes *83 A6* S Norway
Lille *97 D1* N France
Lillehammer *83 B5* S Norway
Lillestrøm *83 B5* S Norway
Lilongwe *76 E4* ● W Malawi
Lima *63 B5* ● W Peru
Limanowa *105 E5* S Poland
Limassol *112 C6* SW Cyprus
Limavady *89 E1* NW Northern Ireland, United Kingdom
Limerick *89 C5* SW Ireland
Límnos *107 F4 island* E Greece
Limoges *97 C4* C France
Limón *55 F6* E Costa Rica
Limón *55 D2* NE Honduras
Limon *47 F5* Colorado, C USA
Limousin *97 C5 cultural region* C France Europe
Limoux *97 D7* S France
Limpopo *76 E5* 〜 S Africa
Linares *65 A6* C Chile
Linares *53 E3* NE Mexico
Linares *99 D5* S Spain
Lincoln *93 E5* E England, United Kingdom
Lincoln *37 G2* Maine, NE USA
Lincoln *43 D5 state capital* Nebraska, C USA
Lincoln Edge *93 E4 ridge* E England, United Kingdom
Lincoln Sea *143 B4 sea* Arctic Ocean
Linden *63 E2* E Guyana
Lindi *75 E7* SE Tanzania
Líndos *107 G6* Rhodes, Dodecanese, Greece
Line Islands *135 island group* E Kiribati
Lingen *101 B3* NW Germany
Lingga, Kepulauan *131 C6 island group* W Indonesia
Linköping *83 C6* S Sweden
Linnhe, Loch *91 C5 inlet* W Scotland, United Kingdom
Linton *43 C2* North Dakota, N USA
Linz *101 E7* N Austria
Lion, Gulf of *97 D7 gulf* S France
Lipari *103 D7 island* Aeolian Islands, Italy
Lipetsk *111 B6* W Russian Federation
Lira *75 C5* N Uganda
Lisala *76 C1* N Dem. Rep. Congo
Lisboa *see* Lisbon
Lisbon *99 A4* ● W Portugal
Lisburn *89 E2* E Northern Ireland, United Kingdom
Lisdoonvarna *89 B5* W Ireland
Lisieux *97 C2* N France
Liski *111 A6* W Russian Federation
Lisnaskea *89 D3* W Northern Ireland, United Kingdom
Lisse *84 C4* W Netherlands
Listowel *89 B5* SW Ireland
Litang *129 D5* C China
Lithgow *137 G6* New South Wales, SE Australia
Lithuania *83 E7* ◆ *republic* NE Europe
Little Alföld *105 D7 plain* Hungary/Slovakia
Little Andaman *127 H5 island* Andaman Islands, SE India
Little Barrier Island *139 D2 island* N New Zealand
Little Cayman *57 C4 island* E Cayman Islands
Little Colorado River *47 D7* 〜 Arizona, SW USA
Little Falls *43 E3* Minnesota, N USA
Littlefield *44 F3* Texas, SW USA
Littlehampton *95 F5* SE England, United Kingdom
Little Inagua *57 E3 island* S Bahamas
Little Minch, The *91 B3 strait* NW Scotland, United Kingdom
Little Missouri River *43 A3* 〜 NW USA
Little Nicobar *127 H6 island* Nicobar Islands, SE India
Little Ouse *95 G2* 〜 E England, United Kingdom
Little Rock *39 B4 state capital* Arkansas, C USA
Little Saint Bernard Pass *97 F5 pass* France/Italy
Little Sandy Desert *137 B4 desert* Western Australia
Littleton *47 F5* Colorado, C USA
Littleton *37 F3* New Hampshire, NE USA
Liuzhou *129 F5* S China
Liverpool *35 F5* Nova Scotia, SE Canada
Liverpool *93 C4* NW England, United Kingdom
Liverpool Bay *93 E1 bay* England/Wales, United Kingdom
Livingston *91 E5* C Scotland, United Kingdom
Livingston *47 D3* Montana, NW USA
Livingston *44 H4* Texas, SW USA
Livingstone *76 D4* S Zambia
Livingstone Mountains *139 A7* ▲▲ South Island, New Zealand
Livingston, Lake *44 H4* ⊠ Texas, SW USA
Livojoki *83 E3* 〜 C Finland
Livonia *40 E5* Michigan, N USA
Livorno *103 B3* C Italy
Lizard Point *95 A6 headland* SW England, United Kingdom
Ljubljana *101 E8* ● C Slovenia
Ljungby *83 C6* S Sweden
Ljusdal *83 C4* C Sweden
Ljusnan *83 C4* 〜 C Sweden
Llandeilo *93 B7* S Wales, United Kingdom
Llandovery *93 B6* S Wales, United Kingdom
Llandrindod Wells *93 C6* E Wales, United Kingdom
Llandudno *93 B4* N Wales, United Kingdom
Llanes *99 D1* N Spain
Llanos *63 C2 physical region* Colombia/Venezuela
Llanwrtyd Wells *93 B6* C Wales, United Kingdom
Lleida *99 F2* NE Spain
Lleyn Peninsula *93 A5 peninsula* NW Wales, United Kingdom
Llucmajor *99 H4* Majorca, Spain
Lobatse *76 D6* SE Botswana
Löbau *101 E4* E Germany
Lobito *76 B4* W Angola
Locarno *101 B8* S Switzerland
Lochboisdale *91 A4* NW Scotland, United Kingdom
Lochdon *91 C5* W Scotland, United Kingdom
Lochem *84 E4* E Netherlands
Lochgilphead *91 C5* W Scotland, United Kingdom
Lochinver *91 C2* N Scotland, United Kingdom
Lochmaddy *91 B3* NW Scotland, United Kingdom
Lochnagar *91 E4* ▲ C Scotland, United Kingdom
Lochy, Loch *91 C4* ◎ N Scotland, United Kingdom
Lockerbie *91 E7* S Scotland, United Kingdom
Lockport *37 C3* New York, NE USA
Lodja *76 C2* C Dem. Rep. Congo
Lodwar *75 D5* NW Kenya
Lodz *105 E4* C Poland
Lofoten *83 C2 island group* C Norway
Logan *47 D4* Utah, W USA
Logan, Mount *33 E5* ▲ Yukon Territory, W Canada
Logansport *40 D6* Indiana, N USA
Logroño *99 E2* N Spain
Loibl Pass *101 E8 pass* Austria/Slovenia
Loire *97 C3* 〜 C France
Loja *63 B4* S Ecuador
Lokitaung *75 D4* NW Kenya
Lokoja *72 E5* C Nigeria
Lola, Mount *49 B6* ▲ California, W USA
Lolland *83 B7 island* S Denmark
Lom *107 E2* NW Bulgaria
Lomami *76 D2* 〜 C Dem. Rep. Congo
Lomas de Zamora *65 C5* E Argentina
Lombardia *see* Lombardy
Lombardy *103 C2 cultural region* N Italy
Lombok, Pulau *131 E8 island* Nusa Tenggara, C Indonesia
Lomé *72 D5* ● S Togo
Lomela *76 C2* C Dem. Rep. Congo
Lommel *84 D6* N Belgium
Lomond, Loch *91 D5* ◎ C Scotland, United Kingdom
Lomonosov Ridge *143 C4 undersea feature* Arctic Ocean
Lompoc *49 C8* California, W USA
Łomża *105 F2* NE Poland
Loncoche *65 A6* C Chile
London *95 G4* ● SE England, United Kingdom
London *35 C6* Ontario, S Canada
London *39 F3* Kentucky, S USA
Londonderry *89 D2* NW Northern Ireland, United Kingdom
Londonderry, Cape *137 C1 cape* Western Australia
Londrina *63 F7* S Brazil
Lone Pine *49 C7* California, W USA
Long Bay *39 H4 bay* North Carolina/ South Carolina, E USA
Long Beach *49 C9* California, W USA
Long Eaton *93 E5* C England, United Kingdom
Longford *89 D4* C Ireland
Long Island *57 E2 island* C Bahamas
Long Island *37 E5 island* New York, NE USA
Long Island Sound *37 F5 sound* NE USA
Longlac *35 B4* Ontario, S Canada
Longmont *47 F5* Colorado, C USA
Longreach *137 G3* Queensland, E Australia
Long Strait *118 H1 strait* NE Russian Federation
Longview *44 H3* Texas, SW USA
Longview *49 B3* Washington, NW USA
Longyan *129 G5* SE China
Longyearbyen *143 C5* ○ W Svalbard
Lons-le-Saunier *97 E4* E France
Loop Head *89 A5 promontory* W Ireland
Lop Nur *129 C3 seasonal lake* NW China
Loppersum *84 F2* NE Netherlands
Lorca *99 E5* S Spain
Lorengau *141 B1* Manus Island, N Papua New Guinea
Loreto *53 B3* W Mexico
Lorient *97 B3* NW France
Lorn, Firth of *91 B5 inlet* W Scotland, United Kingdom
Lörrach *101 B7* S Germany
Lorraine *97 F2 cultural region* NE France Europe
Los Alamos *44 D2* New Mexico, SW USA
Los Amates *55 B3* E Guatemala
Los Ángeles *65 A6* C Chile
Los Angeles *49 C8* California, W USA
Lošinj *107 A2 island* W Croatia
Los Mochis *53 C3* C Mexico
Los Roques, Islas *57 H7 island group* N Venezuela
Lossiemouth *91 E3* NE Scotland, United Kingdom
Los Testigos, Islas *57 J7 island* NE Venezuela
Lot *97 C5 cultural region* C France Europe
Lot *97 C6* 〜 S France
Lotagipi Swamp *75 D4 wetland* Kenya/ Sudan
Louangphabang *131 B3* N Laos
Loudéac *97 B2* NW France
Loudi *129 F5* S China
Louga *72 A3* NW Senegal
Loughborough *93 E5* C England, United Kingdom
Loughrea *89 C4* W Ireland
Louisburgh *89 B3* NW Ireland
Louisiade Archipelago *141 D3 island group* SE Papua New Guinea
Louisiana *39 A5* ◐ *state* S USA
Louisville *39 E2* Kentucky, S USA
Louisville Ridge *14 undersea feature* S Pacific Ocean
Loup River *43 C5* 〜 Nebraska, C USA
Lourdes *97 C6* S France
Louth *89 E3* NE Ireland
Louth *93 F4* E England, United Kingdom
Loutrá *107 E4* N Greece
Louvain-la Neuve *84 C7* C Belgium
Louviers *97 D2* N France
Loveland *47 F5* Colorado, C USA
Lovelock *47 A5* Nevada, W USA
Lovosice *105 B5* NW Czech Republic
Lóvua *76 C3* NE Angola
Lowell *47 C2* Idaho, NW USA
Lowell *37 F4* Massachusetts, NE USA
Lower California *53 B3 peninsula* NW Mexico
Lower Hutt *139 D5* North Island, New Zealand
Lower Lough Erne *89 D2* ◎ SW Northern Ireland, United Kingdom
Lower Red Lake *43 E2* ◎ Minnesota, N USA
Lower Tunguska *118 E4* 〜 N Russian Federation
Lowestoft *95 H2* E England, United Kingdom
Loyauté, Îles *141 G6 island group* S New Caledonia
Lualaba *76 D2* 〜 SE Dem. Rep. Congo
Luanda *76 B3* ● NW Angola
Luangwa *76 E4* 〜 Mozambique/Zambia
Luanshya *76 D4* C Zambia
Luarca *99 C1* N Spain
Lubaczów *105 G5* SE Poland
Lubań *105 B4* SW Poland
Lubango *76 B4* SW Angola
Lubao *76 D2* C Dem. Rep. Congo
Lübben *101 E4* E Germany
Lübbenau *101 E4* E Germany
Lubbock *44 F3* Texas, SW USA
Lübeck *101 C2* N Germany
Lubelska, Wyżyna *105 F4 plateau* SE Poland
Lubin *105 C4* SW Poland
Lublin *105 F4* E Poland
Lubliniec *105 D5* S Poland
Lubny *109 E4* NE Ukraine
Lubsko *105 B4* W Poland
Lubumbashi *76 D3* SE Dem. Rep. Congo
Lucan *89 E4* E Ireland
Lucano, Appennino *103 E6* ▲▲ S Italy
Lucapa *76 C3* NE Angola
Lucca *103 C3* C Italy
Luce Bay *91 C7 inlet* SW Scotland, United Kingdom
Lucena *131 F4* Luzon, N Philippines
Lucena *99 D5* S Spain
Lučenec *105 E7* C Slovakia
Lucknow *127 E3* N India
Luda Kamchiya *107 F3* 〜 E Bulgaria
Lüderitz *76 B6* SW Namibia
Ludhiana *127 D2* N India
Ludington *40 D4* Michigan, N USA
Ludlow *93 C6* W England, United Kingdom
Ludvika *83 C5* C Sweden
Ludwigsburg *101 B6* SW Germany
Ludwigsfelde *101 D4* NE Germany
Ludwigshafen *101 B6* W Germany
Ludwigslust *101 C3* N Germany
Ludza *83 F6* E Latvia
Luena *76 C3* E Angola
Lufira *76 D3* 〜 SE Dem. Rep. Congo
Lufkin *44 I4* Texas, SW USA
Luga *111 A4* NW Russian Federation
Lugano *101 B8* S Switzerland
Luganville *141 G4* C Vanuatu
Lugenda, Rio *76 F4* 〜 N Mozambique
Lugnaquillia Mountain *89 E5* ▲ E Ireland
Lugo *99 B1* NW Spain
Lugoj *109 A6* W Romania
Luhans'k *109 G5* E Ukraine
Lukenie *76 C2* 〜 C Dem. Rep. Congo
Łuków *105 F4* E Poland
Lukuga *76 D3* 〜 SE Dem. Rep. Congo
Luleå *83 D3* N Sweden
Luleälven *83 D3* 〜 N Sweden
Lulimba *76 D2* E Dem. Rep. Congo
Lulonga *76 C1* 〜 NW Dem. Rep. Congo
Luma *51* E American Samoa
Lumberton *39 H4* North Carolina, SE USA
Lumbo *76 F4* NE Mozambique
Lumi *141 A1* NW Papua New Guinea
Lumsden *139 B7* South Island, New Zealand
Lund *83 C7* S Sweden
Lundy *95 B4 island* SW England, United Kingdom
Lüneburg *101 C3* N Germany
Lungué-Bungo *76 C4* 〜 Angola/Zambia
Luninyets *109 C3* SW Belarus
Lunteren *84 D4* C Netherlands
Luoyang *129 F4* C China
Lurgan *89 E2* S Northern Ireland, United Kingdom
Lúrio *76 F4* NE Mozambique
Lúrio, Rio *76 F4* 〜 NE Mozambique
Lusaka *76 D4* ● SE Zambia
Lut, Dasht-e *123 F3 desert* E Iran
Luti *141 E2* NW Solomon Islands
Luton *95 F3* E England, United Kingdom
Łutselk'e *33 G5* Northwest Territories, W Canada
Luts'k *109 C4* NW Ukraine
Lutzow-Holm Bay *142 D3 bay* Antarctica
Luuq *75 E4* SW Somalia
Luwego *75 D7* 〜 S Tanzania
Luxembourg *84 E9* ● S Luxembourg
Luxembourg *84 E8* ◆ *monarchy* NW Europe
Luxor *70 J3* E Egypt
Luza *111 C4* NW Russian Federation
Luzern *101 B8* C Switzerland
Luzon *131 F3 island* N Philippines
Luzon Strait *131 F3 strait* Philippines/Taiwan
L'viv *109 B4* W Ukraine
Lycksele *83 D3* N Sweden
Lyepyel' *109 D2* N Belarus
Lyme Bay *95 C5 bay* S England, United Kingdom
Lyme Regis *95 D5* S England, United Kingdom
Lymington *95 E5* S England, United Kingdom
Lynchburg *39 G2* Virginia, NE USA
Lynn *37 F4* Massachusetts, NE USA
Lynn Lake *33 H6* Manitoba, C Canada
Lynton *95 C4* SW England, United Kingdom
Lyon *97 E5* E France
Lysychans'k *109 G4* E Ukraine
Lytham St Anne's *93 C4* NW England, United Kingdom
Lyttelton *139 C6* South Island, New Zealand

M

Maamturk Mountains *89 B4* ▲▲ W Ireland
Maaseik *84 E6* NE Belgium
Maastricht *84 E6* SE Netherlands
Mablethorpe *93 F4* E England, United Kingdom
Macao *129 G6* S China
Macapá *63 F3* N Brazil
Macclesfield *93 D5* C England, United Kingdom
Macdonnell Ranges *137 D3* ▲▲ Northern Territory, C Australia
Macduff *91 F3* NE Scotland, United Kingdom
Macedonia *107 D4* ◆ *republic* SE Europe
Maceió *63 I5* E Brazil
Macgillycuddy's Reeks *89 B6* ▲▲ SW Ireland
Machala *63 A4* SW Ecuador
Machanga *76 E5* E Mozambique
Machilipatnam *127 E5* E India
Machynlleth *93 B6* C Wales, United Kingdom
Mackay *137 G3* Queensland, NE Australia
Mackay, Lake *137 D3 salt lake* Northern Territory/Western Australia
Mackenzie *33 F4* 〜 Northwest Territories, NW Canada
Mackenzie Bay *142 E4 bay* Antarctica
Mackenzie Mountains *33 E4* ▲▲ Northwest Territories, NW Canada
Macleod, Lake *137 A4* ◎ Western Australia
Macomb *40 B6* Illinois, N USA
Macomer *103 A6* Sardinia, Italy
Mâcon *97 E4* C France
Macon *39 F5* Georgia, SE USA
Macon *43 F6* Missouri, C USA
Macroom *89 B6* SW Ireland
Macuspana *53 H5* SE Mexico
Ma'daba *123 A2* NW Jordan
Madagascar *76 G5* ◆ *republic* W Indian Ocean
Madang *141 B2* N Papua New Guinea
Made *84 C5* S Netherlands
Madeira, Rio *63 E4* 〜 Bolivia/Brazil
Madeleine, Îles de la *35 F4 island group* Québec, E Canada
Madeline *49 C5* California, W USA
Madera *49 C7* California, W USA
Madhya Pradesh *127 E4 state* C India
Madison *43 D4* South Dakota, N USA
Madison *40 B4 state capital* Wisconsin, N USA
Madisonville *39 D2* Kentucky, S USA
Madiun *131 D8* C Indonesia
Madras *see* Chennai
Madre de Dios, Río *65 A1* 〜 Bolivia/Peru
Madre del Sur, Sierra *53 F5* ▲▲ S Mexico
Madre, Laguna *53 F3 lagoon* NE Mexico
Madre, Laguna *44 H6 lagoon* Texas, SW USA
Madre Occidental, Sierra *53 C3* ▲▲ C Mexico
Madre Oriental, Sierra *53 E4* ▲▲ C Mexico
Madrid *99 D3* ● C Spain
Madrid *99 D3 cultural region* C Spain
Madurai *127 D7* S India
Madura, Pulau *131 E8 island* C Indonesia
Maebashi *133 G5* S Japan
Mae Nam Nan *131 B3* 〜 NW Thailand
Maéwo *141 G4 island* C Vanuatu
Mafia *75 E7 island* E Tanzania
Magadan *118 H3* E Russian Federation
Magarida *141 C3* SW Papua New Guinea
Magdalena *65 B1* N Bolivia
Magdalena *53 B2* NW Mexico
Magdalena, Isla *53 B4 island* W Mexico
Magdalena, Río *63 B3* 〜 C Colombia
Magdeburg *101 D4* C Germany
Magee, Island *89 F2 island* E Northern Ireland, United Kingdom
Magelang *131 C8* C Indonesia
Magellan, Strait of *65 B9 strait* Argentina/Chile
Magerøya *83 D1 island* N Norway
Maggiore, Lake *103 B1* ◎ Italy/Switzerland
Maghera *89 E2* C Northern Ireland, United Kingdom
Maglie *103 F6* SE Italy
Magna *47 D5* Utah, W USA
Magnitogorsk *118 C4* C Russian Federation
Magnolia *39 B4* Arkansas, C USA
Magta' Lahjar *72 B3* SW Mauritania
Magtymguly *125 C3* W Turkmenistan
Mahajanga *76 G4* NW Madagascar
Mahakam, Sungai *131 E6* 〜 Borneo, C Indonesia
Mahalapye *76 D5* SE Botswana
Mahanadi *127 F4* 〜 E India
Maharashtra *127 D5 state* W India
Mahbubnagar *127 D5* C India
Mahia Peninsula *139 E4 peninsula* North Island, New Zealand
Mahilyow *109 D2* E Belarus
Mahmud-e Raqi *125 F5* NE Afghanistan
Maidan Shahr *125 F5* NW Afghanistan
Maidenhead *95 F3* S England, United Kingdom
Maidens, The *89 F2 island group* E Northern Ireland, United Kingdom
Maidstone *95 G4* SE England, United Kingdom
Maiduguri *72 G4* NE Nigeria
Maimanah *125 E4* NW Afghanistan
Main *101 C5* 〜 C Germany
Mai-Ndombe, Lac *76 C2* ◎ W Dem. Rep. Congo
Maine *97 C2 cultural region* NW France
Maine *37 F2* ◐ *state* NE USA
Maine, Gulf of *37 G3 gulf* NE USA
Mainland *91 E1 island* N Scotland, United Kingdom
Mainland *91 A6 island* NE Scotland, United Kingdom
Mainz *101 B5* SW Germany
Maitri *142 C3 Indian research station* Antarctica
Maizhokunggar *129 C4* W China
Majorca *99 H4 island* E Spain
Makarov Basin *143 C4 undersea feature* Arctic Ocean
Makassar *131 E7* Celebes, C Indonesia
Makassar Straits *131 E7 strait* C Indonesia
Makay *76 G5* ▲▲ SW Madagascar
Makeni *72 B4* C Sierra Leone
Makhachkala *111 B9* SW Russian Federation
Makiyivka *109 G5* E Ukraine
Makkah *see* Mecca
Makkovik *35 G2* Newfoundland and Labrador, NE Canada
Makó *105 F8* SE Hungary
Makoua *76 B2* C Congo
Makran Coast *123 F4 coastal region* SE Iran
Makrany *109 B3* SW Belarus
Makurdi *72 F5* C Nigeria
Malabo *72 F6* ● Isla de Bioco, NW Equatorial Guinea
Malacca, Strait of *131 B6 strait* Indonesia/Malaysia
Malacky *105 C7* W Slovakia
Maladzyechna *109 C2* C Belarus
Málaga *99 D6* S Spain
Malahide *89 E4* E Ireland
Malaita *141 F3 island* N Solomon Islands
Malakal *75 C3* N South Sudan
Malang *131 D8* Java, C Indonesia
Malanje *76 B3* NW Angola
Mälaren *83 D5* ◎ C Sweden
Malatya *121 E4* SE Turkey
Malawi *76 E4* ◆ *republic* S Africa
Malay Peninsula *131 B5 peninsula* Malaysia/Thailand
Malaysia *131 C5* ◆ *monarchy* SE Asia
Malbork *105 E2* N Poland
Malchin *101 D2* N Germany
Malden *43 G7* Missouri, C USA
Malden Island *135 atoll* E Kiribati
Maldives *127 C9* ◆ *republic* N Indian Ocean
Male *127 C8* ● C Maldives
Malekula *141 G5 island* W Vanuatu
Malheur Lake *49 C4* ◎ Oregon, NW USA
Malheur River *49 C4* 〜 Oregon, NW USA
Mali *72 D3* ◆ *republic* W Africa
Mali Kyun *131 A4 island* Mergui Archipelago, S Myanmar (Burma)
Malin *89 D1* NW Ireland
Malindi *75 E6* SE Kenya
Malin Head *89 D1 headland* NW Ireland
Mallaig *91 C4* N Scotland, United Kingdom
Mallawi *70 I3* C Egypt
Mallorca *see* Majorca
Mallow *89 C6* SW Ireland
Malmberget *83 D2* N Sweden
Malmédy *84 E7* E Belgium
Malmö *83 C7* S Sweden
Malone *37 E2* New York, NE USA
Małopolska, Wyżyna *105 F5 plateau* S Poland
Malozemel'skaya Tundra *111 D3 physical region* NW Russian Federation
Malta *47 E1* Montana, NW USA
Malta *112 A6* ◆ *republic* C Mediterranean Sea
Malta Channel *103 D9 strait* Italy/Malta
Malton *93 E4* N England, United Kingdom
Maluku *see* Moluccas
Malung *83 C5* C Sweden
Malvern Hills *93 C6 hill range* W England, United Kingdom
Mamberamo, Sungai *131 I7* 〜 Papua, E Indonesia
Mamonovo *83 D7* W Russian Federation
Mamoré, Rio *65 B1* 〜 Bolivia/Brazil
Mamou *72 B4* W Guinea
Mamoudzou *76 G4* ○ C Mayotte
Mamuno *76 C5* W Botswana
Manacor *99 H4* Spain
Manado *131 F6* Celebes, C Indonesia
Managua *55 D5* ● W Nicaragua
Managua, Lake *55 D4* ◎ W Nicaragua
Manakara *76 G5* SE Madagascar
Manama *123 D4* ● N Bahrain
Mananjary *76 G5* SE Madagascar
Manapouri, Lake *139 A7* ◎ South Island, New Zealand
Manas, Gora *125 F2* ▲ Kyrgyzstan/Uzbekistan
Manau *141 C2* S Papua New Guinea
Manaus *63 E4* NW Brazil
Manavgat *121 C5* SW Turkey
Manbij *123 B1* N Syria
Manchester *93 D4* NW England, United Kingdom
Manchester *37 F3* New Hampshire, NE USA
Mandalay *131 A2* C Myanmar (Burma)
Mandan *43 B2* North Dakota, N USA
Mand, Rud-e *123 D3* 〜 S Iran
Mandurah *137 B5* Western Australia
Manduria *103 F6* SE Italy
Mandya *127 D6* C India
Manfredonia *103 E5* SE Italy
Mangai *76 C2* W Dem. Rep. Congo
Mangalmé *72 H4* SE Chad
Mangalore *127 D6* W India
Mangerton Mountain *89 B6* ▲ SW Ireland
Mangoky *76 F5* 〜 W Madagascar
Manhattan *43 D6* Kansas, C USA
Manicouagan, Réservoir *35 E4* ◎ Québec, E Canada
Manihiki *135 atoll* N Cook Islands
Manila *131 F4* ● N Philippines
Manisa *120 A3* W Turkey
Manistee River *40 D4* 〜 Michigan, N USA
Manitoba *33 H6* ◐ *province* S Canada
Manitoba, Lake *33 H6* ◎ Manitoba, S Canada
Manitoulin Island *35 C5 island* Ontario, S Canada
Manizales *63 B2* W Colombia
Manjimup *137 B6* Western Australia
Mankato *43 E3* Minnesota, N USA
Manlleu *99 G2* NE Spain
Manmad *127 D4* W India
Mannar *127 E7* NW Sri Lanka
Mannar, Gulf of *127 D8 gulf* India/Sri Lanka
Mannheim *101 B6* SW Germany
Manokwari *131 H6* E Indonesia
Manono *76 D3* SE Dem. Rep. Congo
Manorhamilton *89 C3* NW Ireland
Manosque *97 E6* SE France
Mansa *76 D3* N Zambia
Mansel Island *33 I4 island* Nunavut, NE Canada
Mansfield *93 E5* C England, United Kingdom
Mansfield *40 E6* Ohio, N USA
Mansfield *37 C4* Pennsylvania, NE USA
Mantova *103 C2* NW Italy
Manua Islands *51 island group* E American Samoa
Manurewa *139 D2* North Island, New Zealand
Manus Island *141 B1 island* N Papua New Guinea
Manzanares *99 D4* C Spain
Manzanillo *57 D3* E Cuba
Manzanillo *53 D5* SW Mexico
Manzhouli *129 F1* N China
Mao *72 G3* W Chad
Maó *99 H3* Minorca, E Spain
Maoke, Pegunungan *131 I7* ▲▲ Papua, E Indonesia

◐ Administrative region ◆ Country ● Country capital ◇ Dependent territory ○ Dependent territory capital ▲▲ Mountain range ▲ Mountain Volcano 〜 River ◎ Lake ⊠ Reservoir

MOROCCO

Maoming *129 F6* S China
Maputo *76 E6* ● S Mozambique
Maraa *141 A6* W French Polynesia
Marabá *63 G4* NE Brazil
Maracaibo *63 C1* NW Venezuela
Maracaibo, Lake *63 B2 inlet* NW Venezuela
Maradah *70 G3* N Libya
Maradi *72 F3* S Niger
Maragheh *123 C1* NW Iran
Marajó, Baía de *63 G3 bay* N Brazil
Marajó, Ilha de *63 F3 island* N Brazil
Maranhão *63 G4 state* E Brazil
Marañón, Río *63 B4* ≈ N Peru
Marathon *35 B4* Ontario, S Canada
Marathon *44 E4* Texas, SW USA
Maraza *121 I2* E Azerbaijan
Marbella *99 D6* S Spain
Marble Bar *137 B3* Western Australia
Marburg an der Lahn *101 B5* W Germany
March *95 G2* E England, United Kingdom
Marche *97 D4 cultural region* C France
Marche-en-Famenne *84 D8* SE Belgium
Mar Chiquita, Laguna *65 B5* ◎ C Argentina
Marcy, Mount *37 E3* ▲ New York, NE USA
Mardan *127 C1* N Pakistan
Mar del Plata *65 C6* E Argentina
Mardin *121 F4* SE Turkey
Maré *141 G6 island* Îles Loyauté, E New Caledonia
Mareeba *137 G2* Queensland, NE Australia
Maree, Loch *91 C3* ◎ N Scotland, United Kingdom
Marfa *44 E4* Texas, SW USA
Margarita, Isla de *63 D1 island* N Venezuela
Margate *95 H4* SE England, United Kingdom
Margherita, Lake *75 D4* ◎ SW Ethiopia
Margow, Dasht-e *125 D6 desert* SW Afghanistan
Mari *141 A3* SW Papua New Guinea
María Cleofas, Isla *53 C5 island* C Mexico
Maria Island *137 G7 island* Tasmania, SE Australia
María Madre, Isla *53 C4 island* C Mexico
María Magdalena, Isla *53 C4 island* C Mexico
Mariana Islands *15 island group* Guam/ Northern Mariana Islands
Mariana Trench *15 undersea feature* W Pacific Ocean
Mariánské Lázně *105 A5* W Czech Republic
Maribor *101 F8* NE Slovenia
Maridi *75 B4* S South Sudan
Marie Byrd Land *142 B5 physical region* Antarctica
Marie-Galante *57 K5 island* SE Guadeloupe
Mariental *76 C6* SW Namibia
Mariestad *83 C6* S Sweden
Marietta *39 E4* Georgia, SE USA
Marietta *40 F7* Ohio, N USA
Marília *63 F7* S Brazil
Marín *99 B2* NW Spain
Maringá *63 F7* S Brazil
Marion *40 B8* Illinois, N USA
Marion *43 F4* Iowa, C USA
Marion *40 E6* Ohio, N USA
Mariscal Estigarribia *65 C3* NW Paraguay
Maritsa *107 F3* ≈ SW Europe
Mariupol' *109 G5* SE Ukraine
Marka *75 F5* S Somalia
Market Harborough *93 E6* C England, United Kingdom
Markham, Mount *142 C5* ▲ Antarctica
Markounda *72 H5* NW Central African Republic
Marktredwitz *101 D5* E Germany
Marmande *97 C5* SW France
Marmara, Sea of *120 A2 sea* NW Turkey
Marmaris *120 A5* SW Turkey
Marne *97 E2 cultural region* N France Europe
Marne *97 E3* ≈ N France
Maro *72 H4* S Chad
Maroantsetra *76 G4* NE Madagascar
Maromokotro *76 G4* ▲ N Madagascar
Maroni *63 F2* ≈ French Guiana/ Suriname
Maroua *72 G4* N Cameroon
Marquesas Islands *135 island group* N French Polynesia
Marquette *40 C2* Michigan, N USA
Marrakech *70 C2* W Morocco
Marrawah *137 F7* Tasmania, SE Australia
Marree *137 E5* South Australia
Marsa al Burayqah *70 G3* N Libya
Marsabit *75 D5* N Kenya
Marsala *103 C8* Sicily, Italy
Marsberg *101 B4* W Germany
Marseille *97 E7* SE France
Marshall *43 D3* Minnesota, N USA
Marshall *44 I3* Texas, SW USA
Marshall Islands *135* ◆ *republic* W Pacific Ocean
Marsh Harbour *57 D1* Great Abaco, W Bahamas
Martigues *97 E6* SE France
Martin *105 E6* N Slovakia
Martinique *57 K5 French* ◇ E West Indies
Martinique Passage *57 K5 channel* Dominica/Martinique
Marton *139 D4* North Island, New Zealand
Martos *99 D5* S Spain
Mary *125 D4* S Turkmenistan
Maryborough *137 H4* Queensland, E Australia
Maryland *39 I2* ⬖ *state* NE USA
Maryville *43 E5* Missouri, C USA
Maryville *39 F3* Tennessee, S USA
Masai Steppe *75 D6 grassland* NW Tanzania
Masaka *75 C5* SW Uganda
Masan *133 C6* S South Korea
Masasi *75 D7* SE Tanzania
Masaya *55 D5* W Nicaragua
Maseru *76 D6* ● W Lesotho
Mashhad *123 F1* NE Iran
Masindi *75 C5* W Uganda
Masira, Gulf of *123 F5 bay* E Oman
Mask, Lough *89 B4* ◎ W Ireland
Mason *44 G4* Texas, SW USA
Mason City *43 E4* Iowa, C USA
Masqat *see* Muscat
Massa *103 B3* C Italy
Massachusetts *37 F4* ⬖ *state* NE USA
Massawa *see* Mits'iwa
Massena *37 D2* New York, NE USA
Massenya *72 G4* SW Chad
Massif Central *97 D5 plateau* C France
Masterton *139 D5* North Island, New Zealand
Masuda *133 D7* SW Japan
Masvingo *76 E5* SE Zimbabwe
Matadi *76 B3* W Dem. Rep. Congo
Matagalpa *55 D4* C Nicaragua
Matale *127 E8* C Sri Lanka
Matamata *139 D3* North Island, New Zealand
Matamoros *53 F3* NE Mexico
Matane *35 F4* Québec, SE Canada
Matanzas *57 B2* NW Cuba
Matara *127 E8* S Sri Lanka
Mataram *131 E8* C Indonesia
Mataró *99 G2* E Spain
Matātula, Cape *51 headland* W American Samoa
Mataura *139 B8* South Island, New Zealand
Mataura *139 B7* ≈ South Island, New Zealand
Matautu *141 B5* C Samoa
Matā'utu *141 K4* ○ N Wallis and Futuna
Mataveri *141 C6* Easter Island, Chile
Matera *103 E6* S Italy
Matías Romero *53 G5* SE Mexico
Matlock *93 D5* C England, United Kingdom
Mato Grosso *63 E6 state* W Brazil
Mato Grosso do Sul *63 E7 state* S Brazil
Matosinhos *99 B3* NW Portugal
Matsue *133 D6* SW Japan
Matsumoto *133 F5* S Japan
Matsuyama *133 D7* Shikoku, SW Japan
Matterhorn *101 B9* ▲ Italy/Switzerland
Matthew Town *57 E3* S Bahamas
Maturín *63 D1* NE Venezuela
Mau *127 E3* N India
Maui *51 D2 island* Hawaii, USA
Maun *76 C5* C Botswana
Mauna Loa *51 D3* ▲▲ Hawaii, USA
Mauritania *72 A2* ◆ *republic* W Africa
Mauritius *66* ◆ *republic* W Indian Ocean
Mawlamyine *131 B3* S Myanmar (Burma)
Mawson *142 E4 Australian research station* Antarctica
Maya *55 B2* ≈ E Russian Federation
Mayaguana *57 F3 island* SE Bahamas
Mayaguana Passage *57 E3 passage* SE Bahamas
Mayagüez *57 H4* W Puerto Rico
Maybole *91 D6* W Scotland, United Kingdom
Maych'ew *75 D3* N Ethiopia
Maydan Shahr *125 F5* E Afghanistan
Mayfield *139 C6* South Island, New Zealand
May, Isle of *91 F5 island* E Scotland, United Kingdom
Maykop *111 A8* SW Russian Federation
Maymyo *131 A2* C Myanmar (Burma)
Mayor Island *139 D3 island* NE New Zealand
Mayotte *76 G4 French* ◇ E Africa
Mazabuka *76 D4* S Zambia
Mazar-e Sharif *125 F4* N Afghanistan
Mazatlán *53 D4* C Mexico
Mazury *105 F2 physical region* NE Poland
Mazyr *109 D3* SE Belarus
Mbabane *76 E6* ● NW Swaziland
Mbala *76 E3* NE Zambia
Mbale *75 C5* E Uganda
Mbandaka *76 C2* NW Dem. Rep. Congo
M'Banza Congo *76 B3* NW Angola
Mbanza-Ngungu *76 B2* W Dem. Rep. Congo
Mbarara *75 C5* SW Uganda
Mbé *72 G5* N Cameroon
Mbeya *75 C7* SW Tanzania
Mbuji-Mayi *76 C3* S Dem. Rep. Congo
McAlester *43 D8* Oklahoma, C USA
McAllen *44 G6* Texas, SW USA
McCamey *44 F4* Texas, SW USA
McCammon *47 D4* Idaho, NW USA
McComb *39 C6* Mississippi, S USA
McCook *43 B5* Nebraska, C USA
McDermitt *47 B4* Nevada, W USA
McKinley, Mount *50 D2* ▲ Alaska, USA
McKinley Park *50 E2* Alaska, USA
McLaughlin *43 B3* South Dakota, N USA
M'Clintock Channel *33 G3 channel* Nunavut, N Canada
McMinnville *49 B3* Oregon, NW USA
McMurdo *142 C6 US research station* Antarctica
McNary *44 D4* Texas, SW USA
McPherson *43 D6* Kansas, C USA
Mdantsane *76 D7* SE South Africa
Mead, Lake *47 C7* ▣ Arizona/Nevada, W USA
Meadville *37 B4* Pennsylvania, NE USA
Mecca *123 B5* W Saudi Arabia
Mechelen *84 C6* C Belgium
Mecklenburger Bucht *101 C2 bay* N Germany
Mecsek *105 D8* ▲▲ SW Hungary
Medan *131 B6* E Indonesia
Medellín *63 B2* NW Colombia
Médenine *70 F2* SE Tunisia
Medford *49 B4* Oregon, NW USA
Mediaş *109 B6* C Romania
Medicine Hat *33 G7* Alberta, SW Canada
Medina *123 B4* W Saudi Arabia
Medinaceli *99 E3* N Spain
Medina del Campo *99 D3* N Spain
Mediterranean Sea *112 D4 sea* Africa/Asia/Europe
Médoc *97 B5 cultural region* SW France
Medvezh'yegorsk *111 B3* NW Russian Federation
Medway *95 G4* ≈ SE England, United Kingdom
Meekatharra *137 B4* Western Australia
Meerssen *84 E6* SE Netherlands
Meerut *127 D2* N India
Mehtar Lām *125 G5* E Afghanistan
Mejillones *65 A3* N Chile
Mek'ele *75 D2* N Ethiopia
Meknès *70 C1* N Morocco
Mekong *131 C4* ≈ SE Asia
Mekong, Mouths of the *131 C5 delta* S Vietnam
Melaka *131 B6* SW Malaysia
Melanesia *141 G3 island group* W Pacific Ocean
Melbourne *39 G7* Florida, SE USA
Melbourne *137 F6 state capital* Victoria, SE Australia
Melghir, Chott *70 E2 salt lake* E Algeria
Melilla *69 D1* S Spain
Melita *33 H7* Manitoba, S Canada
Melitopol' *109 F6* SE Ukraine
Melle *84 B6* NW Belgium
Melleray, Mount *89 D6* ▲ S Ireland
Mellerud *83 C6* S Sweden
Mellieha *112 B6* E Malta
Mellizo Sur, Cerro *65 A8* ▲ S Chile
Melo *65 D5* NE Uruguay
Melsungen *101 C5* C Germany
Melton Mowbray *93 E5* C England, United Kingdom
Melun *97 D3* N France
Melville Island *137 D1 island* Northern Territory, N Australia
Melville Island *33 G2 island* Parry Islands, Northwest Territories, NW Canada
Melville, Lake *35 G3* ◎ Newfoundland and Labrador, E Canada
Melville Peninsula *33 H3 peninsula* Nunavut, NE Canada
Memmingen *101 C7* S Germany
Memphis *39 C3* Tennessee, S USA
Menai Bridge *93 B5* NW Wales, United Kingdom
Ménaka *72 E3* E Mali
Menaldum *84 D2* N Netherlands
Mende *97 D6* S France
Mendeleyev Ridge *143 C3 undersea feature* Arctic Ocean
Mendi *141 B2* W Papua New Guinea
Mendip Hills *95 D4 hill range* S England, United Kingdom
Mendocino, Cape *49 A5 headland* California, W USA
Mendoza *65 A5* W Argentina
Menemen *120 A3* W Turkey
Menengiyn Tal *129 F2 plain* E Mongolia
Menongue *76 B4* C Angola
Menorca *see* Minorca
Mentawai, Kepulauan *131 B7 island group* W Indonesia
Meppel *84 E3* NE Netherlands
Merano *103 C1* N Italy
Mercedes *65 C4* NE Argentina
Mercedes *44 G6* Texas, SW USA
Meredith, Lake *44 E2* ▣ Texas, SW USA
Mérida *53 H4* SE Mexico
Mérida *99 C4* W Spain
Mérida *63 C2* W Venezuela
Meridian *39 D5* Mississippi, S USA
Mérignac *97 B5* SW France
Merizo *51* SW Guam
Merowe *75 C2 desert* W Sudan
Merredin *137 B5* Western Australia
Merrick *91 D7* ▲ S Scotland, United Kingdom
Merrimack River *37 F4* ≈ Massachusetts/New Hampshire, NE USA
Mersey *93 C4* ≈ NW England, UK
Mersin *121 D5* S Turkey
Merthyr Tydfil *93 C7* S Wales, United Kingdom
Merton *95 F4* SE England, United Kingdom
Meru *75 D5* C Kenya
Merzifon *121 D2* N Turkey
Merzig *101 A6* SW Germany
Mesa *44 B3* Arizona, SW USA
Messalo, Rio *76 F4* ≈ NE Mozambique
Messina *103 D8* Sicily, Italy
Messina *see* Musina
Messina, Strait of *103 E8 strait* SW Italy
Mestia *121 G1* N Georgia
Mestre *103 D2* NE Italy
Metairie *39 C6* Louisiana, S USA
Metán *65 B4* N Argentina
Metapán *55 B3* NW El Salvador
Meta, Río *63 C2* ≈ Colombia/Venezuela
Métsovo *107 D4* C Greece
Metz *97 F2* NE France
Meulaboh *131 A6* Sumatra, W Indonesia
Meuse *97 E2* ≈ W Europe
Mexborough *93 E4* N England, United Kingdom
Mexicali *53 A1* NW Mexico
Mexico *43 F6* Missouri, C USA
Mexico *53 D3* ◆ *federal republic* N Central America
Mexico City *53 E5* ● C Mexico
Mexico, Gulf of *28 G3 gulf* W Atlantic Ocean
Mezen' *111 C3* ≈ NW Russian Federation
Mezőtúr *105 F8* E Hungary
Mġarr *112 A6* N Malta
Miahuatlán *53 G6* SE Mexico
Miami *39 G9* Florida, SE USA
Miami *43 E7* Oklahoma, C USA
Miami Beach *39 G8* Florida, SE USA
Mianyang *129 E4* C China
Miastko *105 C2* N Poland
Michalovce *105 F6* E Slovakia
Michigan *40 D4* ⬖ *state* N USA
Michigan, Lake *40 C4* ◎ N USA
Michurinsk *111 B6* W Russian Federation
Micronesia *135* ◆ *federation* W Pacific Ocean
Mid-Atlantic Ridge *14 undersea feature* Atlantic Ocean
Middelburg *84 B5* SW Netherlands
Middelharnis *84 C5* SW Netherlands
Middelkerke *84 A6* W Belgium
Middle Andaman *127 H5 island* SE India
Middle Atlas *70 C2* ▲▲ N Morocco
Middlesboro *39 F3* Kentucky, S USA
Middlesbrough *93 E3* N England, United Kingdom
Middletown *37 D6* Delaware, NE USA
Middletown *37 E5* New Jersey, NE USA
Middletown *37 E4* New York, NE USA
Middlewich *93 C5* W England, United Kingdom
Mid-Indian Ridge *15 undersea feature* C Indian Ocean
Midland *35 D5* Ontario, S Canada
Midland *40 E4* Michigan, N USA
Midland *43 B4* South Dakota, N USA
Midland *44 F3* Texas, SW USA
Midleton *89 C6* SW Ireland
Mid-Pacific Mountains *15 undersea feature* NW Pacific Ocean
Midway Islands *27 US* ◇ C Pacific Ocean
Miechów *105 E5* S Poland
Międzyrzec Podlaski *105 G3* E Poland
Międzyrzecz *105 C3* W Poland
Mielec *105 F5* SE Poland
Miercurea-Ciuc *109 C6* C Romania
Mieres del Camín *99 C1* NW Spain
Mī'eso *75 E3* C Ethiopia
Miguel Asua *53 D3* C Mexico
Mijdrecht *84 D4* C Netherlands
Mikhaylovka *111 B7* SW Russian Federation
Mikun' *111 D4* NW Russian Federation
Mikura-jima *133 G6 island* E Japan
Milan *103 B2* N Italy
Milano *see* Milan
Milas *120 A4* SW Turkey
Mildenhall *95 G2* E England, United Kingdom
Mildura *137 F5* Victoria, SE Australia
Miles *137 G4* Queensland, E Australia
Miles City *47 F2* Montana, NW USA
Milford Haven *93 A7* SW Wales, United Kingdom
Milford Haven *93 A7 inlet* SW Wales, United Kingdom
Milford Sound *139 A7* South Island, New Zealand
Mil'kovo *118 I3* E Russian Federation
Milk River *33 G7* Alberta, SW Canada
Milk River *47 E1* ≈ Montana, NW USA
Milk, Wadi el *75 B2* ≈ C Sudan
Milledgeville *39 F5* Georgia, SE USA
Mille Lacs Lake *43 E2* ◎ Minnesota, N USA
Millennium Island *135 atoll* Line Islands, E Kiribati
Millerovo *111 A7* SW Russian Federation
Millford *89 D1* NW Ireland
Millville *37 D6* New Jersey, NE USA
Mílos *107 F6 island* Cyclades, Greece
Milton *139 B8* South Island, New Zealand
Milton Keynes *95 F3* SE England, United Kingdom
Milwaukee *40 C4* Wisconsin, N USA
Minas Gerais *63 H7 state* E Brazil
Minatitlán *53 G5* E Mexico
Minbu *131 A2* W Myanmar (Burma)
Minch, The *91 C2 strait* NW Scotland, United Kingdom
Mindanao *131 G5 island* S Philippines
Mindelheim *101 C7* S Germany
Minden *101 B4* NW Germany
Mindoro *131 F4 island* N Philippines
Mindoro Strait *131 E4 strait* W Philippines
Minehead *95 C4* SW England, United Kingdom
Mineral Wells *44 G3* Texas, SW USA
Mingäçevir *121 I2* C Azerbaijan
Mingaora *127 C1* N Pakistan
Mingulay *91 A4 island* NW Scotland, United Kingdom
Minho *99 B2* ≈ Portugal/Spain
Minicoy Island *127 C7 island* SW India
Minna *72 E4* C Nigeria
Minneapolis *43 E3* Minnesota, N USA
Minnesota *43 D3* ⬖ *state* N USA
Miño *99 B2* ≈ Portugal/Spain
Minorca *99 H3 island* Balearic Islands, Spain
Minot *43 B1* North Dakota, N USA
Minsk *109 C2* ● C Belarus
Minskaya Wzvyshsha *109 C2* ▲▲ C Belarus
Minto, Lac *35 D2* ◎ Québec, C Canada
Miraflores *53 C4* W Mexico
Miranda de Ebro *99 E2* N Spain
Miri *131 D5* E Malaysia
Mirim Lagoon *65 D5 lagoon* Brazil/ Uruguay
Mirjaveh *123 F3* SE Iran
Mirny *142 D5 Russian research station* Antarctica
Mirnyy *118 F4* NE Russian Federation
Mirpur Khas *127 C3* SE Pakistan
Mirtoan Sea *107 E6 sea* S Greece
Miskitos, Cayos *55 F3 island group* NE Nicaragua
Miskolc *105 F7* NE Hungary
Misool, Pulau *131 G7 island* Maluku, E Indonesia
Misratah *70 F2* NW Libya
Mission *43 B4* South Dakota, N USA
Mississippi *39 C5* ⬖ *state* SE USA
Mississippi Delta *39 C7 delta* Louisiana, S USA
Mississippi River *39 C4* ≈ C USA
Missoula *47 C2* Montana, NW USA
Missouri *43 E6* ⬖ *state* C USA
Missouri River *43 C4* ≈ C USA
Mistassini, Lac *35 D4* ◎ Québec, SE Canada
Mistelbach an der Zaya *101 F6* NE Austria
Misti, Volcán *63 C6* ✷ S Peru
Mitchell *137 G4* Queensland, E Australia
Mitchell *49 C3* Oregon, NW USA
Mitchell *43 C4* South Dakota, N USA
Mitchell, Mount *39 F3* ▲ North Carolina, SE USA
Mitchell River *137 F2* ≈ Queensland, NE Australia
Mito *133 G5* S Japan
Mitrovicë *107 D3* N Kosovo
Mitrovica *see* Mitrovicë
Mits'iwa *75 D2* E Eritrea
Mitspe Ramon *123 G7* S Israel
Mitú *63 C3* SE Colombia
Mitumba Range *76 D3* ▲▲ E Dem. Rep. Congo
Miyako *133 G3* C Japan
Miyako-jima *133 G6 island* SW Japan
Miyakonojo *133 D8* SW Japan
Miyazaki *133 D8* SW Japan
Mizen Head *89 A7 headland* SW Ireland
Mjøsa *83 B5* ◎ S Norway
Mława *105 E3* C Poland
Mljet *107 C3 island* S Croatia
Moab *47 D6* Utah, W USA
Moa Island *137 F1 island* Queensland, NE Australia
Moala *141 J5 island* S Fiji
Moanda *76 B2* SE Gabon
Moate *89 D4* C Ireland
Moba *76 D3* E Dem. Rep. Congo
Mobaye *72 H5* S Central African Republic
Moberly *43 F6* Missouri, C USA
Mobile *39 D6* Alabama, S USA
Mochudi *76 D6* SE Botswana
Mocímboa da Praia *76 F3* N Mozambique
Môco *76 B4* ▲ W Angola
Mocuba *76 F4* NE Mozambique
Modena *103 C3* N Italy
Modesto *49 B7* California, W USA
Modica *103 D8* Sicily, Italy
Modimolle *76 D6* NE South Africa
Moe *137 F6* Victoria, SE Australia
Moffat *91 E6* S Scotland, United Kingdom
Mogadishu *75 F5* ● S Somalia
Mogilev *see* Mahilyow
Mogilno *105 D3* C Poland
Mogollon Rim *44 B2 cliff* Arizona, SW USA
Mohammedia *70 C1* NW Morocco
Mohawk River *37 D4* ≈ New York, NE USA
Mohoro *75 D7* E Tanzania
Moi *83 A6* S Norway
Mo i Rana *83 C3* C Norway
Mõisaküla *83 E6* S Estonia
Moissac *97 C6* S France
Mojácar *99 E5* S Spain
Mojave *49 C8* California, W USA
Mojave Desert *49 D8 plain* California, W USA
Mokpo *133 B7* SW South Korea
Mol *84 D6* N Belgium
Mold *93 C5* NE Wales, United Kingdom
Moldavia *see* Moldova
Molde *83 B4* S Norway
Moldo-Too, Khrebet *125 H2* ▲▲ C Kyrgyzstan
Moldova *109* ◆ *republic* SE Europe
Molfetta *103 E6* SE Italy
Mölndal *83 B6* S Sweden
Molodezhnaya *142 E3 Russian research station* Antarctica
Moloka'i *51 C1 island* Hawaii, USA
Molopo *76 C6 seasonal river* Botswana/ South Africa
Moluccas *131 G7 island group* E Indonesia
Molucca Sea *131 F6 sea* E Indonesia
Mombacho, Volcán *55 D5* ✷ SW Nicaragua
Mombasa *75 E6* SE Kenya
Møn *83 B7 island* SE Denmark
Monach Islands *91 A3 island group* NW Scotland, United Kingdom
Monaco *97 F6* ● S Monaco
Monaco *97 F6* ◆ *monarchy* W Europe
Monadhliath Mountains *91 D4* ▲▲ N Scotland, United Kingdom
Monaghan *89 E3* N Ireland
Monahans *44 E4* Texas, SW USA
Mona, Isla *57 H4 island* W Puerto Rico
Mona Passage *57 H4 channel* Dominican Republic/Puerto Rico
Monbetsu *133 G1* NE Japan
Moncalieri *103 A2* NW Italy
Monchegorsk *111 B2* NW Russian Federation
Monclova *53 E3* NE Mexico
Moncton *35 F5* New Brunswick, SE Canada
Mondovì *103 A3* NW Italy
Moneygall *89 D5* C Ireland
Moneymore *89 E2* C Northern Ireland, United Kingdom
Monfalcone *103 D2* NE Italy
Monforte de Lemos *99 B2* NW Spain
Mongo *72 H4* C Chad
Mongolia *129 D2* ◆ *republic* E Asia
Mongu *76 C4* W Zambia
Monkey Bay *76 E4* SE Malawi
Monkey River Town *55 C2* SE Belize
Monmouth *93 C7* SE Wales, United Kingdom
Mono Lake *49 C7* ◎ California, W USA
Monóvar *99 F5* E Spain
Monroe *39 B5* Louisiana, S USA
Monrovia *72 B5* ● W Liberia
Mons *84 C7* S Belgium
Monselice *103 C2* NE Italy
Montana *107 E2* NW Bulgaria
Montana *47 D2* ⬖ *state* NW USA
Montargis *97 D3* C France
Montauban *97 C6* S France
Montbéliard *97 F3* E France
Mont Cenis, Col du *97 F5 pass* E France
Mont-de-Marsan *97 B6* SW France
Monteagudo *65 B3* S Bolivia
Monte Caseros *65 C5* NE Argentina
Monte Cristi *57 F4* NW Dominican Republic
Montego Bay *57 D4* W Jamaica
Montélimar *97 E6* E France
Montemorelos *53 E3* NE Mexico
Montenegro *107 C3* ◆ *republic* SW Europe
Monte Patria *65 A5* N Chile
Monterey *49 B7* California, W USA
Monterey Bay *49 B7 bay* California, W USA
Montería *63 B2* NW Colombia
Montero *65 B2* C Bolivia
Monterrey *53 E3* NE Mexico
Montes Claros *63 G6* SE Brazil
Montevideo *65 C6* ● S Uruguay
Montevideo *43 D3* Minnesota, N USA
Montgenèvre, Col de *97 F5 pass* France/ Italy
Montgomery *93 C6* E Wales, United Kingdom
Montgomery *39 E5 state capital* Alabama, S USA
Monthey *101 A8* SW Switzerland
Monticello *37 D4* New York, NE USA
Monticello *47 E6* Utah, W USA
Montluçon *97 D4* C France
Montoro *99 D5* S Spain
Montpelier *47 D4* Idaho, NW USA
Montpelier *37 E3 state capital* Vermont, NE USA
Montpellier *97 D6* S France
Montréal *35 E5* Québec, SE Canada
Montrose *91 F4* E Scotland, United Kingdom
Montrose *47 E6* Colorado, C USA
Montserrat *57 J5 UK* ◇ E West Indies
Monywa *131 A2* C Myanmar (Burma)
Monza *103 B2* N Italy
Monze *76 D4* S Zambia
Monzón *99 F2* NE Spain
Moonie *137 G4* Queensland, E Australia
Moora *137 B5* Western Australia
Moore *43 D8* Oklahoma, C USA
Moorea *141 A5 island* Îles du Vent, W French Polynesia
Moore, Lake *137 B5* ◎ Western Australia
Moorhead *43 D2* Minnesota, N USA
Moose *47 D3* Wyoming, C USA
Moose *35 C4* ≈ Ontario, S Canada
Moosehead Lake *37 F1* ◎ Maine, NE USA
Moosonee *35 C4* Ontario, SE Canada
Mopti *72 C3* C Mali
Mora *83 C5* C Sweden
Morales *55 B3* E Guatemala
Morar, Loch *91 C4* ◎ N Scotland, United Kingdom
Moratalla *99 E5* SE Spain
Morava *105 D6* ≈ C Europe
Moravia *105 D6 cultural region* E Czech Republic
Moray Firth *91 D3 inlet* N Scotland, United Kingdom
Moreau River *43 B3* ≈ South Dakota, N USA
Morecambe *93 C3* NW England, United Kingdom
Morecambe Bay *93 C3 inlet* NW England, United Kingdom
Moree *137 G5* New South Wales, SE Australia
Morelia *53 E5* S Mexico
Morena, Sierra *99 C5* ▲▲ S Spain
Mórfou *see* Güzelyurt
Morgan City *39 B6* Louisiana, S USA
Morghab, Darya-ye *125 E4* ≈ Afghanistan/Turkmenistan
Moriarty *44 D2* New Mexico, SW USA
Morioka *133 G3* C Japan
Morlaix *97 A2* NW France
Morocco *70 B2* ◆ *monarchy* N Africa

⬖ Administrative region ◆ Country ● Country capital ◇ Dependent territory ○ Dependent territory capital ▲▲ Mountain range ▲ Mountain ✷ Volcano ≈ River ◎ Lake ▣ Reservoir

◆ Administrative region ◆ Country ● Country capital ◇ Dependent territory ○ Dependent territory capital ▲ Mountain range ▲ Mountain ⋇ Volcano ⌁ River ○ Lake ⊡ Reservoir

169

◇ Administrative region   ◆ Country   ● Country capital   ◇ Dependent territory   ◎ Dependent territory capital   ▲ Mountain range   ▲ Mountain   ⚑ Volcano   ✍ River   ◎ Lake   ▣ Reservoir

SALISBURY

Quincy 40 A6 Illinois, N USA
Quito 63 B3 ● N Ecuador
Qurghonteppa 125 F4 SW Tajikistan
Quy Nhon 131 D4 C Vietnam

R

Raahe 83 E3 W Finland
Raalte 84 E3 E Netherlands
Raamsdonksveer 84 D5 S Netherlands
Raasay 91 B3 *island* NW Scotland, United Kingdom
Rába 105 C8 ≈ Austria/Hungary
Rabat 70 C1 ● NW Morocco
Rabat 112 A5 W Malta
Rabaul 141 D1 E Papua New Guinea
Rabinal 55 B3 C Guatemala
Rabka 105 E6 S Poland
Rabyanah Ramlat 70 G4 *desert* SE Libya
Race, Cape 35 H4 *cape* Newfoundland, E Canada
Rach Gia 131 C4 S Vietnam
Racine 40 C5 Wisconsin, N USA
Rádeyilikóé *see* Fort Good Hope
Radom 105 F4 C Poland
Radomsko 105 E4 C Poland
Radzyń Podlaski 105 F4 E Poland
Raetihi 139 D4 North Island, New Zealand
Rafaela 65 B5 E Argentina
Raga 75 B4 W South Sudan
Ragged Island Range 57 D3 *island group* S Bahamas
Ragusa 103 D8 Sicily, Italy
Rahimyar Khan 127 C3 SE Pakistan
Raichur 127 D5 C India
Rainier, Mount 49 B2 🌋 Washington, NW USA
Rainy Lake 43 E1 ◎ Canada/USA
Raipur 127 E4 C India
Rajahmundry 127 E5 E India
Rajang, Batang 131 D6 ≈ East Malaysia
Rajapalaiyam 127 D7 SE India
Rajasthan 127 C3 *state* NW India
Rajkot 127 C4 W India
Rajshahi 127 G3 W Bangladesh
Rakaia 139 C6 ≈ South Island, New Zealand
Raleigh 39 H3 *state capital* North Carolina, SE USA
Râmnicu Vâlcea 109 B7 C Romania
Ramree Island 131 A3 *island* W Myanmar (Burma)
Ramsey 93 B3 NE Isle of Man
Ramsgate 95 H4 SE England, United Kingdom
Rancagua 65 A5 C Chile
Ranchi 127 F4 N India
Randers 83 B6 C Denmark
Rangiora 139 C6 South Island, New Zealand
Rangitikei 139 D4 ≈ North Island, New Zealand
Rangoon *see* Yangon
Rangpur 127 G3 N Bangladesh
Rankin Inlet 33 H4 Nunavut, C Canada
Rannoch Moor 91 D4 *heathland* C Scotland, United Kingdom
Rapid City 43 A3 South Dakota, N USA
Rāpina 83 E5 SE Estonia
Rarotonga 135 *island* S Cook Islands
Rasht 123 D1 NW Iran
Ratän 83 C4 C Sweden
Rathfriland 89 E3 SE Northern Ireland, United Kingdom
Rathkeale 89 C5 SW Ireland
Rathlin Island 89 E1 *island* N Northern Ireland, United Kingdom
Ráth Luirc 89 C6 S Ireland
Rathmelton 89 D1 N Ireland
Rathmore 89 B6 SW Ireland
Rathmullan 89 D1 N Ireland
Rathnew 89 E5 E Ireland
Rat Islands 50 A1 *island group* Aleutian Islands, Alaska, USA
Ratlam 127 D4 C India
Ratnapura 127 E8 S Sri Lanka
Raton 44 E1 New Mexico, SW USA
Rättvik 83 C5 C Sweden
Raufarhöfn 83 B1 NE Iceland
Raukumara Range 139 E3 ⛰ North Island, New Zealand
Raurkela 127 F4 E India
Rauma 83 D5 SW Finland
Ravenglass 93 B3 NW England, United Kingdom
Ravenna 103 C3 N Italy
Ravi 127 C2 ≈ India/Pakistan
Rawalpindi 127 D1 NE Pakistan
Rawa Mazowiecka 105 E4 C Poland
Rawicz 105 C4 C Poland
Rawlinna 137 C5 Western Australia
Rawlins 47 E4 Wyoming, C USA
Rawson 65 B7 SE Argentina
Rayong 131 B4 S Thailand
Razazah, Buhayrat ar 123 B2 ◎ C Iraq
Razgrad 107 F2 N Bulgaria
Razim, Lacul 109 D7 *lagoon* NW Black Sea
Reading 95 F4 S England, United Kingdom
Reading 37 D5 Pennsylvania, NE USA
Real, Cordillera 58 ⛰ C Ecuador
Realicó 65 B5 C Argentina
Rebecca, Lake 137 C5 ◎ Western Australia
Rebun-to 133 F1 *island* NE Japan
Recife 63 I5 E Brazil
Recklinghausen 101 A4 W Germany
Recogne 84 D8 SE Belgium
Reconquista 65 C4 C Argentina
Red Bluff 49 B5 California, W USA
Redcar 93 E2 N England, United Kingdom
Red Deer 33 G7 Alberta, SW Canada
Redding 49 B5 California, W USA
Redditch 93 D6 W England, United Kingdom
Redhill 95 F4 SE England, United Kingdom
Redon 97 B3 NW France
Red River 43 D1 ≈ Canada/USA
Red River 131 B2 ≈ China/Vietnam
Red River 44 G2 ≈ S USA
Red River 39 B6 ≈ Louisiana, S USA
Redruth 95 A6 SW England, United Kingdom
Red Sea 123 A4 *sea* Africa/Asia
Red Wing 43 F3 Minnesota, N USA
Reefton 139 C5 South Island, New Zealand
Ree, Lough 89 D4 ◎ C Ireland
Reese River 47 B5 ≈ Nevada, W USA
Refahiye 121 F3 C Turkey
Regensburg 101 D6 SE Germany
Regenstauf 101 D6 SE Germany
Registan 125 E6 *desert region* S Afghanistan
Reggane 70 D3 C Algeria
Reggio di Calabria 103 E8 SW Italy
Reggio nell'Emilia 103 C3 N Italy
Regina 33 H7 *province capital* Saskatchewan, S Canada
Rehoboth 76 B5 C Namibia
Rehovot 123 G6 C Israel
Reid 137 D5 Western Australia
Ré, Île de 97 B4 *island* W France
Reims 97 E2 N France
Reindeer Lake 33 H5 ◎ Manitoba/Saskatchewan, C Canada
Reinga, Cape 139 C1 *headland* North Island, New Zealand
Reinosa 99 D1 N Spain
Reliance 33 G5 Northwest Territories, C Canada
Rendsburg 101 C2 N Germany
Rengat 131 B6 Sumatra, W Indonesia
Rennell 141 E3 *island* S Solomon Islands
Rennes 97 B3 NW France
Reno 47 A5 Nevada, W USA
Republican River 47 G5 ≈ Kansas/Nebraska, C USA
Repulse Bay 33 I3 Northwest Territories, N Canada
Resistencia 65 C4 NE Argentina
Reşiţa 109 A7 W Romania
Resolute 33 H2 Cornwallis Island, Nunavut, N Canada
Resolution Island 35 E1 *island* Nunavut, NE Canada
Réthymno 107 F7 SE Greece
Réunion 76 H6 *French* ◇ W Indian Ocean
Reus 99 G3 E Spain
Reutlingen 101 B7 S Germany
Reuver 84 E6 SE Netherlands
Revillagigedo, Islas 53 B5 *island group* W Mexico
Rexburg 47 D3 Idaho, NW USA
Reyes 65 A2 NW Bolivia
Rey, Isla del 55 H6 *island* Archipiélago de las Perlas, SE Panama
Reykjavík 83 A1 ● W Iceland
Reynosa 53 F3 C Mexico
Rezé 97 B3 NW France
Rhein *see* Rhine
Rheine 101 B4 NW Germany
Rheinisches Schiefergebirge 101 A5 ⛰ W Germany
Rhine 84 E4 ≈ W Europe
Rhinelander 40 B3 Wisconsin, N USA
Rho 103 B2 N Italy
Rhode Island 37 F5 ◐ *state* NE USA
Rhodes 107 G6 *island* Dodecanese, Greece
Rhodope Mountains 107 E3 ⛰ Bulgaria/Greece
Rhône 97 E6 ≈ France/Switzerland
Rhossili 93 B7 S Wales, United Kingdom
Rhum 91 B4 *island* W Scotland, United Kingdom
Ribble 93 C4 ≈ NW England, United Kingdom
Ribeira 99 A2 NW Spain
Ribeirão Preto 63 G7 S Brazil
Riberalta 65 B1 N Bolivia
Rice Lake 40 A3 Wisconsin, N USA
Richard Toll 72 A3 N Senegal
Richfield 47 D6 Utah, W USA
Richland 49 C3 Washington, NW USA
Richmond 139 C5 South Island, New Zealand
Richmond 93 D3 N England, United Kingdom
Richmond 39 E2 Kentucky, S USA
Richmond 39 H2 *state capital* Virginia, NE USA
Richmond Range 139 C5 ⛰ South Island, New Zealand
Ricobayo, Embalse de 99 B2 ⊠ NW Spain
Ridder 118 D5 E Kazakhstan
Ridgecrest 49 D8 California, W USA
Ridsdale 93 D2 N England, United Kingdom
Ried im Innkreis 101 D7 NW Austria
Riemst 84 D7 NE Belgium
Riesa 101 D4 E Germany
Riga 83 E6 ● C Latvia
Riga, Gulf of 83 E6 *gulf* Estonia/Latvia
Riggins 47 B3 Idaho, NW USA
Riihimäki 83 E5 S Finland
Rijeka 107 B1 NW Croatia
Rijn *see* Rhine
Rijssen 84 E4 E Netherlands
Rimah, Wadi ar 123 C4 *dry watercourse* C Saudi Arabia
Rimini 103 D3 N Italy
Rimouski 35 E4 Québec, SE Canada
Ringebu 83 B4 S Norway
Ringkøbing Fjord 83 A7 *fjord* W Denmark
Ringvassøya 83 C1 *island* N Norway
Ringwood 95 E5 S England, United Kingdom
Rio Branco 63 D5 W Brazil
Río Bravo 53 F3 C Mexico
Río Cuarto 65 B5 C Argentina
Rio de Janeiro 63 H7 SE Brazil
Río Gallegos 65 B9 S Argentina
Río Grande 65 B9 S Argentina
Rio Grande 63 F9 S Brazil
Río Grande 53 D4 C Mexico
Rio Grande 47 F7 ≈ Texas, SW USA
Rio Grande do Norte 63 I4 *state* E Brazil
Rio Grande do Sul 63 F8 *state* S Brazil
Ríohacha 63 C1 N Colombia
Río Lagartos 53 I4 SE Mexico
Riom 97 D5 C France
Río Verde 53 E4 C Mexico
Ripoll 99 G2 NE Spain
Ripon 93 D3 N England, United Kingdom
Rishiri-to 133 F1 *island* NE Japan
Ritidian Point 51 *headland* N Guam
Rivas 55 D5 SW Nicaragua
Rivera 65 C5 NE Uruguay
River Falls 40 A3 Wisconsin, N USA
Riverside 49 D9 California, W USA
Riverstown 89 C6 S Ireland
Riverton 139 A8 South Island, New Zealand
Riverton 47 E4 Wyoming, C USA
Riviera 44 G6 Texas, SW USA
Rivière-du-Loup 35 E5 Québec, SE Canada
Rivne 109 C4 NW Ukraine
Rivoli 103 A2 NW Italy
Riyadh 123 C4 ● C Saudi Arabia
Rize 121 F2 NE Turkey
Rkîz 72 A3 W Mauritania
Road Town 57 I4 ○ C British Virgin Islands
Roag, Loch 91 A2 *inlet* NW Scotland, United Kingdom
Roanne 97 E4 E France
Roanoke 39 G2 Virginia, NE USA
Roanoke River 39 H3 ≈ North Carolina/Virginia, SE USA
Roatán 55 D2 N Honduras
Robin Hood's Bay 93 E3 N England, United Kingdom
Robson, Mount 33 F6 ▲ British Columbia, SW Canada
Robstown 44 H5 Texas, SW USA
Roca Partida, Isla 53 B5 *island* W Mexico
Rocas, Atol das 63 I4 *island* E Brazil
Rochdale 93 D4 NW England, United Kingdom
Rochefort 84 D8 SE Belgium
Rochefort 97 B4 W France
Rochester 43 F4 Minnesota, N USA
Rochester 37 F3 New Hampshire, NE USA
Rochester 37 C3 New York, NE USA
Rockford 40 B5 Illinois, N USA
Rockhampton 137 H4 Queensland, E Australia
Rock Hill 39 G4 South Carolina, SE USA
Rock Island 40 B5 Illinois, N USA
Rock Sound 57 E2 Eleuthera Island, C Bahamas
Rock Springs 47 E4 Wyoming, C USA
Rocky Mount 39 H3 North Carolina, SE USA
Rocky Mountains 28 ⛰ Canada/USA
Roden 84 E2 NE Netherlands
Rodez 97 D6 S France
Rodos *see* Rhodes
Roermond 84 E6 SE Netherlands
Roeselare 84 B6 W Belgium
Rogers 39 B3 Arkansas, C USA
Roi Et 131 C3 E Thailand
Rokiškis 83 F7 NE Lithuania
Rokycany 105 B5 W Czech Republic
Rolla 43 F6 Missouri, C USA
Roma 137 G4 Queensland, E Australia
Roma *see* Rome
Roman 109 C6 NE Romania
Romania 109 B6 ◆ *republic* SE Europe
Rome 103 C5 ● C Italy
Rome 39 E4 Georgia, SE USA
Romford 95 G3 SE England, United Kingdom
Romney Marsh 95 G4 *physical region* SE England, United Kingdom
Romny 109 E4 NE Ukraine
Rømø 83 A7 *island* SW Denmark
Romsey 95 E4 S England, United Kingdom
Ronda 99 C6 S Spain
Rondônia 63 D5 *state* W Brazil
Rondonópolis 63 F6 W Brazil
Rønne 83 C7 E Denmark
Ronne Ice Shelf 142 B4 *ice shelf* Antarctica
Roosendaal 84 C5 S Netherlands
Roosevelt Island 142 C6 *island* Antarctica
Roraima 63 D3 *state* N Brazil
Roraima, Mount 63 D2 ▲ N South America
Røros 83 B4 S Norway
Rosa, Lake 57 E3 ◎ S Bahamas
Rosalia, Punta 141 C5 *headland* Easter Island, Chile
Rosario 65 C5 C Argentina
Rosario 65 C3 C Paraguay
Rosarito 53 A1 NW Mexico
Roscommon 89 C4 C Ireland
Roscommon 40 D4 Michigan, N USA
Roscrea 89 D5 C Ireland
Roseau 57 K5 ● SW Dominica
Roseburg 49 B4 Oregon, NW USA
Rosenberg 44 H4 Texas, SW USA
Rosengarten 101 C3 N Germany
Rosenheim 101 D7 S Germany
Roslavl' 111 A5 W Russian Federation
Rosmalen 84 D5 S Netherlands
Ross 139 B6 SW New Zealand
Rossano 103 E7 SW Italy
Ross Carbery 89 B7 S Ireland
Ross Ice Shelf 142 C5 *ice shelf* Antarctica
Rosslare 89 E6 SE Ireland
Rosslare Harbour 89 E6 SE Ireland
Rosso 72 A3 SW Mauritania
Ross-on-Wye 93 C6 W England, United Kingdom
Rossosh' 111 A7 W Russian Federation
Ross Sea 142 C6 *sea* Antarctica
Rostock 101 D2 NE Germany
Rostov-na-Donu 111 A7 SW Russian Federation
Roswell 44 E3 New Mexico, SW USA
Rother 95 F4 ≈ S England, United Kingdom
Rothera 142 A4 *UK research station* Antarctica
Rotherham 93 E4 N England, United Kingdom
Rothesay 91 C6 W Scotland, United Kingdom
Rotorua 139 D3 North Island, New Zealand
Rotorua, Lake 139 D3 ◎ NE New Zealand
Rotterdam 84 C4 SW Netherlands
Rottweil 101 B7 S Germany
Rotuma 141 I4 *island* NW Fiji
Roubaix 97 D1 N France
Rouen 97 D2 N France
Round Rock 44 G4 Texas, SW USA
Roundstone 89 B4 W Ireland
Roundwood 89 E5 E Ireland
Rousay 91 E1 *island* N Scotland, United Kingdom
Roussillon 97 D7 *cultural region* S France
Rouyn-Noranda 35 D5 Québec, SE Canada
Rovaniemi 83 E3 N Finland
Rovigo 103 C3 NE Italy
Rovuma, Rio 76 F4 ≈ Mozambique/Tanzania
Roxas City 131 F4 C Philippines
Royale, Isle 40 C1 *island* Michigan, N USA
Royal Leamington Spa 93 D6 C England, United Kingdom
Royal Tunbridge Wells 95 G4 SE England, United Kingdom
Royan 97 B4 W France
Royston 95 G3 E England, United Kingdom
Rožňava 105 E6 E Slovakia
Ruapehu, Mount 139 D4 🌋 North Island, New Zealand
Ruapuke Island 139 B8 *island* SW New Zealand
Ruatoria 139 E3 North Island, New Zealand
Ruawai 139 D2 North Island, New Zealand
Rubizhne 109 G4 E Ukraine
Ruby Mountains 47 B5 ⛰ Nevada, W USA
Rudnyy 118 C4 N Kazakhstan
Rufiji 75 D7 ≈ E Tanzania
Rufino 65 B5 C Argentina
Rugby 93 E6 C England, United Kingdom
Rugeley 93 D5 C England, United Kingdom
Rügen 101 D2 *cape* NE Germany
Ruhr Valley 101 A4 *industrial region* W Germany
Rukwa, Lake 75 C7 ◎ SE Tanzania
Rumbek 75 B4 C South Sudan
Rum Cay 57 E2 *island* C Bahamas
Rumia 105 D1 N Poland
Runanga 139 C5 South Island, New Zealand
Runcorn 93 C4 C England, United Kingdom
Rundu 76 C5 NE Namibia
Ruoqiang 129 C3 NW China
Rupel 84 C6 ≈ N Belgium
Rupert, Rivière de 35 D4 ≈ Québec, C Canada
Ruse 107 F2 N Bulgaria
Rushden 95 F2 C England, United Kingdom
Rushmore, Mount 43 A4 ▲ South Dakota, N USA
Russellville 39 B3 Arkansas, C USA
Russian Federation 118 D4 ◆ *republic* Asia/Europe
Rustavi 121 H2 SE Georgia
Ruston 39 B5 Louisiana, S USA
Rutland 37 E3 Vermont, NE USA
Rutland Water 93 E5 ◎ C England, United Kingdom
Rutog 129 A4 W China
Ruvuma 75 D7 ≈ Mozambique/Tanzania
Ruwenzori 75 B5 ⛰ Dem. Rep. Congo/Uganda
Ružomberok 105 E6 N Slovakia
Rwanda 75 B6 ◆ *republic* C Africa
Ryazan' 111 B6 W Russian Federation
Rybinsk 111 B5 W Russian Federation
Rybnik 105 D5 S Poland
Rye 95 G4 SE England, United Kingdom
Rye 93 E3 ≈ N England, United Kingdom
Ryki 105 F4 E Poland
Rypin 105 E3 C Poland
Rysy 105 E6 ▲ S Poland
Ryukyu Islands 133 A7 *island group* SW Japan
Rzeszów 105 F5 SE Poland
Rzhev 111 A5 W Russian Federation

S

Saale 101 D4 ≈ C Germany
Saalfeld 101 C5 C Germany
Saarbrücken 101 A6 SW Germany
Saaremaa 83 D6 *island* W Estonia
Saariselkä 83 E2 N Finland
Šabac 107 D2 W Serbia
Sabadell 99 G2 E Spain
Sabah 131 E5 *cultural region* Borneo, E Malaysia Asia
Sab'atayn, Ramlat as 123 C7 *desert* C Yemen
Sabaya 65 A3 S Bolivia
Saberi, Hamun-e 123 F3 ◎ Afghanistan/Iran
Sabha 70 F3 C Libya
Sabinas 53 E2 NE Mexico
Sabinas Hidalgo 53 E3 NE Mexico
Sabine Lake 39 A6 ◎ Louisiana/Texas, S USA
Sabine River 44 I4 ≈ Louisiana/Texas, SW USA
Sable, Cape 39 G9 *headland* Florida, SE USA
Sable, Île de 141 E5 *island* NW New Caledonia
Sable Island 35 G5 *island* Nova Scotia, SE Canada
Sabzevar 123 E1 NE Iran
Sachsen *see* Saxony
Sachs Harbour 33 F3 Banks Island, Northwest Territories, N Canada
Sacramento 49 B6 *state capital* California, W USA
Sacramento Mountains 44 D3 ⛰ New Mexico, SW USA
Sacramento River 49 B6 ≈ California, W USA
Sacramento Valley 49 B6 *valley* California, W USA
Sa'dah 123 C6 NW Yemen
Sado 133 F4 *island* C Japan
Säffle 83 C5 C Sweden
Safford 44 C3 Arizona, SW USA
Saffron Walden 95 G3 SE England, United Kingdom
Safi 70 B2 W Morocco
Safid Kuh, Selseleh-ye 125 D5 ⛰ W Afghanistan
Saga 133 D7 Kyūshū, SW Japan
Sagaing 131 A2 C Myanmar (Burma)
Sagami-nada 133 G6 *inlet* SW Japan
Saganaga Lake 43 F1 ◎ Minnesota, N USA
Sagar 127 E4 C India
Saginaw 40 E4 Michigan, N USA
Saginaw Bay 40 E4 *lake bay* Michigan, N USA
Sagua la Grande 57 C2 C Cuba
Sagunt *see* Sagunto
Sagunto 99 F4 E Spain
Sahara 72 D2 *desert* Libya/Algeria
Saharan Atlas 70 D2 ⛰ Algeria/Morocco
Sahel 72 E3 *physical region* C Africa
Sahiwal 127 D2 E Pakistan
Saidpur 127 F3 NW Bangladesh
Saimaa 83 F4 ◎ SE Finland
St Albans 95 F3 E England, United Kingdom
Saint Albans 39 F2 West Virginia, NE USA
St Aldhelm's Head 95 E5 *headland* S England, United Kingdom
St Andrews 91 E5 E Scotland, United Kingdom
St Anne 95 H5 Alderney, Channel Islands
St. Anthony 35 G3 Newfoundland, SE Canada
Saint Augustine 39 G6 Florida, SE USA
St Austell 95 B5 SW England, United Kingdom
St Austell Bay 95 B6 *bay* SW England, United Kingdom
St-Barthélemy 57 J4 *island* N Guadeloupe
St Bees Head 93 B3 *headland* NW England, United Kingdom
St-Brieuc 97 B2 NW France
St. Catharines 35 D6 Ontario, S Canada
St Catherine's Point 95 E5 *headland* S England, United Kingdom
St-Chamond 97 E5 E France
Saint Clair, Lake 37 A4 ◎ Canada/USA
St-Claude 97 E4 E France
Saint Cloud 43 E3 Minnesota, N USA
St. Croix 51 *island* S Virgin Islands (USA)
Saint Croix River 40 A3 ≈ Minnesota/Wisconsin, N USA
St David's 93 A7 SW Wales, United Kingdom
St-Dié 97 F3 NE France
St-Egrève 97 E5 E France
Saintes 97 B4 W France
St-Étienne 97 E5 E France
St-Flour 97 D5 C France
St-Gaudens 97 C6 S France
Saint George 137 G4 Queensland, E Australia
Saint George 47 C6 Utah, W USA
St. George's 57 K7 ● SW Grenada
St-Georges 35 E5 Québec, SE Canada
St George's Channel 89 F6 *channel* Ireland/Wales, United Kingdom
Saint Helena 26 *UK* ◇ C Atlantic Ocean
St. Helena Bay 76 B7 *bay* SW South Africa
St Helens 93 C4 NW England, United Kingdom
Saint Helens, Mount 49 B2 🌋 Washington, NW USA
St Helier 95 H6 ○ S Jersey, Channel Islands
Saint Ignace 40 D3 Michigan, N USA
St Ives 95 A6 E England, United Kingdom
St Ives 95 B3 SW England, United Kingdom
St-Jean, Lac 35 E4 ◎ Québec, SE Canada
St. John 35 F5 New Brunswick, SE Canada
St John 95 H6 N Jersey
St. John 51 *island* Virgin Islands (USA)
Saint John River 37 G1 ≈ Canada/USA
St John's 57 J4 ● Antigua, Antigua and Barbuda
St. John's 35 H4 Newfoundland, E Canada
Saint Johns 44 C2 Arizona, SW USA
St John's Point 89 C2 *headland* N Ireland
Saint Joseph 43 E6 Missouri, C USA
Saint Kitts and Nevis 57 I5 ◆ *commonwealth republic* E West Indies
St. Lawrence, Gulf of 35 F4 *gulf* NW Atlantic Ocean
Saint Lawrence Island 50 C1 *island* Alaska, USA
Saint Lawrence River 37 D2 ≈ Canada/USA
St. Lawrence Seaway 35 F4 *seaway* Canada/USA North America Gulf of St.Lawrence N Atlantic Ocean
St-Lô 97 C2 N France
St-Louis 97 F3 NE France
Saint Louis 72 A3 NW Senegal
Saint Louis 43 G6 Missouri, C USA
St Lucia 57 J6 ◆ *commonwealth republic* SE West Indies
St. Lucia Channel 57 K6 *channel* Martinique/Saint Lucia North America Atlantic Ocean
St Magnus Bay 91 A6 *bay* N Scotland, United Kingdom
St-Malo 97 B2 NW France
St-Malo, Golfe de 97 B2 *gulf* NW France
St Margaret's Hope 91 E1 NE Scotland, United Kingdom
St-Martin 57 J4 *island* N Guadeloupe
St Mary 95 H6 Jersey, Channel Islands
St. Matthias Group 141 C1 *island group* NE Papua New Guinea
St. Moritz 101 C8 SE Switzerland
St-Nazaire 97 B3 NW France
St Neots 95 F2 E England, United Kingdom
St-Omer 97 D1 N France
Saint Paul 43 E3 *state capital* Minnesota, N USA
St Peter Port 95 G6 ○ C Guernsey, Channel Islands
Saint Petersburg 111 A4 NW Russian Federation
Saint Petersburg 39 F7 Florida, SE USA
St-Pierre and Miquelon 35 G4 *French* ◇ NE North America
St-Quentin 97 D2 N France
St. Thomas 51 *island* Virgin Islands (USA)
Saint Vincent 57 J6 *island* N Saint Vincent and the Grenadines
Saint Vincent and the Grenadines 57 I6 ◆ *commonwealth republic* SE West Indies
Saint Vincent Passage 57 K6 *passage* Saint Lucia/Saint Vincent and the Grenadines
Sajama, Nevado 65 A2 ▲ W Bolivia
Sajószentpéter 105 F7 NE Hungary
Sakakawea, Lake 43 B2 ⊠ North Dakota, N USA
Sakata 133 F4 C Japan
Sakhalin 118 I4 *island* SE Russian Federation
Saki 121 I2 NW Azerbaijan
Sakishima-shoto 133 A8 *island group* SW Japan
Sala 83 C5 C Sweden
Sala Consilina 103 E6 S Italy
Salado, Río 65 B4 ≈ E Argentina
Salado, Río 65 B5 ≈ C Argentina
Salalah 123 E6 SW Oman
Salamá 55 B3 C Guatemala
Salamanca 65 A5 C Chile
Salamanca 99 C3 NW Spain
Salang Tunnel 125 F4 *tunnel* C Afghanistan Asia
Salantai 83 E7 NW Lithuania
Salavat 111 D6 W Russian Federation
Šalčininkai 83 F7 SE Lithuania
Salcombe 95 C6 SW England, United Kingdom
Sale 137 G6 Victoria, SE Australia
Salé 70 C1 NW Morocco
Salekhard 118 D3 N Russian Federation
Salelologa 141 A5 C Samoa
Salem 127 D7 SE India
Salem 49 B3 *state capital* Oregon, NW USA
Salerno 103 D6 S Italy
Salerno, Gulf of 103 D6 *gulf* S Italy
Salford 93 D4 NW England, United Kingdom
Salihorsk 109 C3 S Belarus
Salina 43 D6 Kansas, C USA
Salina 47 D6 Utah, W USA
Salina Cruz 53 G6 SE Mexico
Salinas 49 B7 California, W USA
Salisbury 95 E4 S England, United Kingdom

◐ Administrative region ◆ Country ● Country capital ◇ Dependent territory ○ Dependent territory capital ⛰ Mountain range ▲ Mountain 🌋 Volcano ≈ River ◎ Lake ⊠ Reservoir

T

◆ Administrative region ◆ Country ● Country capital ◇ Dependent territory ◎ Dependent territory capital ▲ Mountain range ▲ Mountain ﯼ Volcano ↝ River ◎ Lake ▣ Reservoir

◇ Administrative region   ◆ Country   ● Country capital   ◇ Dependent territory   ○ Dependent territory capital   ▲▲ Mountain range   ▲ Mountain   ⛰ Volcano   ⚷ River   ◎ Lake   ▭ Reservoir

X

Y

Z

◆ Administrative region   ◆ Country   ● Country capital   ◇ Dependent territory   ○ Dependent territory capital   ▲ Mountain range   ▲ Mountain   ℞ Volcano   ↝ River   ⊚ Lake   ⊠ Reservoir

NORTH AMERICA

CANADA

UNITED STATES OF AMERICA

MEXICO

BELIZE

COSTA RICA

EL SALVADOR

GUATEMALA

HONDURAS

SOUTH AMERICA

GRENADA

HAITI

JAMAICA

ST KITTS & NEVIS

ST LUCIA

ST VINCENT & THE GRENADINES

TRINIDAD & TOBAGO

COLOMBIA

AFRICA

URUGUAY

CHILE

PARAGUAY

ALGERIA

EGYPT

LIBYA

MOROCCO

TUNISIA

LIBERIA

MALI

MAURITANIA

NIGER

NIGERIA

SENEGAL

SIERRA LEONE

TOGO

BURUNDI

DJIBOUTI

ERITREA

ETHIOPIA

KENYA

RWANDA

SOUTH SUDAN

SOMALIA

EUROPE

SOUTH AFRICA

SWAZILAND

ZAMBIA

ZIMBABWE

DENMARK

FINLAND

ICELAND

NORWAY

MONACO

ANDORRA

PORTUGAL

SPAIN

ITALY

SAN MARINO

VATICAN CITY

AUSTRIA

LIECHTENSTEIN

CROATIA

MACEDONIA

MONTENEGRO

SERBIA

KOSOVO (disputed)

BULGARIA

GREECE

MOLDOVA

ROMANIA

ASIA

ARMENIA

AZERBAIJAN

GEORGIA

TURKEY

IRAQ

ISRAEL

JORDAN

LEBANON

IRAN

KAZAKHSTAN

KYRGYZSTAN

TAJIKISTAN

TURKMENISTAN

UZBEKISTAN

AFGHANISTAN

PAKISTAN

TAIWAN

JAPAN

BRUNEI

INDONESIA

EAST TIMOR

MALAYSIA

SINGAPORE

MYANMAR (BURMA)

AUSTRALASIA & OCEANIA

MAURITIUS

SEYCHELLES

AUSTRALIA

NEW ZEALAND

PAPUA NEW GUINEA

SOLOMON ISLANDS

MARSHALL ISLANDS

MICRONESIA